How To Operate Your Home

Second Edition

Tom Feiza
Mr. Fix-It

**Published
by
Mr. Fix-It Press**

P.O. Box 510724
4620 S. Raven Lane
New Berlin, WI 53151
Phone: (262) 786-7878
Fax: (262) 786-7877
E-mail:Tom@misterfix-it.com
www.howtooperateyourhome.com
or www.htoyh.com

© 2000, 2006
by
Mr. Fix-It Press

NOTICE:

This book is available at special discounts for bulk purchases, sales promotions, premiums, fund-raising, or educational use. For details, contact the publisher.

Second Edition, 2006

ISBN 0-9674759-3-7

Printed in the United States of America

Be Safe

The information in this book has been carefully assembled to ensure that it is as accurate as possible. However, the book provides general information only, and it is sold with the understanding that the publisher and author are not rendering legal or professional services.

This book does not provide product-specific information, and you should consult the manufacturer of the product or equipment for specific information. Operation and maintenance information is provided for general understanding only. Consult the Reference section to learn how to contact manufacturers, or consult with local contractors and professionals.

When attempting a home repair project, always consult professionals and follow label directions. Companies that manufacture equipment and home repair products are the ultimate authorities. Follow their instructions.

Many home repair, operation, and maintenance projects involve a certain degree of risk and should be approached with care. You should only attempt repairs if you have read and understood the instructions for the product, equipment, or tool that you are using. If questions or problems arise, consult a professional or the manufacturer.

Due to the variability of local conditions, construction materials, and personal skills, neither the author nor the publisher assumes responsibility for any injuries suffered or for damages or other losses that may result from the information presented.

Dedication

Who made me Mr. Fix-It?

I owe a lot to Uncle Nick and Uncle Joe in Virgil, Illinois, who put me on the road to being a real fix-it guy. I worked at their dairy farms, racetrack and motorcycle shop and on their many construction projects.

I was nine years old when Uncle Nick began paying me 50 cents a day to work on his farm. When I graduated from Marquette University's engineering school, I was still working for and learning from Nick and Joe and their crews.

They taught me that you "learn by doing" and that the real education takes place working in the trade. From Uncle Nick and Uncle Joe, I learned the value of hard and honest effort.

My mom was also a great fix-it lady who taught me a lot about painting and refinishing.

What is my house like?

Ask Gayle, my wife and best friend. She will tell you we have a lot of fix-it projects waiting for me. Just like every other couple, we operate with a "honey-do" list—you know, "Honey, you need to do this." And when the list gets too long, we talk about hiring a contractor. Our home is just like every other home.

So, this book is dedicated to:

My wife, Gayle, and my kids, Lindsay and Tom III, for putting up with all my fix-it projects and my basement full of stuff; and to my mom, Uncle Nick, and Uncle Joe.

Tom Feiza – "Mr. Fix-It"

Acknowledgements

Special thanks go to all the people who listen to my radio show, watch my television appearances, attend my seminars, use my home inspection service, and read my newspaper column. Your questions, answers, and tips made this book possible.

Many manufacturers have provided me with excellent technical information, and I value their help.

My editor, Leah Carson, took my rough copy and made the information much more useful and user-friendly. Lynn Eckstein designed my Mr. Fix-It logo years ago, and she is responsible for the original cover design. Tom Feiza III created the cover revisions and the wonderful interior layout.

Graphic artist (now architect) Justin Racinowski took my rough drawings and produced the easy-to-understand computer-generated drawings for the first edition. Lindsay Mefford (Feiza) created the artwork for this revised edition from our originals and my rough sketches.

Most importantly, I owe a lot to my wife, Gayle, and our kids, Lindsay and Tom. They helped me keep things in proper perspective by dragging me out of the office for vacations and family time.

Please enjoy my book and have a great fix-It day!

Tom Feiza – "Mr. Fix-It"

Author ....Tom Feiza, a.k.a. Mr. Fix-It

Editor...................................Leah Carson, Excellent Words (luv2cre8@wi.rr.com)

Artwork...............................Justin Racinowski, Lindsay Mefford, Tom Feiza

Layout ....Tom Feiza III (tomfeiza@yahoo.com)

Cover Art ....Tom Feiza III, original by Lynn Eckstein

About the Author

Tom Feiza, Mr. Fix-It, is a "recovering" mechanical engineer and a real life fix-it guy. He personally tests home-related products and evaluates home construction problems.

Tom worked on a dairy farm through grade school, high school and college. After graduating from Marquette University as a mechanical engineer, Tom became licensed as a professional engineer and later as a home inspector. After college, Tom worked for over 20 years in the construction, maintenance and operation of large facilities. He shifted from engineering to become Mr. Fix-It, helping people with their home operation, maintenance and repair problems.

Tom now combines his hobby, his passion and his profession into his unique enterprise—Tom Feiza, Mr. Fix-It, Inc.

Tom hosts a live radio call-in show on AM 620 WTMJ in Milwaukee, Wisconsin. More than 80 newspapers carry his question-and-answer column, and he often appears on television, providing home repair tips.

Tom presents unique and entertaining how-to seminars at home shows, association meetings, and retail events. He also gives entertaining keynotes at dinner meetings and professional conventions.

In another venture that helps him stay in touch with homes, people, and their related problems, Tom provides home inspection services and engineering investigations and evaluations for residential construction.

Contents – Quick Reference

Contents

Contents

Contents

Contents

Introduction

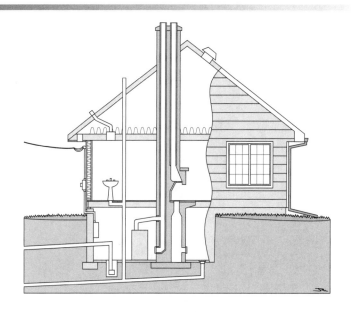

So you have a new home—and no idea what to do next. It's like bringing your first baby home from the hospital. Throughout the pregnancy, everyone was helpful and encouraging. You read all the books and went to all the classes. But now you are home alone with the baby. What do you do next?

Sure, you have that home improvement "Honey Do" list for the painting and decorating tasks that will make the house your home. But what about the furnace, the roof, the garage door opener, the hose bibs, the everything? A home is the most complicated thing you have ever bought. It has more than 5,000 parts and components. Now you own it, and you need to run it.

So where is that operating manual? You didn't get one?! You got one with the new car—and driving a car isn't complicated. For a new home, you're lucky if you get instruction manuals for major systems. For a used home, don't plan on receiving any instructions.

Everyone who owns a home has faced all the same questions and concerns. We never had an operating manual. Most of us just muddled through and eventually got things right. We learned through trial and error and corrected our mistakes. Lucky buyers had a dad, mom or Uncle Nick who was a great resource and would explain what to do and how things work. This book fills the void. It's an operating manual for your new or older home. It won't replace Uncle Nick—but it will come close. The book shares my 35 years of experience around homes, fixing or breaking the complicated stuff that fills them up.

You see, I am a mechanical engineering graduate of Marquette University and a registered professional engineer. I have over 25 years of experience working as an engineer on the maintenance and construction of buildings and equipment. Big deal! Actually, I know stuff about houses because I'm a hands-on guy. My Uncle Nick took me under his wing when I was 9 years old. He was a great teacher with the patience of a saint. Since Uncle Nick, I've regarded homes as a great learning experience.

I have not included all the answers. That is impossible. But all the basic information is here. There are even clues to the mysterious sounds and smells in your home. This book also provides great references in case you need to do a little research on your own.

Enjoy your home. It is the biggest and best investment you have ever made. This book will certainly make your home a little easier to understand, operate and enjoy. Congratulations on your purchase!

Tom Feiza

"Mr. Fix-It"

Chapter 1 – Start It Up and Take That First Spin

Walk Through Before Closing

Just before closing, walk through your new home to observe its condition and contents. This will help avoid surprises and misunderstandings. Your real estate broker may arrange the walk-through and help you make sure everything is in order. Bring your purchase agreement and any related documentation so you can refer to all items that are included in your home purchase.

In addition to the home purchase agreements, check the following:

- Documentation on equipment and utility systems: instruction books, service information, contractor information

- Appliances

- Heating and air conditioning operation

- Potential water leaks in ceilings, basement, water heater, plumbing

- Garage door opener operation and controls

- Home construction documents, if available

- Warrantees or guarantees that may transfer with your home

- Any natural gas smells or sewer odors

- Any physical damage inside and out

- Septic and well maintenance information

- Instruction manuals for equipment and appliances

Home Floor Plan

KITCHEN
DINING
GARAGE
LIVING
CLOSET
FOYER

© Tom Feiza Mr. Fix-It Inc.

M002

Have the owner explain all the features of the home and its systems. Only he or she will know about that special key for the basement storage.....the interior switch that turns off the power to the garage....the emergency release for the garage door.

Utility Services

Prior to closing, arrange a transfer of all utility services to your name. Be ready to answer questions about budget payment or monthly payments. Ask about special electrical controls on air conditioning and water heaters that save you money and reduce utility demands. This is a good time to ask the utility companies for any home operating tips or instructions they may have.

Also, ask the utilities for emergency procedures and phone numbers. Often, they will mail you this information.

Most telephone companies now connect their lines to a junction box at the exterior of your home. This will usually activate the internal jacks that the owner had connected. Any changes inside your home will be your responsibility, and you can hire either the phone company or private contractors to set up the inside wiring.

Garbage, Recycling

In some municipalities, garbage and trash removal is provided by private companies. Arrange this in advance. Your new neighbors will be your best resource for information on private trash contractors that service the area.

You will also need to learn local rules on recycling paper, metal, cardboard, plastic, aerosol cans, and glass. Ask about separation of trash and requirements for containers. Your local municipality and neighbors will be a big help. Also ask about rules on disposal of hazardous materials such as paint, solvents, chemicals, and oil.

Insurance

Prior to closing on your home, you will need a homeowner's insurance policy in force. Your mortgage company will require this, and you should understand all the details of the policy. When you set up this policy, be ready to answer questions about the size of the home, type of construction, security and fire alarm systems, local fire department, wood-burning appliances and other details.

Post Office / Phone Numbers

Remember to plan in advance for a change of address and phone number(s). A quick note to family and friends will take care of the important people. File a change of address form with your current post office.

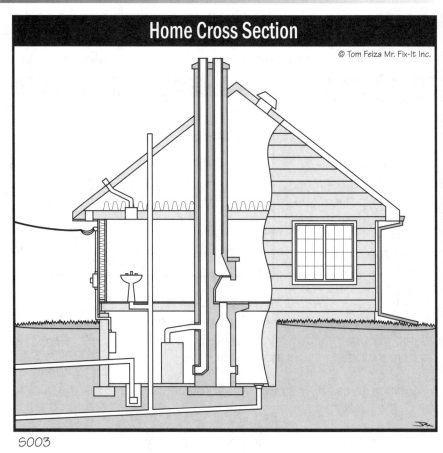

Home Cross Section

© Tom Feiza Mr. Fix-It Inc.

S003

Keys and Locks

When you take occupancy of your new home, you should receive all keys and security codes. Plan on re-keying all locks. Consider keying all exterior door locks to the same key. Find a trusted neighbor or friend who can keep a spare key for an emergency, but don't put your name and address on the key; use a code, first name, or initials only.

For your garage door opener, change the security code on the transmitters and receiver. Most door openers installed in the past 20 years have a security code that can be changed easily; check the instruction manual.

Welcome Wagon / Local Government and Service Groups

Take time to contact your local government office for information on the community. Also, contact the Welcome Wagon and any other local service organizations. They can provide useful information about your new neighborhood.

Safety and Security– Your First Priority

Local Fire, Police and Emergency Numbers

By your first day in your new home, have on hand all local emergency phone numbers for fire, police, ambulance, family physician, poison control center, hospital, eye doctor, utility companies, Mom and Dad at work, schools, and relatives. Keep these listed next to your phone, and make sure your kids know where to find this information. Also, carry a copy of the list with you. Accidents and problems can occur in new and unfamiliar places, so be ready.

Kids—Safety Information and Practice

Take some time with the kids to identify emergency telephone numbers. Walk through the exits and make sure everyone knows how to operate all locks and doors. Test your carbon monoxide, smoke and fire alarms so you all know where they are, how they work, and what they sound like.

It is wise to place smoke and fire detectors on all levels, in sleeping areas, in utility rooms, and at the top of stairs. Test smoke detectors periodically after you move in.

Smoke Detector / Alarm

© Tom Feiza Mr. Fix-It Inc.

Test once per month. Replace batteries yearly. Replace battery if "chirping." Replace unit before 10 years of age.

MO11

Establish an escape plan. All family members should know how to exit your home in an emergency and where to meet outside. Be sure your kids know that they must leave immediately and not return for pets or possessions. Use a sketch of your home's floor plan to identify all escape routes, utility shutoffs, and meeting points. Include your emergency numbers with the plan.

In some homes, a window may be the alternate exit from a second story or lower level. Identify such windows, and practice opening and using them.

Consider adding some battery-powered lights that come on during a power outage. Always have a few flashlights available.

Practice your escape plan with your kids. Activating an alarm helps the kids take a drill seriously. When practicing, keep in mind that emergencies can occur in the night, during a storm, when you are sound asleep, and/or when the power is off.

Fire Extinguishers

Equip your home with a fire extinguisher on each level and in the garage, basement and kitchen. Fire extinguisher have different ratings; select one that's rated "ABC," which means it's good for all common household fires. Contact your local fire department for more information.

Flammable Storage

The best advice for storing flammable materials is "just don't do it." When such storage is necessary, keep it to a minimum. Of course, we all need to store some gasoline for the lawnmower and solvents for household chores, so learn to store and use flammables safely. Use the original container or a container designed for that purpose. Keep flammable materials away from open flames and sources of combustion.

When using flammable solvents or cleaners, follow all safety precautions on the container. Never use a solvent cleaner or finish in a closed area without ventilation or near a source of combustion such as a gas furnace, gas water heater, or electric heater.

Use a spillproof container when storing gasoline. Gasoline should never be stored indoors. Vapors from gasoline are extremely flammable and must never be allowed to accumulate. If gasoline is stored in your garage, the entrance into your home should be up at least one step. Since gasoline vapors are heavier than air, they will settle in low areas. If you have a gas-fired heater or a water heater in the garage, do not store gasoline there.

Tags for Main Utility Valves and Shutoffs

In the event of an emergency, you may need to turn off a utility service to your home. It is important to identify the main shutoffs with tags telling how to turn them off. Make sure everyone in your family knows where to find and how to operate these shutoffs. (See Chapter 9 for information and illustrations on the types of shutoffs and their operation.)

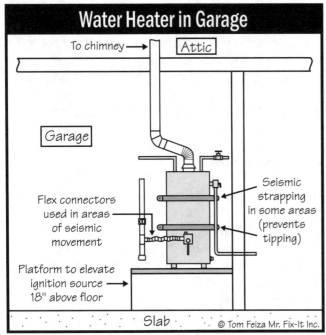

Water Heater in Garage

To chimney → | Attic |

Garage

Flex connectors used in areas of seismic movement

Seismic strapping in some areas (prevents tipping)

Platform to elevate ignition source 18" above floor

Slab

© Tom Feiza Mr. Fix-It Inc.

W013

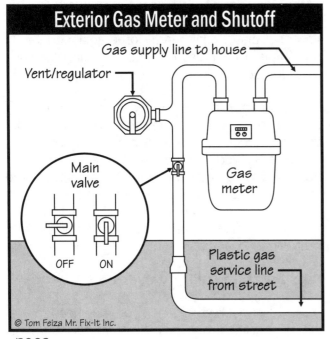

Exterior Gas Meter and Shutoff

Gas supply line to house

Vent/regulator

Main valve

OFF ON

Gas meter

Plastic gas service line from street

© Tom Feiza Mr. Fix-It Inc.

P002

Identify the following:

- Main electrical disconnect: fuse block, breaker or switch

- Main water valve

- Main gas valve or propane valve

In addition, identify shutoffs for individual parts of systems:

- Furnace disconnect switch (electrical)

- Furnace gas or fuel valves

- Air conditioning disconnect switch

- Gas valves for appliances

- Hot water shutoff

- Individual breakers or fuses for branch circuits

- Plumbing valves for appliances and main distribution connections

Garage Door Safety

All garage door openers should have an automatic reverse that stops the door's downward motion if there is an obstruction in its path. This feature helps prevent injury to people or pets beneath the door.

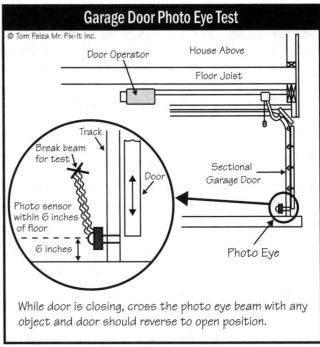

Garage Door Photo Eye Test

© Tom Feiza Mr. Fix-It Inc.

Door Operator House Above

Floor Joist

Track

Break beam for test

Door

Sectional Garage Door

Photo sensor within 6 inches of floor

6 inches

Photo Eye

While door is closing, cross the photo eye beam with any object and door should reverse to open position.

M017

The first day in your home, test the garage door reverse. After that, test it once a month. (For testing instructions, see Chapter 6.)

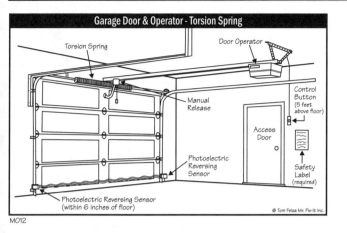

Garage Door & Operator - Torsion Spring

M012

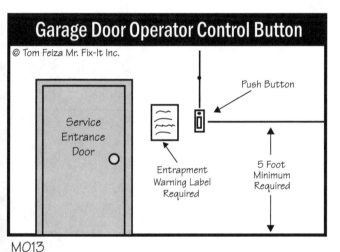

Garage Door Operator Control Button

M013

If your garage door opener does not reverse, take it out of service until it is repaired or adjusted. Look for adjustment instructions on the housing of the opener or in the instruction manual. If you are confused or unsure about how to make these adjustments, consult a professional.

Check the location of the garage door operator button(s). The button should be located at least 5 feet above the floor so children can't reach it. Since these control buttons are low voltage, you can easily relocate them as needed.

Lighting Controls and Exterior Security

A brightly lit entrance is always a welcome sight on a dark evening. Consider adding motion sensor lights to entrances and garage door areas. These inexpensive fixtures replace the existing light fixtures. When anyone drives up or walks up, the unit senses motion and turns on the light.

For further information: Your local fire and police departments can be excellent sources of safety information. You could also contact the National Safety Council, the National Fire Protection Association (NFPA), and/or Underwriters Laboratories, Inc. (UL). See the References chapter for addresses and phone numbers.

Chapter 2 – Environmental and Safety Concerns

Lead

Starting in 1996, federal regulations required land-lords and sellers of single family homes built before 1978 to notify renters and buyers about potential lead hazards. This requirement has raised concerns for everyone.

The regulation affects homes built before 1978 because that is when the manufacture of lead-based paint was banned. Lead-based paint was used almost universally in homes until the 1950s and was used to a lesser degrees in the 1960s and 1970s. If you buy a home built before 1978, you will be given an excellent booklet, "Protect Your Family from Lead in Your Home."

The main concern with lead is that exposure can harm young children, babies, and even unborn children. People can get lead in their bodies by breathing or swallowing lead dust or by eating soil or paint chips with lead in them. If you think your home may have lead hazards, call the National Lead Information Clearinghouse at 1-800-424-LEAD to obtain free information.

Lead-based paint that is in good condition is usually not a hazard, but peeling, chipping, chalking or cracking lead-based paint is a hazard that needs immediate attention. Friction and rubbing points on windows and doors raise the biggest concern. Remodeling and paint removal can increase the risk if the lead-based paint is not handled properly.

Good housekeeping techniques can help reduce the risks of existing lead-based paint surfaces. Clean up paint chips immediately. Clean floors, window frames, windowsills and other surfaces weekly. Use a mop or sponge with warm water and a general all-purpose cleaner or a cleaner made specifically for lead. Thoroughly rinse sponges and mop heads after cleaning.

Wash children's hands often, especially before they eat and before naps and bedtime. Keep children from chewing windowsills or other painted surfaces.

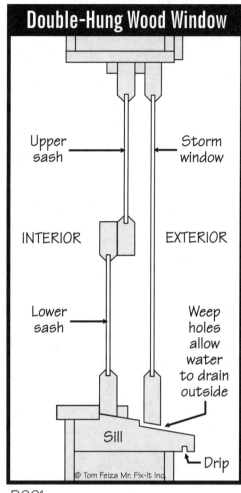

Double-Hung Wood Window

Upper sash

Storm window

INTERIOR

EXTERIOR

Lower sash

Weep holes allow water to drain outside

Sill

Drip

© Tom Feiza Mr. Fix-It Inc.

D001

Lead can also be present in drinking water. Call your local health department or water supplier to find out about testing your water. If your water supply does have lead, follow the recommendation of the local water supplier.

For more information, contact:

- The National Lead Information Center at 1-800-LEAD-FYI

- Your local health department

- The Consumer Product Safety Commission

- The Environmental Protection Agency (EPA)

Also, see the References section for additional contact information.

Asbestos

Asbestos was often used in building materials until the 1970s. However, the mere presence of asbestos in your home is not hazardous. The danger is that asbestos materials may become damaged over time; damaged asbestos may release asbestos fibers that present a health hazard.

Studies show that people exposed to high levels of asbestos fibers have an increased risk of cancer and asbestosis. The risk increases with the number of fibers inhaled. Smokers are also at increased risk.

You may find asbestos fibers in pipe and duct insulation, resilient floor tiles, cement sheeting and shingles, soundproofing, joint compounds, and many fireproof or fire-resistant materials. The only way to determine whether a building material contains asbestos is to have it sampled and tested by a qualified lab.

If you think you have asbestos in your home, don't panic. Usually the best thing you can do with asbestos materials in good shape is to leave them alone. Repairs or remodeling must be done properly to avoid disturbing these materials. Do not sweep, dust or vacuum debris that may contain asbestos; these steps may release asbestos fibers into the air.

For more information, contact:

- Consumer Product Safety Commission

- Environmental Protection Agency

- American Lung Association

- Your state and local health departments

Also, see the References section for additional contact information.

Radon

Radon is a radioactive gas that has been found in homes all over the U.S. It comes from the natural breakdown of uranium in soil, rock and water, and it gets into the air we breathe. Typically, radon moves up through the ground and enters a home's foundation through cracks and holes. Your home can trap this radon.

Testing is the only way to know whether you and your family are at risk from radon. You cannot see, smell or taste it. Breathing air containing radon increases your risk of getting lung cancer. If you smoke and your home has high radon levels, your risk of lung cancer is especially high.

You can conduct a radon test using a small charcoal canister or alpha-track detector. Test kits are available through hardware stores, and the cost usually includes lab analysis. The most accurate testing procedure follows EPA testing requirements. You can also hire a professional testing firm, but make sure it is registered with the EPA and that it follows EPA guidelines. A professional test will cost about $100.

A short-term test over two to four days provides only a quick snapshot of the radon levels in your home. A much better test is a long-term test conducted over more than 90 days.

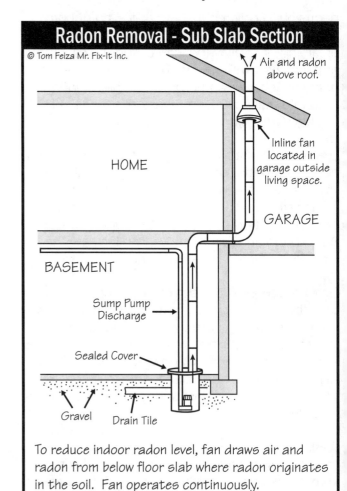

Radon Removal - Sub Slab Section

© Tom Feiza Mr. Fix-It Inc.

Air and radon above roof.

Inline fan located in garage outside living space.

HOME

GARAGE

BASEMENT

Sump Pump Discharge

Sealed Cover

Gravel   Drain Tile

To reduce indoor radon level, fan draws air and radon from below floor slab where radon originates in the soil. Fan operates continuously.

V034

If excessive radon is present, a common solution for a home with a drain-tile system is a sub-slab depressurization system. It removes radon from below the slab.

Radon can also be present in your drinking water. Contact your water supplier for specific information. You can receive more information on radon from several local and federal sources.

For more information, contact:

- The Environmental Protection Agency

- State or local health departments

- The American Lung Association

Carbon Monoxide

Carbon monoxide (CO) should be a concern for all homeowners. The government estimates that 300 people are killed by CO in their homes each year. CO is called a silent killer because it has no taste, color or odor. Almost all CO problems are caused by poor maintenance or improper use of fuel-burning equipment.

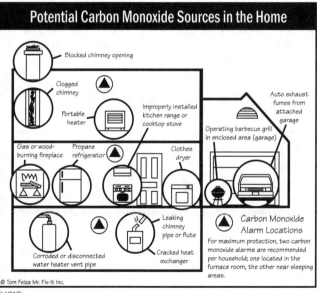

Potential Carbon Monoxide Sources in the Home

M019

You can take simple precautions to protect your family by understanding CO and by properly maintaining combustion equipment in your home.

CO is produced when fuel is burned. Fuel-burning appliances such as your furnace are potential sources. Properly maintained appliances produce very little CO and will not cause a problem. However, improperly operating appliances, your auto, or any non-vented indoor fire can cause CO poisoning.

Proper maintenance of fuel-burning appliances is essential. This includes the furnace, water heater, gas clothes dryer, fireplace, and even a gas range or space heater. All of these appliances should be used as designed, and all need periodic servicing.

Pay particular attention to furnaces and water heaters. Have them serviced regularly, and routinely inspect the flue connections and chimney. Flue pipes should not have holes, rust or soft areas. Flues should not show signs of water streaking or sooting; this indicates that combustion gas is not flowing up the flue into the chimney.

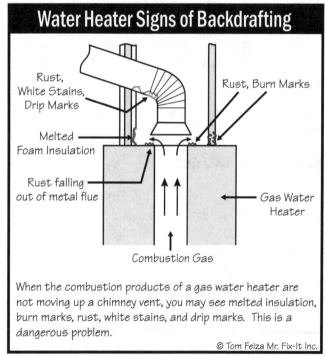

Water Heater Signs of Backdrafting

When the combustion products of a gas water heater are not moving up a chimney vent, you may see melted insulation, burn marks, rust, white stains, and drip marks. This is a dangerous problem.

© Tom Feiza Mr. Fix-It Inc.

V033

Also, know the symptoms of CO poisoning. Initial symptoms are similar to the flu without fever: dizziness, nausea, fatigue, headache and irregular breathing. If you have these symptoms at home and then feel better when you go outside your home, suspect a problem. If all the members of your family have similar symptoms at similar times, suspect a problem.

You can also help protect your family with a CO detector. Buy one similar to a smoke detector. It should have a loud audio alarm. Do not rely on detectors with small dots that turn black when exposed to CO—how often will you look at the dots? Select a top-of-the-line alarm with a digital CO readout so you can monitor the level in your home.

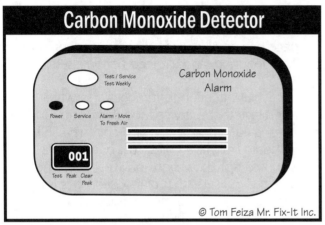

M020

The best location for a CO detector is on a wall in your sleeping area, about 5 feet from the floor. Place it where you will see it every night before you go to bed so you will remember to check the level.

For sources of safety information, see the References section.

Mold and Mildew

Since about 1990, mold has become a serious concern for homeowners. The news media present graphic stories of sick homeowners and homes that must be torn down because of mold contamination. In recent years that message has been reinforced by more and more stories. Some people are even concerned with the small black dots that may appear from time to time in caulk around the bathtub.

Is mold a real problem? Every homeowner needs to think through this issue relative to his or her own home. Mold has been around forever, but recently it has become a big issue. Why? Is it really an important issue?

Recent government and scientific studies have found that mold poses a threat to those who have breathing problems, allergies, or weakened immune systems. Government studies also show that mold does not normally affect healthy people.

We certainly don't want to be exposed to mold and risk our health. So, what do we do? Avoid the conditions that cause mold to grow: moisture, warmer temperatures, and a food source.

Mold is everywhere—inside and outside your home. Mold helps turn leaves and grass back into soil. The green growth on the north side of the tree trunk is—you guessed it—mold.

What has changed? Why is it a problem now?

Older homes are big energy wasters. Air and heat move easily though old homes. Air movement and heat easily dry out old homes if they become wet. (Want to dry your hair? Blow hot air on it.)

Newer homes are tight—wrapped in air barriers and moisture retarders with tight insulation. We have stopped the air movement and heat loss, but now these homes don't dry out. If new homes get wet and don't dry out, there is the potential for mold.

Our First Defense

Our first defense is to keep our homes dry. Without moisture, mold will not grow. This means we can't allow excessive condensation, roof leaks, or plumbing leaks; and if surfaces do get wet, we need to dry them as soon as possible. If soft materials become wet, they should be removed.

What to do if you suspect mold

Look for visible mold growth. Search for areas with a noticeable mold odor. Look for signs of water stains, leaks, standing water, or condensation. Eliminate the water and stop the mold. Most government agencies don't recommend more extensive testing because a simple visual inspection can confirm whether there is a mold or moisture problem. There are no accepted standards for testing and exposure levels for mold. There are no standards relating health issues to levels of exposure. Your best bet is to find the moisture problem, eliminate the moisture, and clean up any mold.

Mold Information – Resources

For good information on investigation, testing, and mold removal, I suggest the following resources:

Minnesota Department of Health

www.health.state.mn.us

Building Science Corporation

www.buildingscience.com

The New York City Health Department

www.ci.nyc.ny.us

Forest Products Laboratory

www.fpl.fs.fed.us

Environmental Protection Agency

www.epa.gov

State of Wisconsin – Department of Health and Family Services – Mold Information

www.dhfs.wisconsin.gov/eh/HlthHaz/fs/moldindx.htm

Chapter 3 – Utility Systems – Heating and Air Conditioning

Utility and General System Notes

This is where your homework starts. Take time to read these chapters. They contain important information about the many systems in your home. The explanation of each system includes operating information, terminology, sketches, main shutoffs, and part names. If you need more specific information, check the References section.

Since some systems are very complicated, they need to be serviced routinely by contractors. Look in the Service Checklists chapter for specifications you can copy and use with service contractors. You can do simple maintenance yourself; this information is provided in utility systems chapters and in Chapter 8 on Service Requirements by the Calendar.

Your home will not have all of the systems shown in this book. For instance, you may have a warm air furnace or a hot water furnace, but not both. You may have either a central air conditioner or a heat pump. As you read, walk around your home to determine the type of equipment you have and identify important valves and switches. If some systems or parts are confusing, ask a professional service contractor or a knowledgeable friend to walk you through the system.

The chapters on emergencies will help you solve problems and perhaps avoid a service call. Many emergencies, strange noises, leaks and smells have simple solutions. I have attempted to include all common problems.

Heating and Air Conditioning

Most homes are heated with a warm air furnace (also called a forced air furnace) because this type of system provides heating and cooling through the same air distribution ducts. A warm air system requires supply grills in most rooms. Some homes are heated with a hydronic (warm water) system that uses radiators, baseboard (convector) elements, or heating pipes buried in walls or floors.

The energy source for heating can be natural gas, propane, or oil. In warmer climates, electrical resistance heating elements may be used in a warm air furnace. Usually, the energy source for air conditioning is electricity, but gas-powered engine systems can also provide cooling.

Some homes have separate heating and cooling systems. One common system combines hydronic heating with ducted air conditioning.

As you review the information on heating and air conditioning, identify the system used in your home.

As with all systems in your home, you must understand the basics of heating and air conditioning so you can perform basic maintenance and operate the system properly and efficiently.

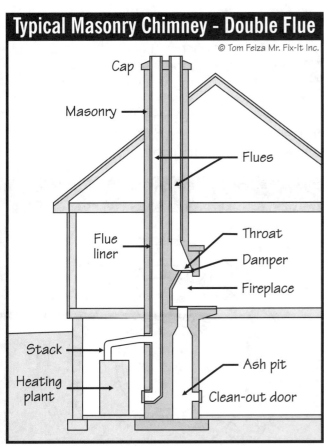

Typical Masonry Chimney - Double Flue

© Tom Feiza Mr. Fix-It Inc.

- Cap
- Masonry
- Flues
- Flue liner
- Throat
- Damper
- Fireplace
- Stack
- Ash pit
- Heating plant
- Clean-out door

F002

Gas Warm Air Furnace

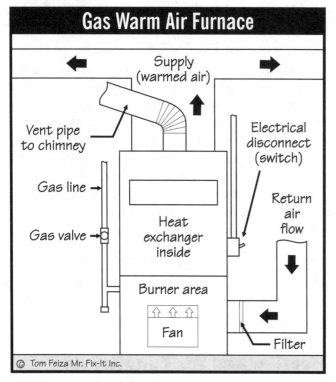

© Tom Feiza Mr. Fix-It Inc.

H001

Must Know / Must Do
Heating and Air Conditioning

- Understand how your heating and cooling system works and who you can call for service.

- Understand the control (thermostat) for the heating and cooling system.

- Perform basic maintenance: filter changes and lubrication.

- Schedule yearly maintenance by a professional.

- Identify and know how to use emergency shutoffs for electricity, gas, oil, and so on.

Thermostat

The thermostat provides automatic control for heating and cooling systems. You set it to the temperature you want to maintain. The thermostat, located in the conditioned (heated and/or cooled) space, senses room temperature, and when the room tem-

perature varies from your setpoint, the thermostat activates the heating or cooling system.

A dual heating/cooling thermostat will have switches that let you change the system from heating to cooling and operate the fan separately. Some thermostats also allow you to turn off the heating and cooling systems.

All heating and cooling thermostats operate with similar buttons and controls. The basic and common controls are as follows:

HEAT – OFF – COOL

This switch will put the system in the heating mode (HEAT), turn the system off (OFF), or switch the system to cooling (COOL) if there is an air conditioning system. Once the system is set to HEAT or COOL, the thermostat temperature setting controls the system based on the room temperature.

FAN – ON – AUTO

This switch allows operation of the fan manually (ON), independent of the heating and cooling system. This allows you to circulate air in your home without operating the heating or cooling system. In the automatic (AUTO) setting the fan will cycle on and off as needed by the heating or cooling system. AUTO is the setting normally used.

Heat Only Thermostat

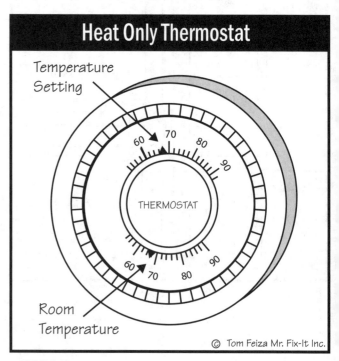

© Tom Feiza Mr. Fix-It Inc.

H024

Heat - Cool Thermostat

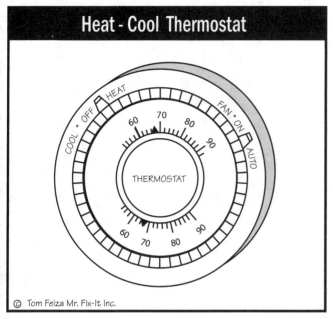

© Tom Feiza Mr. Fix-It Inc.

HO23

The typical home system is either fully on or fully off; it doesn't provide variable heating/cooling. When the thermostat calls for heat, the furnace reacts at 100 percent capacity until the room temperature reaches the setpoint; then the furnace shuts off. Turning the thermostat up higher will not heat the room any faster. When you switch the system to cooling, turning the thermostat lower will not cool the room any faster. (A few homes do have complicated systems in which the furnace is capable of variable heating/cooling, but these are the exception.)

Electronic (or digital) thermostats can be programmed for automatic adjustment of the setpoint temperature based on time of day and day of week. These help conserve energy; they can lower the temperature during sleeping hours or when your home is not occupied.

Thermostats should be installed and maintained by professionals. Special anticipator settings on the thermostat match its operation with the operation of the furnace. If you replace a thermostat, make sure that this anticipator setting is done properly.

Thermostats are very sensitive. Your thermostat should be level, out of direct sunlight, and away from direct heat sources. If a thermostat develops a major problem, the usual recommendation is replacement rather than repair, because much better electronic thermostats with modern setback capabilities are readily available at reasonable prices.

Digital Thermostat

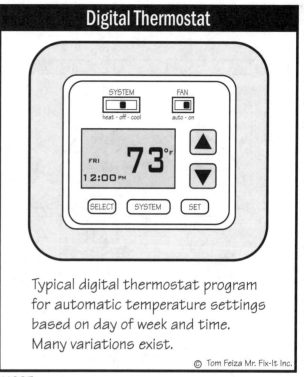

Typical digital thermostat program for automatic temperature settings based on day of week and time. Many variations exist.

© Tom Feiza Mr. Fix-It Inc.

HO25

To obtain detailed information on thermostats, see the References section; many manufacturers will send instructions for a specific thermostat.

Warm Air Furnace

The most common type of warm air (forced air) furnace provides heat by burning a fossil fuel to warm air and then distributing the warm air inside your home. The heat source is confined within a heat exchanger inside the furnace housing. For gas, propane, and oil systems, the fuel is burned inside or below a heat exchanger. The hot products of combustion flow through the heat exchanger and up a chimney or are drawn out through a vent pipe.

The hot products of combustion warm the metal of the heat exchanger. After a minute or so, when the heat exchanger's metal is warm, the circulating (furnace) fan starts. This fan circulates air across the hot metal on the outside of the heat exchanger. The heated air warms your home.

For homes without basements or crawl spaces, warm air furnaces can be located in attics or closet spaces. The typical warm air furnace located in an attic or crawl space uses the same components as a basement (upflow type) furnace but the furnace is often designed to operate horizontally to save space.

Warm Air Furnace and Distribution Ducts

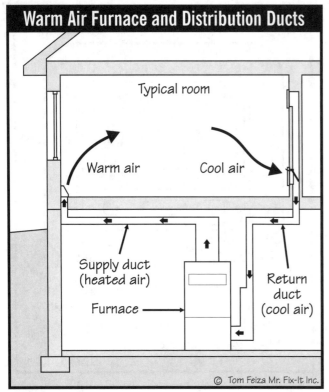

HO10

Furnaces for homes built on a concrete slab are located in the attic or in a closet. For the closet installations, a downflow warm air furnace may be used. These furnaces are similar to the upflow furnace, but the components are reversed. The heat supply ducts are in the floor slab. Homes on slabs can also have a warm air furnace in a closet using a typical upflow furance – the supply ducts will be in the attic and the return will be through the halls or in the floor slab.

The efficiency of gas furnaces has improved dramatically in recent years. Standard (60%) warm air furnaces have been improved with electronic ignition devices to eliminate the standing pilot light and prevent this heat loss. These furnaces have also been improved with a motor-operated flue damper in the pipe that goes to the chimney. When the burner is on, the damper is open. When the burner is off, the damper closes and eliminates the draft up the chimney, saving energy. These improvements will make a 60% furnace operate at about 65 to 70% efficiency.

You will find 80% efficiency furnaces that use a draft fan to force the products of combustion up the chimney. You will find 90%+ efficiency furnaces that vent with plastic PVC pipe. These higher efficiency furnaces squeeze so much energy out of the

Warm Air Furnace with Damper & Ignitor

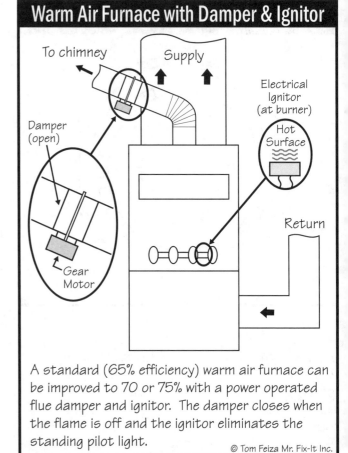

A standard (65% efficiency) warm air furnace can be improved to 70 or 75% with a power operated flue damper and ignitor. The damper closes when the flame is off and the ignitor eliminates the standing pilot light.

© Tom Feiza Mr. Fix-It Inc.

HO41

Warm Air Furnace - Horizontal Flow

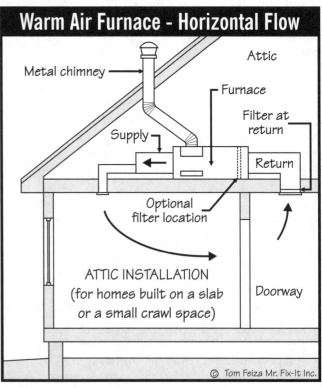

HO11

Warm Air Furnace - Downflow

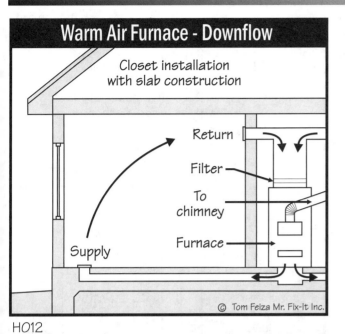

Closet installation with slab construction

Return
Filter
To chimney
Furnace
Supply

© Tom Feiza Mr. Fix-It Inc.

H012

Warm Air Furnace with Oil Burner

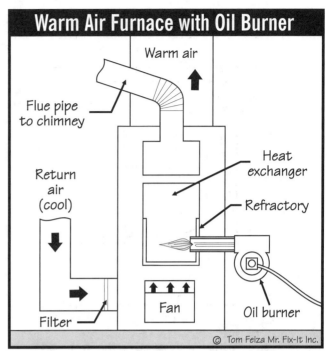

Warm air
Flue pipe to chimney
Heat exchanger
Refractory
Return air (cool)
Filter
Fan
Oil burner

© Tom Feiza Mr. Fix-It Inc.

H013

Warm Air Furnace in Garage

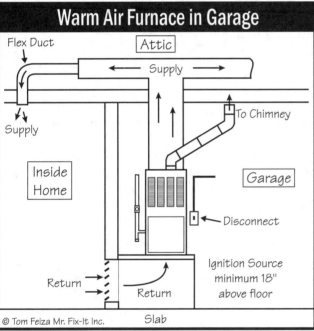

Flex Duct
Attic
Supply
To Chimney
Supply
Inside Home
Garage
Disconnect
Return
Return
Ignition Source minimum 18" above floor
Slab

© Tom Feiza Mr. Fix-It Inc.

H039

Outside Air Supply to Heating Return Duct

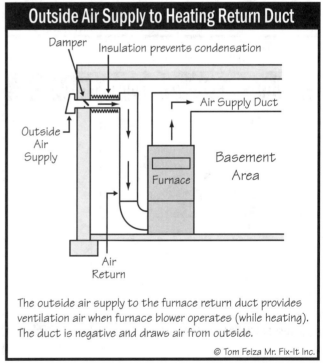

Damper
Insulation prevents condensation
Air Supply Duct
Outside Air Supply
Basement Area
Furnace
Air Return

The outside air supply to the furnace return duct provides ventilation air when furnace blower operates (while heating). The duct is negative and draws air from outside.

© Tom Feiza Mr. Fix-It Inc.

V028

products of combustion that they need special fans to help remove the products of combustion; the combustion gas is not hot enough to naturally draft up the chimney.

In an electric warm air furnace, air circulates directly over an electrical resistance-heating element.

A propane gas furnace is similar to a natural gas furnace but uses a different burner and control system designed for propane.

Oil warm air furnaces have a special oil burner and combustion chamber. The burner pressurizes the oil and sprays it through a small nozzle, forming a mist. The burner also provides an air supply and a high-voltage spark. This results in a very hot flame that is contained in a ceramic combustion chamber. From the combustion chamber, the hot combustion gas flows up through the heat exchanger, just as in a gas furnace.

Outside Air Supply to Heat/Cool Return Duct

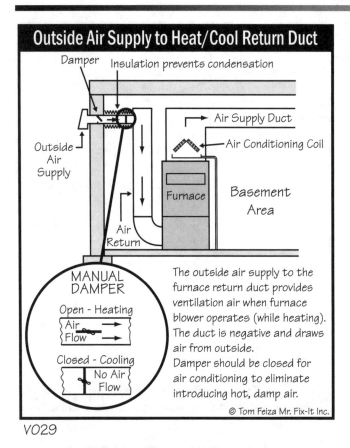

VO29

The outside air supply to the furnace return duct provides ventilation air when furnace blower operates (while heating). The duct is negative and draws air from outside.

Damper should be closed for air conditioning to eliminate introducing hot, damp air.

© Tom Feiza Mr. Fix-It Inc.

Mid-Efficiency Warm Air Furnace

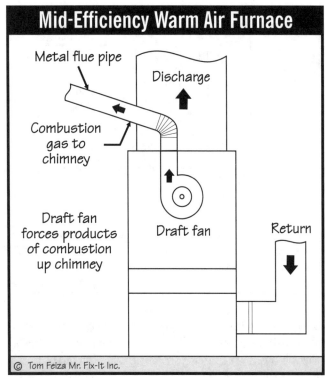

© Tom Feiza Mr. Fix-It Inc.

HOO2

A warm air furnace recirculates air in your home. It does not draw in outside air unless there are special provisions for an outside air supply (which is not common). The fan circulates the air, which is drawn

High-Efficiency Warm Air Furnace

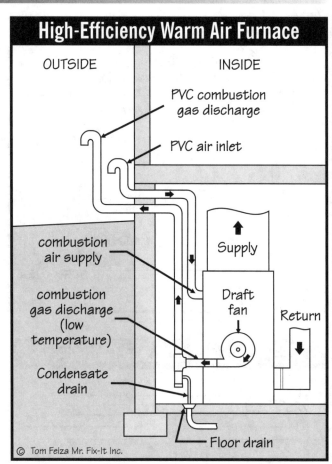

© Tom Feiza Mr. Fix-It Inc.

HOO3

from the return grills and ducts inside your home and discharged through the supply grills. There will be a furnace air filter located near the fan; you must maintain this filter.

Systems for air supply and ducting have changed through the years. The early "gravity" warm air furnace system (commonly called an octopus) did not use a circulating fan. The air was said to move by "gravity"—that is, warm air simply rose up into the rooms. This type of system often has warm supply grills in the center of the home and the cold returns along outside walls.

When furnaces were improved with circulating fans (the forced air/warm air furnace), heating ducts made a transition to the upper portion of the center wall; return ducts were still located along the outer walls. In an older home, you may find a strange combination of supply and return grills, since they were added as heating systems were upgraded or replaced.

Warm air or forced air furnaces have a circulating fan or blower located near the heat exchanger. This fan circulates the house air over the warm metal of the heat exchanger inside the furnace. The fan may be powered directly by a fan motor mounted inside the fan housing. A motor through a belt and pulley arrangement may also power the fan.

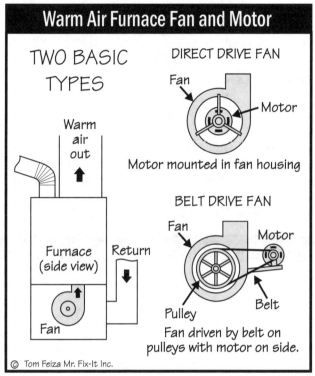

Warm Air Furnace Fan and Motor

TWO BASIC TYPES

Warm air out

Furnace (side view) Return

Fan

DIRECT DRIVE FAN

Fan

Motor

Motor mounted in fan housing

BELT DRIVE FAN

Fan

Motor

Pulley

Belt

Fan driven by belt on pulleys with motor on side.

© Tom Feiza Mr. Fix-It Inc.

H014

For a belt drive fan, you must maintain the belt and belt alignment. Turn off power to the unit before you open the fan chamber. The belt should not be cracked or frayed. If the belt is very hard and shiny on the driving "v" sides, it is old and needs to be replaced. The pulleys should align so the belt runs straight between each pulley.

Proper tension on the belt is required to transmit power. With moderate hand pressure applied on the belt one-half way between the pulleys, the belt should deflect about 1/2 to 3/4 inch. The motor mounting brackets are often adjustable to change the belt tension.

Many older furnaces require lubrication of the bearings on the fan and fan motor. On newer furnaces, bearings may be lubricated for life and will not need additional lubrication. Check your owner's manual or consult with a heating contractor for the specific requirements for your furnace. You can also look at the ends of the fan and the motor; you may see little (1/4-inch) caps over little tubes. These are

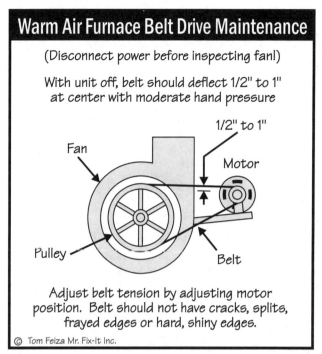

Warm Air Furnace Belt Drive Maintenance

(Disconnect power before inspecting fan!)

With unit off, belt should deflect 1/2" to 1" at center with moderate hand pressure

1/2" to 1"

Fan

Motor

Pulley

Belt

Adjust belt tension by adjusting motor position. Belt should not have cracks, splits, frayed edges or hard, shiny edges.

© Tom Feiza Mr. Fix-It Inc.

H015

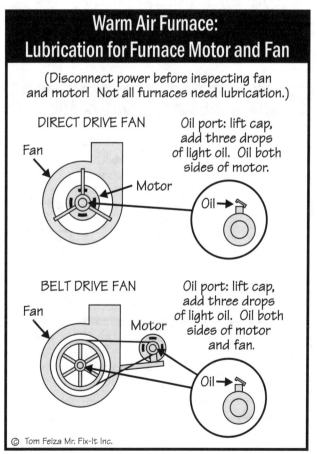

Warm Air Furnace: Lubrication for Furnace Motor and Fan

(Disconnect power before inspecting fan and motor! Not all furnaces need lubrication.)

DIRECT DRIVE FAN

Fan

Motor

Oil port: lift cap, add three drops of light oil. Oil both sides of motor.

Oil

BELT DRIVE FAN

Fan

Motor

Oil port: lift cap, add three drops of light oil. Oil both sides of motor and fan.

Oil

© Tom Feiza Mr. Fix-It Inc.

H016

ports in which to add oil for lubrication. Generally these bearings should be lubricated with a few drops of light oil every few months.

Newer furnaces will also have a safety switch built into the fan access door. When the fan chamber door is removed, this switch shuts the furnace off. This is a safety device that prevents accidental injury from the moving part of the fan system. If you ever have a situation with no heat or no air conditioning, you should check this access door and safety switch. A loose fan access door can inadvertently shut the system down.

An older home may also have a supply grill without a return grill. This is common in the second story of Cape Cod style houses. Often this works well for heating but not for proper air conditioning.

With modern systems, heat ducts are located on the floor or ceiling near the outside walls, windows and doors. Returns are placed on interior walls. If the furnace is in the basement or crawl space, supply grills will be near the floor; if the furnace or supply ducting is in the attic, supply grills will be in the ceiling. This modern arrangement provides for good air distribution and greater comfort. Most modern systems have a return grill in every room except the bathrooms.

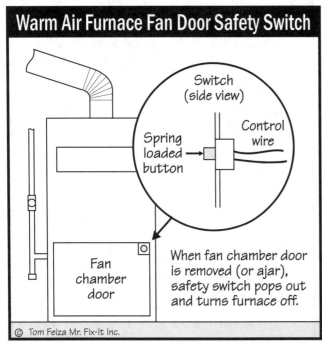

Warm Air Furnace Fan Door Safety Switch

Switch (side view)

Spring loaded button

Control wire

Fan chamber door

When fan chamber door is removed (or ajar), safety switch pops out and turns furnace off.

© Tom Feiza Mr. Fix-It Inc.

H017

Air Filters

Air filters are provided on all forced air furnaces to remove dirt and lint from heated air.

This keeps the fan, heat exchanger and air conditioning coil clean. It also helps clean the air of your home as air circulates through the system (note the direction of the air flow).

Media Filters

ONE-INCH-THICK FIBERGLASS

The standard filter on most furnaces is a nominal 1"-thick media filter. Usually, this filter is made of fiberglass. The filter should be changed when it is visibly dirty—usually every month or two, depending on the quality of the filter and the amount of

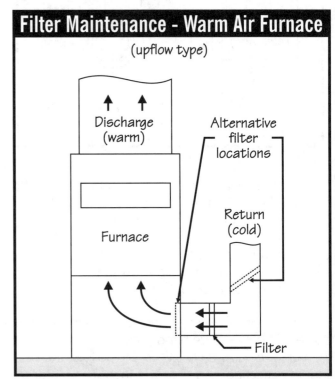

Filter Maintenance - Warm Air Furnace

(upflow type)

Discharge (warm)

Alternative filter locations

Furnace

Return (cold)

Filter

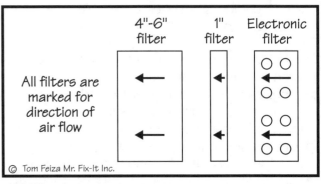

	4"-6" filter	1" filter	Electronic filter
All filters are marked for direction of air flow	←	←	←
	←	←	←

© Tom Feiza Mr. Fix-It Inc.

H009

Fiberglass Filter - Flow Direction

Air Flow Direction

Arrow on filter frame indicates air flow direction

16•20•1

© Tom Feiza Mr. Fix-It Inc.

H026

dirt in your home's air. Children, pets, plants, and activity tend to produce more dirt that finds its way into the heating system.

Be careful about the direction of the air flow through the filter. Filters are designed to be installed with one particular side facing the air stream. Most filters have directions or an arrow telling you which side should be installed toward the furnace. The arrow is the direction of the air flow and should be toward the base or the fan of the furnace.

Must Know / Must Do

Routinely Maintain the Furnace Filter

Maintenance is based on the type of filter, how often the unit is running (heating and cooling), and how you use your home. The three basic types of filters are media, electronic, and electrostatic.

Remember: the furnace filter is also used when you operate the fan and/or central air conditioning, so you should check on the filter during the summer, too.

PAPER

I recommend that you try one of the pleated paper filters. These catch more dirt than inexpensive fiberglass filters. Some even have a static charge to attract dirt. Others have a carbon filter content. Paper filters cost between $3 and $15 and can be found in most hardware stores. You will need to change this type of filter more often because it collects more dirt.

WASHABLE

Washable filters can be made of foam or woven synthetic fiber. They are about as effective as inexpensive fiberglass filters. You can improve the efficiency of a foam filter by spraying it with a special filter coating; this oily/waxy spray helps the filter hold dirt better.

PLEATED, 4- TO 6-INCH THICK

A big improvement over the standard 1"-thick filter is a pleated fiberglass or paper filter.

1 - Inch Pleated Paper Filter

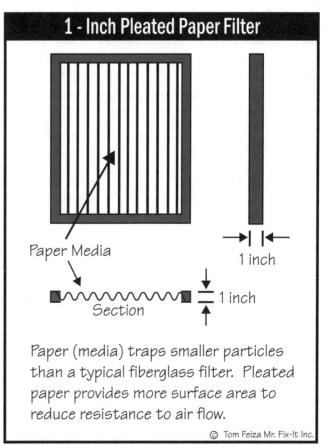

Paper Media

1 inch

Section

1 inch

Paper (media) traps smaller particles than a typical fiberglass filter. Pleated paper provides more surface area to reduce resistance to air flow.

© Tom Feiza Mr. Fix-It Inc.

H027

6 - Inch Pleated Media Filter

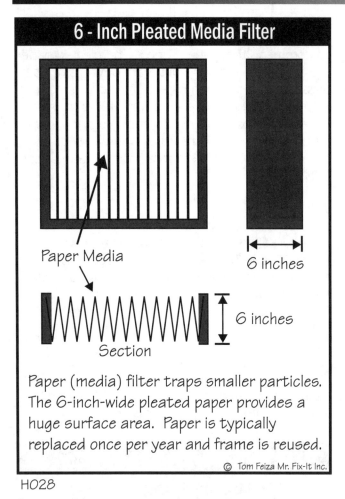

Paper Media

6 inches

6 inches

Section

Paper (media) filter traps smaller particles. The 6-inch-wide pleated paper provides a huge surface area. Paper is typically replaced once per year and frame is reused.

© Tom Feiza Mr. Fix-It Inc.

H028

Electronic Air Filter

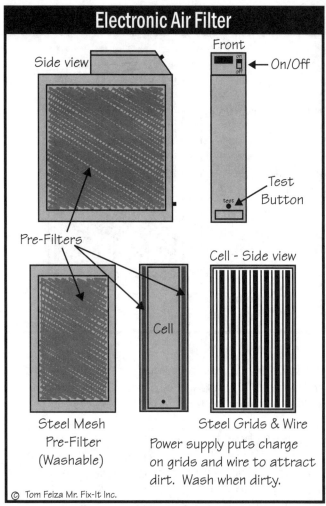

Side view

Front

On/Off

Test Button

Pre-Filters

Cell - Side view

Cell

Steel Mesh Pre-Filter (Washable)

Steel Grids & Wire

Power supply puts charge on grids and wire to attract dirt. Wash when dirty.

© Tom Feiza Mr. Fix-It Inc.

H029

Often, the pleated paper filter is housed in a 6"-thick frame. The paper filter is very fine, and it catches smaller particles of dirt and dust. This type of filter is normally changed once per year, and you replace only the paper element.

A pleated fiberglass filter often is mounted in a throwaway paper frame. The entire unit is replaced about once a year.

Electronic Filters

Electronic filters use electrically charged metal plates and wires that attract dirt. These filters can remove very small particles from smoke and pollen which aren't caught by standard filters. If you have respiratory problems or are sensitive to dust or pollen, you may want to use this type of filter.

Electronic filters cost more than $600 to install. Maintenance involves washing the interior frame and metal plates and wires with detergent or running them through a dishwasher. Most electronic filters have a metal pre-filter that also must be washed. For more specific cleaning instructions, contact a heating contractor or the filter manufacturer. The References section includes contact information.

Electrostatic and Electronic Filters

Many types of washable filters have multiple layers of filtering material; vendors claim these layers contain an electrostatic charge that attracts and traps dirt more effectively than a standard media filter.

Several companies also make a 1"-thick electrostatic/electronic filter as a direct replacement for throwaway filters. This filter may have an electronic power supply and may require particular maintenance procedures.

For more information on filters, look up manufacturers in the References section.

Warm Air Furnace—Maintenance Requirements

All heating equipment should be routinely checked by a qualified service technician. Most furnace manufacturers recommend yearly maintenance.

ROUTINE MAINTENANCE A HOMEOWNER SHOULD PERFORM

Note: Turn off power to the unit before inspection or maintenance.

- Maintain records. Have a professional service the unit yearly. Proper maintenance keeps equipment operating efficiently and ensures safety. Contact the manufacturer of your furnace for specific maintenance requirements. See the References section for contact information.

- Change the filter as required—often every other month.

- Switch high/low returns at the start and end of the heating season. For complete instructions, check the section on "Heating and Cooling Distribution" later in this chapter.

- Check all flue pipes and vents for rust, water leaks, and loose connections.

- Lubricate the fan motor and fan bearing with a few drops of oil twice per year. (This is only required on certain units.)

- Check the belt to make sure it's not cracked or loose. (This is only required with belt-driven fans.)

- Listen to the furnace operate. Follow up on any strange sounds.

- Check drain lines to make sure they are clear and draining properly.

- Look for water leaks or changes in the system.

ROUTINE MAINTENANCE A PROFESSIONAL SHOULD PERFORM

During a routine service call, the service technician should perform the following general maintenance measures. The technician may perform other checks, too, depending on the type of furnace.

- Check and clean burner.

- Check flue pipes, draft diverter, heat exchanger, and chimney.

- Remove burners to clean burners and heat exchanger if necessary.

- Check electrical wiring and connections.

- Check and clean circulating fan. Lubricate fan and motor if necessary.

- For belt drive fans: check for tension, wear and alignment.

- Check supply and returns ducts for air leakage, water stains, rust.

- Check and maintain filter.

- Perform an operational check of furnace and safety controls.

- Test for carbon monoxide in the flue gas and in the air around the furnace.

- Check for gas leaks.

- Check, clean, and adjust pilot light if necessary.

For a high-efficiency furnace, the technician should also:

- Check for water leaks (condensation from combustion).

- Check flue pipes and connections.

- Check for condensation on metal pipes and parts.

- Check for a clean condensate drain line.

- Check operation and condition of draft fan.

Duplicates of the above lists appear in the Service Checklists chapter. You may want to make a photocopy of the professional's list and send it to the service company when you arrange service and/or review the list with the technician at the beginning of the service call.

Hydronic (Hot Water) Heat

Hot water or hydronic systems provide heat by warming water and circulating it through piping to heating devices: radiators, baseboard convectors, radiant pipes in the floors or walls, or even coils with a fan. Older system typically use cast iron radiators; newer systems typically use baseboard convectors (finned tubes).

Hydronic systems usually burn oil, gas, or propane below a cast iron container or coil that holds water. The warmed water is then distributed to the radiators through a network of supply and return piping. Older systems use gravity to move the water—warm water rises, cool water falls. Newer systems use a small circulation pump to move the water.

The distribution system is sealed and should not leak, but water expands as it warms, so there will be an expansion tank to hold the increased volume. Most systems have an automated fill valve and backflow prevention.

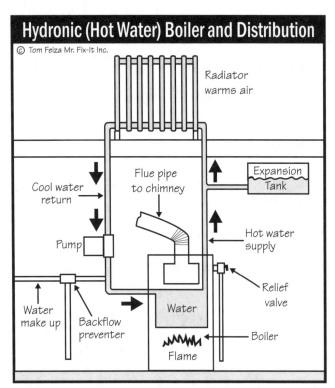

Hydronic (Hot Water) Boiler and Distribution

© Tom Feiza Mr. Fix-It Inc.

Radiator warms air

Cool water return

Flue pipe to chimney

Expansion Tank

Hot water supply

Pump

Relief valve

Water make up

Backflow preventer

Water

Boiler

Flame

H005

The system automatically responds to a thermostat located in the heated space. When the thermostat calls for heat, the boiler and the pump start. Warm water is delivered to the radiators. When the thermostat is satisfied, the boiler is turned off.

There are many variations to hydronic systems: multiple zones provided by thermostat and zone control valves or multiple pumps…boiler temperature water resets based on outside temperature….many control options…and variations in piping systems, to name a few. If you have a complicated system, ask a service technician to explain it to you.

Hydronic Heating— Maintenance Requirements

All heating equipment should be routinely checked by a qualified service technician. Most hydronic boiler manufacturers recommend yearly maintenance to keep equipment operating efficiently and to ensure safety.

Contact the manufacturer of your furnace for specific maintenance requirements. See the References section for contacts.

ROUTINE MAINTENANCE A HOMEOWNER SHOULD PERFORM

Note: Turn off power to the unit before inspection or maintenance.

- Maintain records, and have a professional service the unit yearly.

- Check all flue pipes and vents for rust, water leaks, loose connections.

- Listen to the boiler operate. Follow up on any strange noises.

- Check drain lines to make sure they are clear and draining properly. (This is required only for high efficiency condensing units.)

- Look for water leaks or changes in the system.

- Oil the circulating pump twice per year. (Use just a few drops).

- Check that the temperature/pressure gauge is in the operating range identified by a professional service technician. Mark the proper range on the gauge.

ROUTINE MAINTENANCE A PROFESSIONAL SHOULD PERFORM

A service technician should perform the following general maintenance measures. The service technician may also perform additional checks, depending on the type of furnace.

- Check and clean burner.

- Vent the system at the high points as necessary.

- Check all flue pipes, draft diverter, boiler housing, and chimney.

- Remove burners to clean burners and heat exchanger if necessary.

- Check electrical wiring and connections.

- Check and lubricate circulating pump(s).

- Check for water leaks.

- Check temperature and pressure relief valve.

- Check water supply system and backflow preventer.

- Add backflow preventer if none is present.

- Check expansion tank for proper water level.

- Perform an operational check of controls for temperature, pressure, and safety.

- Test for carbon monoxide in the flue gas and in the air around the furnace.

- Check for gas leaks.

- Check, clean, and (if necessary) adjust pilot light.

Additional checks for a high-efficiency boiler with a draft fan:

- Check draft fan for condensation and rust.

- Check flue pipe for condensation.

- Check condensate drain lines.

Duplicates of the above lists appear in the Service Checklists chapter. You may want to make a photocopy of the professional's list and send it to the service company when you arrange service and/or review the list with the technician at the beginning of the service call.

Steam Heating

A steam heating system is similar to a hydronic boiler system except that it produces steam at low pressure. Because they require more maintenance than hydronic systems, steam systems are rarely installed in newer homes, and older steam systems often are converted to hydronic systems.

Steam systems can use oil, natural gas or propane as an energy source. The burning fuel heats water in the boiler, turning it to steam. The steam, under pressure, rises through the system to the radiators. Vents in the radiators release heated air. The steam condenses back into water as it releases energy in the radiator, and the water flows back to the boiler to be reheated.

While there are variations in the piping systems, almost all residential systems are "one-pipe" systems as described above. You can identify a one-pipe system because it will have only one pipe connected to the radiators.

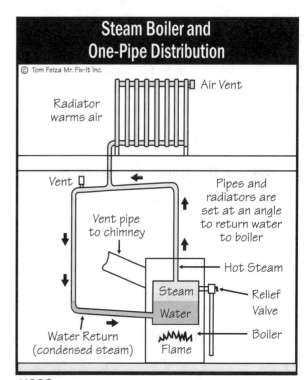

H006

Steam systems should have professional maintenance at least once per year, perhaps more often. Much of the maintenance required by a steam system is too complicated for most homeowners to perform.

ROUTINE MAINTENANCE A HOMEOWNER SHOULD PERFORM

- Maintain records.

- Check all flue pipes and vents for leaks, rust, and loose connections.

- Check the system for any leaks.

- Check the steam gauge. Have your contractor mark the normal range.

- Check the water level every month. The normal range should be marked on a sight glass.

- Make the sure the radiators slope slightly toward the steam inlet pipe. This will help keep the pipe from knocking or pounding.

- Make sure the vents on the radiators are operating; otherwise, radiators may be cold.

ROUTINE MAINTENANCE A PROFESSIONAL SHOULD PERFORM

A service technician should perform the following general maintenance measures. The service technician may also perform additional checks, depending on the type of boiler. (For a gas-fired system, see the information on oil burners, which require additional checks.)

- Check and clean the burner.

- Check all vents on radiators and piping.

- Check all flue pipes, draft diverter, boiler housing and chimney.

- Remove burners to clean them and the heat exchanger if necessary.

- Check electrical wiring and connections.

- Check for water or steam leaks.

- Check the temperature and pressure relief valve.

- Add a backflow preventer if none is present.

- Perform an operational check of controls for temperature, pressure and safety.

- Test for carbon monoxide in the flue gas and the air around the boiler.

- Check for gas leaks.

- Check, clean and if necessary adjust the pilot light.

Duplicates of the above lists appear in the Service Checklists chapter. You may want to make a photocopy of the professional's list and send it to the service company when you arrange service and/or review the list with the technician at the beginning of the service call.

Oil Burner

An oil burner can be used just like a gas burner in warm air furnaces, hydronic systems or even water heaters. All oil burners are essentially the same except for some very old style vaporizing or pot-type burners. Here we will only cover modern pressure burners or gun-type burners.

A modern oil burner pressurizes oil and sprays it through a small nozzle, forming a mist. At the same time, the burner provides an air supply and a high-voltage spark. This results in a very hot flame that is contained in a ceramic combustion chamber. From the combustion chamber, the hot combustion gas flows up through the heat exchanger, just as in a gas-fired appliance.

Oil Heat—Maintenance Requirements

Oil burners can be quite efficient, comparable to gas units. Oil burners require yearly maintenance. Also, never let your oil system run out of fuel. This can cause major problems with the burner, requiring a service call.

Most homeowners find it convenient to arrange for an oil delivery and burner service company to provide automatic oil tank filling and yearly service. This is the best way to ensure that the system is operating properly. You will also be placed at the top of the service call list if you are an established customer.

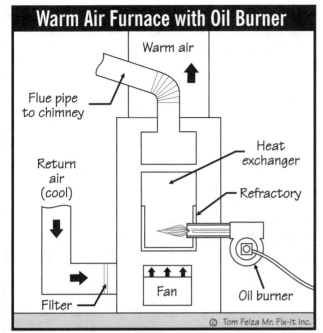

Warm Air Furnace with Oil Burner

Warm air

Flue pipe to chimney

Return air (cool)

Heat exchanger

Refractory

Filter

Fan

Oil burner

© Tom Feiza Mr. Fix-It Inc.

H013

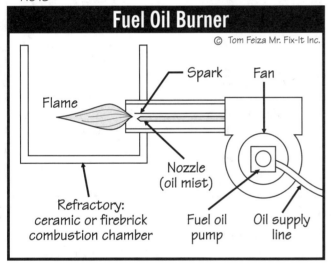

Fuel Oil Burner

© Tom Feiza Mr. Fix-It Inc.

Spark

Fan

Flame

Nozzle (oil mist)

Refractory: ceramic or firebrick combustion chamber

Fuel oil pump

Oil supply line

H007

ROUTINE MAINTENANCE A HOMEOWNER SHOULD PERFORM

Note: Turn off power to the unit before attempting inspection or maintenance.

- Follow the maintenance requirements listed above for warm air or hydronic boiler systems.

- Schedule routine maintenance yearly.

- Lubricate the burner motor if it has oil ports (ask your service technician).

- Make sure the system never, never runs out of fuel oil.

ROUTINE MAINTENANCE A PROFESSIONAL SHOULD PERFORM

A service technician should perform the following general maintenance measures. The service technician may also perform additional checks, depending on the type of furnace.

- Follow applicable maintenance requirements listed above for a hydronic boiler or warm air furnace.

- Remove and clean burner, clean blower blades, replace or clean filter and/or strainer, replace the nozzle, clean flame and heat sensors, check and clean or replace electrodes.

- Lubricate the burner motor.

- Check flue and barometric damper.

- Check for oil leaks.

- Check and clean oil pump.

- Clean and test stack control.

- Check and adjust draft regulator.

- Test for efficiency and make proper adjustments.

Duplicates of the above lists appear in the Service Checklists chapter. You may want to make a photocopy of the professional's list and send it to the service company when you arrange service and/or review the list with the technician at the beginning of the service call.

Central Air Conditioning

Central air conditioning uses a warm air furnace system to cool air and distribute it throughout the home. The air conditioning system uses the fan, filter, thermostat and ducts; the heating portion of the system remains turned off.

When a home has hydronic heat, central air conditioning may be provided by a separate system. In this case, there is no heating equipment in the standard furnace housing; it has only a fan and cooling coil.

Air Conditioning System with Warm Air Furnace

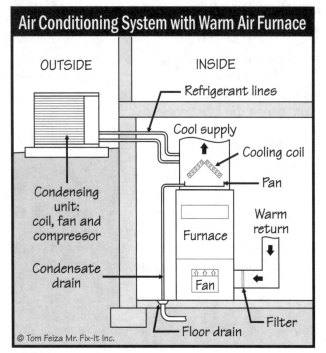

OUTSIDE | INSIDE

Refrigerant lines

Cool supply

Cooling coil

Pan

Condensing unit: coil, fan and compressor

Warm return

Furnace

Condensate drain

Fan

Floor drain

Filter

© Tom Feiza Mr. Fix-It Inc.

A001

Air Conditioning - Exterior Electrical Disconnect

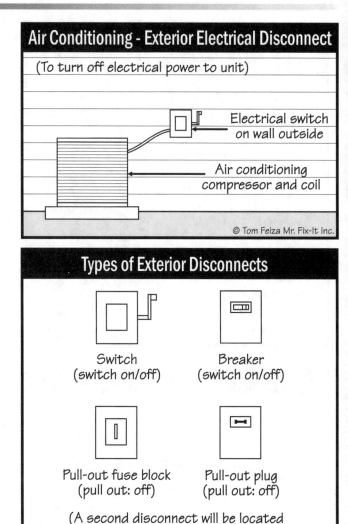

(To turn off electrical power to unit)

Electrical switch on wall outside

Air conditioning compressor and coil

© Tom Feiza Mr. Fix-It Inc.

Types of Exterior Disconnects

Switch (switch on/off)

Breaker (switch on/off)

Pull-out fuse block (pull out: off)

Pull-out plug (pull out: off)

(A second disconnect will be located inside at the main electrical panel)

A004

A central air system includes an interior coil (in the furnace housing) that removes heat from the interior air and an exterior coil that rejects heat into air outside the house.

When the thermostat signals for cooling, this starts up the exterior refrigeration compressor, exterior fan and furnace fan. The exterior compressor moves refrigerant through the closed system of coils and valves to produce a cool coil inside. The furnace fan moves air across this coil. The air cools, and moisture condenses on the coil's surface. This moisture is caught in a pan below the coil and drains away through a hose.

It is not necessary to cover the exterior unit during the winter, since these units are designed to withstand the weather. If you do cover the unit for some reason (for instance, if the unit is located where debris might accumulate on it), it's best to cover only the top of the unit. If you were to securely wrap the sides, moisture could condense in the unit. Also, a wrapped unit provides a perfect winter home for animals that may chew wiring and cause other problems.

When it's time for the winter shutdown, turn off power to the unit to prevent accidental operation. The power disconnect could be the breaker or fuse at the main panel. Or the disconnect may be at the exterior unit, usually as a switch or a fuse block or plug that you pull out to disconnect the power.

Central air conditioning systems should never be operated in cold weather. This can cause serious damage.

Don't start the central air conditioner unless the outdoor temperature has been above 60 degrees for at least 24 hours. Remember to uncover the unit if you added a cover for the winter.

At the start of the cooling season, when you're about to turn on power to the unit, make sure that the thermostat is switched off, and leave the thermostat off for 24 hours before operating the unit. If the unit has a crankcase heater, this procedure allows the heater to warm the unit.

Central Air Conditioning– Maintenance Requirements

Proper maintenance will keep the unit operating properly and save you energy costs. Have your air conditioning system checked yearly by a professional service contractor.

You should also perform basic maintenance. Contact the manufacturer of your furnace/AC unit for specific maintenance requirements; see the References section for contact information.

ROUTINE MAINTENANCE A HOMEOWNER SHOULD PERFORM

Note: Turn off all power and disconnect switches before performing inspections/maintenance.

- Maintain records, and have a professional service the unit yearly.

- Change the filter as often as required (in some cases, every month).

- Switch high/low returns (and adjust ductwork if necessary) at the start and end of the cooling season. For complete instructions, check the section on "Heating and Cooling Distribution" later in this chapter.

- Listen to the air conditioner operate. Follow up on any strange noises.

- Check drain lines from the furnace to make sure they are clear and draining properly.

- Look for water leaks or changes in the system.

- Keep plants and obstructions away from the exterior coil and fan. Allow 3 feet of clearance at the air discharge and 1 foot all around the unit.

- Keep the exterior coil clean.

- Keep the exterior unit level and away from soil or landscape materials.

- Make sure that supply and return registers inside your home are not blocked.

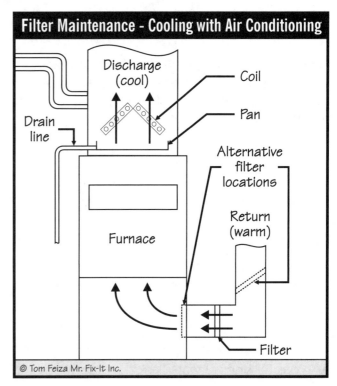

Filter Maintenance - Cooling with Air Conditioning

© Tom Feiza Mr. Fix-It Inc.

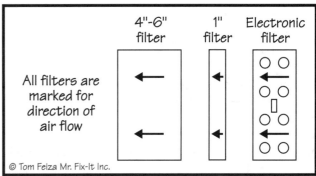

All filters are marked for direction of air flow

4"-6" filter | 1" filter | Electronic filter

© Tom Feiza Mr. Fix-It Inc.

A002

FALL MAINTENANCE

1. Disconnect power to the unit to prevent accidental use.

2. (Optional)—Cover the top of the unit.

SPRING MAINTENANCE

1. Uncover the unit.

2. Turn the power on 24 hours before operation. Keep the thermostat off.

3. Perform the maintenance listed above and arrange for professional service.

ROUTINE MAINTENANCE A PROFESSIONAL
SHOULD PERFORM

A service technician should perform the following procedures during a routine service call. The technician may perform additional checks, depending on the type of air conditioner you have.

- Check filter and replace as needed.

- Check exterior unit for level conditions, a clean coil, clearances, and adequate air flow.

- Check interior temperature drop across the cooling coil (15 to 22 degrees F).

- Check the condensate drain pan and line.

- Check secondary pan and line if unit is located in an attic.

- Look for signs of water leaks or excessive air leaks.

- Lubricate the fan motor and check the belt if required.

- Inspect electrical connections.

- Inspect refrigerant lines for signs of leaks.

- If performance problems exist, the technician-may check for amp draw, clean the coils, check the refrigerant charge, and/or complete general performance tests.

Duplicates of the above lists appear in the Service Checklists chapter. You may want to make a photocopy of the professional's list and send it to the service company when you arrange service and/or review the list with the technician at the beginning of the service call.

Central Air Cooling – Evaporative Cooler

Evaporative coolers, commonly called "swamp coolers," are used for cooling in climates where air temperatures are high and relative humidity is very low. The outside air must be hot and dry for the units to function, so they are only used in hot, arid places like the American Southwest. This type of cooling will not work in humid climates.

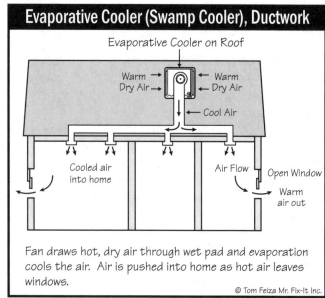

Evaporative Cooler (Swamp Cooler), Ductwork

Fan draws hot, dry air through wet pad and evaporation cools the air. Air is pushed into home as hot air leaves windows.

© Tom Feiza Mr. Fix-It Inc.

V048

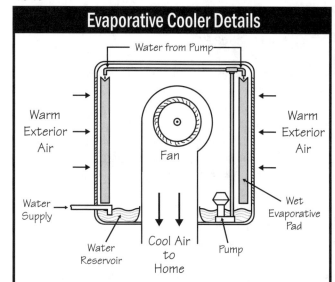

Evaporative Cooler Details

Warm, dry air is drawn across a wet pad by fan. Water evaporates from the pad and cools the air. The pump wets the pads and a water supply fills the reservoir pans with a float for control.

© Tom Feiza Mr. Fix-It Inc.

V049

The evaporative cooler works because hot outside air can be cooled as it absorbs moisture. As hot outside air is drawn across a pad full of water, the water evaporates into the air and the air is cooled as much as 20 degrees. The energy required to change the water into invisible vapor in the air makes the temperature drop.

In the process, the air is also humidified, but because it was so dry to begin with, this additional moisture is not objectionable. The cooled air is circulated through the home and to the outdoors.

The evaporative cooler is typically located on the roof; cooled air is ducted into rooms and out the windows. A cooler can also be mounted in a window or on a concrete pad outside the home.

Evaporative cooling is what cools our bodies in hot climates. As sweat evaporates, it takes heat from our skin. We can speed the cooling process by wetting our skin with a water mist and blowing air across our skin. That is why we feel cooler when we leave a swimming pool and the wind is blowing—we are experiencing evaporative cooling.

The basic evaporative cooler operates as follows:

1. A water pan on the unit is automatically filled by a float, fill valve, and water supply.

2. A small pump in the pan lifts water and distributes it over evaporative pads on the sides of the unit. The excess water drains back into the pan.

3. A large fan draws hot, dry exterior air across the saturated pads.

4. As dry air is drawn across the wet pads, it gains moisture and is cooled. The energy needed to change water into vapor cools the air.

5. The cooler air is pushed into the home and out the windows.

6. In the process, humidity is added to interior air.

7. Since the pads filter the air and trap particles, the systems may flush out deposits through a drain line in the bottom of the water pan.

Evaporative coolers are less expensive to install and operate than refrigerant-based central air conditioning systems, but they must be maintained, and leaks must be prevented to limit any damage to a home.

Evaporative Cooler – Maintenance Requirements

Proper maintenance will keep the unit operating properly and prevent water leaks and contamination. Because the pads filter outside air, pad and pans must be maintained. Specific maintenance requirements for homeowners and for professional service are in Chapter 23: Service Checklists.

Heat Pumps

A heat pump provides heating and cooling. Simply put, a heat pump is a central air conditioner that can cycle in reverse to provide heating.

Local conditions will dictate whether a heat pump is an efficient alternative for heating your home.

A heat pump transfers heat from an exterior coil to an interior coil in the warm air heating system. A heat pump provides efficient heating in areas where exterior temperatures are moderate. In cold winter weather, though, a heat pump is no more efficient than electrical resistance heating, which costs more to operate than a natural gas or oil furnace.

Before you use your heat pump, have a professional explain its operation. Unfortunately, it's easy to accidentally operate the system with emergency electrical heat; in this mode, the heat pump is turned off and electrical resistance heating coils turn on. This method works fine, and you may not observe any problems—until you get your electric bill.

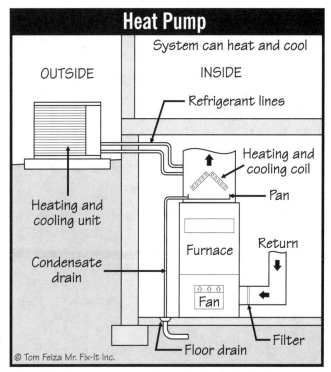

A003

The emergency (electrical resistance) system should only be used when (1) the heat pump is not working, or (2) the outside temperature is so cold (about 30 degrees or lower) that the heat pump would be less efficient than electric resistance heating. When the outside temperature gets this low, emergency resistance heating turns on automatically. You do not need to adjust the controls.

Heat Pump—Maintenance Requirements

Maintenance for a heat pump is similar to that for central air conditioning systems, but because a heat pump is operated winter and summer, it will require more maintenance.

ROUTINE MAINTENANCE A HOMEOWNER SHOULD PERFORM

Note: Turn off all power and disconnect switches before performing inspections/maintenance.

- Schedule professional service yearly.

- Watch for ice forming on the exterior unit. This is a serious problem indicating that the unit needs service.

- Follow all the maintenance recommendations for central air conditioning.

ROUTINE MAINTENANCE A PROFESSIONAL SHOULD PERFORM

A service technician should perform the following procedures during a routine service call. The technician may perform additional checks, depending on the type of heat pump you have.

- Follow all maintenance requirements for central air conditioning.

- Follow specific recommendations by the heat pump manufacturer.

- Check filter and replace as needed.

- Check exterior unit for level conditions, a clean coil, clearances, and adequate air flow.

- Check interior temperature drop across the cooling coil (15 to 22 degrees F).

- Check the condensate drain pan and line.

- Check secondary pan and line if unit is located in an attic.

- Look for signs of water leaks or excessive air leaks.

- Lubricate the fan motor and check the belt if required.

- Inspect electrical connections.

- Inspect refrigerant lines for signs of leaks.

- If performance problems exist, the technician may check for amp draw, clean the coils, check the refrigerant charge, and/or complete general performance tests.

- Follow any specific recommendations by the heat pump manufacturer.

Duplicates of the above lists appear in the Service Checklists chapter. You may want to make a photocopy of the professional's list and send it to the service company when you arrange service and/or review the list with the technician at the beginning of the service call.

Heating and Cooling Distribution: Ducts and Dampers

Warm air heating (and central air conditioning) is distributed throughout your home by a system of ducts, dampers and grills. Supply grills provide conditioned air, and return grills provide a route for the air to return to the central heating/cooling unit. The central fan circulates air through these ducts and grills.

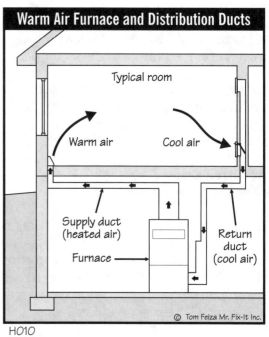

Warm Air Furnace and Distribution Ducts

Typical room

Warm air   Cool air

Supply duct (heated air)

Return duct (cool air)

Furnace

© Tom Feiza Mr. Fix-It Inc.

H010

These ducts may be metal, fiberglass or even flexible plastic. When there is a basement or crawl space, the ducts are often located just below the first floor. When the furnace is in the attic, distribution is routed through the attic. Often, framing in joist or stud spaces forms return ducts. For homes with slab foundations, the ducts may be buried in the foundation slab.

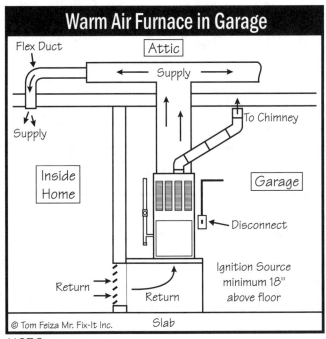

H039

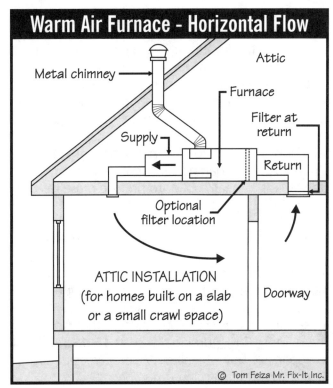

HO11

In warmer climates, for homes with slab construction, the furnace is often located in the attached garage with supply ductwork in the attic and a return in the central hall.

This distribution system often has adjustable dampers that control the air flow to certain points in your home. Frequently, these dampers are adjusted during installation and are never re-adjusted later. At times, though, dampers should be adjusted when switching from heating to cooling or to accommodate a central humidifier that is turned on in winter and off in the summer.

For a two-story home, you may need to make air flow adjustments for winter and summer. In the winter, warm air rises to the second floor, and you don't need as much heating up there. In the summer, warm air still rises, and the hot attic adds more heat, so you'll need more cooling (air flow) to the second floor than the first.

Must Know / Must Do
Ductwork and Dampers

- Never allow openings or holes in ductwork. This wastes energy and makes living spaces uncomfortable.

- You may need to adjust ductwork dampers when switching from heating to cooling or vice versa.

- If your furnace has a damper on the humidifier, you may need to adjust it. Turn it off during summer.

- Ask your service technician if your warm air furnace has a damper for a winter/summer switch.

- Ductwork in attics and crawl spaces should be well insulated to prevent loss of energy.

Dampers are located inside the ducting system. Often, you'll find dampers where round supply ducts connect to the main rectangular ducts. All you will see of a damper is a small lever and lock nut or a small shaft and a wing nut. You can determine the position of the damper by checking the direction of the lever or the screwdriver slot in the end of the shaft. If the lever or slot is parallel to the duct, this means the damper is open. If the lever/slot is perpendicular (at a right angle) to the duct, the damper is closed. Some systems have levers indicating the direction of the damper. Some rectangular ducts have dampers and levers. You can adjust these dampers to close off rooms you don't want to heat/cool or to provide more heating or cooling to specific rooms.

At the start of hot summer weather, you may need to direct more cool air to the second story. Start by fully opening all second-floor dampers. Next, partially close dampers to first floor rooms that are cold and receiving lots of air. The dampers often fit loosely in the ducts, so you may find that closing the damper 50% (turning the shaft 45 degrees) will only partially slow the air flow. Sometimes air will flow through a fully closed damper.

However, don't close off more than one-quarter of all the dampers; operation can be hindered if too little air flows through the system. If you need to make major changes to the system, consult a professional.

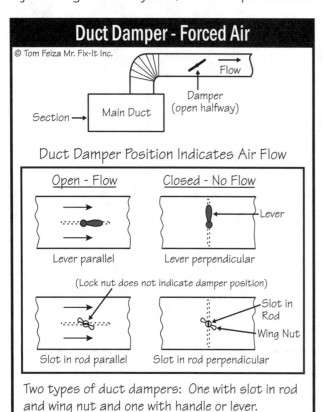

HO42

Once you've found a desirable balance, mark the damper settings for winter and summer.

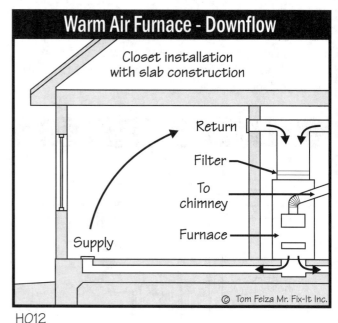

HO12

High and Low Returns

Some distribution systems have "high" and "low" return grills on interior walls. These grills are located one above the other. They aid in air distribution and comfort.

High returns should be opened for cooling. Remember that warm air rises, and you want to return the warm air to the air conditioning coil in the furnace.

During the heating season, the low returns should be open to return cold air at floor level to the furnace.

Outside Air Supply

Since the mid 1990s, the concept of adding an outside air supply to a forced air duct system has become more popular and has been required by some code officials. This involves installing a duct between the home's exterior and the return duct on the forced air system. When the furnace fan operates, it draws a small amount of air from the outside. This outside air duct may have a damper that can be closed in the summer when the unit is used as an air conditioner. The duct is usually insulated to prevent condensation on a cold surface in the winter.

Warm Air Furnace Dampers

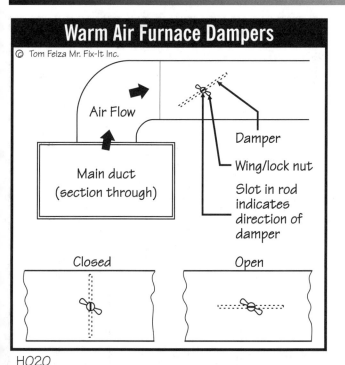

© Tom Feiza Mr. Fix-It Inc.

H020

High and Low Returns

FORCED AIR FURNACE IN BASEMENT

SUMMER (cooling on)

Upper return grill

Air Flow

Return register (fully closed)

Cool air

Supply from furnace — Return to furnace

Exterior wall and window — Interior wall

WINTER (heating on)

Upper return blocked by open lower register damper

Air Flow

Return register (fully open)

Hot air

© Tom Feiza Mr. Fix-It Inc.

Supply from furnace — Return to furnace

H019

The goal of the outside air supply duct is to provide some ventilation air. Since this air is cold and dry during the heating season, it will help dry the home's interior air. As air is introduced into the system, an equal amount of warm damp air leaks out of the home. This also tends to remove moisture from the home.

Outside Air Supply to Heating Return Duct

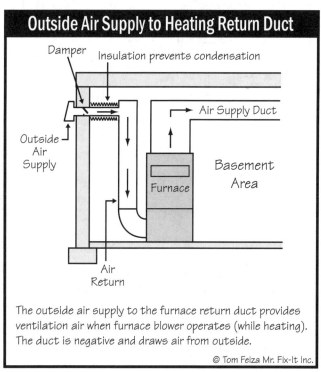

The outside air supply to the furnace return duct provides ventilation air when furnace blower operates (while heating). The duct is negative and draws air from outside.

© Tom Feiza Mr. Fix-It Inc.

V028

Humidifier Controls and Settings

In northern heating climates, homes can become very dry in the winter. As warm air leaks out of our homes, it is replaced with cold, dry air. This is less severe if we have tightened up our homes for energy conservation, but it still can be a problem. Excessive dryness can damage furniture and harm your physical well-being.

The simple way to add moisture to the air of your home is with a central humidifier on your warm air furnace. A modern system is easy to maintain and should not leak. Modern systems have automatic controls that sense humidity level and operate automatically.

Older systems are not the best, but some are serviceable. Do not use the type that employs a water pan with an automatic fill valve. These are hard to maintain, may harbor disease-causing bacteria, and can leak water and ruin a furnace by rusting it out.

Humidifier on Gas Warm Air Furnace

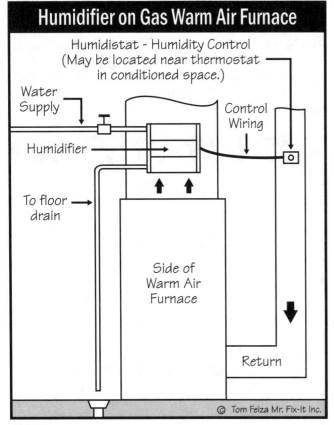

Humidistat - Humidity Control
(May be located near thermostat
in conditioned space.)

Water Supply

Control Wiring

Humidifier

To floor drain

Side of Warm Air Furnace

Return

© Tom Feiza Mr. Fix-It Inc.

H018

The type with a water panel and drain (Aprilaire is a common brand) works well if you maintain it. This system slowly flushes water across a perforated metal panel, where the air picks up moisture. Excessive water drains through a pan and hose. In general, maintenance requires changing the water panel yearly and cleaning the pan and drain lines. Routinely check for water leaks, and keep the drain line clear.

You must also adjust the humidistat to compensate for the outside air temperature. The humidistat looks like a thermostat and is located next to the thermostat or on the ductwork of the furnace. The colder the outside temperature, the lower the interior humidity level should be. Your windows provide a great humidity indicator. If moisture condenses on the windows, the interior humidity level is too high.

Aprilaire offers a humidistat that automatically compensates for outside air temperature.

For more specific information, see the contacts listed in the References section.

Humidifier System and Controls

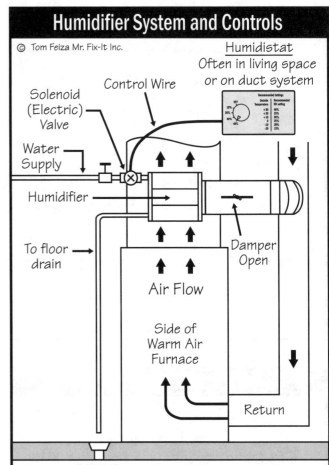

© Tom Feiza Mr. Fix-It Inc.

Humidistat
Often in living space
or on duct system

Solenoid (Electric) Valve

Control Wire

Water Supply

Humidifier

To floor drain

Damper Open

Air Flow

Side of Warm Air Furnace

Return

Humidistat measures indoor humidity (moisture) level and operates humidifier when level is low. Humidifier air is distributed by the forced air furnace.

H034

Humidifier Without Transfer Duct

© Tom Feiza Mr. Fix-It Inc.

Adds moisture to air through forced air furnace.

H030

Must Know / Must Do
Central Humidifier

- Routinely check for leaks in the humidifier. Leaks will ruin the furnace.

- Routinely clean and service the unit to prevent bacteria that endanger the health of those in your home.

- Check that the drain line is clear and draining.

- Turn off the unit and its water supply in the summer.

- Adjust the duct damper on the unit if necessary: off for summer, on for winter.

- If condensation forms on your windows in the winter, lower the humidity setting.

- Newer, tighter homes rarely need a humidifier.

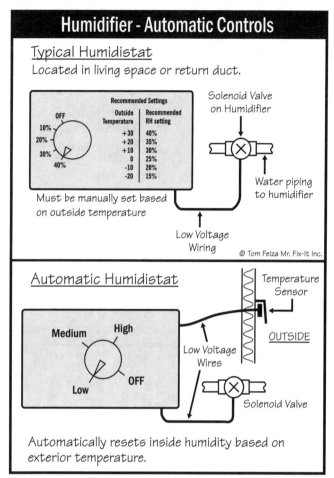

Humidifier - Automatic Controls

Typical Humidistat
Located in living space or return duct.

Recommended Settings

Outside Temperature	Recommended RH setting
+30	40%
+20	35%
+10	30%
0	25%
-10	20%
-20	15%

OFF
10%
20%
30%
40%

Solenoid Valve on Humidifier

Water piping to humidifier

Must be manually set based on outside temperature

Low Voltage Wiring

© Tom Feiza Mr. Fix-It Inc.

Automatic Humidistat

Medium   High
Low   OFF

Temperature Sensor

OUTSIDE

Low Voltage Wires

Solenoid Valve

Automatically resets inside humidity based on exterior temperature.

H035

Chapter 4 – Utility Systems – Electrical

Utility Systems—Electrical

The electrical supply to your home begins outside, where you will see either an overhead feed and piping down the side of your home or (if you have underground service) a metal box near the ground.

The overhead service wire should be clear of trees and other wires. It should be at least 10 feet above any surface you can walk on.

With underground service, you will see a meter mounted on the metal box. This box hides the entrance of the service wire into your home.

In cold, wet climates, the main electrical panel will be located in the basement or utility room. In dry climates, the electrical panel may be outside. From this panel, electricity is divided into circuits through individual breakers or fuses and is fed through the wiring system, outlets and cords to various electrical devices.

Most modern homes have 220-volt systems with a minimum of 100 amps of power. Older houses may have fuses and can have 60-amp systems. Very old houses can have 110-volt, 30-amp systems, but these are rare.

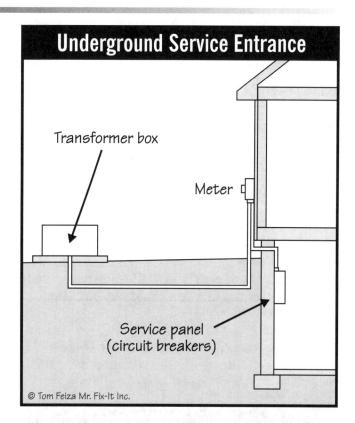

Underground Service Entrance

Transformer box

Meter

Service panel
(circuit breakers)

© Tom Feiza Mr. Fix-It Inc.

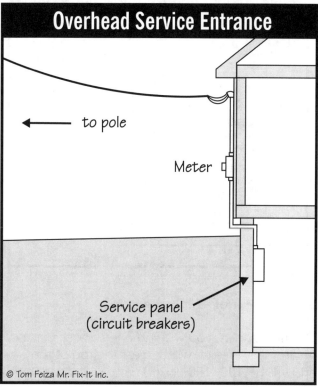

Overhead Service Entrance

to pole

Meter

Service panel
(circuit breakers)

© Tom Feiza Mr. Fix-It Inc.

EOO1

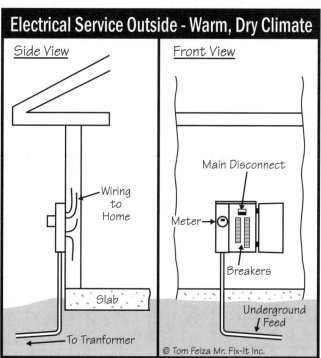

Electrical Service Outside - Warm, Dry Climate

Side View

Wiring to Home

Slab

To Tranformer

Front View

Main Disconnect

Meter →

Breakers

Underground Feed

© Tom Feiza Mr. Fix-It Inc.

E019

Main Panel

Take a tour of your main electrical panel. Do this with a professional or an experienced friend if you are confused or if you have particular questions or concerns.

During this tour, identify the main disconnects so you can turn off power in an emergency. Also, determine how to reset a breaker and/or replace a fuse.

To begin, locate the main panel and open the door. Do not remove the metal cover beneath, since that would expose bare wires.

You will find fuses or breakers but not bare wires or exposed connectors. Breakers look like switches that can be moved from "on" to "off." Fuses will be either a round screw-in type or the larger cartridge type mounted in a fuse block that can be pulled from the main panel.

Other configuration are possible. There may be a combination of fuse panels and breaker panels. There may be "sub-panels" located next to the main panel.

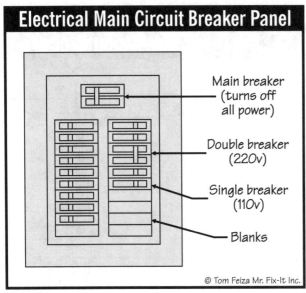

Electrical Main Circuit Breaker Panel

Main breaker (turns off all power)

Double breaker (220v)

Single breaker (110v)

Blanks

© Tom Feiza Mr. Fix-It Inc.

E002

Breaker Panel—Main Switch

On most panels, you will find one breaker marked "main." This breaker will be near the top of the box and will be 100, 150 or 200 amp. If you switch this breaker off, all power in your home will be disconnected, and you will be in the dark. I don't suggest turning off the power.

Must Know / Must Do—Electrical

Properly installed electrical systems are very safe and efficient. To prevent safety problems, though, you should understand the basics.

- Know where the main electrical disconnect is located and how to use it.

- To prevent shocks, any outlets near water (such as next to a sink) and all exterior outlets should have GFCI protection installed. (These outlets are explained below.)

- Know which outlets are GFCI protected. Test GFCI outlets and breakers monthly.

- Avoid using extension cords.

- Never attempt an electrical repair unless you know exactly what you are doing.

- Never perform wiring or re-wiring work. Use a professional.

- Identify which breakers/fuses control which outlets.

- If you replace a fuse, always use the same size—20 amp for 20 amp, 15 amp for 15 amp. Have a few spare fuses on hand.

- Know how to reset a breaker. The usual procedure is to turn it off, then on. Some systems use red indicators or an "off" indicator to show that a breaker has been tripped.

- Never cut or modify electrical plugs or outlets.

An older breaker panel may have several breakers marked as main disconnects. Some may be marked "lighting" or "air conditioning." There may also be a fused main with breakers for distribution circuits.

Breaker Panel–Reset a Breaker

Modern circuit breaker panels are convenient because you can "reset" a breaker if it trips and you don't need to search for a replacement fuse. You do need to use common sense and caution when resetting a breaker. If a breaker trips, there may be an overload on the circuit. Before you switch a breaker back on, check for devices that may be causing the overload: hair dryers, electrical resistance heaters, power tools or other devices that use a lot of power. Remove the device before you reset the breaker. If the breaker trips a second time, consult a professional.

There are several types of breakers and methods to reset breakers. Most breakers flip to an "off" position when an overload occurs. For these breakers, you flip the switch back to the "on" position. Some breakers also have a little window that shows a red "flag" when the breaker is tripped.

Other breakers flip to a center position when tripped. The handle will be halfway between "on" and "off". You will need to look carefully to find this type of tripped breaker. This type of breaker often requires you to move the breaker handle to the "off" position and then back to the "on" position to reset the breaker.

Fuse Panel—Main Switch

You will see a main fuse block, about 4" x 3", with a small handle. Turning off ("pulling") this main turns off all power to your home.

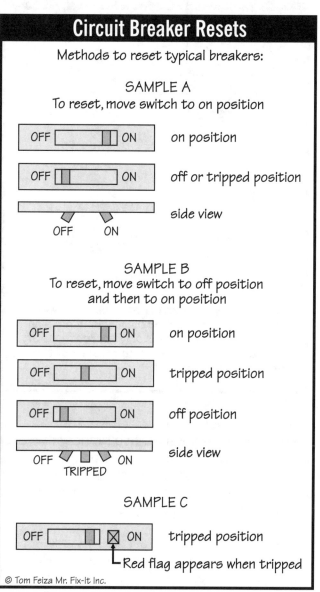

Circuit Breaker Resets

Methods to reset typical breakers:

SAMPLE A
To reset, move switch to on position

OFF [ ] ON — on position
OFF [ ] ON — off or tripped position
side view
OFF   ON

SAMPLE B
To reset, move switch to off position and then to on position

OFF [ ] ON — on position
OFF [ ] ON — tripped position
OFF [ ] ON — off position
side view
OFF   ON
TRIPPED

SAMPLE C

OFF [ ] ☒ ON — tripped position
Red flag appears when tripped

© Tom Feiza Mr. Fix-It Inc.

E013

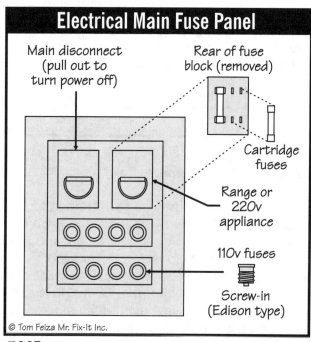

Electrical Main Fuse Panel

Main disconnect (pull out to turn power off)

Rear of fuse block (removed)

Cartridge fuses

Range or 220v appliance

110v fuses

Screw-in (Edison type)

© Tom Feiza Mr. Fix-It Inc.

E003

Some older systems have multiple main disconnects—instead of pulling one main, you must pull multiple fuse blocks to turn off all power. Main disconnects should be clearly identified at the fuse blocks or on the cover of the panel. They may be marked "lighting main," "range," "dryer," "air conditioner," and so on. Usually, each 220-volt appliance has its own main.

If this sounds confusing, review the sketches I've provided. If you still don't understand your system, or if it's not well-marked, go over the panel with a professional and rewrite the markings.

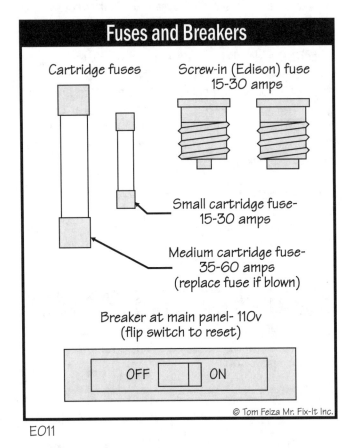

Fuses and Breakers

Cartridge fuses

Screw-in (Edison) fuse
15-30 amps

Small cartridge fuse-
15-30 amps

Medium cartridge fuse-
35-60 amps
(replace fuse if blown)

Breaker at main panel- 110v
(flip switch to reset)

OFF | ON

© Tom Feiza Mr. Fix-It Inc.

EO11

Fuses and Replacement

Typical screw-in type fuses are called Edison base fuses. They fit into a threaded socket just like a light bulb. If a fuse "blows," it will appear dark or burned in the cover window. To replace a fuse, you unscrew the old fuse and screw in a new fuse of a matching amperage rating. The "blown" fuse is discarded. You should always match the amperage rating and never put a larger fuse in the socket. For example, a 15-amp fuse must be replaced with a 15-amp fuse, *not* a 20-amp fuse.

You can improve the safety of your fuse system by adding S-Type fuse bases. This base is a special socket that is threaded into the standard size Edison socket. Once in place, it will only accept the correct size fuse. Each S-Type fuse has a unique threaded base. Safety is ensured because a 20-amp fuse will not fit in a 15-amp S-Type fuse socket.

Wiring and Flow of Electricity

Distribution wiring is what routes electrical power to lights, outlets and appliances. Most of this wiring is buried in walls and attics, but some will be visible near the main panel and in basements and crawl spaces. Since the 1970s, plastic shielded wiring (Romex is a common brand) has been used in residential construction. Older homes may have cloth-shielded wiring, BX or flexible metal-shielded wiring, or even conduit (metal pipe). There are many variations and exceptions.

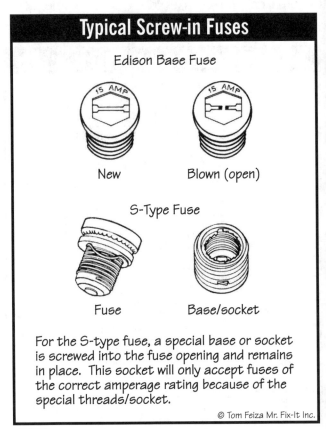

Typical Screw-in Fuses

Edison Base Fuse

15 AMP

New

15 AMP

Blown (open)

S-Type Fuse

Fuse

Base/socket

For the S-type fuse, a special base or socket is screwed into the fuse opening and remains in place. This socket will only accept fuses of the correct amperage rating because of the special threads/socket.

© Tom Feiza Mr. Fix-It Inc.

EO15

Homes built around 1910 may have "knob and tube" wiring that consists of two strands of wire run parallel. This wiring is strung on knobs, around corners, and through tubes in framing. It should only be modified by a professional. If your home has this type of wiring, plan for an upgrade.

Electricity flows like water, so it requires at least two wires: it pushes through the live wire and returns through the neutral wire. This is why all electrical devices have plugs with at least two prongs. Modern systems add a third (ground) wire for safety.

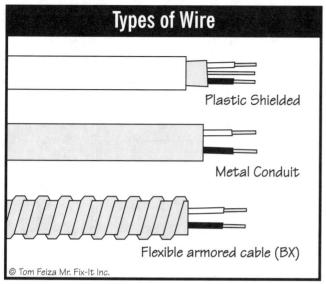

Types of Wire

Plastic Shielded

Metal Conduit

Flexible armored cable (BX)

© Tom Feiza Mr. Fix-It Inc.

E004

Devices like electric ranges run on 220 volts and require two power wires (110v plus 110v) plus the neutral wire. Some 220-volt appliances have four wires: two power, one neutral, and one ground. All newer 240v appliances are now four-wire.

Sound complicated? It is. Don't modify or tamper with the system. Consult a professional when repairs are needed. Experience and knowledge are necessary when working with electricity. Electricians spend at least six years in school and training just to learn the basics of their trade.

Outlets, Cords, 110 vs. 220

220 volt—what? Is that 110, 220, 240 or 90210? Terminology used with electrical systems is confusing, but you really don't need to sweat it. In fact, electric utility companies don't provide an exact voltage. Just remember this:

Electricity is provided to your home with a nominal (approximate) voltage of 110 to 120 volts per wire. When you connect between the two live wire feeds, you double the voltage to about 220 or 240 volts. So you can call it 110 or 120 volts for smaller appliances and 220 or 240 volts for large appliances.

How can you tell the difference? 110 volt is provided to all convenience outlets, light switches, and lighting fixtures in your home. The standard electrical outlet is 110 volt.

Large appliances like stoves and electric clothes dryers use 220/240-volt outlets. These are the big clunky outlets. Electric water heaters, central air conditioners, and heat pumps are directly connected to 220/240-volt power without a plug. Some large electric appliances may also be directly wired.

Electrical code changes implemented around 2002 require all 240-volt dryer and range outlets to be four-wire, so they are a grounded 240-volt outlet. This will require re-wiring the outlet and appliance to provide a ground on new installations.

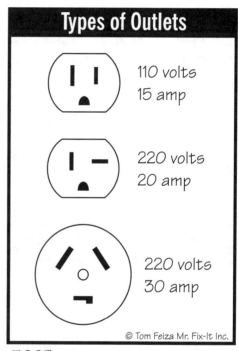

Types of Outlets

110 volts
15 amp

220 volts
20 amp

220 volts
30 amp

© Tom Feiza Mr. Fix-It Inc.

E005

Just to confuse you, you may find a funny looking small outlet and plug that is the same size but a different shape than a standard 110-volt outlet. These are 20 amp, 220/240-volt outlets. These are not common but they may be found for large window air conditioners, woodworking equipment, and shop air compressors. A standard plug will not fit into a 220/240-volt outlet.

Service Disconnects

Electrical equipment is often connected to the electrical system with a plug or service disconnect as a safety measure. All equipment must have a readily available means of disconnection from the electrical system in case the unit needs servicing.

Common service disconnects:

- Furnace—"light switch" on the side of the unit

- Central air conditioner—switch or pull-out in a box next to the exterior unit

- Dishwasher—"light switch" above the kitchen counter.

Know where the service disconnects are located and how to use them.

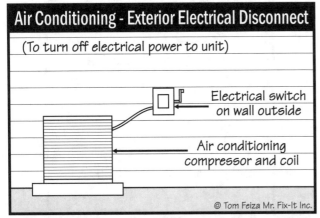

Air Conditioning - Exterior Electrical Disconnect

(To turn off electrical power to unit)

Electrical switch on wall outside

Air conditioning compressor and coil

© Tom Feiza Mr. Fix-It Inc.

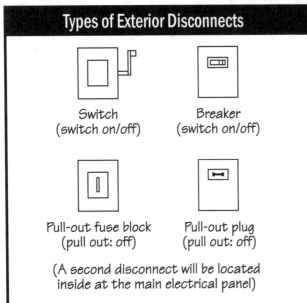

Types of Exterior Disconnects

Switch (switch on/off)

Breaker (switch on/off)

Pull-out fuse block (pull out: off)

Pull-out plug (pull out: off)

(A second disconnect will be located inside at the main electrical panel)

A004

Electrical Polarity

Polarity is an important concept. For safety's sake, you need to understand the basics.

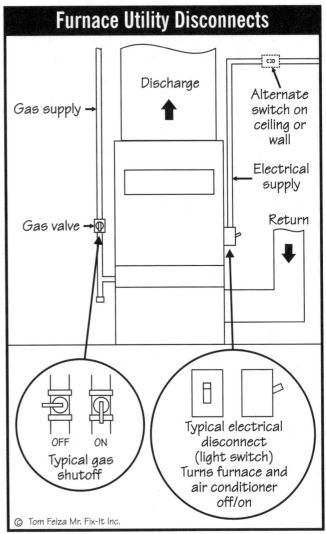

Furnace Utility Disconnects

Gas supply →

Discharge

Alternate switch on ceiling or wall

Electrical supply

Gas valve →

Return

OFF   ON
Typical gas shutoff

Typical electrical disconnect (light switch) Turns furnace and air conditioner off/on

© Tom Feiza Mr. Fix-It Inc.

H008

Electricity circulates through wires just like water moves through a hose. In the case of a lamp, for instance, electricity pushes through the "hot" wire, lights the bulb, and returns through the neutral wire. Got it?

Plugs on modern lamps and other devices have one wide blade and one narrow blade so that they can be plugged into an outlet in the correct position only—unlike plugs on old lamps, which could be reversed. Electrical devices with three-prong plugs have a ground wire; these, too, can only be plugged into an outlet in one position.

You may find a modern electrical tool with a plug that has two narrow blades that can be inserted in either direction. These are special "double insulated" tools with plastic housings that isolate the electrical components from contact with your skin.

Dishwasher - Water & Electrical Supply

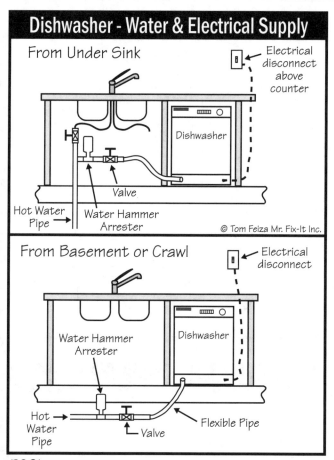

From Under Sink

Electrical disconnect above counter

Dishwasher

Valve

Hot Water Pipe

Water Hammer Arrester

© Tom Feiza Mr. Fix-It Inc.

From Basement or Crawl

Electrical disconnect

Water Hammer Arrester

Dishwasher

Hot Water Pipe

Valve

Flexible Pipe

P061

Outlet - Old Style

Polarized, Non-Grounded

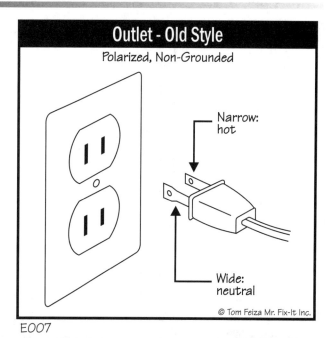

Narrow: hot

Wide: neutral

© Tom Feiza Mr. Fix-It Inc.

E007

Outlet With Ground

© Tom Feiza Mr. Fix-It Inc.

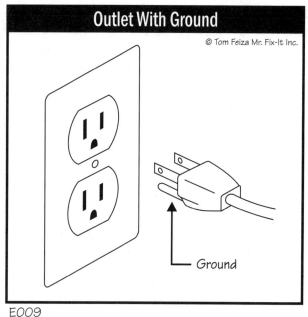

Ground

E009

What happens if you power a device with "reversed polarity"—that is, with the plug reversed? Stereo equipment may buzz; electrical and computer equipment may be damaged. Lights and lamps pose a serious hazard. When turning off the switch, you would be turning off the neutral (return) wire, not the live (hot) wire. This means that even when the lamp is off, the ring around the base of the bulb is still live, and if you touch the ring you can get a serious shock.

What does all this mean to you? Never change a plug or outlet unless you understand polarity and know exactly what you are doing.

Electrical Grounding

Electrical devices with metal housings—stoves, dryers, tools—often have a grounded plug. A grounded plug has a third, round connector. Grounded plugs provide an extra level of safety by grounding the metal housing of the device. Never remove the grounding device from a grounded plug. Never use adapters that convert a grounding plug to a standard two-prong plug. If your electrical device

has a grounded plug, it should only be used with a grounded outlet. If there's no grounded outlet where you need it, have one installed.

Ground Fault Circuit Interrupters

A ground fault circuit interrupter (GFCI) is a valuable safety device that should be installed in bathrooms, kitchens, sink locations, the garage, and exterior outlets. GFCIs have been required in new construction and remodeling since the mid-'70s. If you are remodeling, add GFCI outlets in the bathroom and any other damp or wet location. Have an electrician perform this work.

Polarity - Correct

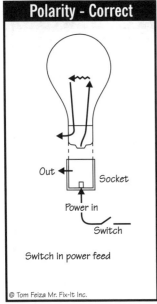

Out

Socket

Power in

Switch

Switch in power feed

© Tom Feiza Mr. Fix-It Inc.

E008

Polarity - Reversed

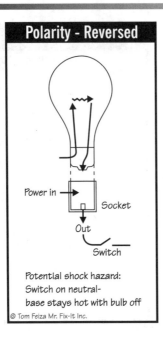

Power in

Socket

Out

Switch

Potential shock hazard:
Switch on neutral-
base stays hot with bulb off

© Tom Feiza Mr. Fix-It Inc.

Ground Fault Circuit Interrupter (GFCI)

© Tom Feiza Mr. Fix-It Inc.

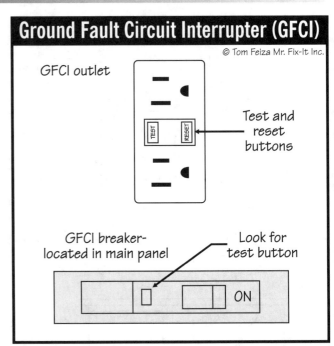

GFCI outlet

TEST RESET

Test and reset buttons

GFCI breaker-
located in main panel

Look for test button

ON

E016

GFCI Breaker Reset

Ground fault circuit interrupter (GFCI) breaker
found in main electrical panel

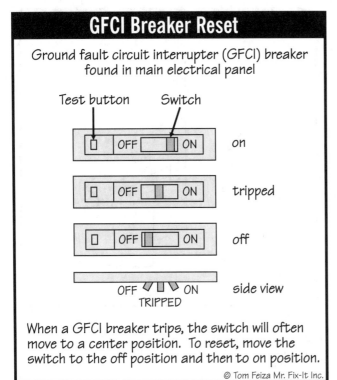

Test button   Switch

| OFF | ON | on

| OFF | ON | tripped

| OFF | ON | off

OFF TRIPPED ON   side view

When a GFCI breaker trips, the switch will often
move to a center position. To reset, move the
switch to the off position and then to on position.

© Tom Feiza Mr. Fix-It Inc.

E014

GFCI outlets or circuit breakers provide a high level
of safety for very little cost. The GFCI outlet costs
less than $10 and can be installed in a few minutes
in most locations.

A tiny imbalance in the power and neutral lines will
trip the GFCI. The imbalance indicates potential current leakage that could deliver a shock.

GFCI Protects Outlets Downstream

© Tom Feiza Mr. Fix-It Inc.

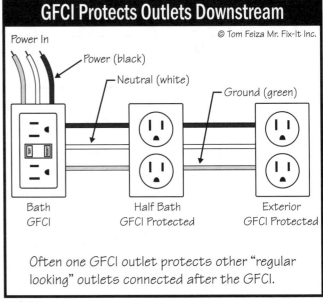

Power In

Power (black)

Neutral (white)

Ground (green)

Bath
GFCI

Half Bath
GFCI Protected

Exterior
GFCI Protected

Often one GFCI outlet protects other "regular
looking" outlets connected after the GFCI.

E022

Don't confuse a GFCI with the fuse or circuit breaker in the basement. The fuse or breaker protects the
wire from overloads, overheating and burning. A
fuse will allow 15 or 20 amps to flow through the
circuit before it trips. This is more than enough
power to electrocute you.

Once the GFCI is installed, test it monthly with the
test/reset button on the face of the breaker or outlet. Testing is simple and essential. Push the test button, and the GFCI will trip. Reset the GFCI outlet by
pressing the reset button on the face of the outlet.

Reset a GFCI breaker (at the main panel) by moving the switch from the center "tripped position" to fully "off" and then to the "on" position.

Unfortunately, most outlets are not tested. I provide home inspection services, and I find that 5% to 10% of existing GFCI outlets are not working properly.

Arc Fault Circuit Interrupters (AFCI)

An Arc Fault Circuit Interrupter (AFCI) is an electrical safety device that started to appear in residential construction codes and some homes about 1999. It is designed to prevent fires by detecting an arc (spark) and then disconnecting the power before a fire starts.

An arc or spark may occur between two wires without tripping a standard circuit breaker because the current flow may not be high enough. Yet while the spark may not trip the breaker, it can ignite building materials. The AFCI contains sophisticated electronic circuitry that detects arc faults.

When required by code or installed by a conscientious electrical contractor, the AFCI usually protects circuits in bedrooms. A dangerous arc fault is likely to occur with damaged or frayed electrical cords. The AFCI is installed in the main circuit panel or as a special outlet and has a reset button on its face. Typically, the device protects several outlets.

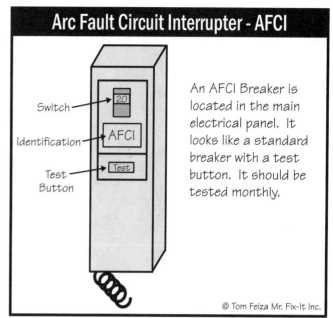

Arc Fault Circuit Interrupter - AFCI

Switch

Identification

Test Button

An AFCI Breaker is located in the main electrical panel. It looks like a standard breaker with a test button. It should be tested monthly.

© Tom Feiza Mr. Fix-It Inc.

E020

Unlike a Ground Fault Circuit Interrupter (GFCI), the AFCI is designed to prevent fires. The GFCI is designed to prevent electrical shock. If your home has an AFCI, you should test it periodically with the test button. Most manufacturers suggest testing once per month. When the AFCI is tripped, there should be no power at the outlet or the circuit.

Chapter 5 – Utility Systems – Plumbing, Water Supply

Water Service—Municipal

Most homes in urban areas receive water from municipal water systems. The original water source may be a lake, a river, or large, deep wells and storage facilities. Municipalities are required to test water for safety and purity. Often they filter the water and treat it with chemicals. If you have questions about the quality of your water supply, contact your local water utility.

In a cold climate municipal system, water is distributed through piping mains beneath the streets. It enters your home under the basement slab or at the first floor slab. In cold climates, piping is buried below the frost line.

Inside the house, there is usually a shutoff valve, a meter, and then a second shutoff valve. You can use either of these valves to turn off the water, but the second valve is used more often. Sometimes the valve on the street side of the meter can only be operated with a wrench.

In many cases there is no basement, and the water meter may also be installed in a shallow box near the street. Often the main water shutoff is located on the side of the home near the street, and the meter and additional valves will be located in shallow boxes near the curb. Any of these valves will turn off all water to the home.

Water is distributed through the house by steel, plastic or copper piping. Check your system, identify valves, and look for any potential problems. Locate the main that feeds the water heater, and check for a shutoff valve before the water heater in case you need to turn off all hot water in your home.

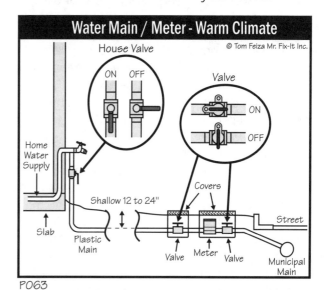

P063

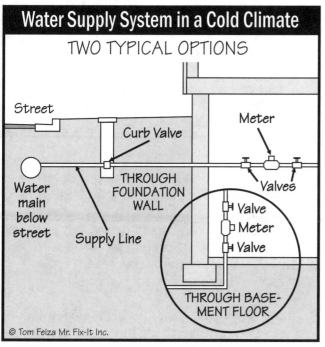

P005

In a warm climate, we don't need to worry about frozen ground and frozen pipes, so water mains can be installed just below the surface of the soil.

P064

Must Know / Must Do Municipal Water Supply

- Make sure that all adults in your home know how to turn off the main water shutoff valve.

- If the valve is old, rusted or leaking, have it serviced by a plumber so it will function when needed.

Water Service—Your Own Well

Well, well, well...OK, that's pretty corny; but if your home has a sick water delivery system, you can lose your water supply and spend hundreds of dollars on repairs.

Most damage to private wells comes from lack of basic homeowner knowledge. As one service company representative told me, "Waterlogged pressure tanks sell more replacement pumps than any marketing I could possible do."

Do you know the symptoms of a waterlogged tank? Can you correct simple well problems? Do you know how to turn off your well water system?

Let's walk through the basics of a residential well water system and discuss how you can recognize common problems and correct them. We will discuss the most common systems in residential use. If you are presently on a municipal water system, fine—you still may enjoy the information or save it for your brother up north. You should also know that most municipal water systems are just larger versions of residential systems.

The Basic System

Most wells have a 6" steel casing that is drilled into the ground to reach a clean water supply. The well casing may extend several hundred feet to reach a clean and adequate water supply. Water rises to a static level of equilibrium inside the steel casing and surrounds smaller internal piping. This internal piping is connected to a pump that lifts the water from the well and delivers it under pressure to your home plumbing system.

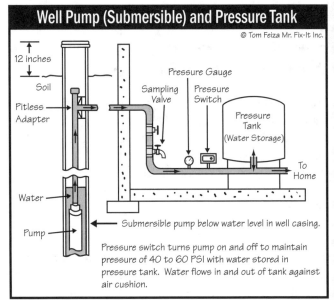

Well Pump (Submersible) and Pressure Tank

© Tom Feiza Mr. Fix-It Inc.

Pressure switch turns pump on and off to maintain pressure of 40 to 60 PSI with water stored in pressure tank. Water flows in and out of tank against air cushion.

P055

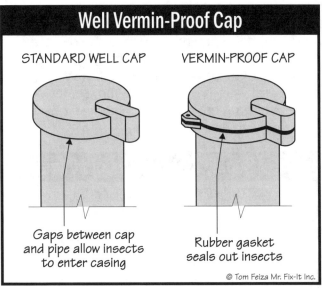

Well Vermin-Proof Cap

STANDARD WELL CAP

VERMIN-PROOF CAP

Gaps between cap and pipe allow insects to enter casing

Rubber gasket seals out insects

© Tom Feiza Mr. Fix-It Inc.

P030

The top of the well casing is covered with a cap and should be 12" above the surrounding soil to prevent contamination from surface water and other sources. The cap should be securely fastened to prohibit tampering. Recently, problems with insects have prompted many people to replace older caps with modern vermin-proof caps.

From the well casing, piping extends underground into your home, entering the basement near a pressure tank. The piping may be steel, copper, or plastic and is installed at least 6 feet below the surface to prevent freezing.

The Pump

For shallow wells and older systems, a jet-type centrifugal pump lifts water out of the well and delivers it to your home's piping. This type of pump is surface mounted in a pit near the well head or the pressure tank in the basement. The pump is driven by an electrical motor and is connected to the piping.

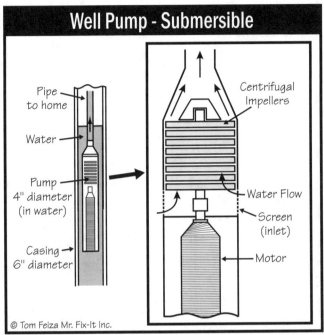

P053

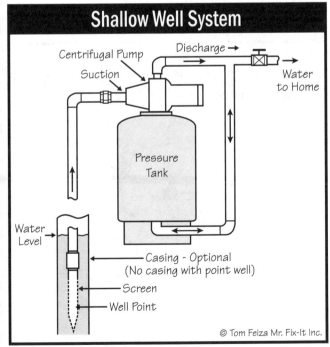

P059

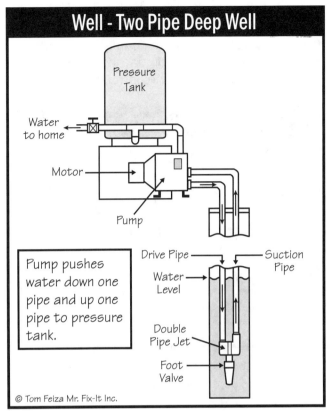

P058

Deeper wells and newer systems use submersible pumps that are placed under the water's surface inside the well casing. This kind of pump is long and slender—normally only 4" in diameter—and hangs from the supply piping. This type of pump pushes water up and out of the well.

When you "pull" a pump, you physically remove the cap of the well casing and pull the submersible pump out of the hole by the supply pipe.

Working Under Pressure

A pressure tank, normally located in the basement, stores water and prevents the pump from turning on and off every time you use water. There is a compressed air cushion above the water in the tank; it expands and compresses with changes in pressure. As you use water in your home, the air cushion in the tank expands to maintain pressure and force water into your piping.

The cushion of air generally varies in pressure within a normal operating range of about 40 to 60 pounds per square inch (psi). As water is used, the pressure decreases; when it reaches 40 psi, an automatic pressure sensing switch turns on the electricity to the pump. With the pump running, water is forced into the tank, raising the pressure of the air and water. As the tank is fully recharged with water, the pressure approaches 60 psi, and the pressure switch turns the pump off.

Well Pressure Tank Problems

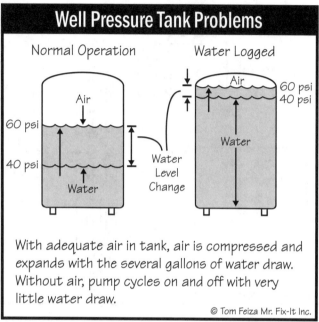

Normal Operation — Water Logged

With adequate air in tank, air is compressed and expands with the several gallons of water draw. Without air, pump cycles on and off with very little water draw.

© Tom Feiza Mr. Fix-It Inc.

P054

This pumping cycle repeats automatically as you use water from the tank. If you use a small amount of water, the pump will not need to start. You may notice a slight variation in pressure in your home as the system cycles slowly between 40 and 60 psi. When the system operates properly, the slow pressure changes are barely noticeable. A larger tank will draw more water per cycle, and there will be less pressure variation.

Tank Types Make a Difference

There are four basic types of pressure tanks. The conventional or galvanized "air over water" tank, generally found on systems over 30 years old, holds water in direct contact with the air cushion. This tank loses its air cushion as air is absorbed in the water, so you will need to service it several times per year to maintain the air cushion. You will recognize this type as a large, upright, galvanized steel tank.

An improved galvanized tank separates the air from the water with a floating disc. This tank will not lose air to the water as quickly, but it still requires routine maintenance.

Well Tank with Bladder
SEQUENCE OF OPERATION

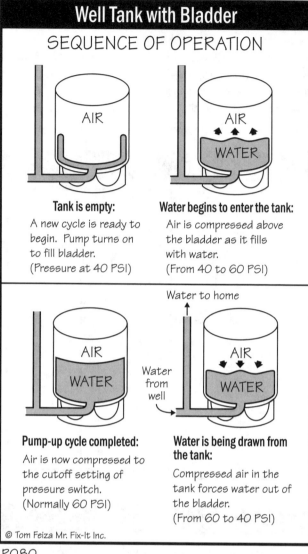

Tank is empty:
A new cycle is ready to begin. Pump turns on to fill bladder.
(Pressure at 40 PSI)

Water begins to enter the tank:
Air is compressed above the bladder as it fills with water.
(From 40 to 60 PSI)

Pump-up cycle completed:
Air is now compressed to the cutoff setting of pressure switch.
(Normally 60 PSI)

Water is being drawn from the tank:
Compressed air in the tank forces water out of the bladder.
(From 60 to 40 PSI)

© Tom Feiza Mr. Fix-It Inc.

P080

Well Tank with Air Volume Control

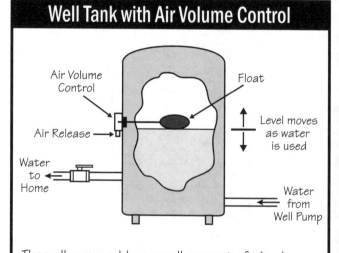

The well pump adds a small amount of air when it starts. If there is excessive air in the tank, the float drops and releases air.

© Tom Feiza Mr. Fix-It Inc.

P057

Well Pressure Tanks

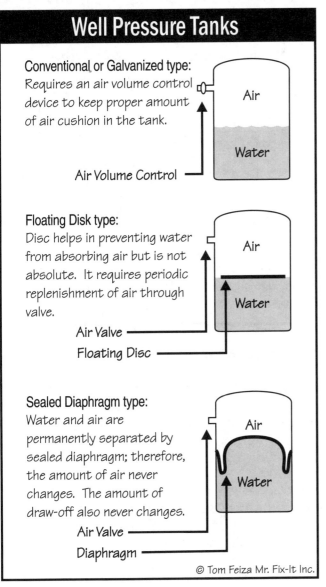

Conventional or Galvanized type:
Requires an air volume control device to keep proper amount of air cushion in the tank.

Air

Water

Air Volume Control

Floating Disk type:
Disc helps in preventing water from absorbing air but is not absolute. It requires periodic replenishment of air through valve.

Air

Water

Air Valve

Floating Disc

Sealed Diaphragm type:
Water and air are permanently separated by sealed diaphragm; therefore, the amount of air never changes. The amount of draw-off also never changes.

Air

Water

Air Valve

Diaphragm

© Tom Feiza Mr. Fix-It Inc.

POO6

Some systems are designed with a pump that adds a small amount of air to the system each time to pump starts. This system has a special air release tank, and every time the pump starts you will hear a little "gurgle" or "burp" if you are standing next to the tank. The "burp" results as air enters the tank.

This special air release or air volume control tank never needs additional air because the pump constantly maintains the air supply. If the system has too much air, a float in the tank drops with the water level and allows air to be released from the side of the tank. You will see a small plastic fitting on the side of the tank, and you may notice some water staining below the fitting. When air is released from the tank, some water is often released as well.

A tank with an air volume control is often installed when the well water has contaminates and odor problems. Because the tank eliminates the rubber bladder to hold water, it tends to reduce these problems.

Modern tanks are a big improvement over the older tanks. They are smaller and usually are made of painted steel. Inside the tank, the elements are separated by a sealed diaphragm or bladder which holds either the air or the water. Since there is no direct air/water contact, this tank system maintains the air cushion indefinitely.

Steps to Well Wellness

The best route to a trouble-free well is to become familiar with the system's important parts and know how it is supposed to look and sound when running properly. Take the time to identify the components of your system and to watch it operate. Read any instructions and information available for your system. Look for the pressure tank, pressure switch, and gauges. Find the circuit breaker or switch that turns off the power to the pump.

Turn on a faucet and watch the pressure gauge to see the system's pressure vary. As it approaches 40 psi, you will hear a click when the pressure switch turns the pump on. With a submersible pump, you may hear a hum while the pump runs. When the pump is on, water flow into the tank will gradually increase the pressure to about 60 psi; then the pump will click off. It should take a minute or two for the pressure to increase from 40 to 60 psi.

If your system operates as described, now you know how a properly operating system responds when water is used.

The Helpful Turn-Off

It's important to know how to turn off the system completely. To stop the water flow to your home, you must turn off both the house service valve and the electrical supply to the pump. At least two people in your household should know how to do this.

Trace your home's piping back toward the pressure tank. The large valve in the line between the tank and the house piping is your house service valve.

Well - Main Water Disconnects

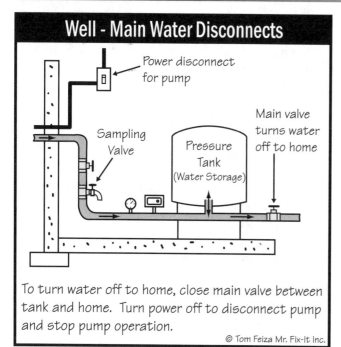

To turn water off to home, close main valve between tank and home. Turn power off to disconnect pump and stop pump operation.

© Tom Feiza Mr. Fix-It Inc.

P056

If you turn off only the power to the pump, all the water under pressure in the tank will still flow into the piping system. If you turn off only the valve, the pump and electrical system can still malfunction.

Spotting a Waterlogged Tank

The most common and damaging problem in this system is a waterlogged pressure tank. A tank is waterlogged (full of water) when there is no air cushion in the tank. Without an air cushion, there is no air pressure to push water out of the tank into the home's piping. The pressure will vary quickly whenever a small amount of water is used.

This quick change in pressure causes the pump to start and stop almost every time you use water. As soon at the pump starts, the pressure will go up very quickly. For instance, if you are running a yard sprinkler, the pump will constantly turn on and off, and you will notice the pressure change at the spray of the sprinkler. If the pump is allowed to continue turning on and off (short cycling), eventually it will be ruined.

You can identify a waterlogged tank by quick changes in pressure and the way the pump switches on almost every time water is used. You must correct this situation to prevent damage to the pump.

Well Pressure Tank Problems

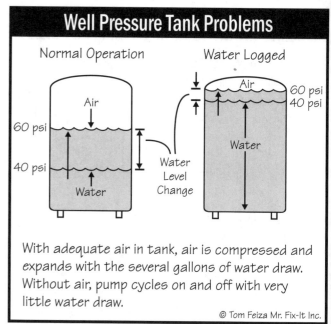

With adequate air in tank, air is compressed and expands with the several gallons of water draw. Without air, pump cycles on and off with very little water draw.

© Tom Feiza Mr. Fix-It Inc.

P054

Correcting a Waterlogged Tank

If you need to correct a waterlogged tank but don't fully understand your well system's operation, call a service company. Watch their repair person service the tank. Ask lots of questions, and take notes so you can do it yourself next time.

The bladder-type tank should not lose its air cushion unless there is a bladder failure or a valve stem leak. If there is an air leak, you will need to recharge this bladder-type tank.

When an air-over-water tank requires replacement of the air cushion, follow these steps:

1. Turn off the electrical power to the pump.

2. Turn off the house service valve.

3. Open the drain valve at the bottom of the tank and drain off all the water under pressure. Normally, a hose is connected to this valve, and water is routed to a drain.

4. Using an air compressor or bicycle pump, add compressed air to the tank through its tire-stem-type fill valve.

5. Continue adding air until all the water is out of the tank and air flows from the drain valve.

6. Close the drain valve.

7. Pressurize the tank to about 5 psi below the normal operating range of the system. (In our example of a pump with a range of 40 to 60 psi, this would mean a pressure of 35 psi.)

8. Turn the electrical power to the pump back on and watch the pressure increase to the normal range as the pump fills the tank with water.

9. Open the drain valve again to drain away any debris that may have loosened inside the pipes and tank when they were under low pressure. Close the valve.

10. Slowly open the house service valve.

If your tank frequently becomes waterlogged, an air leak in the tank is probably the culprit. To check for this, make sure the tank has a full charge of air; then sponge a strong solution of soapy water on the tank and its parts. Check the air fill valve, fittings, and weld joints. Bubbles will indicate an air leak. Fittings and valves can be replaced or sealed to eliminate leaks. However, if the tank welds are leaking, you may wish to replace the unit with a modern bladder-type tank.

Other Problems

Many other problems can occur with well systems. Jet pumps can lose their prime. Pressure switches can fail. Fuses can blow. Pipes can freeze. Excessive air can be pumped into the system. As with any home system, the list of potential problems goes on and on, and most of the more serious problems should be solved by a professional.

However, a properly maintained system will work smoothly and provide years of trouble-free service. Ironically, that may eventually lead to trouble, for we take the system for granted and forget to watch for symptoms of problems. We may fail to perform simple maintenance or notice quick changes in pressure.

What, Me Worry?

Even so...don't worry, be happy. Modern pumps and systems are almost trouble-free. Do your homework and understand your system. Consult a professional if you have any concerns or problems you don't understand. Watch for that water-logged tank—it can cost you a new pump.

Consider replacing an old tank with a modern bladder-type tank if you don't like routinely replacing the air cushion.

Watch for any changes in the water; changes in water clarity, color, and odor can all indicate problems. You should also have your water tested for bacteria at least semi-annually. Some wells require routine chlorination.

Must Know / Must Do
Your Own Well

- Make sure that all adults in your home know how to turn off the main water valve and the electrical power to the well pump.

- If water pressure varies as you draw a small amount of water, this indicates a pressure tank problem: the pump is "short cycling." Add air to the pressure tank, or call for service.

- Have your water tested routinely—perhaps once per year.

For detailed informational brochures on wells, water, and water treatment, contact your local municipal health department or plumbing inspector or your state's department of natural resources. You can also obtain operational information from the companies that manufactured your well pump, tank, and pressure switch. Well service companies are another good source of information.

Water Heaters

A water heater is simply that—a device to heat water. It consists of a storage tank with a gas, electric or oil heat source. If your home has an oil-fired hydronic boiler, there may be a coil in the boiler that heats water. Sometimes hot water is referred to as domestic hot water or potable water.

Water heaters work year after year with very little maintenance, so it is easy to ignore them. Yet routine maintenance checks should be performed on electric, gas and oil water heaters.

Typical Water Heater Parts - Gas

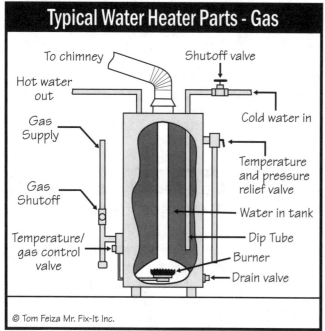

To chimney

Shutoff valve

Hot water out

Cold water in

Gas Supply

Temperature and pressure relief valve

Gas Shutoff

Water in tank

Dip Tube

Temperature/ gas control valve

Burner

Drain valve

© Tom Feiza Mr. Fix-It Inc.

P082

Typical Water Heater Parts - Electric

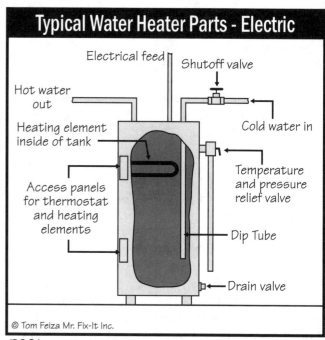

Electrical feed

Shutoff valve

Hot water out

Heating element inside of tank

Cold water in

Access panels for thermostat and heating elements

Temperature and pressure relief valve

Dip Tube

Drain valve

© Tom Feiza Mr. Fix-It Inc.

P081

Water Scalding Chart

Set water heater to 120 degrees or less for safety!

TEMPERATURE	TIME TO PRODUCE SERIOUS BURN
120 degrees (hot)	More than 5 minutes
130 degrees	About 30 seconds
140 degrees	Less than 5 seconds
150 degrees	About 1 1/2 seconds
160 degrees (very hot)	About 1/2 second

© Tom Feiza Mr. Fix-It Inc.

W008

The water heater has a temperature dial. Keep it at a low or middle setting, and check your water temperature at the faucet. It should be about 120 degrees to prevent scalding.

The temperature dial controls a thermostat in the water tank. When the water cools, the burner or electrical heating element is switched on. When the

Electric Water Heater Temperature Dial

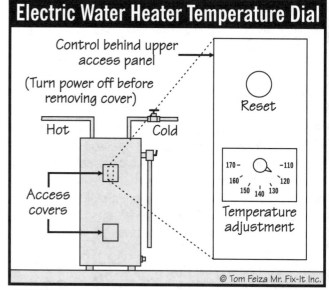

Control behind upper access panel

(Turn power off before removing cover)

Hot   Cold

Access covers

Reset

170 – 110
160   120
150 140 130

Temperature adjustment

© Tom Feiza Mr. Fix-It Inc.

W003

water reaches the specified temperature, the heating unit shuts off. The water heater's tank stores hot water, giving you a reservoir to draw from.

Routinely check your water heater for leaks. A leak is a sign of an impending failure, and you should replace the unit as soon as possible.

Also, routinely check the temperature and pressure (T and P) relief valve. This valve, which has a small lever, will be located on the top or side of the heater tank; the relief pipe should extend from the

Gas Water Heater Temperature Dial

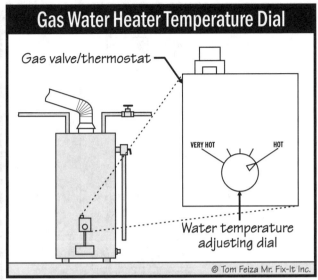

Gas valve/thermostat

VERY HOT   HOT

Water temperature adjusting dial

© Tom Feiza Mr. Fix-It Inc.

W004

Temperature and Pressure Valve

(T & P) RELIEF VALVE

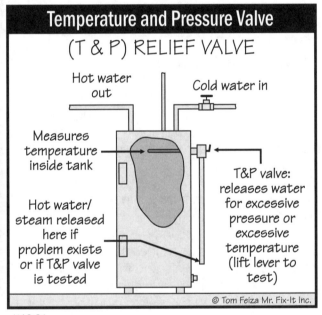

Hot water out

Cold water in

Measures temperature inside tank

Hot water/ steam released here if problem exists or if T&P valve is tested

T&P valve: releases water for excessive pressure or excessive temperature (lift lever to test)

© Tom Feiza Mr. Fix-It Inc.

W001

valve to within 6" of the floor. If water leaks from the relief valve, the valve should be replaced, because a leak may plug the valve with scale and debris. A plugged valve may fail to open if the tank overheats—a dangerous situation.

Manufacturers of T and P valves recommend testing the valve periodically by lifting the lever and allowing water to flow from the valve. They recommend this as a safety measure so you will know whether the valve will work if needed. But there's a risk that the valve won't close properly and will keep leaking, and then it will need to be replaced. When you do test the relief valve, do it when you can buy a replacement or get quick service from a plumber.

Temperature and Pressure (T & P) Valve

T & P Valve in Water Heater

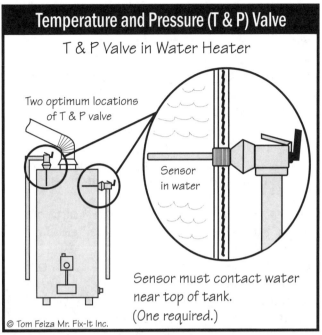

Two optimum locations of T & P valve

Sensor in water

Sensor must contact water near top of tank. (One required.)

© Tom Feiza Mr. Fix-It Inc.

W010

Must Know / Must Do
Water Heater

- Know how to operate the hot water shutoff valve.

- Know how to turn off the gas, oil or electrical power.

- Inspect the flue of a gas water heater yearly.

- Routinely check the water heater for leaks.

- Have an oil-fired water heater serviced yearly.

- Make sure the temperature and pressure valve is not leaking.

- Check the water temperature at the faucet; set the water heater temperature to about 120 degrees F.

- Whenever you have your furnace serviced, ask the technician to check the water heater, too.

- For information on how to contact water heater manufacturers, see the References section.

Manufacturers also recommend that you periodically drain water from the valve at the base of the water heater. This is a good procedure to follow if there is sediment in your water supply—but, again, few people follow this procedure, because their water systems have little sediment. If you do drain the tank, use a hose to direct water to a drain. Be careful—the water will be hot. If you haven't used the drain valve in several years, it probably won't close properly because of sediment buildup. If the valve leaks, you must replace it or cap it with a hose cap.

For a gas water heater, routinely inspect the metal flue pipe to the chimney. It should be free of rust, and it must be securely fastened to the water heater and the chimney. Also, have a contractor routinely inspect and clean the burner. A burner covered with rust indicates that the unit is not drafting well; the internal flue pipe is rusty, and the unit could be producing carbon monoxide. Every time you have your gas furnace tested and tuned, ask the service technician to test the gas water heater and check the flue gas for carbon monoxide.

For an oil-fired water heater, follow maintenance procedures (including yearly service by a professional) recommended in the section on the oil burner furnace.

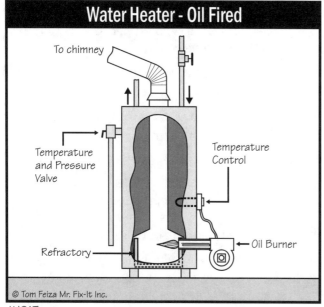

W015

The following problems should be corrected by a professional: difficulties with the T and P valve; lack of hot water; failed electrical elements; and problems with the anode, dip tube, thermocouple, or pilot light.

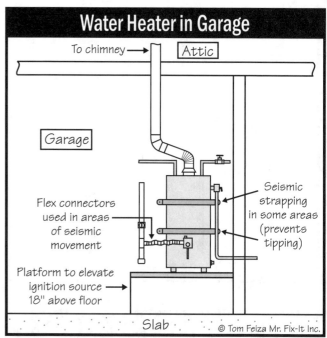

W013

Piping and Valves

Operating your home also requires a basic understanding of plumbing valves and piping. You may need to turn off the water in an emergency. You may need to shut off water to one sink or tub while it's being serviced.

Pipes route water from the main feed to individual fixtures. Piping can be galvanized steel, copper or plastic. Each type of piping has elbows, tees, couplings and reducers to connect lengths of pipe and route them through walls and framing. Take a look at your system. You will notice that it starts with 3/4" or 1" pipes and reduces to pipes of smaller diameters as fewer fixtures are served.

Valves control the flow of water and enable you to disconnect parts of the system. You will find a combination of valves. Take a good look at your plumbing system to identify valves, determine what they control, and learn how they operate. It is a great idea to place a small tag on each valve identifying what it controls. See Chapter 24 for tags.

Piping – Distribution

Let's trace the water flow from the municipal supply in the street or from your private well system. Water enters your home at the municipal main pipe or through the underground pipe connected to your private well system. You should locate the main valve and tag it for future use. Everyone in your home should know where this valve is located and how to operate it. We have provided tags in Chapter 24.

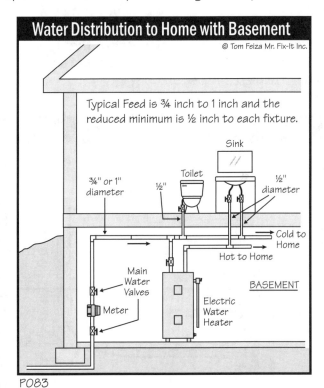

Water Distribution to Home with Basement

© Tom Feiza Mr. Fix-It Inc.

Typical Feed is ¾ inch to 1 inch and the reduced minimum is ½ inch to each fixture.

Sink

Toilet

¾" or 1" diameter

½"

½" diameter

Cold to Home

Hot to Home

Main Water Valves

Meter

Electric Water Heater

BASEMENT

P083

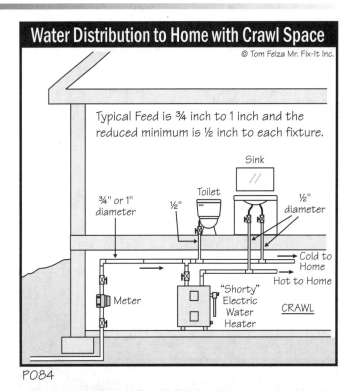

Water Distribution to Home with Crawl Space

© Tom Feiza Mr. Fix-It Inc.

Typical Feed is ¾ inch to 1 inch and the reduced minimum is ½ inch to each fixture.

Sink

Toilet

¾" or 1" diameter

½"

½" diameter

Cold to Home

Hot to Home

Meter

"Shorty" Electric Water Heater

CRAWL

P084

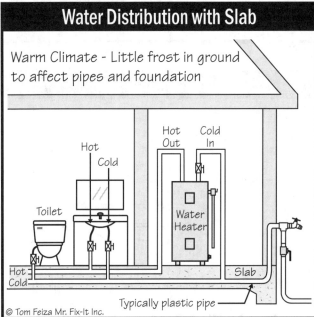

Water Distribution with Slab

Warm Climate - Little frost in ground to affect pipes and foundation

Hot Out

Cold In

Hot

Cold

Toilet

Water Heater

Hot

Cold

Slab

Typically plastic pipe

© Tom Feiza Mr. Fix-It Inc.

P085

For homes with basements, the feed pipe enters through the basement floor or wall. The main feed will then have several valves at the meter in the basement or at the well storage tank. From there the water is fed to the water heater, and the system has two distinct feeds into the home—hot and cold water. If the water is hard and needs treatment, a piping system may also distribute softened water to the water heater and other fixtures. Typically, soft water is not provided to the kitchen sink and exterior hose connections.

In homes with crawl spaces, the main feed pipe enters through the floor or a side wall. The meter and main valves may be in the crawl space, in a closet, in the utility room, or outside. Distribution piping is usually routed through the crawl space and up the fixtures. If you are lucky, you will find a shutoff valve at each fixture or appliance.

In homes built on a concrete slab, modern construction usually places the piping in the slab. The pipes are laid out, and then concrete is poured around the piping. Some homes built on a slab will have pipes run in the attic instead, and repairs or retrofit piping may also be run in the walls or the attic.

Material used for water distribution piping have changed over the years. In the early 1900s, lead piping was used. About 1910, this changed to galvanized steel, and around 1950 it changed to copper. The changes were made as better materials became available and companies looked for ways to reduce labor on installation.

Since about 1970, various plastic piping systems have been used. Some plastic piping systems have

Metal Distribution Piping

Lead - 1900s
- Soft, gray color
- Pre-formed bends
- Decorative fasteners

Galvanized Steel - 1920s
- Silver coating over steel pipe
- Screwed fittings
- Pipe dope, sealer at joints

Copper - 1950s
- Copper or brown color
- Soldered fittings
- Green corrosion for solder flux

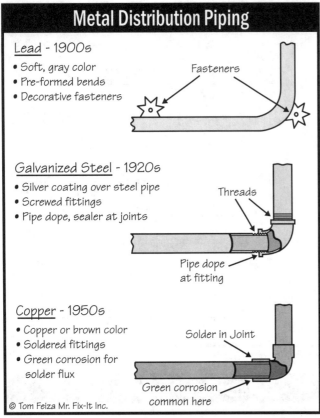

Fasteners

Threads

Pipe dope at fitting

Solder in Joint

Green corrosion common here

© Tom Feiza Mr. Fix-It Inc.

P086

Plastic Distribution Piping

Rigid Plastic Pipe
- PVC - Polyvinyl Chloride
  - white color
- CPVC - Chlorinated Polyvinyl Chloride
  - cream color
- Solvent welded joints

Flexible Plastic Pipe
- PEX - Cross-linked Polyethylene
- PB - Polybutylene
- Bent around corners
- Compression fittings

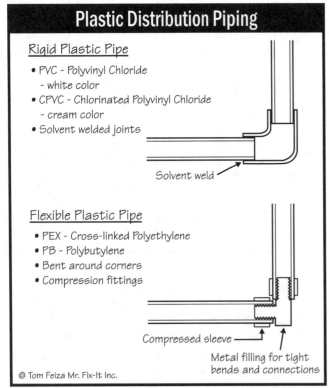

Solvent weld

Compressed sleeve

Metal filling for tight bends and connections

© Tom Feiza Mr. Fix-It Inc.

P087

plastic-welded fittings and are installed much like metal pipe by starting with a large feed and reducing the pipe size toward the end of the run.

PEX is a unique piping system. It is installed with a large main feed pipe to a header (manifold). Small tubes feed each fixture. The piping is flexible and can be bent around some corners without fittings. Tight corners require fittings. Often, copper pipe is used for connections through walls and at fixtures. Fittings are compression type, installed by special tools.

PEX Piping - Manifold

PEX - Cross-linked Polyethylene
Small, flexible plastic tubes are run to each fixture from a manifold

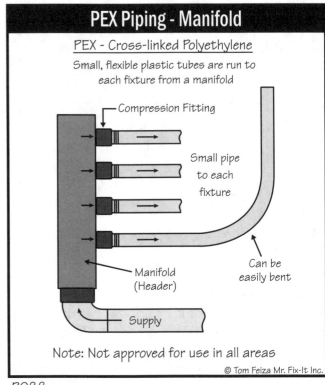

Compression Fitting

Small pipe to each fixture

Can be easily bent

Manifold (Header)

Supply

Note: Not approved for use in all areas

© Tom Feiza Mr. Fix-It Inc.

P088

Ball Valve

Ball valves are used where full flow is required. This valve is unique in that it turns fully on and fully off with a 90-degree turn of a short lever. When the lever is parallel to the pipe, the water is on; when the lever is perpendicular, the water is off. Ball valves are often used at the main feed line and the water heater.

Gate Valve

As you turn the handle, a "gate" inside the valve closes, controlling water flow. A gate valve is designed to be completely open or closed. It is often used at the main feed line.

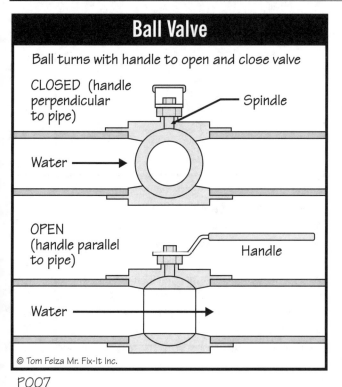

Ball Valve

Ball turns with handle to open and close valve

CLOSED (handle perpendicular to pipe) — Spindle

Water

OPEN (handle parallel to pipe) — Handle

Water

© Tom Feiza Mr. Fix-It Inc.

P007

Globe Valve

A globe valve uses a washer and a set. It can be throttled to control water volume, but generally it is not used in the main shutoff.

Saddle Valve

This is a small valve mounted on the side of a pipe like a saddle mounts on a horse. Saddle valves are frequently found on the water supply line for ice-makers and humidifiers. They provide only a low flow of water and are prone to leaks.

Hose Bib

A hose bib is an exterior hose connection valve. You may also find a hose bib at a utility sink. The hose bib has a threaded end to accept a garden hose. More information about hose bibs appears later in this chapter and in the section "Dripping Water Hoses" in the chapter on Plumbing Mysteries and Secret Solutions.

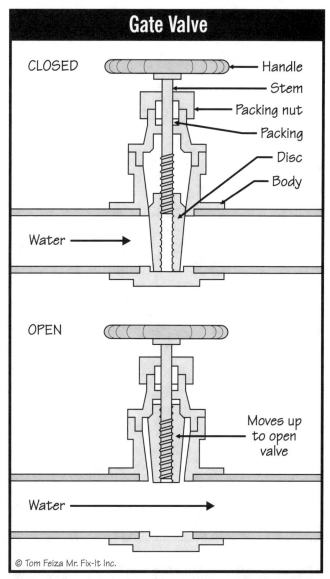

Gate Valve

CLOSED — Handle
— Stem
— Packing nut
— Packing
— Disc
— Body

Water

OPEN

Moves up to open valve

Water

© Tom Feiza Mr. Fix-It Inc.

P008

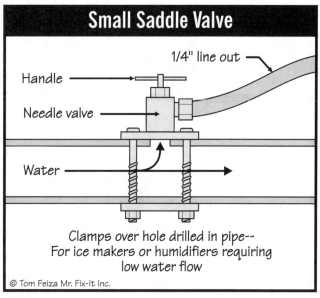

Small Saddle Valve

1/4" line out

Handle

Needle valve

Water

Clamps over hole drilled in pipe--
For ice makers or humidifiers requiring low water flow

© Tom Feiza Mr. Fix-It Inc.

P011

Globe Valve

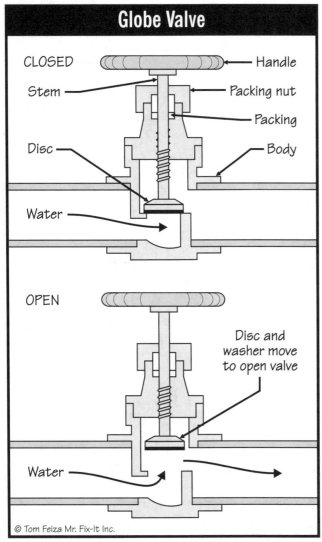

CLOSED

Handle
Stem
Packing nut
Packing
Disc
Body
Water

OPEN

Disc and washer move to open valve

Water

© Tom Feiza Mr. Fix-It Inc.

P009

Hose Bibs - Parts

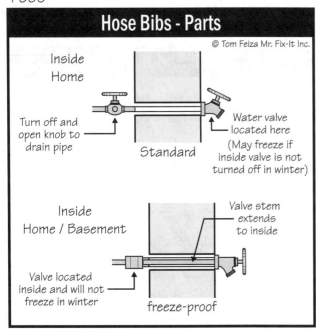

© Tom Feiza Mr. Fix-It Inc.

Inside Home

Turn off and open knob to drain pipe

Water valve located here (May freeze if inside valve is not turned off in winter)

Standard

Inside Home / Basement

Valve stem extends to inside

Valve located inside and will not freeze in winter

freeze-proof

P077

Hose Bibs

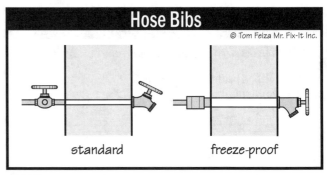

© Tom Feiza Mr. Fix-It Inc.

standard

freeze-proof

P010

Water Softener

If your home has hard water (minerals in the water), you'll probably want to use a water softener. Hard water can corrode piping and fixtures and cause a buildup of deposits. It leaves spots on dishes cleaned in the dishwasher, makes surfaces hard to clean, and interferes with detergents in the clothes washer and shampoos you use on your hair.

A water softener removes the offending minerals, calcium and magnesium and adds a small amount of sodium. A softener can also remove small concentrations of iron.

There are two basic types of salt brine water softeners. One has two separate tanks: a salt brine tank and a resin tank. Salt pellets are placed in the brine tank and soaked in water, creating salt brine. The salt brine is flushed through the resin on a routine basis, based on a time clock or usage meter. Salt ions attach to the resin. As hard water flows through the resin tank, hard water elements such as magnesium and calcium precipitate onto the resin surface. In the process, a small amount of salt is added to the water.

The second type of salt brine water softener has the resin tank located inside the brine tank. The system operates as described above. The only difference is that from the outside, the softener looks like it has only one tank. If you open the cover, you will see the second tank.

The softener is often located near the water main. Normally, it is connected to hot water and bathroom fixtures. It is not routinely connected to tap water in the kitchen because of the slight amount of sodium being added to the water. Also, the softener is not routinely connected to exterior hose piping because there is no need to soften exterior water.

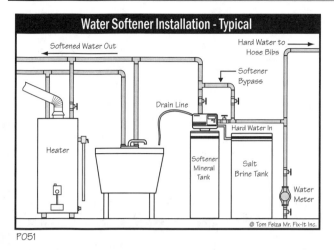

Water Softener Installation - Typical

Softened Water Out

Hard Water to Hose Bibs

Softener Bypass

Drain Line

Heater

Hard Water In

Softener Mineral Tank

Salt Brine Tank

Water Meter

© Tom Feiza Mr. Fix-It Inc.

P051

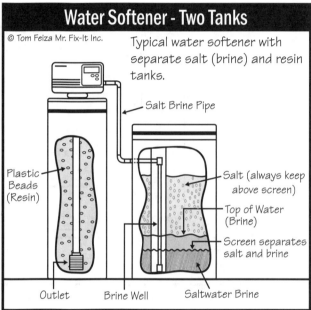

Water Softener - Two Tanks

© Tom Feiza Mr. Fix-It Inc.

Typical water softener with separate salt (brine) and resin tanks.

Salt Brine Pipe

Plastic Beads (Resin)

Salt (always keep above screen)

Top of Water (Brine)

Screen separates salt and brine

Outlet

Brine Well

Saltwater Brine

P089

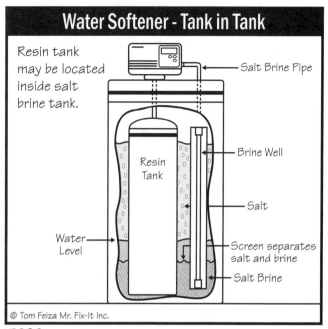

Water Softener - Tank in Tank

Resin tank may be located inside salt brine tank.

Salt Brine Pipe

Brine Well

Resin Tank

Salt

Water Level

Screen separates salt and brine

Salt Brine

© Tom Feiza Mr. Fix-It Inc.

P090

Must Know / Must Do
Water Softener

- Use the proper salt, and keep some salt in the brine tank at all times.

- Watch for leaks.

- If spots appear on dishes and the water doesn't feel "slippery," your softener is not working. Check the salt supply first.

- If the unit cycles on a timer, make sure it's set properly for the number of people in your home. Review the manufacturer's instructions.

A professional should test water for hardness and estimate the amount of water usage, then set up the softener. Some of the better models of softener will base their cycle on the amount of water used. Others cycle on a timer device.

To maintain a water softener, you must keep a supply of salt in the salt brine tank. Use salt that has been processed into pellets, or whatever salt is recommended by the manufacturer. Do not use plain rock salt; it contains small amounts of impurities that will ruin the system over time.

Water treatment systems are almost always installed with a method to "bypass" the system for maintenance and repairs. The bypass involves three valves that are opened or closed to route the water through the system or to bypass the system.

Several types of water softeners have a bypass hidden behind the control panel on top of the softener. Sliding a control lever operates this type of bypass. The lever switches both the hard and soft lines and provides a passageway for water to bypass the softener. These valves are marked with the correct directions for operation, but to find them you must look behind the softener control panel.

Water Softener Bypass

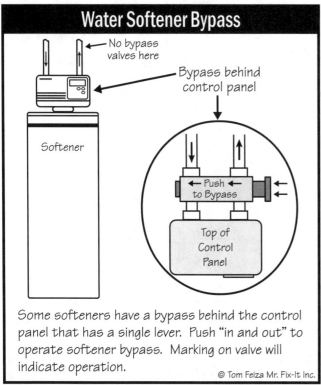

No bypass valves here

Bypass behind control panel

Softener

← Push ← to Bypass →

Top of Control Panel

Some softeners have a bypass behind the control panel that has a single lever. Push "in and out" to operate softener bypass. Marking on valve will indicate operation.

© Tom Feiza Mr. Fix-It Inc.

PO91

Water Conditioner: Typical Bypass Valving

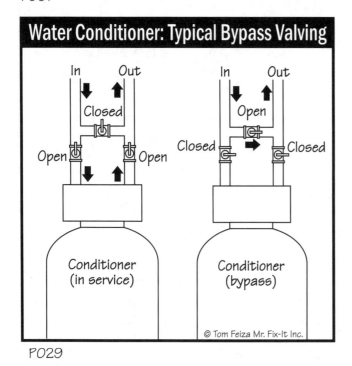

In   Out

Closed

Open   Open

Conditioner (in service)

In   Out

Open

Closed   Closed

Conditioner (bypass)

© Tom Feiza Mr. Fix-It Inc.

PO29

Other Water Treatment Options

If your home has water problems beyond basic hard water, consult a professional. Treatments for problem water include special iron filters, sediment filters, and reverse osmosis.

Iron Removal

Iron creates a difficult problem with many private water systems. Often a simple filter or softener will not remove large quantities of iron. Special treat systems are available; they are expensive but very effective. They use two treatment tanks, an air pump, and sometimes, additional chemical treatment. These systems should be installed and maintained by a professional.

Iron Removal System

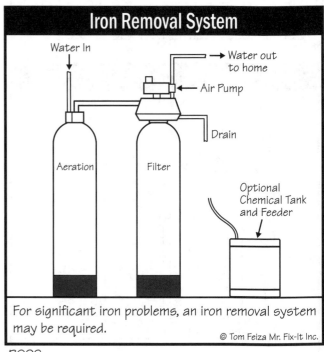

Water In

Water out to home

Air Pump

Drain

Aeration   Filter

Optional Chemical Tank and Feeder

For significant iron problems, an iron removal system may be required.

© Tom Feiza Mr. Fix-It Inc.

PO92

Water Filter

Some water contains a small amount of sediment or particles that can be removed with a simple cartridge filter. Similar to the oil filter in your car, it passes water through a filtering element and removes particles. When the filter becomes plugged, the cartridge must be removed and replaced. Often, the housing is made of clear plastic so you can see the condition of the filter.

Reverse Osmosis

A reverse osmosis water treatment system is a very fine and specialized filter that may be used to treat drinking water and perhaps the water used to create ice cubes in your refrigerator's icemaker. These specialized filters remove most of the particular matter in water. Often they utilize a small storage tank because the water is processed at a relatively slow rate. Some systems use a chemical treatment, while others use electronic monitoring. This system needs to be provided and installed by a professional.

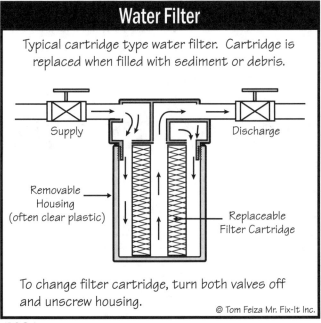

Water Filter

Typical cartridge type water filter. Cartridge is replaced when filled with sediment or debris.

Supply

Discharge

Removable Housing (often clear plastic)

Replaceable Filter Cartridge

To change filter cartridge, turn both valves off and unscrew housing.

© Tom Feiza Mr. Fix-It Inc.

P094

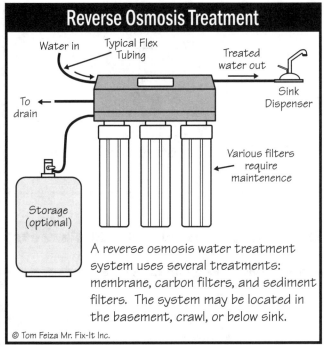

Reverse Osmosis Treatment

Water in

Typical Flex Tubing

Treated water out

To drain

Sink Dispenser

Various filters require maintenence

Storage (optional)

A reverse osmosis water treatment system uses several treatments: membrane, carbon filters, and sediment filters. The system may be located in the basement, crawl, or below sink.

© Tom Feiza Mr. Fix-It Inc.

P093

The system may be located in the basement, in the crawl space, or below the sink. Water may be routed to a small dispenser at the kitchen sink with a small plastic tube. A small tube and supply may also be provided to the icemaker in the refrigerator.

Garbage Disposal

A garbage disposal is a simple device that grinds food and washes it down the sewer system. I suggest that you use the disposal sparingly, placing larger quantities of food waste in the garbage or in a compost pile. Remember that any waste you put down the sewer system must be treated in a municipal sewage treatment facility or in your own private septic system.

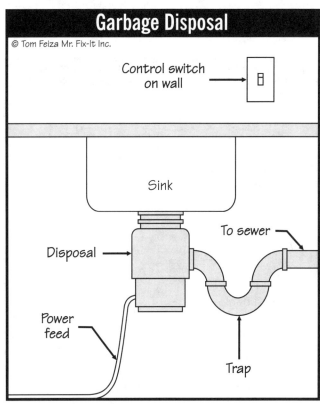

Garbage Disposal

© Tom Feiza Mr. Fix-It Inc.

Control switch on wall

Sink

To sewer

Disposal

Power feed

Trap

P012

Most experts suggest that you do not install a garbage disposal if you have your own septic or mound system. Introducing excess food waste can cause premature failure of the system. If you do use a garbage disposal, have the system pumped more often.

The key to using a disposal is to run the water before you add waste. Run a strong flow of cold water, turn on the unit, then slowly feed waste into it. Keep running water for several seconds after grinding stops to make sure all waste is flushed away. Never fill the unit and then turn it on—you will have a big, big mess of clogged pipes.

When a loud noise comes from the unit while operating, it usually means that a metal object like a spoon is caught in it. Turn the unit off and remove the object with tongs. Never put your hand in the disposal.

If you switch the disposal on and nothing happens (not even a hum), the thermal overload may have tripped. Under the sink, check the body of the unit for a small red or black button that may be marked "reset" or "overload." Turn off power to the disposal by flicking the "light switch" above the kitchen counter and then push in this button. Now try the unit again. If it just hums without running, it is stuck and needs to be cleared.

Garbage Disposal Reset

© Tom Feiza Mr. Fix-It Inc.

Control switch on wall

Sink

Disposal

Reset button

When reset button "trips," turn off at wall switch and push reset button. Clear any obstruction before starting.

PO13

Must Know / Must Do
Garbage Disposal

- Always run a strong flow of cold water and start the disposal before you feed any waste into it.

- Never put your hand in the disposal.

- Know how to use the reset button and service wrench.

To clear the unit, turn off the power again. Look inside the unit for foreign objects, and if you see any, remove them with tongs. Next, look under the sink for a small six-sided wrench (usually stored in a plastic pouch near the disposal). Insert the bent end of this tool into a recessed hole at the center bottom of the disposal. Turn the wrench several revolutions in both directions until the shaft spins freely. Remove the wrench, turn the power back on, and try the unit again.

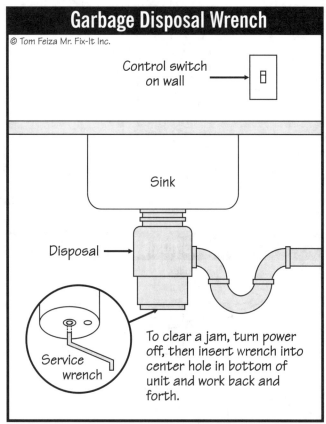

Garbage Disposal Wrench

© Tom Feiza Mr. Fix-It Inc.

Control switch on wall

Sink

Disposal

Service wrench

To clear a jam, turn power off, then insert wrench into center hole in bottom of unit and work back and forth.

PO14

Hose Bibs (Exterior Hose Faucets)

A hose bib is an exterior faucet. There are several types.

In a cold climate, the hose bib valve may extend up to 12" into the house. When you turn off this type of hose bib, you are actually turning off a valve inside your home…but (and this is important), it may not drain properly and could freeze during cold weather if there is a hose connected to it. To prevent this problem, some older installations provide an additional shutoff valve in the basement. Properly turning off water in the winter requires that you (1) turn off the inside valve, (2) open the outside valve, and (3) open the small drain knob (if there is one) on the inside valve to drain off the pipe.

Hose Bibs - Parts

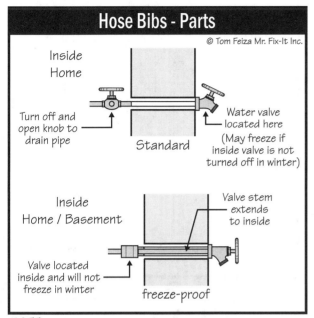

© Tom Feiza Mr. Fix-It Inc.

Inside Home

Turn off and open knob to drain pipe

Standard

Water valve located here (May freeze if inside valve is not turned off in winter)

Inside Home / Basement

Valve stem extends to inside

Valve located inside and will not freeze in winter

freeze-proof

P077

A newer home may have a backflow preventer on the outside hose bib. This could trap water in the pipe and cause a freeze-up. To release water from the pipe, you must either push the little button in the center of the backflow preventer to release the pressure, or open the small knurled knob at the inside shutoff valve to drain water from the pipe.

Every hose bib should have a backflow preventer or an anti-siphon device to keep contaminated water from the hose out of your drinking water system. To find out if such a device is required in your area, check with your water utility, plumbing inspector, or health department.

Must Know / Must Do
Hose Bibs

- Keep all backflow devices in good working order.

- In colder climates, before winter begins, turn off the water supply to all exterior pipes and hose connections, and drain the pipes properly.

Hose Bib - Backflow Prevention

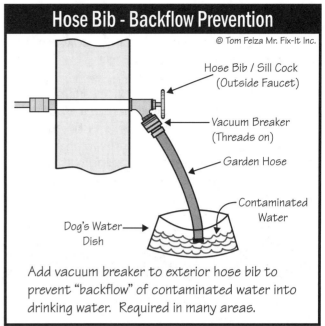

© Tom Feiza Mr. Fix-It Inc.

Hose Bib / Sill Cock (Outside Faucet)

Vacuum Breaker (Threads on)

Garden Hose

Contaminated Water

Dog's Water Dish

Add vacuum breaker to exterior hose bib to prevent "backflow" of contaminated water into drinking water. Required in many areas.

P034

Hose in Laundry Tub - Prevent Contamination

Possible contamination through cross connection of clean and dirty water.

Vacuum Breaker

Vacuum breaker prevents "backflow" of dirty water into drinking water. Removing the hose is the best solution.

© Tom Feiza Mr. Fix-It Inc.

P042

Water Hammer Arresters

Modern plumbing systems have water hammer arresters (anti-water-hammer devices) that prevent water pipes from pounding when water is quickly turned off. Basically, these are air chambers that can be compressed by moving water.

When halted quickly—for example, by an electrically-operated valve in a washing machine—water has lots of energy to dissipate. If the water can bounce against an air cushion, pipes won't pound. (For you electrical/electronic designers: this is equivalent to a capacitor in an electrical circuit.)

In older homes, anti-hammer devices are located near the main valve. In newer homes they are located near the washing machine, dishwasher, laundry tubs, and perhaps near the water main. They look like a short length of piping with a cap on the end. In a newer home, an anti-hammer device may be a small, specially designed chamber about 1" around and 4" long.

Modern Water Hammer Arrester

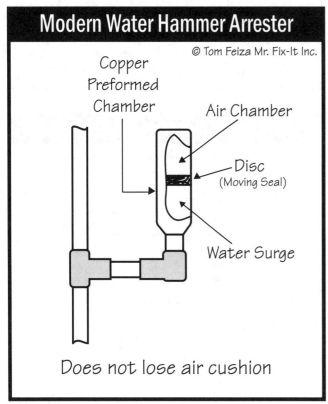

© Tom Feiza Mr. Fix-It Inc.

Copper Preformed Chamber

Air Chamber

Disc (Moving Seal)

Water Surge

Does not lose air cushion

P032

If your pipes pound or bang when the water shuts off, add water hammer arresters or check any existing arresters. Old-style arresters may have filled with water and need to be drained. Before you try this, though, be sure the main valve is in good working order. If it leaks, is hard to turn, or has excessive corrosion, call a plumber. Also, be aware that in older homes with steel piping, turning off the water may loosen sediment inside the pipes; you may see rust and debris in the water. And since this technique introduces air into the system, an air/water mix may shoot out of the faucets when you turn them on again.

Water Hammer Arresters

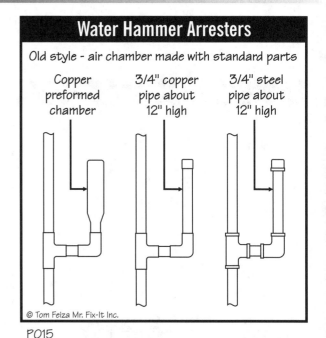

Old style - air chamber made with standard parts

Copper preformed chamber

3/4" copper pipe about 12" high

3/4" steel pipe about 12" high

© Tom Feiza Mr. Fix-It Inc.

P015

Must Know / Must Do
Water Hammer Arresters

- If pipes pound or bang when the water shuts off, check water hammer arresters.

- Consider draining the system to restore air in the chambers of water hammer arresters.

- If the main valve is hard to operate, don't drain the system; call a plumber instead.

To drain the system and restore air to the arresters, turn off the water main, shutting off all water to your home. Then open all faucets and allow all water to drain from them. Next, slowly open the main valve part way and close the faucets one by one as the water runs steadily. After all faucets are closed, fully open the main valve.

Drainage, Waste and Vent System

After water is used in your home, it exits through a drainage, waste and vent (DWV) system. Large pipes allow wastewater to flow by gravity from your home to a municipal sewer or private septic system. A series of traps and vents allow wastewater to flow freely while preventing sewer gas from entering your home.

Drainage, Waste and Vent (DWV) System

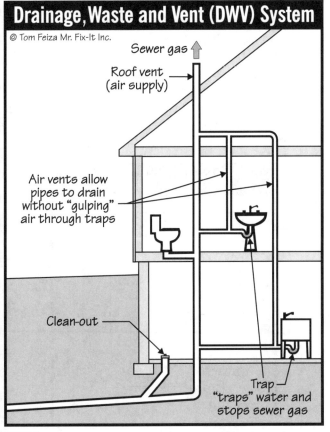

© Tom Feiza Mr. Fix-It Inc.

Sewer gas

Roof vent
(air supply)

Air vents allow
pipes to drain
without "gulping"
air through traps

Clean-out

Trap
"traps" water and
stops sewer gas

P016

Older systems are constructed of cast iron and gal-vanized steel piping. Newer systems are made of plastic. Copper was used for some systems built about 1970.

The sketch shows common components of a DWV system, which uses pipes that are larger than those in the water-supply plumbing system. The pipes range from 1-1/2" to 4", with the larger pipes installed where the system exits your home. Horizontal pipes are angled to allow for proper waste flow.

The vent portion of the system starts with the vent pipe or stack routed through the roof. This open pipe allows air to enter the system so all pipes can drain properly. Think of the drainage system as a big straw. If you fill a straw with water, cover the top end with your finger and pick it up, water will not drain from the straw. When you release your finger and allow air to "vent" the straw, water drains quickly.

S Trap Not Allowed

In older systems or systems installed by an amateur, you may see a sink drained with an "S" trap. This type of trap has an S-shaped pipe below the sink, and instead of draining into the wall, it drains into the floor. Since there is no vent and no air supply, the trap will drain with a long slurp as air is drawn through it. The trap seal also may be lost.

S Trap - Not Allowed

Water draining through the "S" trap will siphon out the water seal and allow sewer gas and vermin into home.

Will drain with a "glug - glug."

© Tom Feiza Mr. Fix-It Inc.

P037

Air Admittance Valve

In systems installed since about 2000, when plumbing codes changed, a new device called an air admittance valve may be added to the drain line. This valve allows air to enter the drainage system but does not allow sewer gas to escape. The device will be located in the horizontal run from a sink in place of a plumbed vent. It must be visible and accessible for maintenance. This valve may not be allowed on certain fixtures and may be prohibited in some communities.

Plumbing Vent of Island Sink

Island sinks present a special problem for running a typical vent pipe up a wall and into the attic, because there is no wall available. Island sinks have either a special vent arrangement with a vent loop under the sink or an air admittance valve if it is allowed.

Air Admittance Valve

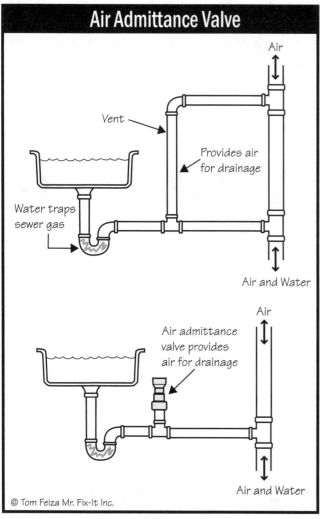

Air

Vent

Provides air for drainage

Water traps sewer gas

Air and Water

Air admittance valve provides air for drainage

Air

Air and Water

© Tom Feiza Mr. Fix-It Inc.

P035

Plumbing Vent of Island Sink

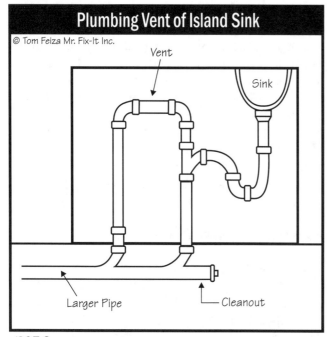

© Tom Feiza Mr. Fix-It Inc.

Vent

Sink

Larger Pipe

Cleanout

P036

All piping and fixtures must be vented. If problems occur with the venting system, drains will "glug-glug" and empty slowly.

Each fixture has a trap—a P-shaped device below a sink (or built into the base of a toilet) that remains full of water. "Trapping" water creates a seal that prevents sewer gas from entering through the drain. If a trap dries up, you will notice a sewage smell.

Floor Drain Trap

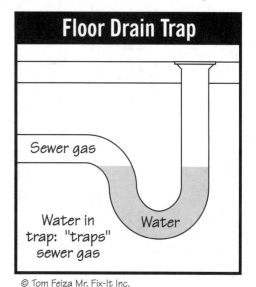

Sewer gas

Water in trap: "traps" sewer gas

Water

© Tom Feiza Mr. Fix-It Inc.

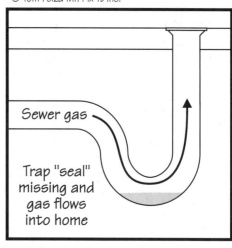

Sewer gas

Trap "seal" missing and gas flows into home

P026

Traps are designed to be dismantled to remove blockages or retrieve lost objects. Drain piping has covers ("clean-outs") that can be removed to help clean out clogged pipes. The main system cleanout will be located in the basement floor or where the main pipe exits your home.

If you have a septic system, this cleanout will be outside, about 4 feet below the soil. With slab construction, the cleanout will be in the slab or outside.

Sanitary Sewer Check Valve

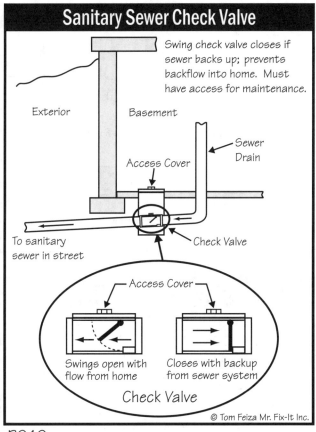

Swing check valve closes if sewer backs up; prevents backflow into home. Must have access for maintenance.

Exterior

Basement

Sewer Drain

Access Cover

To sanitary sewer in street

Check Valve

Access Cover

Swings open with flow from home

Closes with backup from sewer system

Check Valve

© Tom Feiza Mr. Fix-It Inc.

P040

Sanitary Sewer Cleanout

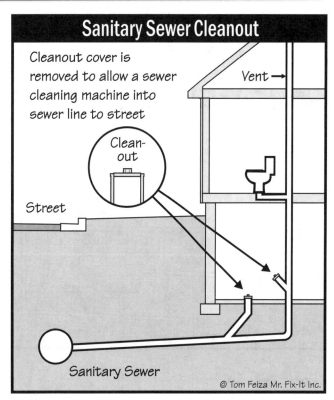

Cleanout cover is removed to allow a sewer cleaning machine into sewer line to street

Vent →

Clean-out

Street

Sanitary Sewer

© Tom Feiza Mr. Fix-It Inc.

P028

Must Know / Must Do
Drainage, Waste and Vent System

- If you notice a sewage smell, check for a dry trap.

- If a sink or other fixture backs up, there's a blockage in the trap.

- If your whole system backs up or wastewater backs up out of the lowest fixture, this indicates a problem with the main drainage line. Call a plumber.

- Any leaks from the waste system are potentially dangerous and should be repaired as soon as possible.

If the sewer drainage system is subject to backups from the municipal connection, the municipality may allow the installation of a sanitary sewer check valve. Typically this valve is located below the basement floor or wherever the main sewer line exits the structure. The valve is located in a box with a cover so the check valve can be maintained. Maintenance involves visual inspection of the operation, as well as clearing of any debris that would prevent the valve from closing.

Under normal conditions, the valve swings open to allow sewage to flow out of your home. When there is no flow, or if a backup occurs in the sewage system, the swing check valve drops closed, preventing sewage from backing up into your home.

Sewer and Septic Systems

After wastewater leaves your home, it must be treated and cleaned before it is released into the environment. In a municipal sewage system, wastewater is routed to a treatment facility. If you live in the country, your home will have its own private treatment system—a septic or mound system.

Sewer System

Municipal sewer systems collect sanitary waste (sewer water) through pipes below the street. Wastewater flows through a series of pipes that increase in size as they approach the treatment facility. Pipes can be 6 feet or more in diameter.

In many systems, all sewage flows by gravity until pumping stations "lift" (pump) it into the treatment facility. Once treated, the water is released to rivers and streams.

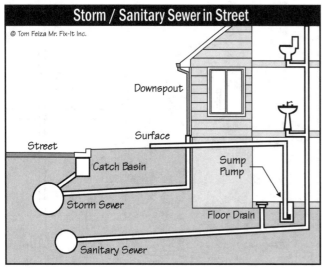

PO17

Septic System

In rural areas without a municipal sewage treatment facility, residential sewage is treated in a septic system—a large underground tank and absorption field. Bacteria in the tank break down sewage solids. This treated sewage becomes sludge that settles at the bottom of the tank. Grease, fat and soap scum rise to the top of the tank, where they are trapped by baffles.

As wastewater enters the tank, processed water is released to a drain field or absorption field consisting of a series of perforated pipes that release the water into soil. The soil then filters the wastewater; soil microorganisms decompose many contaminants in the wastewater.

Although the septic system works automatically through the actions of bacteria, microorganisms, tank and piping, you must arrange for a professional to pump and inspect the tank.

Generally, a family of four should have the tank pumped and inspected every 2 years, but this varies with the type and size of the system and with local conditions. A professional septic service company can determine when your system should be pumped. Pumping the tank involves removing the sludge and scum before an excess builds up.

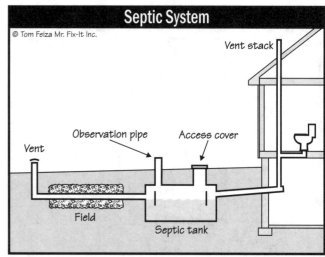

PO18

Conventional Septic Tank & Field

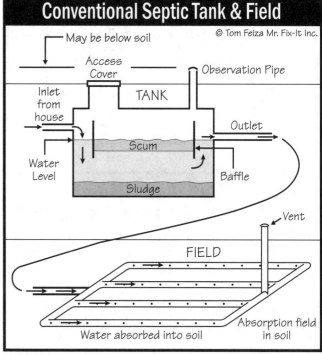

PO78

Must Know / Must Do
Septic System

- Understand how your system works.

- Have the system pumped and serviced routinely.

- Do not put contaminants in the system.

- Learn ways to conserve water.

You also must limit the amount of water that enters the system. Use fixtures (toilets, showerheads) that limit water use. Repair all plumbing leaks promptly. Don't connect the sump pump discharge to the septic system—the sump handles clear rainwater that doesn't need treatment. Divert surface water away from the septic drainage field so it can work properly.

Never put grease, fat, coffee grounds, paper towels, food waste, sanitary napkins, or disposable diapers down the drains—they will clog the system. Also, do not put toxic substances like solvents, oils, paints, disinfectants, or pesticides down the drains.

Most experts agree that "sweeteners" or septic system "starters" are not useful.

For more information, consult local health officials, the local plumbing inspector, or your nearest department of natural resources.

Mound System

Mound systems are installed in rural areas where the soil can't accept water from a standard septic system. A mound system usually has a second holding tank/pump tank. After sewage is processed in the septic tank, water flows into the pump tank, which lifts the water to the top of the mound.

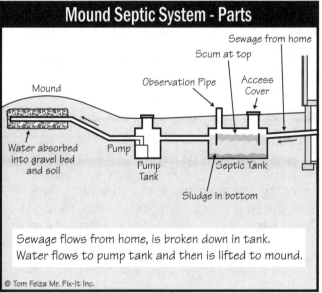

Mound Septic System - Parts

Mound
Sewage from home
Scum at top
Observation Pipe
Access Cover
Water absorbed into gravel bed and soil
Pump
Pump Tank
Septic Tank
Sludge in bottom

Sewage flows from home, is broken down in tank. Water flows to pump tank and then is lifted to mound.

© Tom Feiza Mr. Fix-It Inc.

PO79

The mound is specially constructed of gravel and soil that's mounded above the surrounding surface. The mound functions the same as the absorption field in a conventional septic system, and the requirements for maintenance are the same as those described above for a septic system.

You should understand the operation of the pump/second holding tank. Also, there may be an alarm that goes off if the pump is not working. If the alarm sounds, contact professional help.

Sewage Ejector

In most homes with basements and septic systems, sanitary system drainage will exit the basement 4 feet below the exterior soil depth, or about halfway up the basement wall. Sewage flows by gravity through the drainage pipe. But if there is a laundry tub, sink, bathroom, or floor drain in the basement, their wastewater must be pumped up to the main waste line. In this case, a sewage ejector or wastewater pump lifts the sewage water.

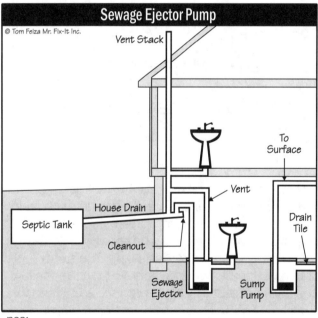

Sewage Ejector Pump

© Tom Feiza Mr. Fix-It Inc.

Vent Stack
To Surface
Vent
House Drain
Septic Tank
Drain Tile
Cleanout
Sewage Ejector
Sump Pump

PO21

You can tell if your home has a sewage ejector by looking for a sealed crock with piping that leads to the septic system. Modern systems are sealed and vented. An older system may consist of an open crock if it just services a laundry tub or floor drain.

These pumps and crocks require little maintenance, but if the pump fails or water leaks from the crock, stop using water in the lower level, and call a plumber.

Sometimes a home that's on a municipal sewage system will have a sewage ejection pump. This depends on the height of the main sewer line in the street and the height of the connection to the home.

Storm Sewer—Municipal or None?

Modern municipalities have two distinct sets of piping beneath roads and streets: sanitary sewers and storm sewers. The sanitary (municipal) sewer system routes all toilet, sink and drain water to a sewage treatment plant for processing, after which the clean water is released to rivers, lakes and streams.

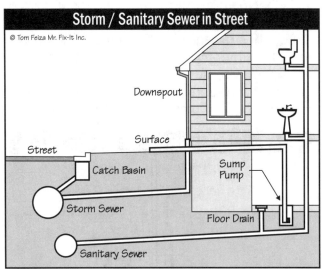

Storm / Sanitary Sewer in Street

© Tom Feiza Mr. Fix-It Inc.

Downspout

Surface

Street

Catch Basin

Sump Pump

Storm Sewer

Floor Drain

Sanitary Sewer

P017

Cities, and some subdivisions, also have a separate system—the storm sewer system—that handles rainwater. This system directly discharges untreated rainwater/runoff into rivers and streams. Your sump pump and rain gutters may be connected to this system through an underground pipe. The storm sewer line in your basement may look just like the sanitary sewer line except that it's not connected to toilets and sinks and doesn't have a vent on the roof.

If your sump pump is routed to the sanitary sewer system instead, you are sending clean rainwater to the sewage treatment plant. That overloads the plant and creates an unnecessary treatment expense. So don't connect your sump pump to the laundry tubs, because this water is routed to the sanitary sewer.

In rural areas, storm water may be routed into an open ditch beside the road. In densely populated areas, storm sewer piping below the street handles rainstorm runoff from hard surfaces like roofs, drive-

ways, and parking lots. Such runoff is too great to be absorbed by the limited area of exposed soil in the city. Whenever you see sewer grates in the street, you are looking at parts of an underground storm sewer system.

Palmer Valve

In some metropolitan areas, homes built between the 1920s and the 1950s had a "palmer valve" that routed clear storm water into the sanitary sewer lines. This practice is no longer permitted in new home construction. We cannot afford to treat clear water in the sewer treatment plants. We also can't size sanitary sewer systems to accept large quantities of storm water during heavy rains.

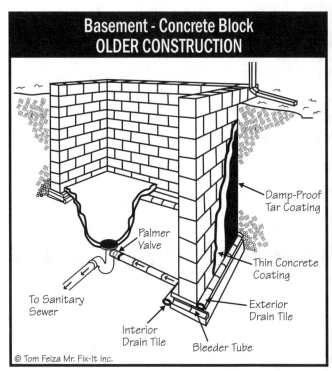

**Basement - Concrete Block
OLDER CONSTRUCTION**

Damp-Proof Tar Coating

Palmer Valve

Thin Concrete Coating

To Sanitary Sewer

Exterior Drain Tile

Interior Drain Tile

Bleeder Tube

© Tom Feiza Mr. Fix-It Inc.

B002

If your house doesn't have a sump pump, it probably has a palmer valve— and if so, you should maintain it. In the basement, remove the cover from the floor drain and shine a bright flashlight down into it. The palmer valve is a round brass disc at the side of the vertical pipe, just above the water in the trap.

Hook the lower edge of the palmer valve brass disc with a stiff wire or tool to make sure it moves freely—the brass disc should swing easily from the hinge at its top. If this disc is stuck closed (and most of them are), water that collects in the basement drain tile system cannot be drain away. You may end up with water rising in your basement. See Chapter 25 – Keep Your Basement Dry.

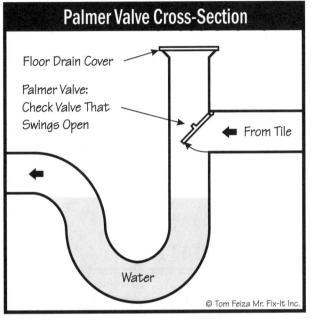

Palmer Valve Cross-Section

Floor Drain Cover

Palmer Valve:
Check Valve That
Swings Open

From Tile

Water

© Tom Feiza Mr. Fix-It Inc.

B001

To loosen a stuck palmer valve, spray it with lubricating oil a few times over several days, and bang it with a stick or tool. Try to hook the bottom and lift it up. You could also grab it with your hand if you are a brave soul. Or hire a plumber to free the valve.

Irrigation Systems

Landscape irrigation systems come in all designs and types. They are not common in northern climates, although they may be used for more expensive housing. In dry southern climates, drip systems often are buried to deliver moisture to soil below the plants.

In northern climates, water must be drained from an underground system to prevent winter freezing. A professional best performs this service. In addition, the system will need routine maintenance of sprinkler heads, automatic valves, and piping.

Most systems receive water from the home's drinking (potable) water system. In this case the irrigation system must be separated from the drinking water with a vacuum breaker or a backflow prevention device. Typically this device is located at least 12 inches above the soil in the feed pipe to the system. The backflow preventer stops any backflow that would contaminate the drinking water.

Where homes are on a metered municipal water system and a municipal sanitary sewer system, the irrigation system or even the exterior hose bib connections may be separately metered. This involves two water meters—one for the total amount of water used and one for the irrigation water. This allows the municipality to determine how much water is used for irrigation so the homeowner will not have to pay a sewer charge on it.

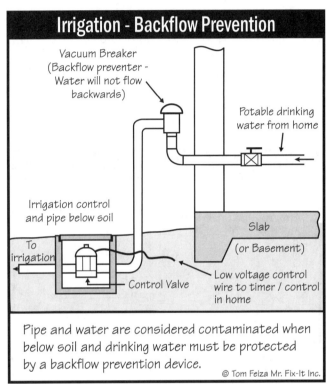

Irrigation - Backflow Prevention

Vacuum Breaker
(Backflow preventer -
Water will not flow
backwards)

Potable drinking
water from home

Irrigation control
and pipe below soil

Slab

To
irrigation

(or Basement)

Control Valve

Low voltage control
wire to timer / control
in home

Pipe and water are considered contaminated when below soil and drinking water must be protected by a backflow prevention device.

© Tom Feiza Mr. Fix-It Inc.

P098

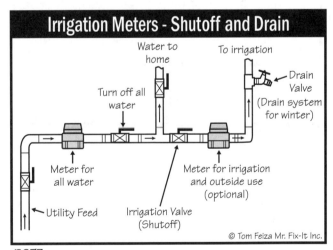

Irrigation Meters - Shutoff and Drain

Water to
home

To irrigation

Drain
Valve
(Drain system
for winter)

Turn off all
water

Meter for
all water

Meter for irrigation
and outside use
(optional)

Utility Feed

Irrigation Valve
(Shutoff)

© Tom Feiza Mr. Fix-It Inc.

P073

Natural Gas and Propane

Natural gas and propane are commonly used in central heating systems and may also be used for cooking, drying clothes, and operating fireplaces. Know the basics of the distribution system in your home and how to turn off the system in an emergency.

Natural Gas

Natural gas is provided by a public utility in many areas. Underground piping distributes the gas, and a small line brings it to the house through a metering/control system outside or in the basement. Gas enters your home at very low pressure. There is a main shutoff valve near the meter, and the system has a relief valve and vent piping for safety.

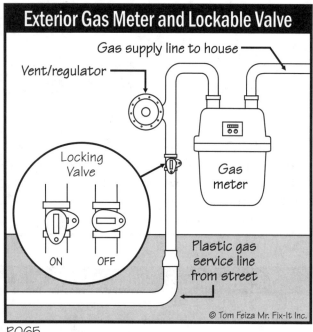

Exterior Gas Meter and Lockable Valve

Gas supply line to house

Vent/regulator

Locking Valve

ON   OFF

Gas meter

Plastic gas service line from street

© Tom Feiza Mr. Fix-It Inc.

P065

Inside your home, natural gas may be distributed by "black iron" steel-screwed pipes. It can also be distributed by brass or copper pipes, depending on local requirements.

Natural gas piping should be well-supported and protected from damage. There should be a shutoff valve at each appliance connection to the piping. Most fixed gas appliances like the furnace or water heater will be directly connected to the gas piping without a flexible connector. Most connections will include a "drip leg," a small vertical pipe below the appliance connection that catches any contamination before it reaches the gas control valves.

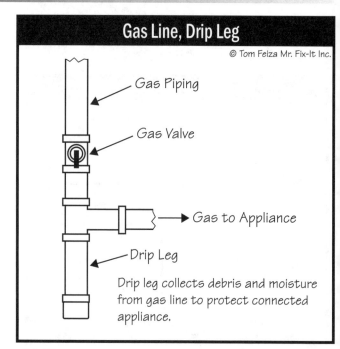

Gas Line, Drip Leg

© Tom Feiza Mr. Fix-It Inc.

Gas Piping

Gas Valve

Gas to Appliance

Drip Leg

Drip leg collects debris and moisture from gas line to protect connected appliance.

P043

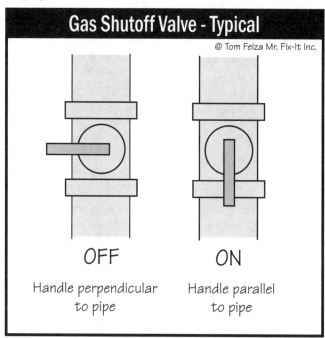

Gas Shutoff Valve - Typical

© Tom Feiza Mr. Fix-It Inc.

OFF
Handle perpendicular to pipe

ON
Handle parallel to pipe

P076

All flexible connectors should be the modern type that extend directly from the gas piping and shutoff valve to the appliance. Normally, flexible connectors are used only with appliances like stoves or dryers that can be moved for maintenance, but areas prone to earthquakes may allow or require flexible connectors at furnaces and water heaters.

The Consumer Product Safety Commission advises that older flexible gas connectors made of uncoated brass can leak. Your connectors should be made

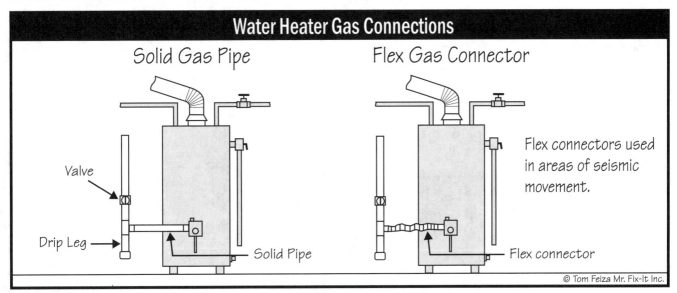

Water Heater Gas Connections

Solid Gas Pipe

Valve

Drip Leg →

— Solid Pipe

Flex Gas Connector

Flex connectors used in areas of seismic movement.

— Flex connector

© Tom Feiza Mr. Fix-It Inc.

P047

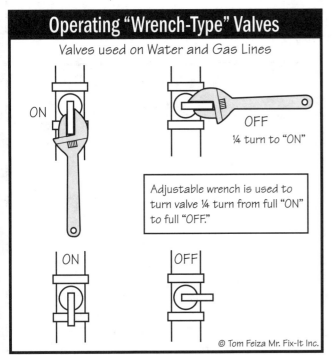

Operating "Wrench-Type" Valves

Valves used on Water and Gas Lines

ON

OFF
¼ turn to "ON"

Adjustable wrench is used to turn valve ¼ turn from full "ON" to full "OFF."

ON

OFF

© Tom Feiza Mr. Fix-It Inc.

P066

of plastic-coated brass or stainless steel. The CPSC advises that any uncoated brass connector should be immediately replaced by a professional. You will recognize uncoated brass by its coppery color, even if it's old. Older connectors made of flexible aluminum or aluminum piping also should be replaced. See the References section to find out how to contact the CPSC for more information.

If a gas appliance is removed from the system, have a professional turn off the gas valve, cap the line beyond the valve, and check for leaks.

Gas valves turn off with a quarter-turn. When the valve handle is parallel to the piping, the valve is on. When the handle is perpendicular to the piping, the valve is off. Many valves must be turned with an adjustable wrench or pliers.

Propane

Propane is a gas that's similar to natural gas, except that propane is provided in a storage tank on your property. Distribution piping is similar to that for natural gas except that there is no meter; you pay for the gas when it's placed in the tank.

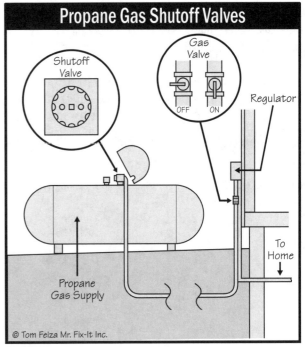

Propane Gas Shutoff Valves

Shutoff Valve

Gas Valve

OFF   ON

Regulator

To Home ↓

Propane Gas Supply

© Tom Feiza Mr. Fix-It Inc.

P075

The main shutoff often is at the top of the tank. It may be a valve that requires several turns to shut off the gas. Review the valve and the rest of the system with your supplier. Follow all precautions noted above for natural gas.

It's wise to sign up with a supplier who automatically fills the tank as needed. Often, the supplier can also service your heating equipment.

Must Know / Must Do
Natural Gas and Propane

- Identify the main shutoff valve and know how it operates.

- Identify the shutoff for every gas appliance.

- Inspect all flexible gas connectors per CPSC standards (noted above).

- If you smell gas, leave the house. Don't light a match, and don't turn on a light. Use a neighbor's phone to call the gas supplier.

Heating Oil

Oil can be used in a heating system and may also be used to heat water. An oil system consists of a storage tank, valve, filter, and distribution piping. A fill and vent line will extend to the exterior of the house.

The oil storage tank often is located in the basement, but it may also be underground in your yard. If your tank is underground, contact the oil supplier or your municipality or state to check maintenance requirements and code regulations. Usually, underground storage tanks are tightly regulated because of the potential for a spill that could contaminate the environment.

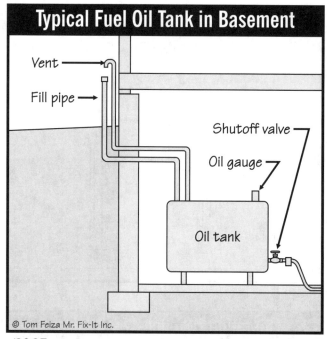

Typical Fuel Oil Tank in Basement

Vent

Fill pipe

Shutoff valve

Oil gauge

Oil tank

© Tom Feiza Mr. Fix-It Inc.

P003

Must Know / Must Do
Heating Oil

- Identify the shutoff valve and know how to operate it.

- Never allow the system to run out of oil.

- The system should not smell or leak. Fix all leaks promptly.

- For underground tanks: contact municipal or state agency for registration and maintenance requirements.

Arrange to have a supplier automatically fill the tank and maintain the oil burner. Never, never, never let the system run out of oil—this can lead to a very expensive service call.

Chapter 6 – General Home Systems

Foundation Basics

A foundation provides a stable, rigid base to support a home. The foundation supports the frame and structure and protects it from moisture and contact with the soil. The foundation must rest on firm soil and be protected from water entry or excessive dampness.

Full Depth Basement, Crawl Spaces

Foundation types vary with local weather conditions and accepted local practices. In northern climates, the foundation must be deep enough to extend below the frost line. This can be 4 feet or more, so full basements are common. (Frost causes soil to expand, and the foundation must be below the frost line so it won't move with this expansion.) In warmer climates that have little or no frost, the foundation may be a crawl space or concrete slab poured "on grade" or directly on the soil. In a coastal region, the foundation may be piers or posts that raise the house above potential high water levels. In some areas, foundations are made of pressure-treated wood.

Foundation Wall Sections

© Tom Feiza Mr. Fix-It Inc.

Concrete block

Poured concrete

Crawl space

Slab on grade

S004

Must Know / Must Do— Foundations

- Understand the type of foundation that supports your home.

- Protect your foundation from water damage. Never allow water to pond around the foundation.

- Protect your foundation and the rest of your home from insects.

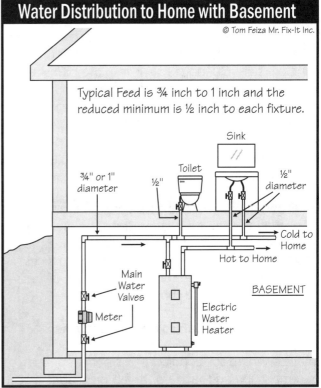

Water Distribution to Home with Basement

© Tom Feiza Mr. Fix-It Inc.

Typical Feed is ¾ inch to 1 inch and the reduced minimum is ½ inch to each fixture.

Sink

Toilet

¾" or 1" diameter

½"

½" diameter

Cold to Home

Hot to Home

Main Water Valves

Meter

BASEMENT

Electric Water Heater

P083

The majority of homes in northern climates are built on foundations that form a crawl space or full basement. The basement rests on a footing that supports the home's weight. Foundation walls are constructed of brick, concrete block, poured concrete, clay tile, stone, or similar materials. The basement floor usually consists of poured concrete. Crawl spaces often have a dirt floor.

Full-depth basements are the most complicated type of foundation because of potential water problems and the pressure of soil outside the basement walls. While full-depth basements require the most maintenance, crawl spaces and slab foundations must also be protected from excessive moisture. See Chapter 25 – Keep Your Basement Dry.

Slab Foundations

In warmer climates, a foundation must be placed on firm soil for proper support, but frost is not an issue. In warmer climates, houses often rest on a "slab on grade," meaning that the foundation is a slab of concrete poured directly on grade. Often these types of foundations are thicker at the edge, and reinforcing steel is set inside the slab to provide structural strength and to resist cracking and movement. With this type of foundation, plumbing, heating and utility lines may be set in the slab.

A slab foundation may also be reinforced with steel cables pulled tightly inside tubes that are set in the concrete slab. During construction, the tubes and steel cables are set in place; concrete is poured, and it sets. Special hydraulic jacks stretch the cables, and they are fastened at the edges of the concrete with special tapered steel wedges. These "post tensioned" steel cables compress the concrete and provide rigidity and strength to the concrete slab.

Local conditions must be considered in maintaining a foundation. Slab foundations must be protected from changes in water in the soil supporting the slab to prevent heaving and cracking. Excessive moisture can make the soil swell, and lack of moisture can make the soil shrink.

Pier, Post, Pile, Caisson Foundations

In areas where soil conditions will not support a basement spread footing or a slab on grade, a post and beam foundation is an option. Generally, pier,

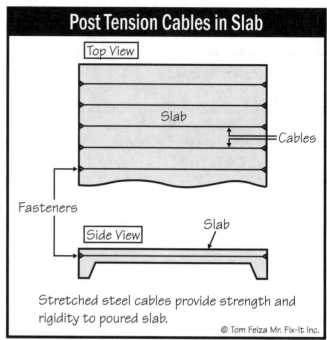

Post Tension Cables in Slab

Top View

Slab

Cables

Fasteners

Side View — Slab

Stretched steel cables provide strength and rigidity to poured slab.

© Tom Feiza Mr. Fix-It Inc.

S034

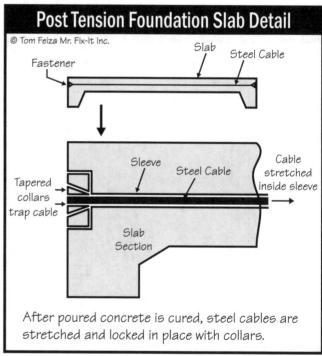

Post Tension Foundation Slab Detail

© Tom Feiza Mr. Fix-It Inc.

Fastener — Slab — Steel Cable

Tapered collars trap cable

Sleeve — Steel Cable

Cable stretched inside sleeve

Slab Section

After poured concrete is cured, steel cables are stretched and locked in place with collars.

S035

post and caisson refer to a vertical post set into the soil down to a firm bearing soil or rock. These types of foundations are well suited for soft soils, soils that expand, and coastal or hillside construction. Usually, the post is constructed of poured reinforced concrete, and it supports a beam that forms the base of the home.

The hole may be drilled for the caisson, and then a steel-reinforced concrete post is poured. A pile is driven into the ground until it reaches suitable soil or rock that provides proper support. This type of construction requires a site evaluation and engineering design.

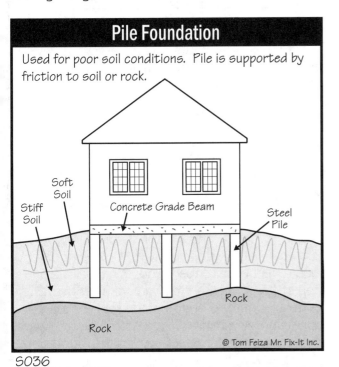

Pile Foundation

Used for poor soil conditions. Pile is supported by friction to soil or rock.

Soft Soil
Stiff Soil
Concrete Grade Beam
Steel Pile
Rock
Rock

© Tom Feiza Mr. Fix-It Inc.

S036

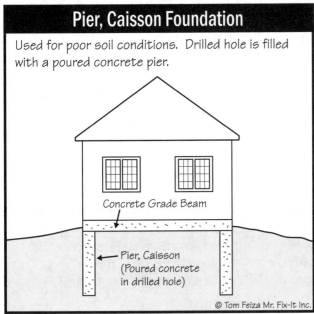

Pier, Caisson Foundation

Used for poor soil conditions. Drilled hole is filled with a poured concrete pier.

Concrete Grade Beam

Pier, Caisson (Poured concrete in drilled hole)

© Tom Feiza Mr. Fix-It Inc.

S037

I will focus on the construction and maintenance of full-depth foundations. The necessary maintenance of crawl spaces is similar. For slabs on grade, follow the recommendations for protecting the foundation from water.

Protecting Your Basement Foundation

Basements foundations require simple, routine maintenance to prevent damage that requires costly repairs. Since most damage to basements occurs slowly, over many years, if you ignore routine maintenance you may not notice a problem until there is a water leak or a major crack and wall movement. So take some time to inspect your basement and its environment. A little common sense and simple maintenance will prevent potentially serious problems and extend the trouble-free performance of your basement.

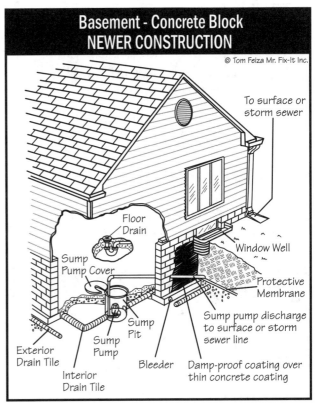

Basement - Concrete Block NEWER CONSTRUCTION

© Tom Feiza Mr. Fix-It Inc.

To surface or storm sewer
Floor Drain
Window Well
Sump Pump Cover
Protective Membrane
Sump Pit
Sump pump discharge to surface or storm sewer line
Exterior Drain Tile
Sump Pump
Bleeder
Damp-proof coating over thin concrete coating
Interior Drain Tile

B005

Over the years, your home's original water diversion systems require maintenance and repair. They simply can't be ignored. Let's walk through the basics of maintaining your hole in the ground.

Grading to Protect the Foundation

Proper grading around the house is your best protection against seepage into the basement that may cause expensive damage. When a home is built, workers dig the excavation several feet larger than the basement walls to allow for construction clearances.

Most of the hole around your basement is filled with soil from the site. This may contain gravel, rock, wood, paper, and unfortunately almost anything no longer useful for home construction. For the next 20 years, this soil and "stuff" settles around your basement walls. It settles quickly for the first few years and more slowly after that.

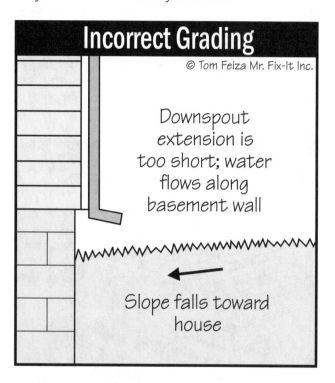

Incorrect Grading

© Tom Feiza Mr. Fix-It Inc.

Downspout extension is too short; water flows along basement wall

Slope falls toward house

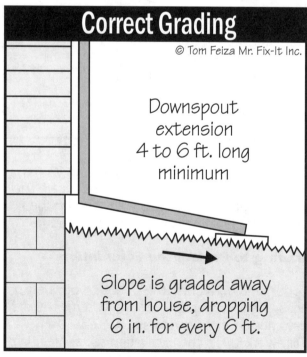

Correct Grading

© Tom Feiza Mr. Fix-It Inc.

Downspout extension 4 to 6 ft. long minimum

Slope is graded away from house, dropping 6 in. for every 6 ft.

BOO3

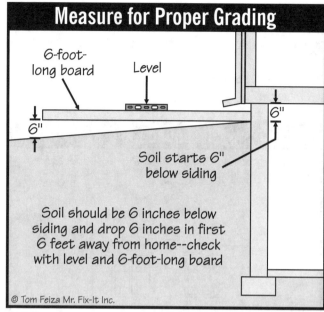

Measure for Proper Grading

6-foot-long board

Level

6"

6"

Soil starts 6" below siding

Soil should be 6 inches below siding and drop 6 inches in first 6 feet away from home--check with level and 6-foot-long board

© Tom Feiza Mr. Fix-It Inc.

B011

To divert surface water, the soil should pitch away from your home with a 1" pitch per linear foot for about 6 feet beyond the foundation. That is a 6" drop in 6 feet. You can measure this with a level and a straightedge held on top of the soil next to the foundation. At a minimum, the pitch should always have some slope for 6 feet beyond the foundation.

The soil should also be 6" below siding and wood trim to prevent water and insect damage. If wood siding touches the ground, water will wick up and rot the siding and framing.

To improve the grade, you have several options, depending on the landscape materials near your home.

Bushes near the foundation, planted above the original foundation hole, often settle. If there is bare soil under the bushes, just add more soil. However, adding more than a few inches of soil can damage bushes by eliminating air from the roots. Check with a professional landscaper on the potential damage to your type of bushes. You may need to raise the bushes and fill under them.

If the area around the foundation has a planting bed or bushes with a ground cover, the soil under the ground cover must pitch away from the foundation. Dig through the ground cover in several areas to check the grade of the soil. To improve this situation, remove the ground cover and fill with soil. Then replace the ground cover.

You may wish to use a fabric weed barrier or black plastic over the soil. The weed barrier will stop weeds while allowing air and water movement— good for plants but not ideal for the basement.

Black plastic does the best job of deflecting water and protecting your basement, but it can be hard on plants. If you use black plastic, cut large holes for plants to improve access to moisture and air.

If there is sod next to the foundation, cut it with a sod cutter and fold it away from the foundation. Add soil, then lay the sod back in place. You could add soil directly over the sod, but that would require re-seeding, and the area will settle as the buried sod decomposes. Cover the sod only if it is in very poor condition or if you need a dramatic change in grade. For flower beds and bare soil, just add topsoil fill.

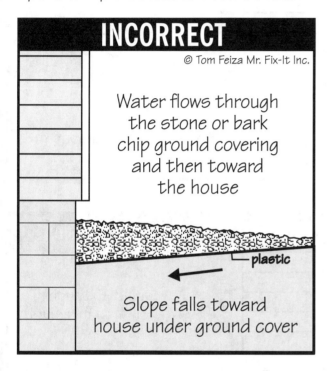

INCORRECT

© Tom Feiza Mr. Fix-It Inc.

Water flows through the stone or bark chip ground covering and then toward the house

plastic

Slope falls toward house under ground cover

Grading - Negative, Problem

Poor pitch of slab causes basement problems

INCORRECT

© Tom Feiza Mr. Fix-It Inc.

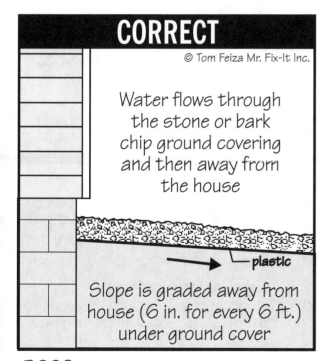

CORRECT

© Tom Feiza Mr. Fix-It Inc.

Water flows through the stone or bark chip ground covering and then away from the house

plastic

Slope is graded away from house (6 in. for every 6 ft.) under ground cover

B009

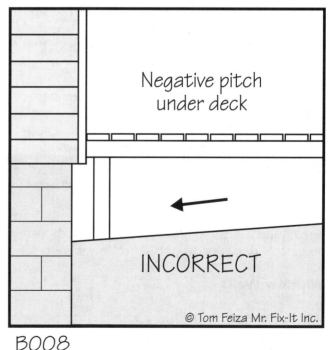

Negative pitch under deck

INCORRECT

© Tom Feiza Mr. Fix-It Inc.

B008

When grading, don't use a light moss-type soil; it will settle too much and hold moisture. In areas where you will not be planting, you can use clay. In planting beds use a blended or brown planting soil, or garden soil. This heavier mixture will not wash away into the yard.

Don't forget to grade areas under decks. You can use black plastic over the properly graded soil to deflect water and stop weeds. A thin cover of gravel or stone will hold down the plastic and make the area more attractive.

All hard surfaces such as walks and driveways should also be pitched away from your foundation. The good news is that only a slight grade, as little as 1/4" per foot, is adequate for hard surfaces.

Check Gutters and Downspouts

Gutters collect tremendous quantities of water from the roof and must deliver that water away from the foundation. Keep your downspouts extended at least 6 to 8 feet away from the foundation to a spot where the natural grade of the soil continues moving the water away.

If your area has underground storm sewers, make sure all downspouts are properly connected to the visible pipe fittings and that water flows into the storm sewer pipe during rainstorms. If this pipe backs up during a storm, it indicates that the storm sewer line is plugged or broken. Test the line by running a hose into the gutter. You can have this line cleaned by a sewer cleaner.

If dampness and seepage appear on basement walls near an underground storm sewer connection, a broken storm sewer line may be the cause. You can run water into the gutter during a dry spell; if moisture seeps into the basement, it indicates that the underground line is damaged. A sewer cleaner can evaluate and repair the line.

Keep gutters clean to prevent plugging and over-flowing of downspouts and storm sewer lines.

Window Wells

Window wells hold soil away from foundation windows as the grade is raised. The window well should fit tightly against the foundation wall to pre-

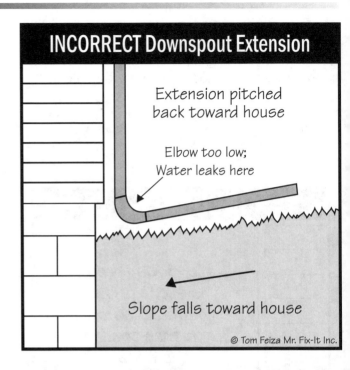

INCORRECT Downspout Extension

Extension pitched back toward house

Elbow too low; Water leaks here

Slope falls toward house

© Tom Feiza Mr. Fix-It Inc.

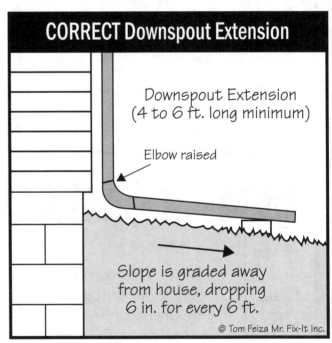

CORRECT Downspout Extension

Downspout Extension (4 to 6 ft. long minimum)

Elbow raised

Slope is graded away from house, dropping 6 in. for every 6 ft.

© Tom Feiza Mr. Fix-It Inc.

B019

vent leaks. The grade around the well should pitch away so water isn't directed into the well. If a window well fills with water, check the fit of the well and the grade around it.

Keep window wells clean and free of all plant material. Fill the bottom of the well with gravel to allow for good drainage and to stop any plant growth.

Downspout to Storm Sewer

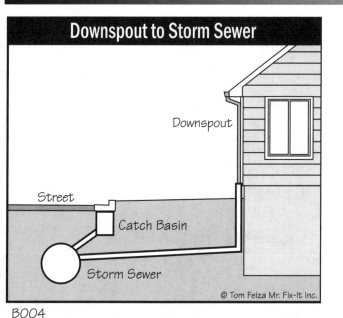

B004

Downspout Lateral Broken

Wet Wall in Basement

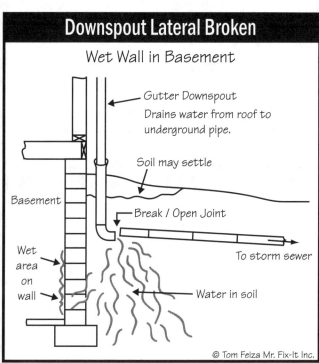

B061

If the grade and fit around the window well are in good condition but the well still fills with water, dig out the bottom of the well about 18" and fill with washed stone. The stone will ensure proper drainage to the tile system. If you have a problem window well, dig down several feet inside it with a post hole digger; then fill the hole with washed stone. This channel helps drain the window well to the basement tile. However, you should only dig this channel if you know the drain tile system is working. If it isn't, you will create a tube of frozen water that can push against the basement wall.

Window Well

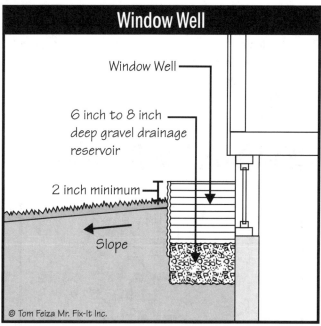

B010

Foundations—The Bottom Line

If you follow these simple inspection and maintenance tips, your basement will perform for many years without failure. All foundations have some problem symptoms, but if you maintain your foundation, minor problems will not become major crises. If you notice severe drainage problems, wall cracks or wall movement, contact a professional home inspector or basement consultant to evaluate your specific situation.

If a major problem is identified, don't feel threatened, and don't jump at the first evaluation or repair proposal. It often takes years for a basement or faoundation problem to develop, and the situation will not require immediate repair. Take time to solicit several evaluations and repair proposals. Check each contractor's references, and make sure the contractor belongs to a professional builders' or remodelers' organization. For complete detail on basement maintenance, see Chapter 25 – Keep Your Basement Dry.

Termite Protection

In warmer climates, the wood structure of a home must be protected from termites and other pests. This often requires special construction techniques and constant diligence to check for potential problems. Often a pest control contractor should be hired on a routine basis.

Homeowners must eliminate soil contact with the wood structure of the home. Potential entry points for pests include contact points of trees and shrubs as well as firewood stacked against a home. In areas where termites are a problem, special precautions like a termite shield can separate the wood structure from the soil to prevent insect movement.

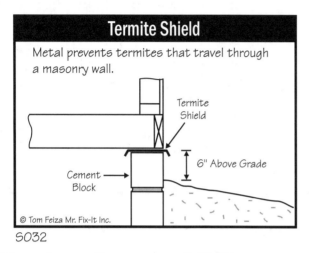

Termite Shield

Metal prevents termites that travel through a masonry wall.

Termite Shield

6" Above Grade

Cement Block

© Tom Feiza Mr. Fix-It Inc.

S032

Structure, Frame and Siding

The structural frame of your home rests on the foundation or basement and holds up the floors, interior walls, and roof. Most homes in the U.S. are framed with wood, but a few are built with a brick or block support structure. Once the frame and structure are properly designed and installed, little maintenance is needed except to protect the structure from water and insects.

Platform Framing

Most homes are built with platform framing. The framing starts with a "platform" of floor joists built over the foundation wall. The joists support the deck. There is usually a beam down the center of the foundation that supports the center of the joists. Posts rest on footings and the foundation wall support beam.

The wooden structure of the home is built to transfer weight loads to the foundation structure. Normally this includes load-bearing interior walls that run parallel to the supporting beam. The exterior walls also carry loads. Some interior walls are partition walls and don't support the structure; they just divide or partition the space. Don't modify any walls without evaluating where the loads of the structure are supported.

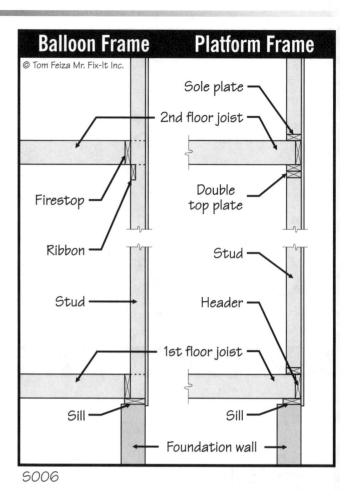

Balloon Frame | **Platform Frame**

© Tom Feiza Mr. Fix-It Inc.

Sole plate
2nd floor joist
Firestop
Double top plate
Ribbon
Stud
Stud
Header
1st floor joist
Sill
Sill
Foundation wall

S006

Load Bearing Walls

© Tom Feiza Mr. Fix-It Inc.

Partition Wall
Joist Overlap
No Load
Load Bearing
Load Path
Joist Overlap
Beam
Poured Wall
Steel Post
Footing
Soil pushes up

Load bearing walls are exterior walls and typically walls above the center beam of a home.

S038

Building up from the foundation structure, the floors are supported by floor joists covered with some type of subflooring material spanning the joists. Exterior walls are placed on the subflooring, and a second floor is added in a similar fashion. Exterior walls and the interior load-bearing walls support the roof structure and ceiling. Various materials have been used for floor joists and beams through the years.

Floor joists can be wood lumber or manufactured I-Joist systems. Wood joists have been constructed since wood or "stick" framing techniques started around 1880. Recently, I-Joist systems have been used because they enable longer spans and provide more dimensional stability than natural wood. Trusses can also be placed to provide floor support, allowing long spans and often eliminating the center beam or center support structure.

Subflooring covers the floor joist system and supports the floor loads. Materials used for subflooring have varied through the years. Until about 1960, solid 1" x 6" wood was used for subflooring.

Beams - Types

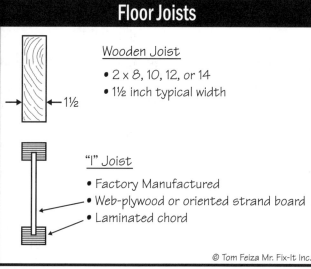

Laminated Veneer Lumber (LVL)

Laminated Lumber (Factory Glued)

Timber (Solid Wood)

Steel "I" Beam

Built Up (Site Built)

© Tom Feiza Mr. Fix-It Inc.

S039

Floor Joists

Wooden Joist
- 2 x 8, 10, 12, or 14
- 1½ inch typical width

1½

"I" Joist
- Factory Manufactured
- Web-plywood or oriented strand board
- Laminated chord

© Tom Feiza Mr. Fix-It Inc.

S040

Floor Truss Systems

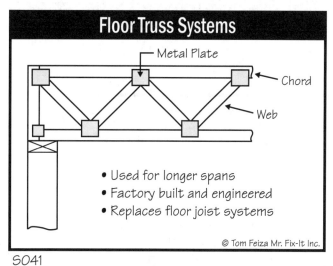

Metal Plate

Chord

Web

- Used for longer spans
- Factory built and engineered
- Replaces floor joist systems

© Tom Feiza Mr. Fix-It Inc.

S041

Subflooring - Typical Options

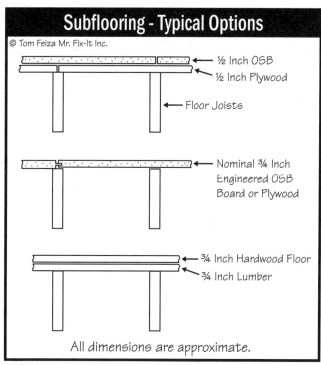

© Tom Feiza Mr. Fix-It Inc.

½ Inch OSB

½ Inch Plywood

Floor Joists

Nominal ¾ Inch Engineered OSB Board or Plywood

¾ Inch Hardwood Floor

¾ Inch Lumber

All dimensions are approximate.

S042

Around 1960, plywood became popular, and multiple layers of materials were often used. Now, specially designed, single-layer oriented strand board panels are used for subflooring.

Ceramic tile flooring presents a special challenge for wood frame construction. It requires additional support because any movement in the subfloor will create cracks in tile and grout and will loosen the tile. Years ago, subflooring was designed to hold a layer of poured concrete or grout to support the tile. Today, stronger subflooring and cement boards are used as a base for tile.

Subfloor for "Mud-Set" Ceramic Tile

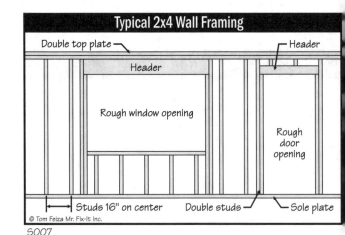

Tile
Mud Set Tile
Grout
1" Concrete (Mud)
Building Paper
1 x 3 Blocking
¾" Lumber

"Mud" or grout can be the base for ceramic tile. On wood framing, it is set over about 1 inch of concrete on lumber flush with the top of the joists.

© Tom Feiza Mr. Fix-It Inc.

S043

The rest of the structure arises above this first platform. It is supported with 2 by 4 or 2 by 6 exterior walls and interior support walls. For a two-story home, a second platform is built above the first floor walls, and then more walls are framed above this platform. Finally, a roof is framed above the wall framing.

The basic platform frame has many possible variations. An older home may have "balloon" framing in which exterior wall studs extend from the foundation to the roof without platforms. Some homes are built with post and beam framing like that used for barns. Some homes have brick or block exterior walls that support the structure.

Since your home's framing is completed, all you need to know (if it's performing well) is that you shouldn't modify the structure of your home without contacting a professional.

Must Know / Must Do Structure

- Understand the basic structure of your home.

- Never modify or remove structural framing without an expert's advice.

- Protect the structure from water and insects.

- Excessive cracking or movement indicate structural problems to be investigated.

Exterior Walls

The exterior walls are framed to support the structure, allow for window and door openings, and protect the structure from the elements. Most exterior walls are framed with 2 by 4 studs spaced 16" on center. The studs are braced in the corners and doubled around window and door openings. Special "headers" are placed over openings to support the weight above the opening.

Exterior wall framing allows space for electrical, cable, telephone and heat distribution components. The framing also supports exterior siding or cladding and includes space for insulation.

Typical 2x4 Wall Framing

Double top plate
Header
Header
Rough window opening
Rough door opening
Studs 16" on center
Double studs
Sole plate

© Tom Feiza Mr. Fix-It Inc.

S007

Siding

Many options exist for siding homes: brick, stone, wood, aluminum, vinyl, cement, asbestos, logs,

On-Center Framing

Typical 16 & 24 inch on-center framing

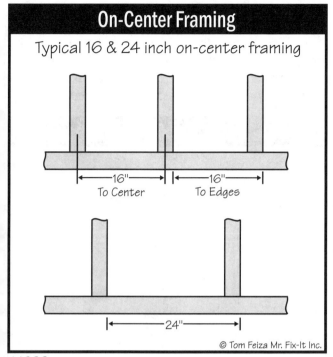

|←—16"—→| |←—16"—→|
To Center   To Edges

|←————24"————→|

© Tom Feiza Mr. Fix-It Inc.

M029

steel siding, wood products, stucco, and even steel panels. Identify the type of siding you have, and maintain the surface. This usually requires caulking and painting. Watch for excessive movement, water leaks and excessive paint damage.

Remember that homes built before 1978 may be painted with lead-based paints. Take special precautions if these finishes chip and flake or if you need to remove them. See the chapter on Environmental and Safety Concerns as well as the References section for more information on lead hazards.

Must Know / Must Do–Siding

- Maintain all painted surfaces.

- Maintain caulk and sealants.

- Be aware of potential lead hazards.

Brick

So you have an all-brick home, and it is beautiful, low-maintenance, cozy and warm. Brick homes are beautiful and valuable, but very few really have a brick structure; rather, they're brick veneer. Don't worry, you want a home that's brick veneer.

If your home was built before 1900, there is a chance that it actually has a brick structure. That means the exterior wall is solid brick, several layers thick, and the brick supports the home's framing and floors. Very few modern brick homes are built this way.

A typical modern brick home has a wood frame that supports the structure. The brick is applied as a veneer or siding over the outside. This method allows for better insulation of walls and a more user-friendly stucture that meets the needs of modern construction.

With brick veneer, you do need to watch for cracking and movement, as well as deterioration of mortar joints. Most brick veneer performs well for years with little maintenance.

Non-Load-Bearing Masonry Veneer

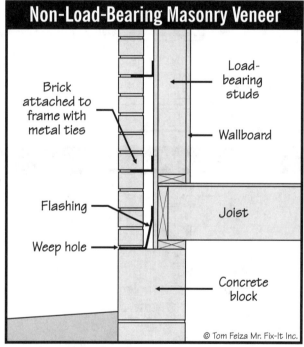

Brick attached to frame with metal ties

Flashing

Weep hole

Load-bearing studs

Wallboard

Joist

Concrete block

© Tom Feiza Mr. Fix-It Inc.

S008

One important element of maintenance involves the steel lintels over window and door openings. A lintel is a steel angle iron or beam that supports the masonry above the opening. Since window frames and door frames are not designed to support masonry, the lintel spans the opening and transfers the load to the masonry on either side. The exposed steel of the lintel must be painted with exterior metal paint to prevent rust. If the lintel rusts, the metal expands, creating cracks in the mortar joints at the top corners of the openings. If excessive rust builds up, the lintel will fail and must be replaced.

Must Know / Must Do—Brick

- Maintain steel lintels.

- Watch for cracks or excessive movement.

- Maintain caulk and sealants at penetrations and windows/doors.

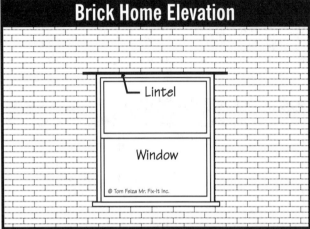

Brick Home Elevation

Lintel

Window

© Tom Feiza Mr. Fix-It Inc.

© Tom Feiza Mr. Fix-It Inc.

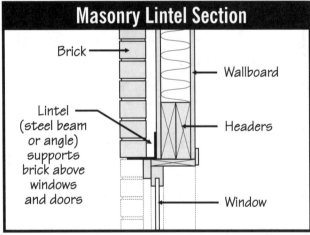

Masonry Lintel Section

Brick

Wallboard

Lintel (steel beam or angle) supports brick above windows and doors

Headers

Window

S009

Look at any brick building and you'll probably see many rusted lintels causing mortar cracking and failure. You may also see that in some buildings, arches, cast concrete or large stones span the openings, eliminating the need for a metal lintel.

Stucco – Cement

Older homes and new homes in dry, warmer climates often have traditional cement stucco siding.

Typically, this stucco consists of a three-part system applied over rigid sheathing material. Often a wire mesh is applied to the sheathing and over a building paper or drainage plane. The stucco is applied in three coats—base coat, scratch coat and a finish coat which often has a decorative surface.

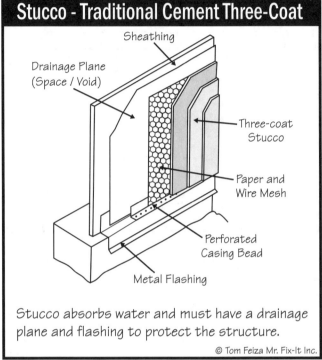

Stucco - Traditional Cement Three-Coat

Sheathing

Drainage Plane (Space / Void)

Three-coat Stucco

Paper and Wire Mesh

Perforated Casing Bead

Metal Flashing

Stucco absorbs water and must have a drainage plane and flashing to protect the structure.

© Tom Feiza Mr. Fix-It Inc.

X014

Synthetic Stucco or Exterior Insulation Finish System – EIFS

Since about 1980, synthetic stucco material has been adapted to wood frame construction. This exterior insulation finish system, often referred to as EIFS, is a thin acrylic coating applied over rigid insulation board or cement board. Corners and joints are taped with a special mesh, and the finish is applied in two coats. The material looks like cement stucco or concrete. It can be painted and textured. In some cases, problems have occurred with moisture intrusion, and a specialized third-part inspector often evaluates this material. Properly installed, the material is effective and energy efficient.

Vinyl and Aluminum Siding

Many homes are covered with aluminum or vinyl siding that provides an economical and attractive surface. Since 1990, vinyl has because the more popular product because it maintains its color and

EIFS - Synthetic Stucco

Exterior Insulation Finish System (EIFS)

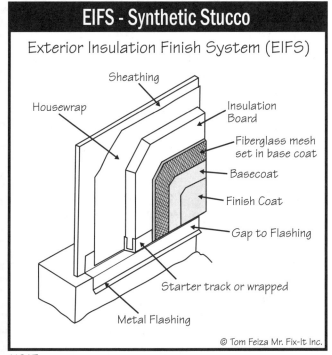

X015

does not dent. If your home has siding, you must maintain caulk where needed. Remember that fading aluminum siding can be easily cleaned or even cleaned and then painted with latex paint. Don't put the barbecue grill too close to the vinyl siding—the siding can melt.

Plywood, Wood Fiber, Wood Siding

All of these materials require routine maintenance of caulk and paint finishes. Watch for horizontal flashing at trim and windows. Often the flashing is not properly designed or installed, and rot can develop if you don't maintain caulk and paint.

Horizontal Trim Flashing and Problems

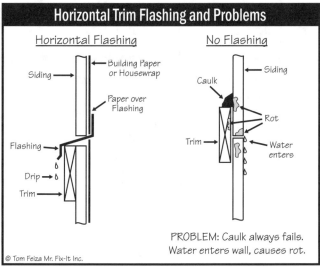

X007

Plywood or panel siding can present a unique problem with caulk at horizontal joints. These joints should have a "Z" or cap flashing, and there should be no caulk at the top of the metal flashing. This is left open to allow water to drain.

Horizontal Panel Flashing and Problems

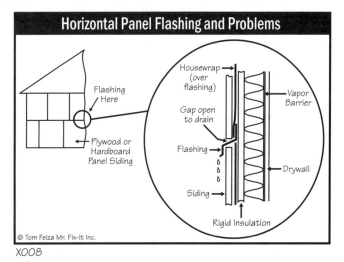

X008

"Z" Flashing - Panel Siding

© Tom Feiza Mr. Fix-It Inc.

X006

Cement Board

Cement board is a fiber and cement panel designed to replace wood siding, wood panels and trim. The siding is durable and needs minimal maintenance. The surface must be periodically painted, and caulk joints must be maintained. Currently this is the best alternative to cedar siding, and its texture and appearance imitate real cedar.

Windows and Doors

It would take an entire book to cover all types of windows and doors and their maintenance. I will cover basic types and provide important maintenance tips. For specific information on maintaining and repairing the windows and doors in your home, contact the manufacturer. The References section contains information on manufacturers and after-market repair parts.

Maintenance information and parts are readily available for windows and doors produced in the last 20 years. For older windows and doors, you will rarely find information and must rely on after-market products. Thousands of companies produced windows and doors through the years, and many are no longer in business.

Windows

Windows come in all shapes, sizes and types. Various types include double-hung, casement, sliders, hopper, fixed, garden, bow and bay. The list goes on and on.

Materials used for window frames include wood, steel, aluminum, vinyl, and combinations of these products. Higher-cost windows have wood framing on the inside for enhanced appearance and a metal coating on the outside for low maintenance.

There are also many glass options. In older homes you will find the basic single-pane glass, usually with a separate storm window. From there we have insulated glass consisting of two panes with a sealed air space between layers. Newer insulated glass is improved with an invisible "low E" coating on one side that lowers heat transmission. Glass can also be tripled-glazed, meaning there are three sealed panes. Other modern advances include a special inert gas that fills the space between panes; special coatings; and insulating spacers.

The keys to maintaining your window are to (1) keep exterior portions of the window weathertight, and (2) maintain painted and varnished surfaces.

On the outside, maintain all painted surfaces and the glazing compound that seals the window glass to the sash. Make sure that caulk which seals the window frame to the brick or siding is tight and

secure. Investigate excessive mildew or peeling paint—these are signs of moisture problems.

The spacing between the primary (interior) window and the storm window on an older system can cause problems. Most storms have a small slot or hole on the lower edge, next to the wooden sill. This "weep hole," which is 1/4" or smaller, allows condensation and water to drain ("weep") to the outside, preventing rot and mildew that could cause serious damage. However, well-intentioned homeowners sometimes caulk weep holes shut, hoping to save energy. Weep holes should always be left open.

Meticulously check and maintain the condition of painted wood-framed windows and doors. Pay special attention to south-facing surfaces because the sun accelerates deterioration of caulk, paint and glazing products. Check the corners and ends of wood framing; this is where wood rot starts, and it can cause serious problems.

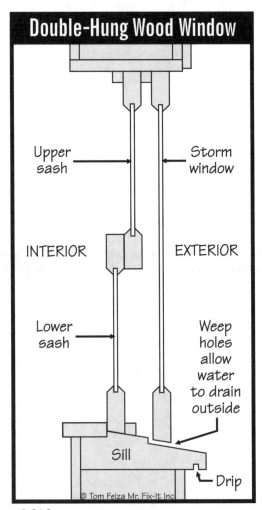

Double-Hung Wood Window

Upper sash

Storm window

INTERIOR

EXTERIOR

Lower sash

Weep holes allow water to drain outside

Sill

Drip

© Tom Feiza Mr. Fix-It Inc

S010

Caution

Double-hung windows have a cord and a weight or spring that balances the weight of the window to keep it open. If the spring or cord breaks, the sash can crash shut, causing serious injury. If your window slams shut, repair the cord or spring, or secure the window to the frame with a metal clip and screw to prevent anyone from opening the window and getting injured.

If you are lucky enough to have casement windows—great. They seal tightly and work well. But when they stick, it is easy to damage the crank mechanism. If you are trying to open a sticky casement window, never force the crank. It will break. Remove the screen and then gently force the window open with your hand, not with the crank.

To open a sticky double-hung or slider window, try to jar the window closed by striking the frame with a closed fist. Be careful. Don't hit it so hard that you break the glass. If the window is painted shut, you must break away all the paint before you try to open it.

Must Know / Must Do Windows

- Maintain paint, putty, caulk and glazing compounds.

- Check the "weep holes" of storm windows.

- Repair broken sash cords and springs to prevent injury.

- Peeling paint on older windows may be a lead hazard–See Chapter 2.

Garage Doors

Garage doors are made of hundreds of possible combinations of materials, rollers, tracks, operators, springs, locks, and other options. Your main responsibilities are to maintain finishes, tighten hardware, and test the safety of operation.

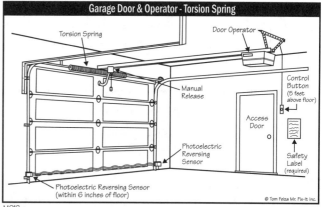

M012

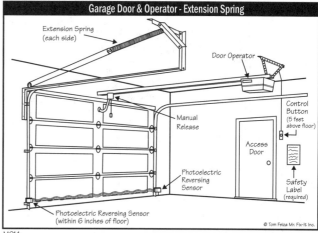

M014

Many garage doors are made of wood and wood products that require routine painting. When you paint a garage door, paint all six sides of each panel. Don't neglect the inside of the door panel, and don't neglect the edges.

Hardware—rollers, hinges and tracks—requires routine maintenance. Because the doors are open and closed so often, hardware and fasteners are always being jarred and bounced, which loosens bolts, screws and other fasteners and eventually affects the smooth operation of the door. Tighten all hardware on your garage door at least twice a year. Put the door in the closed position, make sure all hinges and rollers are aligned, and then tighten bolts and nuts. Inspect rollers to make sure that they line up with the tracks. Tracks should be parallel to the edges of the door. Replace any rollers that have damaged bearings. Lubricate rollers and hinges with a special garage door lubricant, silicone spray, or light oil.

If the door has damaged springs, pulleys or cables, have them repaired by a professional. These springs store tremendous amounts of force, and they can cause serious injury if not handled properly. Professional service is also a good option if the door is not properly aligned to the tracks and the frame opening.

Must Know / Must Do
Garage Door

- Maintain painted finishes on the door.

- Tighten hardware twice a year.

- Hire a professional for repair of springs, cables and rollers.

- Check with the manufacturer of your door for specific maintenance information. See References section.

Garage Door Openers

Many of us take our garage door openers for granted: push the button, and we drive into our dry and lighted garage. These openers provide many years of trouble-free service, but they do require routine maintenance and safety tests. An improperly maintained garage door opener poses a safety hazard.

Contact the manufacturer of your opener for specific safety and maintenance requirements. See the References section.

Follow these safety precautions:

- Do not stand or walk under a moving door. Do not try to rush under a door as it closes.

- Keep the remote control units away from children.

- Explain to children that garage doors are not toys and that the door can hurt them.

- Mount the pushbutton control at least 5 feet from the floor to keep it out of reach of children.

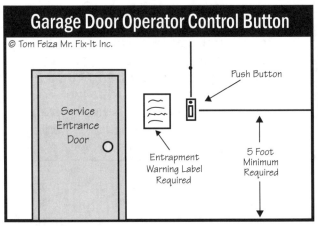

Garage Door Operator Control Button
© Tom Feiza Mr. Fix-It Inc.

Service Entrance Door

Push Button

Entrapment Warning Label Required

5 Foot Minimum Required

M013

- When closing the door, observe it until it is fully closed.

- Check the safety reverse once monthly.

Every garage door should have a safety device that reverses the door if it meets resistance while closing. Very old units may not have a safety reverse; these should be replaced.

Must Know / Must Do
Garage Door Openers

- Follow all safety precautions.

- Perform monthly safety tests of the automatic reverse.

- Check the balance of the door once a year.

- Always consult a professional for repair of springs, pulleys and cables.

- Contact the manufacturer for specific safety and maintenance recommendations. See the References section for contact information.

Openers manufactured after April 1, 1982, must have a safety reverse that activates after striking a 1"-high object. Openers manufactured before that time were required to reverse off a 2" object. If your door does not reverse with the 1" test, replace it.

Openers sold after 1993 also have a photocell. When anything blocks or crosses the photocell beam as the door is closing, the door reverses. If your garage door opener doesn't have this optical safety device, I suggest you replace it with one that does.

Here's the procedure for the monthly safety reverse test. (Check with the manufacturer of your operator for more specific details)

1. With the door open, place a 1"-thick block under the center of the door. Use an actual 1"-thick object, not a nominal 1" piece of wood that is actually 3/4" thick. A 2 by 4 laid flat is often used for this test.

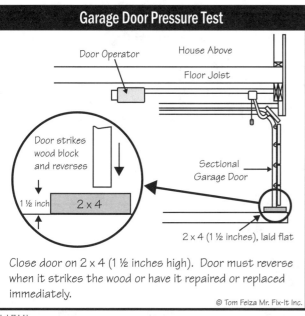

Garage Door Pressure Test

Door Operator

House Above

Floor Joist

Door strikes wood block and reverses

Sectional Garage Door

1 ½ inch   2 x 4

2 x 4 (1 ½ inches), laid flat

Close door on 2 x 4 (1 ½ inches high). Door must reverse when it strikes the wood or have it repaired or replaced immediately.

© Tom Feiza Mr. Fix-It Inc.

M016

2. Activate the opener to close the door.

3. When the door hits the piece of wood, it should reverse and reopen.

4. Activate the opener again. This time, as the door closes, hold up the bottom of the door with your hand. The door should reverse with a few pounds of pressure.

5. If your door has a photocell safety control, perform the test again by breaking the beam as the door closes. The door should reverse itself. You can test the door with a 6 by 12 inch object placed progressively along the door opening. With the object in place, the door should stop and reverse to the full open position.

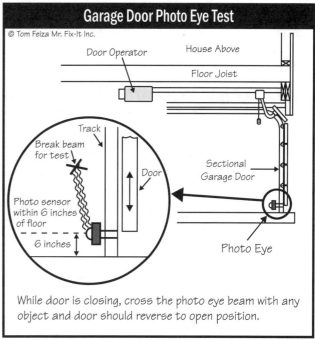

Garage Door Photo Eye Test

© Tom Feiza Mr. Fix-It Inc.

Door Operator

House Above

Floor Joist

Track

Break beam for test

Door

Sectional Garage Door

Photo sensor within 6 inches of floor

6 inches

Photo Eye

While door is closing, cross the photo eye beam with any object and door should reverse to open position.

M017

6. If the opener fails any of these tests, consult a qualified professional for adjustments and repair.

If the remote control fails to operate your garage door, first check for a weak or dead battery in the remote unit. A cold receiver unit with a weak battery could also cause this problem. If batteries are good, check the transmitter and receiver codes and the antenna on the receiver.

Your garage door opener is designed to open and close a balanced garage door. Strong springs provide lift that balances the weight of the door. If the operator unit sounds loud and works very hard to open or close the door, the door may be unbalanced or there may be a broken spring or damaged hardware.

Inspect the springs and hardware. If there is any damage, consult a professional.

You can also test the balance of the door if the springs appear to be in good condition. Start with the door closed. If you start with the door open, it can crash shut, causing damage and possible injury. With the door closed, disconnect the release mechanism—a cord or lever where the operator arm attaches to the operator frame. You should then be able to lift the door with little resistance; the door should "balance" around the center of its motion. If the door is hard to lift and does not balance, consult a professional to adjust the spring mechanism. Don't attempt to adjust the springs yourself. They store a dangerous amount of energy and can easily injure you.

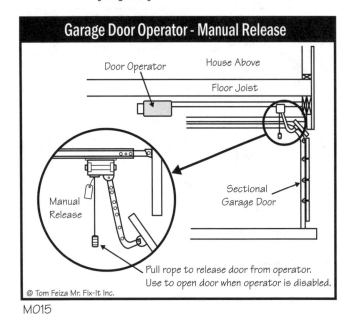

Pull rope to release door from operator. Use to open door when operator is disabled.

M015

If your garage has an automatic door operator but no service or entry door, how can you open the door when the power is out or the remote control is dead? For this type of situation, there should be a key-operated garage door release on the outside of the overhead door. To open the door, remove the lock cylinder and pull the attached cable to release the door from the operator. Now you can lift the door manually.

Insulation and Ventilation

All homes are insulated in some fashion to protect against heat loss and gain. Older homes may have little insulation; newer homes have insulation that meets government standards for energy efficiency.

Ventilation systems remove excessive moisture and protect insulation from moisture damage. Vapor retarders or barriers prevent moisture from flowing into insulation.

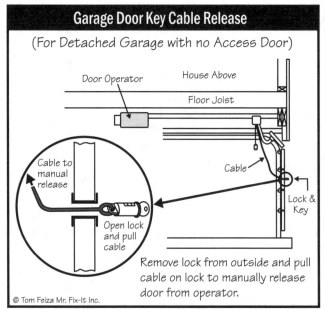

Remove lock from outside and pull cable on lock to manually release door from operator.

M018

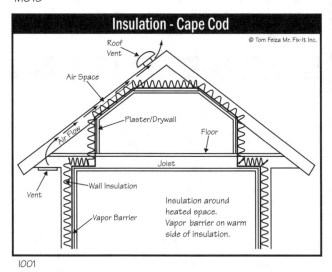

I001

Insulation

Most newer homes are insulated with fiberglass, cellulose fiber, rigid plastic foam, or a combination of these products. Older homes may have vermiculite, wood shavings, paper products, and other types of insulation. Often, homeowners add insulation to walls and attics of older homes to increase energy efficiency.

A note of caution: vermiculite insulation has been found to contain asbestos in some cases. If your home has vermiculite insulation, it should not be disturbed and you should never breathe any related dust. Vermiculite looks like tan and gold gravel particles of about 1/4 to 3/4 inch. It is lightweight, like foam. If you think your home has vermiculite, have it tested by a professional.

Insulation is rated with an R-value, which simply indicates the resistance to heat flow. The higher the R-value, the higher the resistance. The key thing to remember is that when you double the R-value, you cut the heat loss in half; so the first several inches of insulation result in huge energy savings.

Insulation vs. Heat Loss

Typical cost of heat loss through 1 square foot of exterior surface.

Material	R Value	Heat Cost / Sq. Ft.
Single Glass	R1	$2.40
Double Glass	R2	$1.20
4" of Wood	R4	$0.60
Basement w/ 1" Foam	R8	$0.30
Typical Wall	R20	$0.12
Attic Insulation	R40	$0.06

Double the R value and cut the heat loss (cost) in half. Actual cost will change based on climate and heat source. The relationship is constant.

© Tom Feiza Mr. Fix-It Inc.

1004

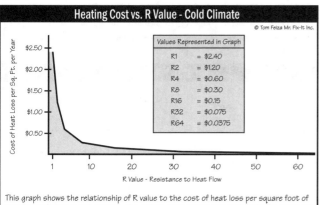

Heating Cost vs. R Value - Cold Climate

© Tom Feiza Mr. Fix-It Inc.

Values Represented in Graph	
R1	= $2.40
R2	= $1.20
R4	= $0.60
R8	= $0.30
R16	= $0.15
R32	= $0.075
R64	= $0.0375

This graph shows the relationship of R value to the cost of heat loss per square foot of exterior surface in a cold climate. The actual cost will vary; the relationship is constant.

1003

Most fiberglass is rated at about R-3 per inch of thickness. A 6"-thick section is fiberglass would be rated about R-19. The R-value for rigid foam ranges from 5 to 7 per inch. Cellulose and mineral wool provide about R-3 per inch.

Insulation recommendations vary with climate conditions and state code requirements. In northern climates, attics are insulated to R-38 or more, and walls are insulated to R-19 or more. In southern zones, attics are insulated to about R-26 and walls to R-11.

Typical Wall Section (2x6 Framed)

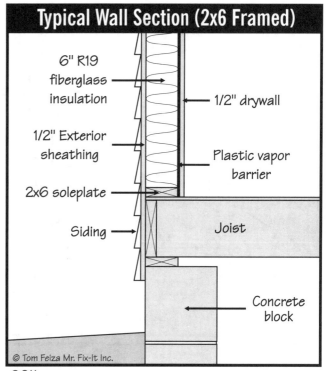

6" R19 fiberglass insulation

1/2" Exterior sheathing

2x6 soleplate

Siding

1/2" drywall

Plastic vapor barrier

Joist

Concrete block

© Tom Feiza Mr. Fix-It Inc.

S011

Vapor Barriers

Vapor barriers or vapor retarders protect insulation and structural framing from moisture damage. Vapor barriers are usually made of polyethylene film. They can also be aluminum foil or kraft paper (brown paper coated with tar).

The vapor barrier, placed behind drywall, plaster or wood flooring and in front of insulation, prevents moisture from moving through the surface and penetrating the insulation. The barrier also prevents air movement through walls and floors; air movement carries tremendous amounts of water vapor.

If moisture were allowed to enter the insulation, it would condense on the cold wood framing of the exterior, causing water damage and potential rot.

In hot and humid climates, such as southern Florida, vapor barriers are not used because the relative humidity outdoors is greater than that in the home, and moisture tends to move into the house. If you have questions about requirements for vapor barriers in your area, consult the local building inspector.

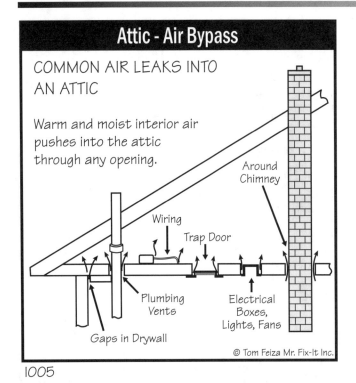

Attic - Air Bypass

COMMON AIR LEAKS INTO AN ATTIC

Warm and moist interior air pushes into the attic through any opening.

Around Chimney

Wiring

Trap Door

Plumbing Vents

Electrical Boxes, Lights, Fans

Gaps in Drywall

© Tom Feiza Mr. Fix-It Inc.

I005

Attic Ventilation

No matter how well a home is constructed, moisture will reach the attic; it's impossible to completely seal this area. So ventilation is necessary to remove moisture and excessive heat from the attic. This is achieved through various combinations of roof vents, soffit vents, gable end vents, ridge vents, and ventilation fans.

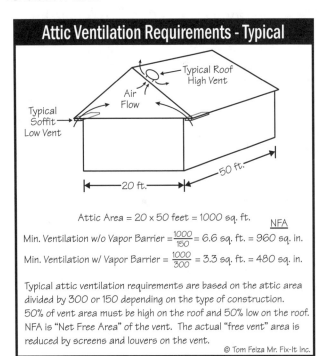

Attic Ventilation Requirements - Typical

Typical Roof High Vent

Air Flow

Typical Soffit Low Vent

50 ft.

20 ft.

Attic Area = 20 x 50 feet = 1000 sq. ft.

$$\text{Min. Ventilation w/o Vapor Barrier} = \frac{1000}{150} = 6.6 \text{ sq. ft.} = 960 \text{ sq. in.}$$

$$\text{Min. Ventilation w/ Vapor Barrier} = \frac{1000}{300} = 3.3 \text{ sq. ft.} = 480 \text{ sq. in.}$$

Typical attic ventilation requirements are based on the attic area divided by 300 or 150 depending on the type of construction. 50% of vent area must be high on the roof and 50% low on the roof. NFA is "Net Free Area" of the vent. The actual "free vent" area is reduced by screens and louvers on the vent.

© Tom Feiza Mr. Fix-It Inc.

V042

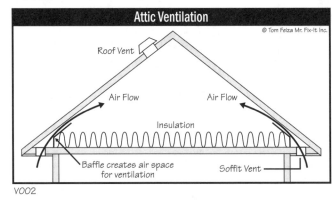

Ventilation - Two Basic Types

ATTIC VENTILATION

Roof Vent

Air Flow

Air Flow

Insulation

Baffle creates air space for ventilation

Soffit Vent

Removes heat and moisture from the attic space.

POINT (SOURCE) VENTILATION

Damper in Fan

Damper

Bath Exhaust Fan

Fan removes heat, contaminants, and moisture from point source to outside home.

© Tom Feiza Mr. Fix-It Inc.

V030

Attic Ventilation

© Tom Feiza Mr. Fix-It Inc.

Roof Vent

Air Flow

Air Flow

Insulation

Baffle creates air space for ventilation

Soffit Vent

V002

For proper air flow, ventilation must be provided both high and low on the roof. Heat and wind help the vents move air through the attic. As an additional benefit, ventilation reduces the temperature inside the attic, lowering the cost of air conditioning and extending the life of an asphalt shingle roof.

Bathroom and kitchen exhaust fans are needed to remove excessive moisture, but they must be routed to an exterior wall or through the roof. Make sure that the exhaust fans in your home aren't dumping moist air into the attic.

Must Know / Must Do
Attic Ventilation

- Check the attic periodically for signs of moisture condensation. Black or gray mildew stains indicate a need for increased ventilation.

- Make sure that the access door to the attic is insulated and weather-stripped to block air entry.

- Don't walk through the attic without taking special precautions. You could fall through the ceiling.

- Make sure that bathroom and kitchen exhaust fans aren't dumping moist air into the attic.

Vapor Barrier in Crawl Space

A crawl space or dirt floor in the basement can release significant amounts of moisture in your home. Even if the soil looks dry, moisture may evaporate from the surface. Cover any bare dirt with a thick (6-mil) poly vapor barrier. The barrier should provide a continuous cover with joints overlapped 12". Edges should lap up several inches on the foundation wall. Place stones or gravel atop the barrier to keep it in place.

Bathroom Ventilation

Ventilation for bathrooms has been required for many years. The minimum requirement is a window or an exhaust fan. Most of us would prefer, and our homes would like, a dedicated exhaust fan controlled by a switch in the bathroom. This allows us to effectively remove excessive moisture from showers and baths.

Confirm the discharge location of your fan. Make sure it discharges moisture through an exterior wall or through the roof. These fans remove a tremendous amount of moisture, and you don't want that moisture in your attic.

Homes built prior to 1980 often have ventilation fans that exhaust into the attic space. These should

be rerouted through the roof with a simple vent kit available at building supply centers.

Often, bath exhaust fans can't keep up with the steam of a hot shower, and the bathroom remains full of moisture. This can cause excessive condensation, mildew, peeling paint, and damage to windows. A simple solution is to replace the ordinary fan switch with a timer switch—the type found on heat lamps. Use a timer that will operate for 1 or 2 hours, and run the fan for a timed period after you leave.

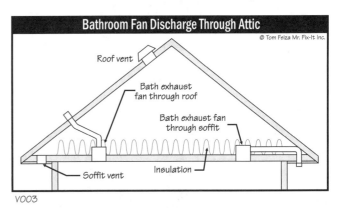

Bathroom Fan Discharge Through Attic
© Tom Feiza Mr. Fix-It Inc.
Roof vent
Bath exhaust fan through roof
Bath exhaust fan through soffit
Soffit vent
Insulation

VOO3

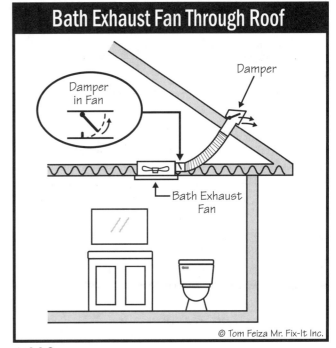

Bath Exhaust Fan Through Roof
Damper
Damper in Fan
Bath Exhaust Fan
© Tom Feiza Mr. Fix-It Inc.

VOO6

Roofs and Gutters

Roof framing and roofing materials contribute significantly to the look and style of your home. The roof also protects your home from the elements. While a roof is easy to ignore, its components do need routine maintenance.

Roof Terms

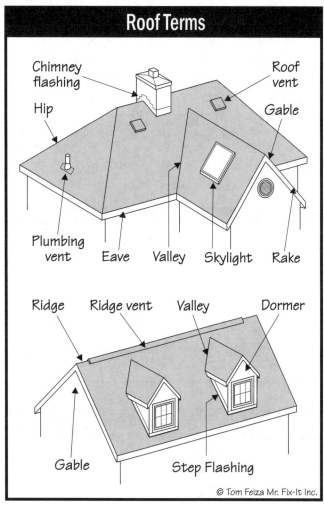

Chimney flashing
Roof vent
Hip
Gable
Plumbing vent
Eave
Valley
Skylight
Rake

Ridge
Ridge vent
Valley
Dormer
Gable
Step Flashing

© Tom Feiza Mr. Fix-It Inc.

R004

Types of Roofs

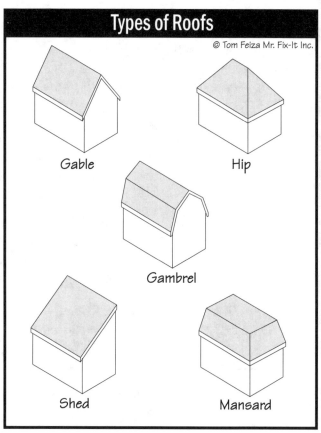

© Tom Feiza Mr. Fix-It Inc.

Gable
Hip
Gambrel
Shed
Mansard

R003

Performing this maintenance requires access to the gutters and valleys and may involve walking on the roof. It's essential to follow all safety precautions for working at heights and climbing ladders. While some homeowners are comfortable with ladders and heights, others are not. If you are not completely comfortable with the idea of working on your roof, hire a professional. For complete information on evaluating and replacing your roof, see Chapter 27 – Replace Your Roof.

Roof Styles and Framing

Many roof designs are dictated by the style of the home and the spans between exterior walls. Roofs are also designed to accommodate snow loads, winds, and other environmental factors.

All roofs have structural framing of joists or trusses that support a wood deck. The deck may be boards, plywood or oriented strand board. Roofing material is attached to the wood deck.

In general, the two basic styles are sloped and low-slope (or flat) roofs.

Sloped roofs are those with a slope greater than 4" in 12" or 4/12. This is equivalent to a 1/4 slope (just convert the fraction), meaning that the roof drops 1 foot for every 4 feet of horizontal run. To determine the slope of your roof, level a 4-foot board and measure the drop at the outer edge. If the pitch drops 4 feet within this 4-foot length, the slope is 4 in 4—and, by extension, 12 in 12. This is often expressed as a 12/12 roof. Styles of sloped roofs include gable, shed, hip, gambrel, mansard, and combinations of various types.

Low-slope or flat roofs have a slope that is less than 4 in 12. These require special waterproof or membrane materials because they do not shed water as well as roofs with a steeper slope. Most "flat" roofs do have a slight pitch to drain water to the edges or to roof drains.

Other components of a roof include valley and sidewall flashings, edge flashings, and flashings at all roof penetrations. The roof will have a ventilation system and may have a gutter and drainage system.

Roof Framing - Joist, Truss

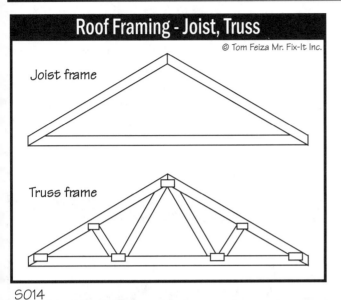

© Tom Feiza Mr. Fix-It Inc.

Joist frame

Truss frame

S014

Roof - 4/12 Slope

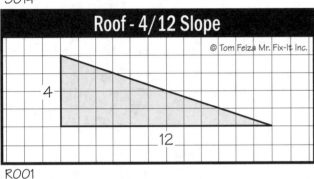

© Tom Feiza Mr. Fix-It Inc.

4

12

R001

Roof Slope - Roof Material Type

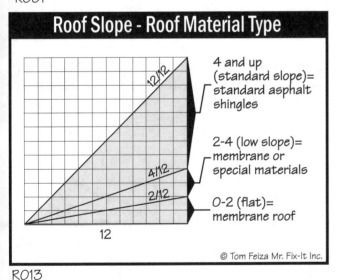

12/12

4 and up
(standard slope)=
standard asphalt
shingles

4/12

2/12

2-4 (low slope)=
membrane or
special materials

0-2 (flat)=
membrane roof

12

© Tom Feiza Mr. Fix-It Inc.

R013

Roofing Materials

Asphalt shingles are the material most commonly used on conventional pitched roofs (1 in 4 and greater). An organic or fiberglass "mat" that forms the body of the shingle is covered with granules to protect the mat from the sun and add color and visual variety. A typical asphalt shingle will last from 15 to 40 years, depending on the original quality

and local weather conditions. Asphalt shingles come in many shapes and sizes. Some are designed to imitate wood or tile.

Other materials used for pitched roofs include wood shakes, wood shingles, cement asbestos, tile, slate, metal, and cement tile. All of these are more expensive than asphalt shingles, but they offer unique design qualities and potentially longer life. Tile, slate and cement often last 50 years or more and are highly resistant to sun damage, wind and fire. However, heavier roof materials require special structural designs.

Components of an Asphalt Shingle Roof

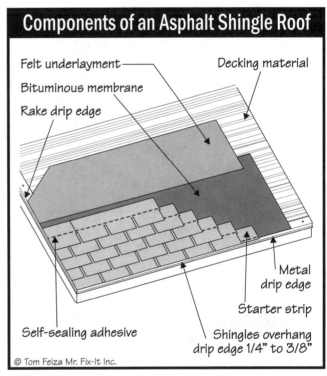

Felt underlayment

Decking material

Bituminous membrane

Rake drip edge

Metal drip edge

Starter strip

Self-sealing adhesive

Shingles overhang drip edge 1/4" to 3/8"

© Tom Feiza Mr. Fix-It Inc.

R005

Wood Roofs

Years ago, most roofs had wood shingles. These flat, smooth shingles were applied without any tar paper beneath them. Today, most wood shingle roofs have been removed or covered with asphalt shingles.

Today when we see a wood roof, it is almost always a wood shake roof. Wood shakes are generally rougher and more irregular than wood shingles. A wood shake roof provides a watertight covering because of the tar paper under the wood shakes. The wood shakes reject some water and protect the tar paper from the ultraviolet rays of the sun. The tar paper provides a watertight covering. Wood shake roofs need routine maintenance. The shakes must be kept clear of debris, and a periodic treatment may extent the life of the shakes.

Wood roof maintenance information is available at the Cedar Bureau: www.cedarbureau.org. Also, see the References chapter.

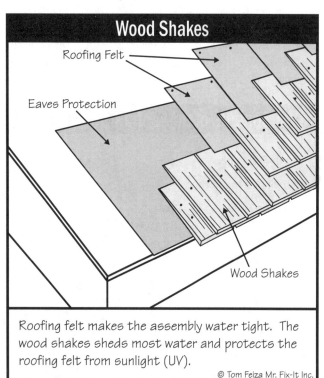

Wood Shakes

Roofing Felt

Eaves Protection

Wood Shakes

Roofing felt makes the assembly water tight. The wood shakes sheds most water and protects the roofing felt from sunlight (UV).

© Tom Feiza Mr. Fix-It Inc.

R017

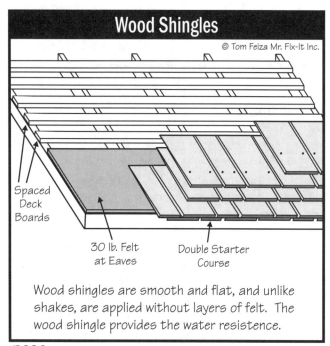

Wood Shingles

© Tom Feiza Mr. Fix-It Inc.

Spaced Deck Boards

30 lb. Felt at Eaves

Double Starter Course

Wood shingles are smooth and flat, and unlike shakes, are applied without layers of felt. The wood shingle provides the water resistence.

R020

Tile Roofs

Tile roofs are found on older, expensive homes and on homes in the South or Southwest. Tile roofs are durable and resistant to sun damage. Because tile is slippery and fragile, you should never walk on a tile roof. Maintenance involves keeping gutters and valleys clear and watching for physical damage to the tile. Today some tile roofs are made from cement-based products in various styles and cross-sections.

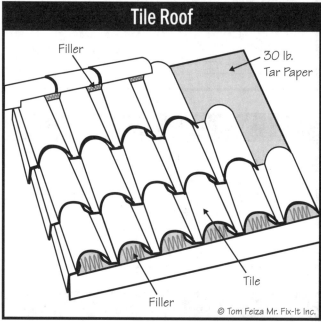

Tile Roof

Filler

30 lb. Tar Paper

Tile

Filler

© Tom Feiza Mr. Fix-It Inc.

R018

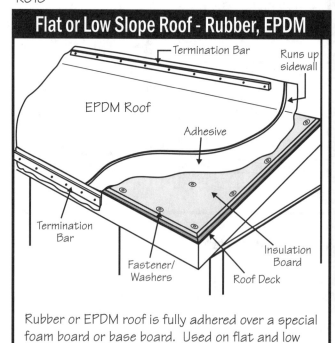

Flat or Low Slope Roof - Rubber, EPDM

Termination Bar

Runs up sidewall

EPDM Roof

Adhesive

Termination Bar

Fastener/ Washers

Roof Deck

Insulation Board

Rubber or EPDM roof is fully adhered over a special foam board or base board. Used on flat and low slope roofs.

© Tom Feiza Mr. Fix-It Inc.

R019

Low-slope or flat roofs require a special roofing material to seal against moisture. Since the slope is low, water does not easily run from the surface. Materials used include single-ply rubber, roll roofing, torch down (a modified bitumen), metal, and built-up roofing. Rubber roofing is quite common; technically, this material is ethylene propylene diene monomer, or EPDM. All of these materials require special installation and maintenance by experienced contractors.

A flat roof should have a slight slope to prevent ponding of water. Roof drains may be placed along the edges or in the center. For information on replacing a roof, see Chapter 27 – Replace Your Roof.

Gutters and Downspouts

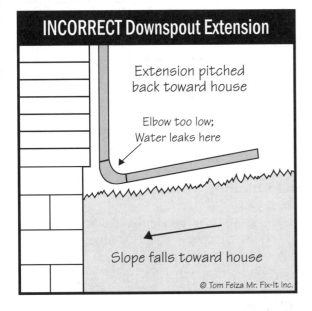

INCORRECT Downspout Extension

Extension pitched back toward house

Elbow too low; Water leaks here

Slope falls toward house

© Tom Feiza Mr. Fix-It Inc.

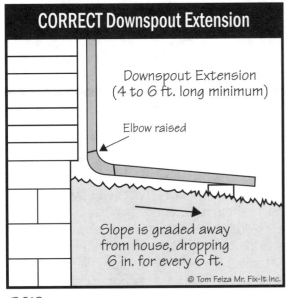

CORRECT Downspout Extension

Downspout Extension (4 to 6 ft. long minimum)

Elbow raised

Slope is graded away from house, dropping 6 in. for every 6 ft.

© Tom Feiza Mr. Fix-It Inc.

B019

When it rains, your roof sheds a tremendous quantity of water that must be moved away from the foundation to protect the basement or crawl spaces. Gutters, downspouts and downspout extensions serve this function.

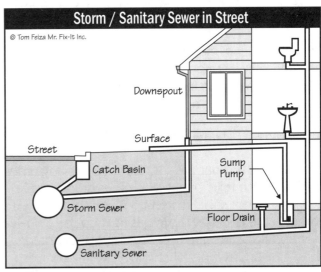

Storm / Sanitary Sewer in Street

© Tom Feiza Mr. Fix-It Inc.

Downspout

Surface

Street

Catch Basin

Storm Sewer

Sanitary Sewer

Sump Pump

Floor Drain

P017

Must Know / Must Do
Roof, Gutters and Downspouts

- Inspect (or hire a professional to inspect) the roof and flashings twice a year.

- Gutters must be cleaned and kept clear of debris. Sometimes twice a year is enough. At other times this must be done once a week, depending on the prevalance of leaves and other materials.

- Keep the drains of a flat roof clear of debris.

- Make sure all downspouts are directed away from the foundation.

- Downspouts routed underground must be cleared or repaired if they "back up."

- Check the roof for wear every few years. Plan for eventual replacement based on professional advice.

Gutters may drain to the surface of your yard. They may be channeled underground to drain into a lower area of your yard. In urban areas, where storm systems collect rainwater, gutters may drain underground into the storm sewer system. For more information on storm sewers, see the section about basements.

Roofing material manufacturers provide excellent free information in printed materials and on their websites. See the References section for details on how to contact them.

Chimney, Flue and Vent

When you burn natural gas, oil, wood or any other fossil fuel, the toxic smoke and other products of combustion must be vented from your home through the chimney. Toxic gas rises up the chimney and flows outside because the gas is lighter than air. Various types of chimneys will accomplish this effect. You should understand chimney basics and know how to recognize problems.

Masonry Chimney

An older home may have a masonry or brick/stone chimney. This type of chimney can vent a wood-burning fireplace as well as an appliance like a furnace or water heater. The clay tile liner of a masonry chimney provides a smooth, uninterrupted surface that eases the flow of combustion gas. The liner harnesses combustion products and protects the brick of the chimney from heat and moisture.

You can view the tan or red tile liner by looking down into the chimney from the top or peering up the fireplace with a flashlight. It's common for a masonry chimney to have several flue liners. Gas and oil appliances often share a liner but cannot use the same flue as a wood-burning fireplace.

A home built before 1900 may have a masonry chimney with no clay tile liner; instead, the inside has exposed brick and some mortar coating. Never use this type of chimney without evaluation by a specialist. Also, be aware that this chimney can't be used to vent a gas appliance.

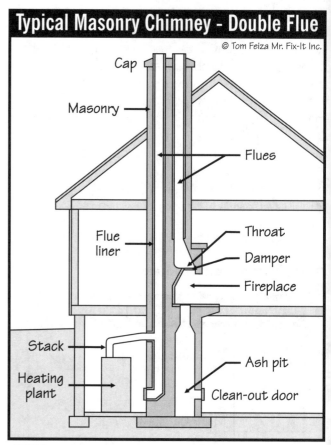

Typical Masonry Chimney - Double Flue

© Tom Feiza Mr. Fix-It Inc.

Cap

Masonry

Flues

Flue liner

Throat

Damper

Fireplace

Stack

Ash pit

Heating plant

Clean-out door

F002

Metal Chimney

A newer home may have a metal chimney, which may be a simple round chimney pipe with a metal liner. A metal chimney might be built into a masonry or wood chimney structure.

All Chimneys

Chimneys look simple, but they are actually complex devices, designed and installed with safety in mind. Chimney designs take into account the type of fuel burned, the heat of the fire, the size of the burner or fireplace, the height of the chimney, the horizontal distance to any appliance they vent, and other factors.

A flue pipe or smoke pipe connects gas- and oil-fired appliances to a chimney. This pipe, specifically sized for the appliance, must be pitched upward into the chimney. The gas appliance also has a special draft hood or draft diverter that allows air to enter the flue pipe, helping to create a proper draft up the chimney. At the chimney, the flue pipes are connected to the flue liner by special metal connectors or mortar.

Chimney Parts - Good Design

(Solid, thick cap)

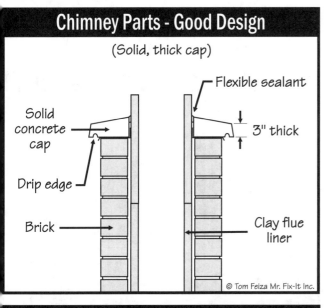

- Solid concrete cap
- Drip edge
- Brick
- Flexible sealant
- 3" thick
- Clay flue liner

© Tom Feiza Mr. Fix-It Inc.

Chimney Parts - Poor Design

(Damaged cap causes brick and mortar damage)

- Thin mortar cracks and breaks away
- Mortar damage
- No flexible seal
- Brick with moisture damage

© Tom Feiza Mr. Fix-It Inc.

F008

Backdrafting

Proper operation of combustion appliances and chimneys requires a supply of combustion air and dilution air. A burning fire consumes oxygen from the air supply and draws additional air up the chimney. This additional (dilution) air is provided by the draft hood or opening in the flue pipe or above the burner in the housing of the appliance.

The air that's exhausted up the chimney must be replaced somehow. This may occur as air enters through small leaks in the structure of the house. If you've ever built a large fire in the fireplace and then opened the front door, you may have noticed

Must Know / Must Do Chimneys and Vent Pipes

- Never modify a chimney or flue pipe. Hire a professional for repairs and maintenance.

- Frequently inspect the vent pipe and draft hood. It should not be corroded, loose or leaking.

- Vent pipes are hot. Provide adequate clearance—at least 6" away from any combustible material. Don't use vent pipes as storage shelves or as racks to dry rags.

- Schedule professional inspection and cleaning for wood-burning stoves and fireplaces. The frequency of the need for maintenance depends on how often you build fires. Annual inspections are the norm.

- Routinely check the condition of the chimney top. A masonry chimney must have tile, brick mortar, flashings and the concrete cap in excellent condition to prevent serious moisture problems. A metal chimney must have a cap in good condition. Chimney damage can create safety problems.

- Install a carbon monoxide alarm.

- Add a rain cap to your chimney to keep out rain and animals.

Flue Pipe to Masonry Chimney

(Also called smoke pipe or vent connection)

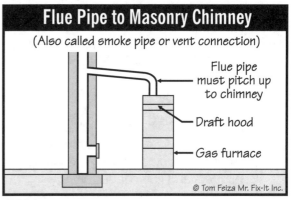

- Flue pipe must pitch up to chimney
- Draft hood
- Gas furnace

© Tom Feiza Mr. Fix-It Inc.

F004

that air rushes in to help replace air flowing up the chimney. This same exhaust process occurs with all combustion appliances.

Also, install a carbon monoxide alarm. It's good insurance against a backdrafting problem that allows carbon monoxide into your home.

Typical Metal Chimney

© Tom Feiza Mr. Fix-It Inc.

Gas furnace

F003

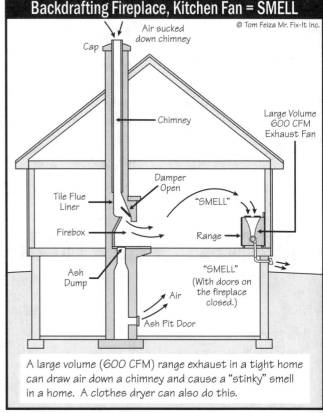

Backdrafting Fireplace, Kitchen Fan = SMELL

© Tom Feiza Mr. Fix-It Inc.

Cap

Air sucked down chimney

Chimney

Large Volume 600 CFM Exhaust Fan

Tile Flue Liner

Damper Open

"SMELL"

Firebox

Range

Ash Dump

"SMELL" (With doors on the fireplace closed.)

Air

Ash Pit Door

A large volume (600 CFM) range exhaust in a tight home can draw air down a chimney and cause a "stinky" smell in a home. A clothes dryer can also do this.

V031

As we build our homes tighter and tighter to aid energy conservation, we limit the number of air leaks and decrease the supply of combustible air. Exhaust fans in the bathroom and kitchen, clothes dryers, and downdraft cooktops also draw air out of the home. This can create problems with backdrafting and spillage of combustion products into the home. For instance, combustion gas from an appliance can be drawn back down the chimney, and if the appliance isn't operating properly, dangerous carbon monoxide can linger indoors.

What can you do to prevent this? Watch for signs of backdrafting. Check flue pipes for rust or water stains, and look for rust or burn marks at draft diverters. If you notice these signs, contact a specialist. Have gas appliances serviced yearly, and ask the contractor to check all chimneys and flue connectors.

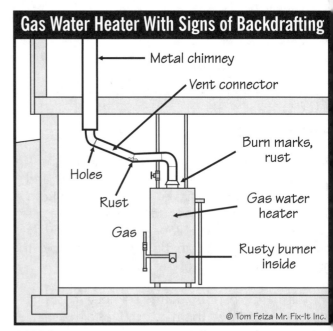

Gas Water Heater With Signs of Backdrafting

Metal chimney

Vent connector

Burn marks, rust

Holes

Gas water heater

Rust

Gas

Rusty burner inside

© Tom Feiza Mr. Fix-It Inc.

W006

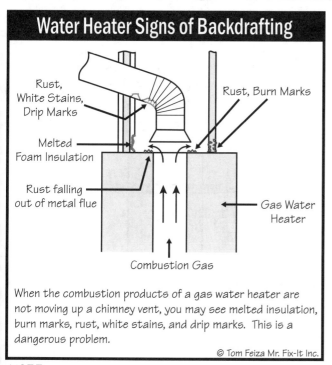

Water Heater Signs of Backdrafting

Rust, White Stains, Drip Marks

Rust, Burn Marks

Melted Foam Insulation

Rust falling out of metal flue

Gas Water Heater

Combustion Gas

When the combustion products of a gas water heater are not moving up a chimney vent, you may see melted insulation, burn marks, rust, white stains, and drip marks. This is a dangerous problem.

© Tom Feiza Mr. Fix-It Inc.

V033

No Chimney for a Gas Appliance?

A modern gas furnace may have a sealed combustion system that doesn't require a chimney; the furnace is vented by plastic pipes to the exterior. Some gas water heaters also direct-vent through a side wall with plastic pipe or a special metal vent. Newer gas fireplaces can vent directly through a side wall, and some have their own combustion air supply.

With today's tighter homes, always consider using fuel-burning appliances that have a built-in combustion supply that draws in air from outside.

Some states allow the installation of gas fireplaces without any vent or chimney, but many states forbid this type of installation because of the potential for safety problems. If you have any questions about the requirements in your area, check with the local building inspector.

For more specific information, look up the Chimney Safety Institute of America in the References section.

Orphaned Water Heater in Masonry Chimney

Today many high-efficiency furnaces are installed to replace inefficient old furnaces. The new efficient furnace vents outdoors through a plastic pipe, and

the old furnace connection to the masonry chimney is eliminated. Sounds great, right?

Well, it is great to use a high efficiency furnace, but you can't just remove the exhaust flue from the masonry chimney if the chimney is shared with a gas water heater. The old furnace operated at only 50 to 65 percent efficiency. That means a lot of the energy from the gas flame went up the chimney, keeping the chimney nice and warm. When you remove this heat source, the chimney stays cold and the remaining (orphaned) water heater can't keep the chimney warm.

This results in condensation of the products of combustion in the chimney. Since water (steam) is a major component of the combustion gas, water condenses inside the chimney flue. This condensation will damage the chimney and can even leak into your home. Eventually, significant damage will occur. Repairing or rebuilding a masonry chimney is very expensive. Safety is also an issue. An oversized chimney can cause backdrafting of combustion gas at the water heater.

You can solve the problem by adding a lightweight metal liner to the chimney. This thin, flexible metal liner runs from the water heater to the top of the chimney. The liner quickly warms from the combustion gas of the water heater, and condensation does not occur.

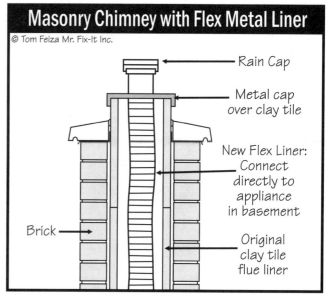

Masonry Chimney with Flex Metal Liner

© Tom Feiza Mr. Fix-It Inc.

Rain Cap

Metal cap over clay tile

New Flex Liner: Connect directly to appliance in basement

Brick

Original clay tile flue liner

F012

Sesmic Movement

In certain parts of the country, earthquakes and tremors are a real concern. When a home shakes, piping can break, causing a major gas or water leak. In areas prone to seismic movement, water heaters often are strapped to the structure to prevent tipping, and flexible gas and water lines are attached to fixed appliances to accommodate movement. (Interestingly, flexible gas lines to fixed appliances are not allowed in some areas of the country.)

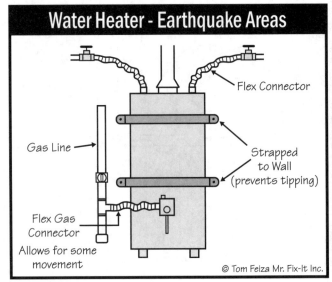

Water Heater - Earthquake Areas

Flex Connector

Gas Line

Strapped
to Wall
(prevents tipping)

Flex Gas
Connector
Allows for some
movement

© Tom Feiza Mr. Fix-It Inc.

W014

Chapter 7 – Fun Yet Serious Systems

Fireplaces and Wood Stoves

Before modern heating sources were available, fireplaces were a primary source of heating. Today a fireplace can't compete with a modern heating system. Fireplaces and wood stoves are great fun and provide a cozy, romantic amenity to our homes, but you do need to understand their basic components and how they operate.

Poor maintenance and improper operation can cause a fire inside your home. Fireplaces and wood stoves can produce dangerous products of combustion, such as carbon monoxide.

Basic Fireplace Types

There are three basic types of fireplaces: masonry, prefabricated metal and direct vent. Masonry fireplaces are designed to burn wood and can be adapted for a gas log set. Prefabricated metal fireplaces can be designed to burn wood, wood and gas, or just gas. Direct vent fireplaces are sealed high-efficiency units that only burn gas. We will look at each type and learn what's involved in safe operation.

A wood stove or fireplace insert should not be operated until a professional has checked it and determined that it conforms to local building codes and requirements. If you have any concerns or specific questions about your fireplace or wood stove, contact a local member of the Chimney Safety Institute of America (CSIA). Local fireplace and wood stove dealers can also provide assistance. For more information, see the References section.

Masonry Fireplace

Masonry fireplaces have been the standard method of home heating for centuries. Since about 1900, when efficient central heating systems were developed, fireplaces have taken on the role of a desirable feature that adds value to our homes and provides a gathering place for family and friends.

A standard masonry fireplace is constructed of brick, firebrick, cement block and clay tile to contain the fire and products of combustion. The fire-

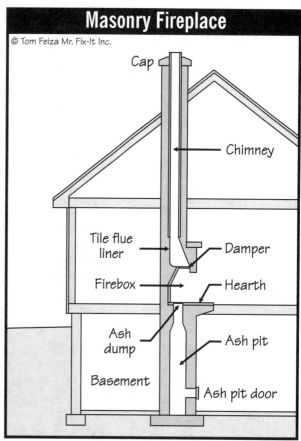

F005

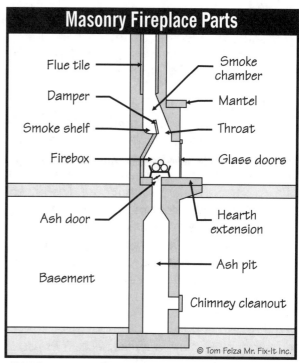

F006

131

place is custom built on-site by skilled masons. The design has changed little over the last 100 years, and masonry fireplaces aren't a very efficient source of heat.

Before you build a fire, you should understand the components of your masonry fireplace. Start by examining the firebox (the area where the fire is built). You will notice that the box is built of smooth brick or firebrick. If the wall of the firebox is metal, you have a metal framed or metal fabricated fireplace.

Look inside the top of the firebox and you will see a metal damper (metal plate) and a handle that operates the damper. Most dampers are made of cast iron and are pushed open with a handle or pulled open with a chain. With the chain-operated units you will often see a pull marked "O" for open and "S" for shut. Pull the chain or push the lever to open the damper. Keep your face and body away from the damper as it opens, because soot may fall from the opening.

With the damper open, you should be able to peer up the clay tile flue and see part of the way up the chimney. You may notice some soot- and tan-colored fluff or deposit. This is creosote. If you see a heavy buildup that is 1/16" to 1/4" thick, have your chimney and fireplace cleaned before you build a fire.

When you build a fire, the hot gases of combustion flow past the damper and up the chimney flue. The firebrick and firebox contain the heat of the fire and radiate some heat back into the room.

A variation on a solid masonry fireplace uses a metal firebox placed inside a masonry fireplace frame. The metal firebox replaces the firebox constructed of firebrick. These units often were constructed with an air passage around the metal box and air duct connections to the room. The lower duct opening draws air from the room at the base of the fireplace. The metal firebox warms the air, which then flows upward through a duct above the fireplace and enters the room through a grill. This gives the fireplace some heating capacity, warming the air of the room.

You might also find a wood-burning metal stove insert fitted inside a masonry fireplace. These custom-designed units provide heat to a room. Often,

such a unit has a partially sealed combustion chamber. It requires a special flue and custom installation. This kind of unit needs yearly maintenance; flue gases exit at a lower temperature, and the unit is prone to a buildup of deposits in the stove and chimney flue.

Metal-Framed Prefabricated Fireplace

Many fireplaces built since about 1970 consist of a metal fireplace and flue built in a factory, which is then installed in a wood frame inside the home. These are called metal-framed, zero clearance, prefabricated, or factory-built fireplaces. They are designed and tested as a unit. Don't be confused by a solid brick or masonry front and mantle on such a fireplace; many metal fireplaces have a masonry front.

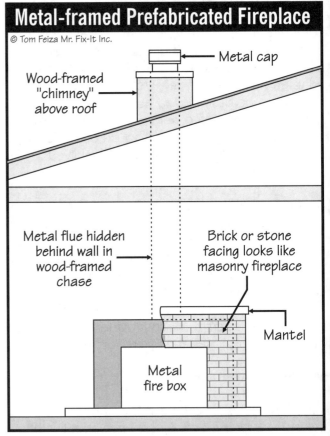

Metal-framed Prefabricated Fireplace

© Tom Feiza Mr. Fix-It Inc.

Metal cap

Wood-framed "chimney" above roof

Metal flue hidden behind wall in wood-framed chase

Brick or stone facing looks like masonry fireplace

Mantel

Metal fire box

F007

If yours is a factory-built fireplace, you will see a metal firebox with refractory panel liners, metal damper and a metal flue. The refractory panels will look like brick cast into a flat panel on three sides of the firebox. The side of the firebox may show the manufacturer's data and nameplate. Outside the house, there will not be a brick chimney; instead, you will see a wood-framed chimney chase and a metal-capped flue pipe. The flue or discharge pipe at the top of the chimney will be metal. The chase can also be covered with masonry materials, but this is not common.

A prefrabricated fireplace functions like a masonry fireplace but doesn't require the foundation and more expensive masonry construction. Glass doors are often included with the firebox, and the fireplace may have an outside air supply that provides combustion air for the fire. This reduces the need for inside air for combustion and makes the fireplace more efficient.

Many prefabricated fireplaces are equipped with a fan to circulate room air around the firebox so that the fire provides some heat in the room. The grills for air circulation are often placed directly above and below the glass doors.

Direct Vent Fireplace

Around 1985, fireplaces were greatly improved as heating appliances when "direct vent" and "sealed combustion" fireplaces started to become popular. These are natural gas or propane burning fireplaces that vent combustion gases directly through a side-wall or up a special metal chimney. They use an outside air supply for combustion. The front glass is totally sealed.

This fireplace may have a pilot light or ignition device, just like a gas furnace. With a good set of gas logs, it provides an attractive flame and is an efficient source of heat. Some of these units are rated heating appliances, just like a warm air furnace, and can be connected to a thermostat for automatic control. The fireplace will have a fan to circulate heated air into the room. Many units are almost as efficient at heating the room as a good warm-air furnace.

Gas Fireplace Logs

A "gas" fireplace generally refers to a set of ceramic logs, a gas burner, and related equipment that allows the feel and look of a real fire while burning natural gas or propane. The advantages of a gas fireplace are that it requires no fuss and creates no mess. You can have an instant fire, and when you

turn it off, you know the fire is out. There is no wood to haul in and no ash to clean up.

Gas fireplace logs are often adapted to a wood-burning masonry fireplace or to a metal-framed fireplace that is designed to burn wood.

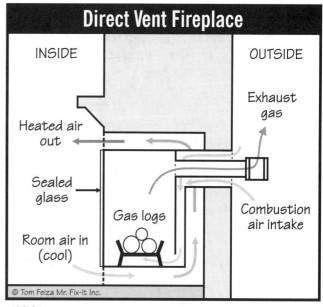

F001

Since each system is a little different, refer to the manufacturer's instructions for your unit. Some will have a pilot light or an automatic ignition device. Some use a wall switch or even a remote control.

With most manually operated gas fireplace logs, the first step is to open the damper in the flue above the logs. Then you place a match or flame in the log set. Use a long fireplace match or a lighter with a long handle. Carefully and slowly open the gas valve after there is a flame in the log set.

If you smell gas near the gas fireplace, do not attempt to light the unit. Turn off the gas valve located in the floor or in the firebox near the log set. Call for service. There should also be another safety valve in the basement or near the fireplace.

If you intend to burn real wood in a gas fireplace, consult a specialist first. Some metal-framed fireplaces are rated for gas only and won't burn wood. If your unit has a gas log set and gas piping, it would be very dangerous to burn real wood without converting the unit.

How to Build a Real Wood Fire

Masonry fireplaces and wood burning metal-framed fireplaces are safe and easy to use if you follow a few simple steps.

First, get everything ready:

1. Assemble a simple set of tools for maintaining the fire. At a minimum, you need some type of poker to move logs as needed when the fire is hot.

2. Always use a grate in the fireplace. The grate raises the wood off the base of the firebox to allow for air circulation, which aids complete combustion. Place the grate to the rear of the firebox.

3. Use dry or seasoned hardwood. This wood will burn hotter and prevent excessive smoke and soot from building up in the chimney flue. Dry or seasoned wood will have been cut and stored out of the weather for about 12 months. It will feel dry and will have cracks and splits in the end grain.

4. Never burn treated wood, Christmas trees, plastic, or trash in a fireplace. Never use a flammable liquid.

5. Remove ashes as they build up below the grate. There must be room for air circulation below the grate. If yours is a real masonry fireplace, you can put cold ashes down the ash pit door. Leave a base layer of about one inch of ash in the fireplace.

Now, to build the fire:

1. Open the damper. Take a look up the flue with a flashlight to make sure the damper is open. (Once you have mastered the operation of the damper, you can stop checking with the flashlight.)

2. If your home is very "tight," you may need to open a window to allow for combustion air to reach the fire. You will learn about this as you use the fireplace; if there is a poor draft, or if smoke builds inside your home, try opening a window.

3. Start loading the fireplace with small pieces of scrap wood (kindling) on the grate. Using small pieces of dry wood for kindling is the key. Woodworking scraps are ideal. These will light quickly, spreading the fire easily to the logs.

4. Add three or four small logs in the grate atop the kindling. Arrange the logs so there is space for air and fire circulation between them.

5. Place wadded newspaper below the grate.

6. You may need to help start the draft with a torch made from rolled newspaper. Light the paper and hold it up near the damper until there is a strong draft. The flame will warm the air in the flue and start a draft (a draw) up the chimney. After you have burned a few fires, you will know whether you can skip this step.

7. Once there is a draft up the chimney, light the crumpled paper below the grate.

8. Keep the screen closed while you are burning a fire.

9. Add and move the logs if needed. Don't build a huge fire.

10. Monitor the fire as it burns. Allow it to burn out before you leave the room. If your fireplace has glass doors, close them when you leave the fire.

11. Don't close the damper until the next day, and make sure the grate and remnants of logs are totally cold. A wood fire can smolder for a long time, and if you close the damper when the fire is still burning, you will trap smoke and dangerous products of combustion inside your home.

Fireplace Draft Problems

One problem with fireplaces in newer, more airtight homes is that they lack combustion air unless a window is open. This was not a problem with older homes, which had so many air leaks around windows, doors and framing that there was plenty of air for combustion.

This condition can be dangerous: as a fire is starting or burning out, it may lack draft, and it can back up dangerous carbon monoxide into your home.

A fire with a strong draft can cause gas-fired appliances such as a water heater or furnace to back-

Backdrafting Fireplace, Kitchen Fan = SMELL

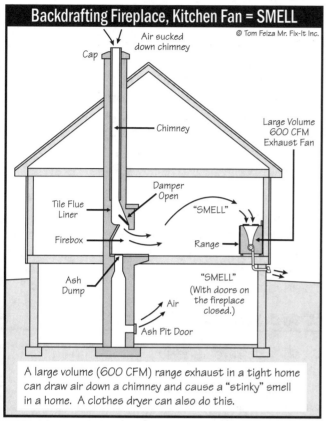

© Tom Feiza Mr. Fix-It Inc.

A large volume (600 CFM) range exhaust in a tight home can draw air down a chimney and cause a "stinky" smell in a home. A clothes dryer can also do this.

V031

Masonry Fireplace - Outside Air Supply

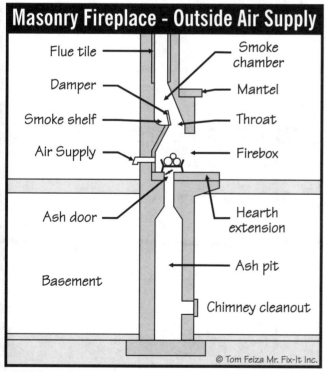

© Tom Feiza Mr. Fix-It Inc.

F009

draft combustion fumes into your home. Any gas-burning appliance vented by gravity up a chimney could be affected. The draft of a fire can overcome the natural venting of these gas appliances.

An air supply directed into the firebox would be a good solution. Consult a qualified brickmason, fireplace contractor or chimney sweep for the installation. This is definitely not a do-it-yourself project. The vent must penetrate an outside wall and the side or front of the fireplace. The vent may also need to be combined with fireplace doors.

Remember that when most natural fireplaces are operated in cold weather, most of the heat goes up the chimney.

There is one situation when a fireplace works well: if the home has excessive moisture levels in the winter, the fireplace will draw lots of air into your home for ventilation (provided that a window is open!)

Must Know / Must Do
Building a Fire

1. Keep the damper open overnight after burning a wood fire.

2. Routinely have the fireplace and flue cleaned by a professional.

3. Watch for soot and creosote buildup.

4. Consider glass doors; they're a great addition to your fireplace. They contain the fire and help prevent excessive room air from entering the fireplace.

5. Never light a gas fireplace if you smell gas. Treat this as a serious safety hazard.

6. If you see cracks, crumbling, or movement of the masonry surface inside the firebox or flue, have them checked by a professional.

7. A professional should check excessive rust on a metal-framed fireplace.

8. If you are not sure how to use your gas or wood-burning fireplace, get help from a professional.

Fireplace Cleaning

The ideal schedule for cleaning your fireplace and chimney depends on many factors. How often do you use your fireplace? What type of wood do you burn? Is the wood always dry hardwood? Is your home in a wooded area? Is there a cap on the chimney? Have you had problems in the past? Do you close the glass doors? Is there always a good draft? Is the chimney in the center of the home or on an outside wall?

If you live in a wooded area, you may wish to have the chimney checked every year just to make sure that no animals or their nests have blocked the flue.

You should inspect your fireplace, damper and flue every year. Operate the damper to see that it opens fully and latches open. The damper should also close tightly. Peer up the flue while shining a bright flashlight on it. You should not see any buildup of creosote or soot on the sides of the firebox or liner. The shelf behind the damper should not be full of debris. Proper inspection also includes looking at the top of the chimney, inspecting the cap, and peering down the flue with a bright light.

Creosote buildup creates a fire hazard. Creosote, a black or brown deposit, can be crusty and flaky, tar-like, or shiny and hardened. You might see different types of buildup on one fireplace. If creosote builds up in sufficient quantities, it can burn, destroying the chimney and even burning down your home.

Wet wood, restricted air for combustion, and cool chimney temperatures all increase the buildup of creosote, so no general rule of thumb can be safely determine when a fireplace needs to be cleaned.

Have your fireplace cleaned, and ask the chimney sweep for recommendations on routine maintenance. He or she can determine how often your chimney needs cleaning, based on all the variables in your case. Select a sweep who belongs to the National Chimney Sweep Guild and is certified by the Chimney Safety Institute of America (CSIA). A chimney sweep must pass an examination to be certified. Remember that it's the worker, not the company, who should be certified. To find the names of certified members in your area, call the CSIA at (317) 837-5362 (www.csia.org).

"Rain" in the Fireplace

To avoid severe condensation problems that mimic rain in the fireplace, check the fit of the fireplace damper. If the damper leaks (or is left open) during the winter, warm moist air will flow up the chimney. This warm air will condense into water on the flue if the chimney is cold from lack of use; when temperatures are below freezing, the condensation will turn to ice on the flue. When you build a fire, this ice can fall like "rain."

"Rain" that falls onto your fire could also result from a leak in the flashing, a damaged cap, damaged brick and mortar, or a liner problem. If the problem persists, hire a certified chimney sweep to do an inspection.

Wood Stoves

Wood stoves, wood heaters, wood-burning fireplace inserts and related wood-burning devices have become popular over the years. Many are well-designed and safe to use. Some are home-made contraptions that are not safe. Some are excellent factory-built units installed by amateurs in an unsafe fashion.

If your home has any type of wood-burning device other than a professionally installed fireplace, have it checked by a professional before you use it. It may not be safe.

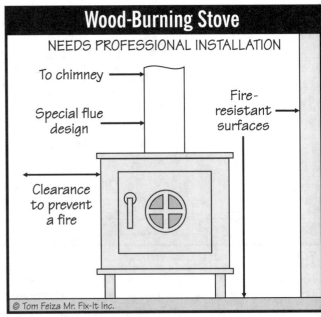

F010

Whirpool Bath

A whirlpool bath is a tub fitted with a circulating pump, jets, air induction, and possibly a heater. The tub can be small or large and is usually located in a bathroom. Most whirlpool tubs let you adjust the direction and amount of air in the jets for a more invigorating flow of water. Water is recirculated through the pump, the jets and a return opening.

The pump system usually is controlled by a switch on the side of the tub that uses pneumatic operation for safety. There may also be a timer and disconnect switch mounted on the wall away from the tub. The electrical system must be protected by a ground fault circuit interrupter (GFCI) outlet or breaker.

To use the tub, fill it with comfortably warm water to a level above the jets; then turn on the airflow to the jets, which should be pointed downward unless you want water spraying into your adjacent closet. You can adjust the jets to vary the amount and strength of the airflow. Adjust the temperature to your liking by adding more hot or cold water.

Whirlpool tubs should be flushed periodically, up to twice per month depending on usage. Debris can build up in the piping system if the unit is not used and flushed periodically.

The Kohler Co., a premier manufacturer of plumbing fixtures and whirlpool tubs, provides excellent information on whirlpool operation and maintenance information at its website, www.kohler.com. According to Kohler, whirlpool flushing should be done as follows:

1. Adjust the jets fully clockwise so there is no air induction.

2. Fill the bath with warm water to a level 2" above the highest jets, or leave water in the bath after using.

3. Add 2 teaspoons of a low-foaming dishwasher detergent and 20 ounces of household bleach (5 to 6 percent sodium hypochlorite) to the water.

4. Run the whirlpool for 5 to 10 minutes. Then shut off the whirlpool and drain the water.

5. If desired, rinse bath surfaces with water.

Must Know / Must Do – Whirlpool Tubs

- Periodically flush and clean the unit.

- Test the GFCI routinely.

- Never use bubble bath or similar detergents.

- Never allow children to use the tub without supervision.

Whirlpool Tub

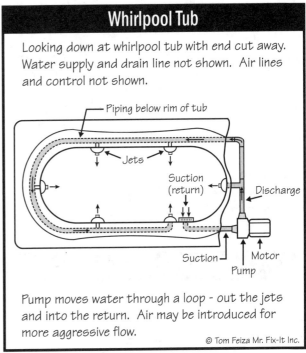

Looking down at whirlpool tub with end cut away. Water supply and drain line not shown. Air lines and control not shown.

Piping below rim of tub

Jets

Suction (return)

Discharge

Suction

Motor

Pump

Pump moves water through a loop - out the jets and into the return. Air may be introduced for more aggressive flow.

© Tom Feiza Mr. Fix-It Inc.

P104

6. Clean bath surfaces as needed with recommended cleaners.

Hot Tub/Spa

A hot tub or a spa is heated, water-filled tub that circulates water and often air through jets below the water line. Water is not drained from a hot tub as it is from a bathroom whirlpool tub.

The hot tub can be made of fiberglass, wood, acrylic or even poured concrete as part of a pool system. Hot tubs vary in size, shape, type and location. They have automatic controls and require routine maintenance.

A hot tub requires carefully controlled treatment with chemicals to maintain water quality. Ozone is also used to treat spa water. There are numerous methods for chemical treatment; some are manual and some are sophisticated, automated systems.

Self-contained (sometimes called portable) spas include the tub and all related equipment—heater pump, jets, filter, air system and automatic controls. They may also include some type of automatic chemical treatment. Usually the heater is electrical and the unit requires a large 240-volt electrical service with ground fault circuit interrupter (GFCI) protection. In most climates these tubs are fitted with a cover to conserve energy and water and maintain the chemical balance. Automatic controls maintain the temperature and operate pumps and heaters.

An in-ground spa installed with a pool usually has a separate pump, filter, heater, air system and chemical treatment. The equipment is often located outside but can be located in a pool room or basement. The heater for this type of spa is usually gas-fired—basically, it's a small gas boiler.

You may wish to hire a contractor for routine maintenance and chemical treatment. The chemicals and equipment must be carefully controlled to provide a safe system and to prevent equipment damage.

Hot Tub, Spa - Equipment

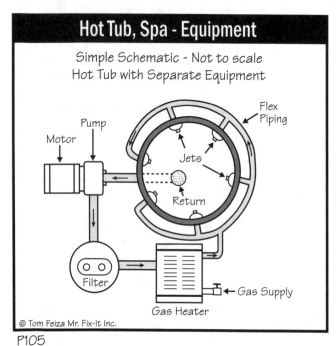

Simple Schematic - Not to scale
Hot Tub with Separate Equipment

Motor
Pump
Flex Piping
Jets
Return
Filter
Gas Supply
Gas Heater

© Tom Feiza Mr. Fix-It Inc.

P105

Swimming Pools

A swimming pool is a man-made tub of water designed for recreation, swimming and staying cool on a hot summer day. Swimming pools comes in all types, shapes and sizes. Some are above ground, some below. Most of them share common systems and components.

Most pools include a pump, filter, strainer, skimmer, drain, valves, and piping that connects all these components. In addition, a pool may have a heater, lights and an automatic treatment system. The treatment may be chemical, salt or oxygenation.

Pools are constructed of poured reinforced concrete, vinyl lined in ground or above ground, or a spray of cement and sand over a metal framework. Some pools are covered with ceramic tile, and some are surrounded with concrete or concrete and tile walking surfaces.

The basic operation of a pool starts with a skimmer and water return lines from the pool. Water from the pool runs through a screen to remove larger debris like leaves and swimming suits (just kidding). From the screen, water is routed through an electrically operated pump and into a filter. After the water is filtered it may be heated, treated, and then returned to the pool through an opening in the side of the pool.

Swimming Pool Equipment

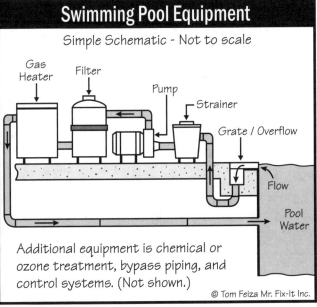

Simple Schematic - Not to scale

Gas Heater · Filter · Pump · Strainer · Grate / Overflow · Flow · Pool Water

Additional equipment is chemical or ozone treatment, bypass piping, and control systems. (Not shown.)

© Tom Feiza Mr. Fix-It Inc.

P106

Routine maintenance of the mechanical equipment requires cleaning the screen to remove debris. The filter is replaced, backwashed or cleaned, depending on the type of filter. To perform any maintenance, you must understand how your specific system operates, and you must use valves to turn off or bypass equipment as needed. Often, pool maintenance is best left to professionals. At the least, the homeowner should be trained by a professional and obtain specific operating and maintenance instructions.

Water treatment is required to limit bacteria and kept the water clean. Often, chlorine compounds are used as a disinfectant. It is important to keep the pH of the pool within a certain range so the chlorine remains useful.

Your pool should be protected by a pool cover. The cover limits evaporation of water and loss of chemicals. It also helps protect the pool from leaves and debris.

Must Know / Must Do – Swimming Pool

- Hire a service contractor to routinely check equipment.

- Establish a maintenance routine based on your equipment.

- Maintain chemical balance, treatment and water chemistry.

- Keep records on maintenance and water chemistry.

- Routinely check for leaks at piping and other systems.

- Regularly change or clean filters and screens.

- Never allow children to use the pool without adults present.

- Use an alarm to alert you to water movement when the pool is not in use.

- Secure the pool with a proper enclosure, and maintain the enclosure.

- Periodically test the GFCI and related safety equipment.

Pool Safety

Children must always be supervised when using a swimming pool. It is a good idea to

have more than one adult around when using a pool. A fence with locking and self-closing gates should protect the pool. All doors to living areas should be equipped with self-closing hardware and locks at least 54 inches above the floor. An electronic or automated safety monitoring system should be in place to detect water movement when the pool is not in use. A pool cover may also be used for additional safety.

All electrical outlets must be spaced away from the water and be protected by a ground fault circuit interrupter (GFCI). Overhead electrical conductors must be eliminated. All systems must be grounded and bonded. If you have any concerns with the electrical system, have it checked by a qualified electrician.

Pool owners should ensure that all safety requirements of the local municipality and state are followed. You may wish to have the local building inspector check the pool and its equipment for safety. It is a good idea to have a phone near the pool with local emergency assistance numbers next to it.

Waterfront Property and Seawalls

Property on lakes and streams must be protected from erosion of soil adjoining the water. This may require some type of retaining wall or rock. Surface water drainage also must be directed around or channeled through any retaining wall to prevent damage. Your local municipality or Department of Natural Resources can provide information on requirements and maintenance.

Property on major bodies of water with wave action may need special protection. Often an engineered and specially constructed seawall is used. Seawalls may consist of poured concrete, steel sheet pile, concrete block, rock or timber. The seawall or bulkhead protects banks by separating the earth or sand behind them from water movement. Provisions must be made to allow surface drainage around or through a seawall.

Generally, seawalls do not protect the shore in from of them from water movement. Your state or municipality can provide local requirements and restrictions for a seawall barrier.

Chapter 8 – Service Requirements by the Calendar

Service Requirements by the Calendar

Home operation and maintenance is easy if we understand our home systems and stay organized. A home operates just like a car—with the right maintenance, you can avoid major problems and efficiently run your home for many years. The key is preventing problems or catching small problems before they become home disasters.

If you don't change the filter on the furnace on a routine basis, you can freeze up the coil, and you will come home to a very warm house. If you don't turn off the exterior hose connection in the winter, you can come home to a flood.

This chapter provides that little bit of organization that helps us all remember to perform important preventive maintenance tasks. It offers lists of maintenance tasks to be performed on a routine basis. Refer to specific chapters in the book for detailed information on the specific tasks. Follow manufacturers' instructions for all service.

Remember, not every maintenance item will be applicable to your home or its systems. You need to do the homework here—study and understand the systems in your home.

Exercise caution before attempting inspection, maintenance or repairs. Turn off the power and disconnect other utility services. Follow any owner's manual supplied by the equipment manufacturer. If you don't understand a problem or system, consult a professional.

Daily and Weekly

Be aware of any changes or strange sounds in your home. If the automatic garage door opener is groaning, the door and track may need lubrication, or perhaps a roller is broken. If you smell sewer gas in the basement, it may be due to a dried-out floor drain trap. If the central air conditioner is squeaking, this may indicate a bad bearing on the fan motor. If a gutter is overflowing, expect water in the basement or crawl space. Just watch for changes, and address issues as they arise.

Be watchful during drastic weather changes. Weather can have a huge effect on our homes. A big snowstorm may make it necessary to clear your furnace's intake and discharge vent pipes. During periods of heavy rain, it is wise to check gutters and downspouts and make sure that the sump pump is working properly. If the furnace runs constantly or more often than you expect, check for a problem.

Furnace Utility Disconnects

Discharge

Gas supply →

Alternate switch on ceiling or wall

Electrical supply

Gas valve →

Return

OFF   ON

Typical gas shutoff

Typical electrical disconnect (light switch) Turns furnace and air conditioner off/on

© Tom Feiza Mr. Fix-It Inc.

H008

Monthly

When these systems are in use, perform the following checks monthly.

System	Check	Condition
❐ Fire and smoke alarms	Test alarm.	_____
❐ Fire extinguishers	Check pressure; service as needed.	_____
❐ Carbon monoxide alarm	Test alarm, and check reading.	_____
❐ Warm air heating system	Check and change or wash filter (unless it is a special type).	_____ _____
❐ Furnace, high efficiency	Check condensate drain to make sure it is clear and draining.	_____ _____
❐ Gas heat, water heater	Check flue pipe (smoke pipe) to chimney for rust or other damage.	_____ _____
❐ Air conditioning	Check and change or wash filter (unless it is a special type); check condensate drain to make sure it is clear and draining.	_____ _____ _____ _____
❐ Heat pump	Check and change or wash filter (unless it is a special type).	_____ _____
❐ Steam heating system	Check water level. Service as needed.	_____
❐ Shower and tub drains	Clear out hair and other debris.	_____
❐ GFCI	Test GFCI (Ground Fault Circuit Interrupter) outlets and breakers.	_____ _____
❐ Plumbing	Check for any leaks at fixtures, traps and piping.	_____ _____
❐ Water softener	Check salt supply.	_____
❐ Clothes dryer	Clean lint from filter (after every use) and check duct for lint.	_____ _____
❐ Garage door operator	Test auto-reverse safety feature.	_____

Spring

System	Check	Condition
☐ Air conditioning	Schedule professional service. Check that the unit is level and clean and has proper clearance. Adjust main duct dampers if needed.	_____ _____ _____ _____
☐ Humidifier	Turn off unit and water supply. Switch humidifier's duct damper from winter to summer setting as needed.	_____ _____ _____
☐ Duct dampers	Adjust dampers for a switch from heating to cooling if necessary.	_____ _____
☐ High and low returns	Open high returns and close low returns for cooling season.	_____ _____
☐ Whole house fan	Check belt; lubricate and clean.	_____
☐ Gutters, downspouts	Clean gutters, and make sure downspouts are attached and extended.	_____ _____
☐ Roof	Inspect for damage. Trim trees if needed.	_____
☐ Roof vents	Inspect for damage or bird nests.	_____
☐ Chimney	Inspect for damage to cap, flashing and masonry.	_____ _____
☐ Sump pump	Test sump pump to make sure it removes water from the crock.	_____ _____
☐ Exterior, general	Check condition of paint, caulk and putty.	_____
☐ Exterior, grounds	Check that grading of soil and hard surfaces slopes away from the basement.	_____ _____
☐ Attic	Check for signs of leaks, mildew, condensation.	_____ _____
☐ Basement	Check for signs of leaks, cracks, movement, rot, mildew.	_____ _____
☐ Crawl space	Check for adequate ventilation to remove excess moisture.	_____ _____
☐ Dehumidifier	Clean; start operation in basement as needed.	_____ _____
☐ Plumbing	Open outside hose connection shutoff.	_____

Spring (continued)

System	Check	Condition
❏ Clothes dryer	Clean lint from duct and from unit per manufacturer's instructions.	_____ _____
❏ Refrigerator	Clean coil, clean drain pan, and check drain.	_____ _____
❏ Range hood	Clean filter, wash fan blades.	_____
❏ Bathroom exhaust fans	Clean grill and fan.	_____
❏ Bathroom tile	Check grout, caulk and tile for damage.	_____
❏ Water heater	Draw sediment from tank as needed.	_____
❏ Sprinklers, irrigation	Service and start system.	_____
❏ Decks	Clean and seal as needed.	_____

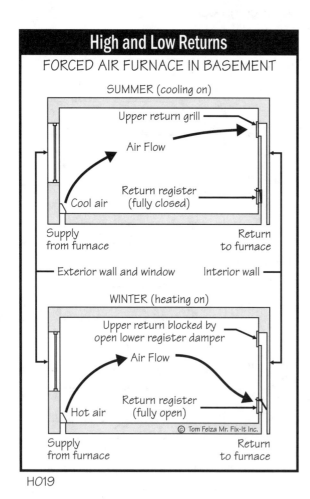

High and Low Returns

FORCED AIR FURNACE IN BASEMENT

SUMMER (cooling on)

Upper return grill

Air Flow

Cool air

Return register (fully closed)

Supply from furnace — Return to furnace

Exterior wall and window — Interior wall

WINTER (heating on)

Upper return blocked by open lower register damper

Air Flow

Hot air

Return register (fully open)

Supply from furnace — Return to furnace

© Tom Feiza Mr. Fix-It Inc.

H019

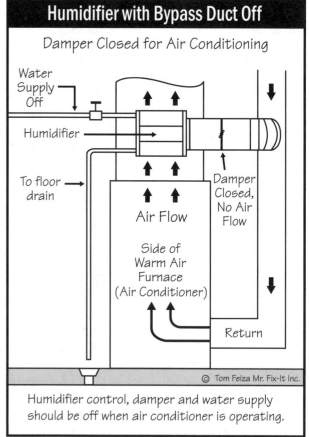

Humidifier with Bypass Duct Off

Damper Closed for Air Conditioning

Water Supply Off

Humidifier

To floor drain

Air Flow

Damper Closed, No Air Flow

Side of Warm Air Furnace (Air Conditioner)

Return

© Tom Feiza Mr. Fix-It Inc.

Humidifier control, damper and water supply should be off when air conditioner is operating.

H033

Summary

System	Check	Condition
☐ Air conditioner	Keep bushes and plant material clear of unit. Maintain air conditioner's filter on furnace. Keep drain lines clear.	_____
☐ Gutters, downspouts	Clean gutters, and make sure downspouts are attached and extended.	_____
☐ Sump pump	Test sump pump to make sure it removes water from the crock.	_____
☐ Exterior	Complete any major paint, putty, wood repair and caulking projects.	_____
☐ Fireplace	Schedule professional cleaning and service as needed.	_____
☐ Wood stoves	Schedule professional cleaning and service.	_____
☐ Chimney and roof	Schedule professional service as needed.	_____
☐ Exterior metal	Check metal railings. Paint as needed.	_____

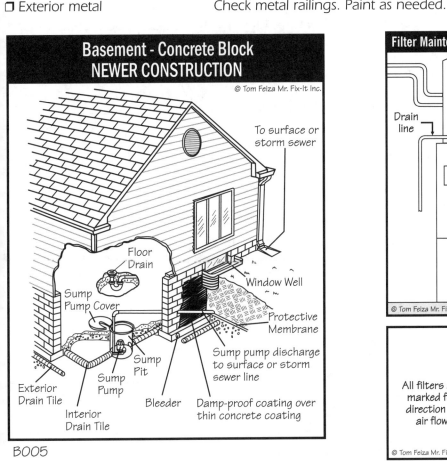

Basement - Concrete Block NEWER CONSTRUCTION

© Tom Feiza Mr. Fix-It Inc.

To surface or storm sewer

Floor Drain

Window Well

Sump Pump Cover

Protective Membrane

Sump pump discharge to surface or storm sewer line

Sump Pit

Sump Pump

Exterior Drain Tile

Bleeder

Damp-proof coating over thin concrete coating

Interior Drain Tile

B005

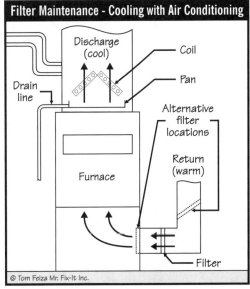

Filter Maintenance - Cooling with Air Conditioning

Discharge (cool)

Coil

Pan

Drain line

Alternative filter locations

Return (warm)

Furnace

Filter

© Tom Feiza Mr. Fix-It Inc.

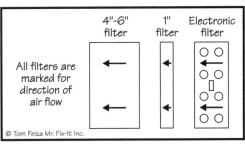

	4"-6" filter	1" filter	Electronic filter
All filters are marked for direction of air flow	←	←	○ ○

© Tom Feiza Mr. Fix-It Inc.

A002

Fall

System	Check	Condition
❐ Air conditioning	Cover top of unit if desired at end of cooling season.	_____
❐ Heating	Schedule professional service; lubricate fan, motor, and pumps.	_____
❐ Oil heat	Arrange for maintenance and oil delivery.	_____
❐ Water heater	Service gas and oil water heaters. Draw sediment from tank as needed. Check for carbon monoxide.	_____
❐ Humidifier	Service, clean, and change water panel as needed. Switch duct damper as needed from summer to winter setting.	_____
❐ Duct dampers	Adjust dampers for the switch from cooling to heating if necessary.	_____
❐ High and low returns	Open low returns and close high returns for heating season.	_____
❐ Gutters, downspouts	Clean gutters, and make sure downspouts are attached and extended.	_____
❐ Roof	Inspect for damage; trim trees as needed.	_____
❐ Roof vents	Inspect for damage or bird nests.	_____
❐ Chimney	Inspect for damage to cap, flashing and masonry.	_____
❐ Sump pump	Test sump pump to make sure it removes water from the crock.	_____
❐ Exterior, general	Check condition of paint, caulk and putty.	_____
❐ Weatherstripping	Check and repair weatherstripping on windows and doors.	_____
❐ Exterior, grounds	Check that grading of soil and hard surfaces slopes away from basement.	_____
❐ Basement	Check for any signs of leaks, cracks, movement, rot, mildew.	_____
❐ Crawl space	Check for adequate ventilation to remove excess moisture.	_____

Fall (continued)

System	Check	Condition
❒ Plumbing	Close outside hose connection shutoff.	_____
❒ Clothes dryer	Clean lint from duct and unit per manufacturer's instructions.	_____
❒ Bathroom tile	Check grout, caulk and tile for damage.	_____
❒ Garage door	Tighten all hardware, and lubricate moving parts.	_____
❒ Fireplace	Check flue, damper, firebox.	_____
❒ Sprinklers, irrigation	Drain and service system.	_____
❒ Room air conditioner	Remove unit, or install cover.	_____
❒ Swimming pool	Service and close.	_____
❒ Hoses	Remove from hose bibs; drain to prevent freezing.	_____

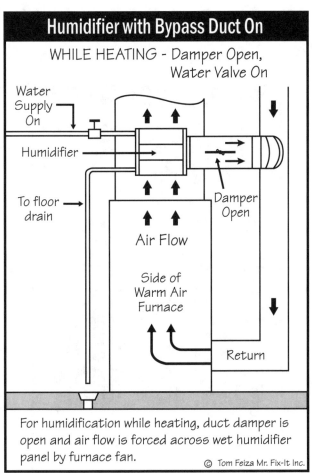

Humidifier with Bypass Duct On

WHILE HEATING - Damper Open, Water Valve On

Water Supply On

Humidifier

To floor drain

Damper Open

Air Flow

Side of Warm Air Furnace

Return

For humidification while heating, duct damper is open and air flow is forced across wet humidifier panel by furnace fan.

© Tom Feiza Mr. Fix-It Inc.

HO32

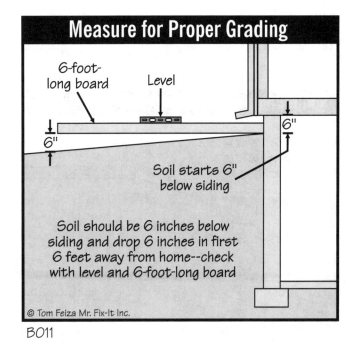

Measure for Proper Grading

6-foot-long board

Level

6"

6"

Soil starts 6" below siding

Soil should be 6 inches below siding and drop 6 inches in first 6 feet away from home--check with level and 6-foot-long board

© Tom Feiza Mr. Fix-It Inc.

B011

Winter

System	Check	Condition/Date
❑ Fire and smoke alarms	Change batteries, vacuum to remove dust, and test.	_____ _____
❑ Carbon monoxide alarms	Change batteries, and test.	_____
❑ Roof and gutters	Monitor for ice dams, and record problems for future corrective work.	_____ _____
❑ Sump pump	Test sump pump to make sure it removes water from the crock.	_____ _____
❑ Furnace	Lubricate fan, motor, and pumps as required at mid-season.	_____ _____
❑ Washing machine	Check supply hoses for damage. Clean screens in hose connections.	_____ _____
❑ Doors and hardware	Lubricate hinges and moving parts.	_____
❑ Boiler	Lubricate pump twice per year.	_____
❑ Steam boiler	Check water level.	_____
❑ Gutters	Keep downspouts extended.	_____

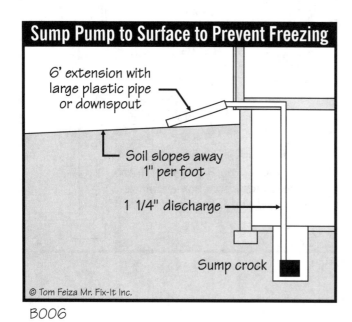

Sump Pump to Surface to Prevent Freezing

6' extension with large plastic pipe or downspout

Soil slopes away 1" per foot

1 1/4" discharge

Sump crock

© Tom Feiza Mr. Fix-It Inc.

B006

Electronic Air Filter

Side view

Front

On/Off

Test Button

Pre-Filters

Cell - Side view

Cell

Steel Mesh Pre-Filter (Washable)

Steel Grids & Wire
Power supply puts charge on grids and wire to attract dirt. Wash when dirty.

© Tom Feiza Mr. Fix-It Inc.

H029

Periodic Maintenance and Service as Needed

System	Check	Condition/Date
❏ Septic system	Schedule professional pumping and inspection at least every 2 years.	_____ _____
❏ Water softener	Clean brine tank and screens or filters as needed.	_____ _____
❏ Well system	Test water for bacteria and other contaminants. Check pressure tank operation.	_____ _____ _____
❏ Fire and smoke alarms	Replace alarms every 10 years.	_____
❏ Fireplace	Schedule cleaning and inspection as needed, depending on use.	_____ _____
❏ Water filters	Replace as needed.	_____
❏ Water treatment units	Replace and service as needed.	_____
❏ Electric baseboard	Vacuum and clean based on usage.	_____
❏ Gas appliances	Check flexible gas connectors for stove, dryer, etc., yearly.	_____ _____
❏ Range hood	Clean filter and fan.	_____
❏ Shutoffs	Periodically review all utility disconnects with your family.	_____ _____
❏ Termites and other pests	Schedule professional inspections and service as needed.	_____ _____
❏ Electrical	Eliminate extension cords. Check for damaged cords, plugs or outlets.	_____ _____
❏ Water heater	Test temperature and pressure relief valve. Replace leaking valves.	_____ _____
❏ Plumbing	Test main water shutoff. If it is hard to operate, call a plumber.	_____ _____

Chapter 9 – Emergencies & Simple Solutions

No Heat

What can you do if you wake up to a cold house and the furnace will not run? Follow these checklists before you call a service company.

For a Gas-Fired Furnace or Boiler

1. Check the thermostat. Is it set to "heat"? Is it set higher than the room temperature indicated on the dial? If it's a digital thermostat, is the battery dead?

2. Check the on-off switch on the side of the furnace or near the furnace.

3. Check the furnace pilot light. If it's out, light it, following the instructions on the furnace. If there is no pilot light, you have spark ignition or a hot surface igniter; the igniter should be hot or sparking as the furnace attempts to fire.

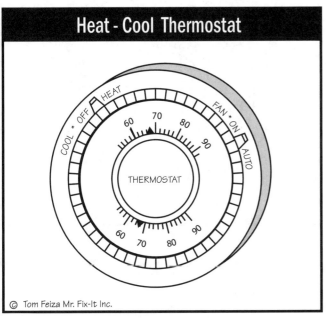

Heat - Cool Thermostat

© Tom Feiza Mr. Fix-It Inc.

H023

4. Is the gas off at the furnace or to your home? If you have a gas stove, you can check this by seeing if the stove's gas supply is on.

5. Is the breaker or fuse to the furnace turned off? Reset the breaker or replace the fuse; but if it trips again, call a service technician.

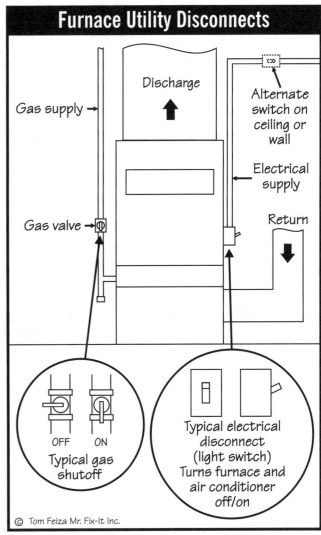

Furnace Utility Disconnects

© Tom Feiza Mr. Fix-It Inc.

H008

6. Check the furnace fan compartment door. Some units have a safety switch that turns the furnace off when the door is ajar.

7. Check for a broken belt or a severely clogged air filter.

For an Oil-Fired Furnace or Boiler

1. Check the thermostat. Is it set to "heat"? Is it set higher than the room temperature indicated on the dial? If it's a digital thermostat, is the battery dead?

2. Check the on-off switch on the side of the unit or near the unit.

Warm Air Furnace Fan Door Safety Switch

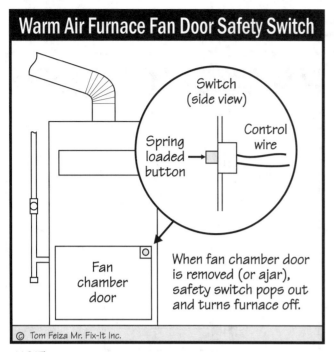

Switch (side view)

Spring loaded button

Control wire

Fan chamber door

When fan chamber door is removed (or ajar), safety switch pops out and turns furnace off.

© Tom Feiza Mr. Fix-It Inc.

HO17

Warm Air Furnace with Oil Burner

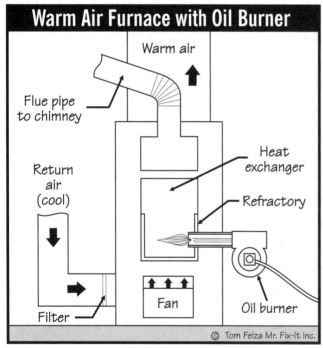

Warm air

Flue pipe to chimney

Heat exchanger

Refractory

Return air (cool)

Fan

Oil burner

Filter

© Tom Feiza Mr. Fix-It Inc.

HO13

3. Is the breaker or fuse to the furnace turned off? Reset the breaker or replace the fuse; but if it trips again, call a service technician.

4. Check the fan compartment door. Some units have a safety switch that turns the furnace off when the door is ajar.

5. Check for a broken belt or a severely clogged air filter.

6. Check the oil supply in the storage tank. If you are out of oil, arrange for oil delivery and burner service. An oil burner that runs out of oil will need service to restart.

7. Check the valve and filter on the tank.

8. Press the reset button of the ignition safety control on the stack or burner. (Try this once only.)

9. Press the restart button on the motor. (Try this once only.)

For a Heat Pump

1. Check the thermostat. Is it set to "heat"? Is it set higher than the room temperature indicated on the dial? If it's a digital thermostat, is the battery dead?

Heat - Cool Thermostat

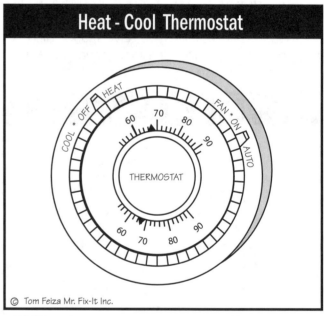

THERMOSTAT

© Tom Feiza Mr. Fix-It Inc.

HO23

2. Check the on/off switch on the side of the furnace or near the furnace.

3. Check the fan compartment door. Some units have a safety switch that turns the furnace off when the door is ajar.

4. Check for a broken belt or a severely clogged air filter.

5. Check whether the outside unit is iced up. If it is, call for service.

Furnace Utility Disconnects

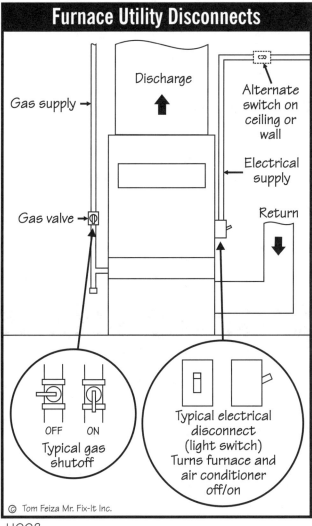

Discharge

Gas supply →

Alternate switch on ceiling or wall

Electrical supply

Return

Gas valve →

OFF   ON

Typical gas shutoff

Typical electrical disconnect (light switch) Turns furnace and air conditioner off/on

© Tom Feiza Mr. Fix-It Inc.

H008

Warm Air Furnace Belt Drive Maintenance

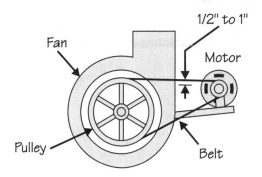

(Disconnect power before inspecting fan!)

With unit off, belt should deflect 1/2" to 1" at center with moderate hand pressure

1/2" to 1"

Fan

Motor

Pulley

Belt

Adjust belt tension by adjusting motor position. Belt should not have cracks, splits, frayed edges or hard, shiny edges.

© Tom Feiza Mr. Fix-It Inc.

H015

6. Check for tripped main fuses or breakers on the disconnect at the unit and at the main distribution panel.

No Air Conditioning

1. Check the thermostat. Is it set to cooling or AC? Is it set lower than the room temperature indicated on the dial? If it's a digital thermostat, is the battery dead?

Air Conditioning System with Warm Air Furnace

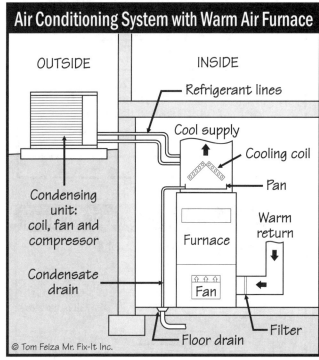

OUTSIDE   INSIDE

Refrigerant lines

Cool supply

Cooling coil

Pan

Condensing unit: coil, fan and compressor

Warm return

Furnace

Condensate drain

Fan

Floor drain

Filter

© Tom Feiza Mr. Fix-It Inc.

A001

2. Check the on/off switch on the side of the furnace or near the furnace. (Remember, the furnace distributes air for the air conditioning and must be switched "on".)

3. Is the disconnect switch outside at the AC unit switched off, disconnect pulled or fuse blown?

4. Is the main breaker or the 220-volt breaker or fuse for the air conditioner off? Reset the breaker or replace the fuse; but if it trips again, call a service technician.

5. Check the fan compartment on the furnace door. Some units have a safety switch that turns the furnace off when the door is ajar.

6. Check for a broken belt or a severely clogged air filter on the furnace.

Digital Thermostat

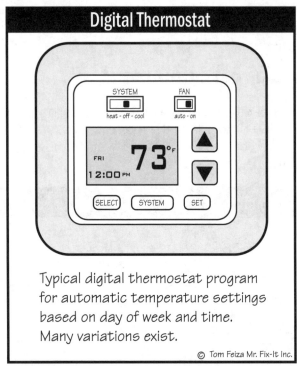

Typical digital thermostat program for automatic temperature settings based on day of week and time. Many variations exist.

© Tom Feiza Mr. Fix-It Inc.

H025

Air Conditioning - Exterior Electrical Disconnect

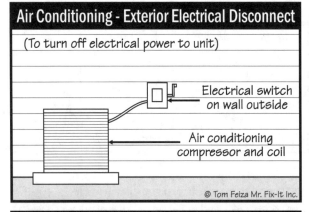

(To turn off electrical power to unit)

Electrical switch on wall outside

Air conditioning compressor and coil

© Tom Feiza Mr. Fix-It Inc.

Types of Exterior Disconnects

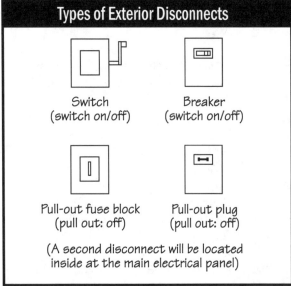

Switch
(switch on/off)

Breaker
(switch on/off)

Pull-out fuse block
(pull out: off)

Pull-out plug
(pull out: off)

(A second disconnect will be located inside at the main electrical panel)

A004

7. Is the coil above the furnace iced up? Call for service.

8. Is the exterior coil dirty or blocked by plants? Service the unit.

No Electricity

1. Find out whether the outage affects only your home. Check with your neighbors. If the whole area is without power, notify the electric utility.

2. If your whole house is without power but your neighbors have power, you may have tripped the main breaker or fuse. Inspect the panel to make sure there is no water or visible signs of damage. Then try to diagnose the problem; dis-

Circuit Breaker Resets

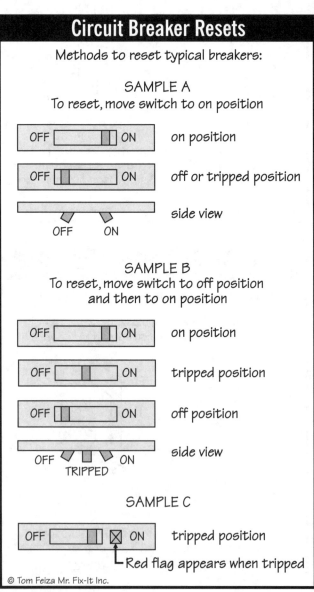

Methods to reset typical breakers:

SAMPLE A
To reset, move switch to on position

OFF [   ] ON   on position

OFF [   ] ON   off or tripped position

OFF _____ ON   side view
OFF   ON

SAMPLE B
To reset, move switch to off position and then to on position

OFF [   ] ON   on position

OFF [   ] ON   tripped position

OFF [   ] ON   off position

OFF _____ ON   side view
TRIPPED

SAMPLE C

OFF [   ] ⊠ ON   tripped position
Red flag appears when tripped

© Tom Feiza Mr. Fix-It Inc.

E013

connect any heater or electrical device that may have tripped the breaker. Reset the main breaker or replace the main fuse. If it trips a second time, call an electrician.

3. If only a part or section of your home has no power, one of the branch circuits has tripped. Check the main box for signs of water or damage. Disconnect a heater or electrical device that may be causing the problem. Reset the tripped

breaker or replace the blown fuse. If it trips again, call an electrician, and temporarily disconnect electrical devices connected to that circuit.

4. If power is out in the bathrooms, near the kitchen sink, in the garage, or at the exterior outlets, this indicates that a Ground Fault Circuit Interrupter (GFCI) has been tripped. You will find the reset button on the affected outlet; or there may be a reset button on a single bath-

GFCI Breaker Reset

Ground fault circuit interrupter (GFCI) breaker found in main electrical panel

Test button   Switch

OFF [   ] ON   on

OFF [   ] ON   tripped

OFF [   ] ON   off

OFF ╲╱╲╱ ON   side view
TRIPPED

When a GFCI breaker trips, the switch will often move to a center position. To reset, move the switch to the off position and then to on position.

© Tom Feiza Mr. Fix-It Inc.

E014

Electrical Main Fuse Panel

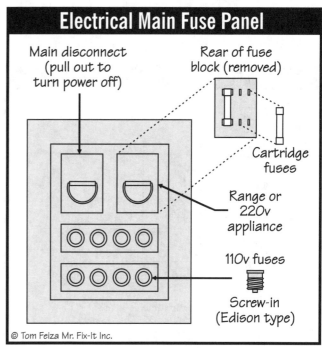

© Tom Feiza Mr. Fix-It Inc.

E003

Electrical Main Circuit Breaker Panel

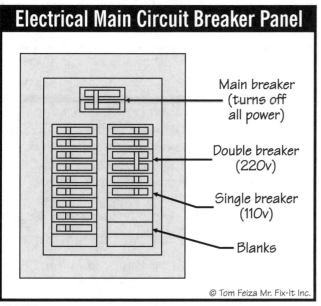

Main breaker (turns off all power)

Double breaker (220v)

Single breaker (110v)

Blanks

© Tom Feiza Mr. Fix-It Inc.

E002

Ground Fault Circuit Interrupter (GFCI)

© Tom Feiza Mr. Fix-It Inc.

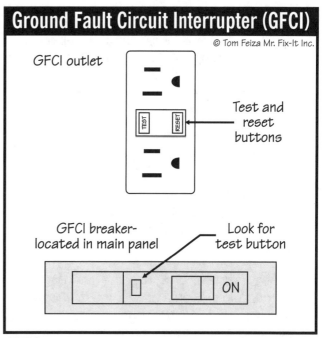

GFCI outlet

Test and reset buttons

GFCI breaker- located in main panel

Look for test button

E016

room outlet that controls all bathroom and exterior outlets; and occasionally a GFCI breaker is located in the main circuit panel (it will have a "test" button). Try resetting the GFCI once or twice; after that, replace the appliance that is causing the problem, or call an electrician. The usual procedure is to turn a GFCI breaker fully off, then on again.

No Water / Frozen Pipes

1. If you're on a municipal system, check with the neighbors to see if the whole area is out of water. Call the water utility.

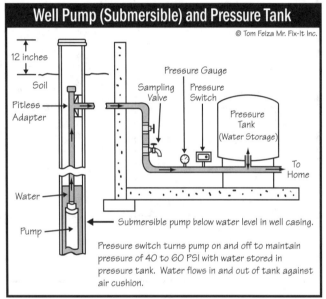

PO55

2. If you have a private well system, check the switch and breaker or fuse for the well pump. Check the pump if it is accessible. If the pump is hot, you need professional repair. If the pump seems okay, try resetting the breaker or replacing the fuse. If the overload device trips again, call for service.

3. In very cold weather, suspect a frozen pipe—either a main line or a smaller line inside your home. Turn off the water to a frozen pipe, because the pipe may be broken and will sprout a major leak when it thaws. Call a plumber.

4. If there is water flowing near the main or from the pressure tank on a private system, this indicates a major leak or damaged piping. Turn off the water and/or the pump, and call for service.

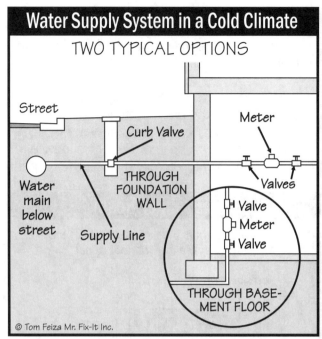

PO05

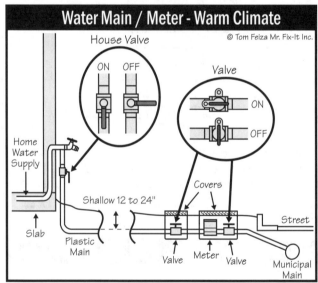

PO63

No Hot Water

1. If you have a gas water heater, check the pilot light. If you smell gas, turn off the gas supply to the water heater and call for service. Never, ever attempt to light a water heater pilot if you smell gas. If you do not smell gas, you may attempt to re-light the pilot, following the instructions on the water heater. If the pilot light keeps going out, the unit needs service.

2. Check to make sure the gas supply is on. Check other gas appliances in your home, or ask your neighbors if their gas supply is working.

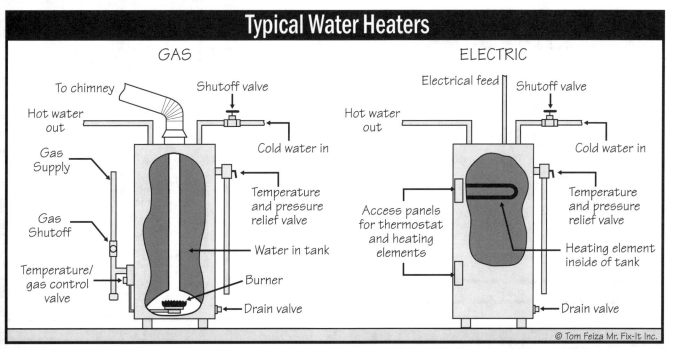

Typical Water Heaters

GAS

To chimney
Shutoff valve
Hot water out
Gas Supply
Cold water in
Temperature and pressure relief valve
Gas Shutoff
Water in tank
Temperature/ gas control valve
Burner
Drain valve

ELECTRIC

Electrical feed
Shutoff valve
Hot water out
Cold water in
Access panels for thermostat and heating elements
Temperature and pressure relief valve
Heating element inside of tank
Drain valve

© Tom Feiza Mr. Fix-It Inc.

W007

3. For an electric water heater, check the circuit breaker or fuse. Reset the breaker or fuse once if there is no visible damage at the water heater or the electrical panel. If the overload trips again, call for service.

4. An electric water heater has a high-limit switch under the heater's top cover on the upper thermostat. You can remove the upper cover and reset this switch once by pushing in the button. You should only attempt this if you feel confident opening the panel and possibly exposing live electrical connections.

Leaking Water Heater

1. If water is leaking from the tank on the floor, the water heater has failed. Turn off the water supply, the electrical power and/or the gas supply and call for service. The supply valve is usually found on the piping on top of the water heater. You will still have cold water in your home when you turn off this valve. If water continues to leak or spray from the unit, open the lowest hot faucet in the system to attempt to drain water and relieve pressure.

2. If the water is leaking from the temperature and pressure (T and P) valve and running down the pipe on the side of the unit, the water heater may be overheating or the valve may have

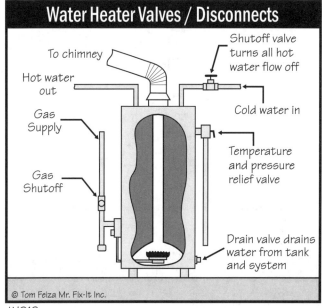

Water Heater Valves / Disconnects

To chimney
Shutoff valve turns all hot water flow off
Hot water out
Gas Supply
Cold water in
Gas Shutoff
Temperature and pressure relief valve
Drain valve drains water from tank and system

© Tom Feiza Mr. Fix-It Inc.

W012

failed. Carefully open a hot water faucet and check for overheated water or even steam. If the water is excessively hot, disconnect power and gas to the unit and call for service.

3. If there is a slow leak from the T and P valve drain line and the water is not excessively hot, have the valve replaced soon. Once the valve has leaked, it needs replacement; sediment may have built up in the valve.

4. If there is a small drip from the drain valve on the side of the unit, try screwing a hose cap and

Gas Shutoff Valve

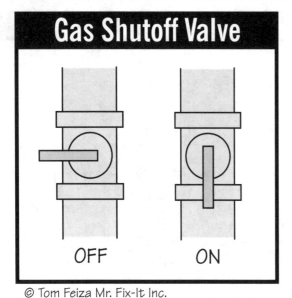

OFF   ON

© Tom Feiza Mr. Fix-It Inc.

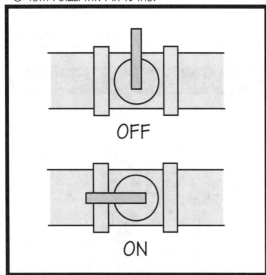

OFF

ON

P001

Gas Water Heater Temperature Dial

Gas valve/thermostat

VERY HOT   HOT

Water temperature adjusting dial

© Tom Feiza Mr. Fix-It Inc.

W004

Temperature and Pressure Valve

(T & P) RELIEF VALVE

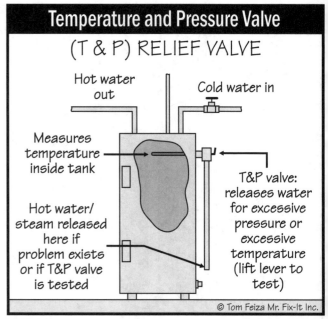

Hot water out

Cold water in

Measures temperature inside tank

Hot water/ steam released here if problem exists or if T&P valve is tested

T&P valve: releases water for excessive pressure or excessive temperature (lift lever to test)

© Tom Feiza Mr. Fix-It Inc.

W001

washer on the fitting to stop the leak. Normally, this valve does not need to be replaced.

Gas Odors

If you smell gas anywhere in your house (natural gas or propane), take the following steps.

1. Get everyone out of the house.

2. Don't light matches or use electrical switches or devices.

3. Call the gas (or propane) company from a neighbor's house.

4. Once outside, turn off the gas main. It is located near the meter. Give the valve a quarter-turn with a wrench until the valve is perpendicular to the piping.

5. Wait for help from the gas company.

Oil Leak

If your home has an oil tank and piping to a heating system, a leak may develop. You may notice an oily smell and see the oil.

1. Locate the oil valve at the oil tank and turn it off.

2. Place a container to catch the oil leak.

Exterior Gas Meter and Shutoff

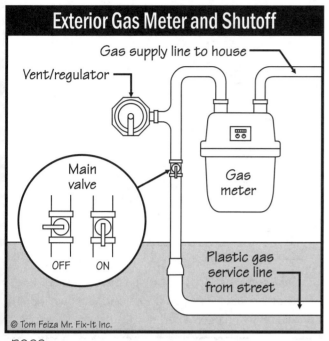

PO02

Propane Gas Shutoff Valves

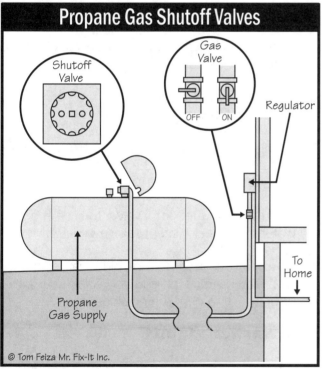

PO75

3. Turn off the oil burner on the boiler, furnace or water heater. Never run an oil burner without an oil supply.

4. If your home has an underground tank, turn off the valve in the lines entering your home or turn off the small pump system on the line into your home.

Typical Fuel Oil Tank in Basement

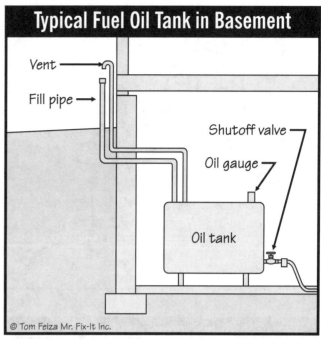

PO03

5. Call for service. Usually, your oil supply company will repair leaks. Plumbers also do these repairs.

Water Leak Anywhere

1. Quickly try to find a local valve that will isolate the leak.

2. If hot water is leaking, turn the water off at the top of the water heater.

3. Or turn off the main water valve—this will turn off all water to your home; later you can locate the specific valve for the leaking pipe.

4. If your home has a well system, you should also turn off the electrical supply to the pump when you turn off the main valve.

5. If your home has a well system, be sure to turn off the valve after the tank in the line feeding your home. If you turn off the valve between the pump and the tank, water in the tank will still empty into your home. When in doubt, turn off both valves.

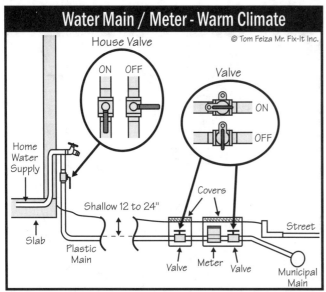

Water Main / Meter - Warm Climate

House Valve
ON OFF
Valve
ON
OFF
© Tom Feiza Mr. Fix-It Inc.
Home Water Supply
Covers
Shallow 12 to 24"
Street
Slab
Plastic Main
Valve   Meter   Valve
Municipal Main

P063

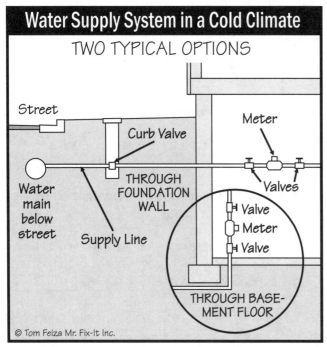

Water Supply System in a Cold Climate

TWO TYPICAL OPTIONS

Street
Meter
Curb Valve
Water main below street
THROUGH FOUNDATION WALL
Valves
Supply Line
Valve
Meter
Valve
THROUGH BASE-MENT FLOOR
© Tom Feiza Mr. Fix-It Inc.

P005

Leaking Toilet

A leak from the toilet tank can be caused by several problems.

1. Turn off the small plumbing valve below and behind the toilet.

2. If you can't find the toilet valve, turn off the main water supply valve.

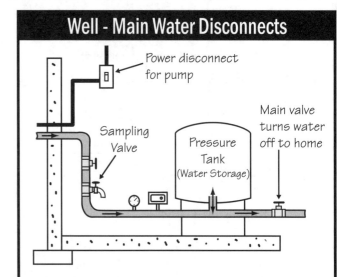

Well - Main Water Disconnects

Power disconnect for pump
Main valve turns water off to home
Sampling Valve
Pressure Tank (Water Storage)

To turn water off to home, close main valve between tank and home. Turn power off to disconnect pump and stop pump operation.
© Tom Feiza Mr. Fix-It Inc.

P056

3. Flush the toilet to remove water from the tank.

4. If water continues to drip from the tank, remove water from the tank with a towel.

Leaking Hose Bib (Exterior Faucet)

1. Locate the pipe feeding the hose bib and turn off the valve just inside the heated space of your home.

2. If you can't find the local valve, turn off the water main (see "Water Leak Anywhere").

3. If the leak occurred during cold weather, the pipe may have frozen and you will find a split or open fitting near the outside wall.

Dishwasher Flood

1. Turn off the electrical switch for the dishwasher.

2. Turn off the water supply located under the kitchen sink or below the dishwasher and floor framing.

3. If you can't find the local valve, turn off the water main (see "Water Leak Anywhere").

Toilet - Water Shutoff

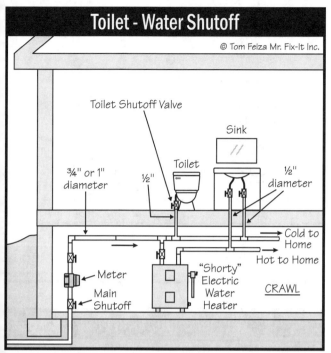

© Tom Feiza Mr. Fix-It Inc.

P107

Hose Bibs - Parts

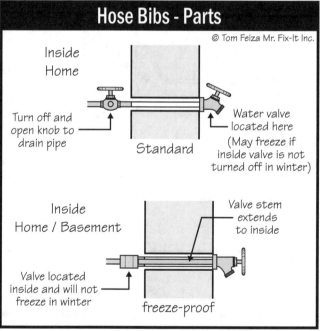

© Tom Feiza Mr. Fix-It Inc.

P077

Refrigerator Leak

1. A significant leak will be caused by the water supply to the icemaker. Locate the valve behind the refrigerator or in the floor framing just below the refrigerator.

2. If you can't find the local valve, turn off the water main (see "Water Leak Anywhere").

Dishwasher - Water & Electrical Supply

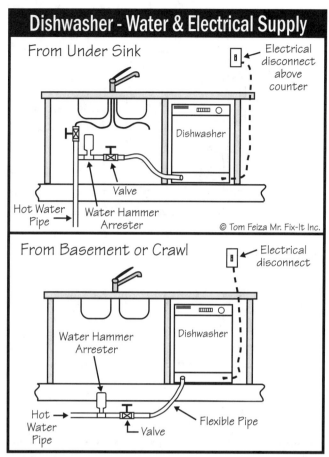

© Tom Feiza Mr. Fix-It Inc.

P061

4. If the leak is very small, it could be an overflow in the drain pan below the refrigerator, a plugged internal drain line, condensation on door gaskets, or a defrosting problem. Check the operation of the refrigerator and the pan below the refrigerator. Normally the lower front grill can be removed.

5. Condensation of the door gaskets during hot, humid weather can be eliminated by turning the gasket heater on. Look for a switch inside the refrigerator labelled "heat" or "hot/cold weather" or "door heater."

Leak At Washing Machine

Hoses to a washing machine have the potential for major leaks.

1. Locate the valves at the start of the flexible hoses and turn them off.

2. If you can't find or locate the feed lines, turn off the main water supply as described above (see "Water Leak Anywhere").

Ice Maker Water Supply (Shutoff Valve)

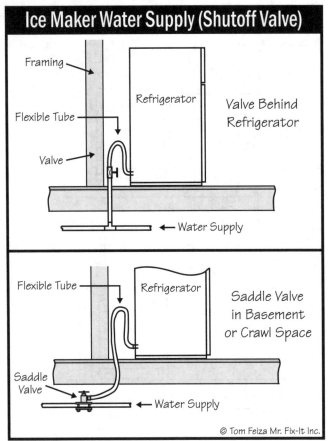

Framing

Refrigerator

Valve Behind
Refrigerator

Flexible Tube

Valve

← Water Supply

Flexible Tube

Refrigerator

Saddle Valve
in Basement
or Crawl Space

Saddle
Valve

← Water Supply

© Tom Feiza Mr. Fix-It Inc.

P062

3. A leak can also occur inside the washing machine. Turn off the washer and the feed lines, and call for service.

4. A major leak can also occur if the drain line is blocked. Check the tub or drain and look for the source of the water. If the drain is leaking, turn off the washer and clear the blockage.

Washer Shutoff - Tub

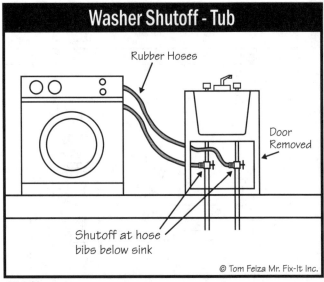

Rubber Hoses

Door
Removed

Shutoff at hose
bibs below sink

© Tom Feiza Mr. Fix-It Inc.

P108

Washer Shutoff - In Wall

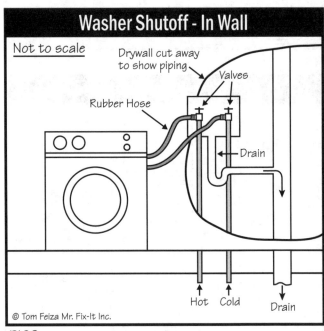

Not to scale

Drywall cut away
to show piping

Valves

Rubber Hose

Drain

Hot   Cold   Drain

© Tom Feiza Mr. Fix-It Inc.

P109

Chapter 10 – Common Problems & Simple Solutions

Wobbling Ceiling Fan

When properly installed and balanced, a ceiling fan should not wobble excessively. Make sure your fan has been mounted properly; there should be an electric box or special bracing to support the fan's weight and movement. You may be able to stop the wobble by switching blade positions and balancing the fan (see below). Contact the manufacturer of your fan for specific instructions, and ask if a balancing kit is available.

For information on how to contact the manufacturer, see the References section.

Typical balancing instructions:

1. Check that the fan is properly installed and that the blades are securely attached.

2. Run the fan on high speed (set to downdraft) and observe the wobble. Stop the fan; switch positions of two adjacent blades. If this improves the balance of the fan, leave it as is and use balancing weights.

3. With the fan stationary, attach the manufacturer's balancing clip on the leading edge of one blade, halfway between the outer tip of the blade and the attachment bracket. (A balancing clip, available from most fan manufacturers, is a small plastic weight that firmly clips to the blade.)

4. Run the fan on high speed, set to downdraft, and observe the wobble. Stop the fan; move the clip to the next blade. Again run the fan and observe the wobble. Repeat this for all fan blades.

5. Move the clip back to the blade where you noticed the least wobble. This time, attach the clip to the leading edge of the blade near the blade bracket. Run the fan and observe the wobble. Stop the fan and move the clip outward toward the end of the blade in small increments until you find the position where the fan runs best.

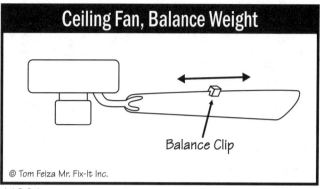

Ceiling Fan, Balance Weight

Balance Clip

© Tom Feiza Mr. Fix-It Inc.

M004

6. Attach a permanent balancing weight on the blade next to the clip. (Weights are often self-stick lead strips provided by the fan manufacturer.)

7. Remove the clip and run the fan. If the wobble was not completely corrected, you may be able to further improve the balance by repeating the above steps and adding more weights.

Doorbell Problems

Don't be afraid to try to repair the doorbell. All of its parts are low voltage—12 to 24 volts—and can't really hurt you. However, you should not attempt to repair or replace the transformer for the unit, which will be located in the basement or near the main power panel. It converts a 110-volt supply to 12 or 24 volts.

Most often, the chime unit consists of an electro-magnetic plunger that strikes a chime when activated—one sliding movement (and one chime) for the rear door and two movements for the front door's double chime.

Some door chimes consist of a low-voltage buzzer or a vibrating hammer on a bell. Others have huge chimes and complicated parts best left to a service company.

If the doorbell thumps or hums when you press the button, you need to clean the chime and plunger.

If pressing the button doesn't trigger any sound, the button itself is probably at fault. The doorbell button is the most common source of problems because of its exposure to weather. For a button that's flush with the wood trim, slip a screwdriver or putty knife under the edge to pry the button out of its hole. If the button is screwed to the frame, remove the screws.

Now you can see the low-voltage wires. If they are loose or broken, this could be why the doorbell isn't working.

If the wires look okay, disconnect their ends and touch them together to complete the circuit. If the doorbell rings now, you have found the problem— a bad button. You can easily replace the button with a matching button from the hardware store.

If the doorbell does not ring when you manually complete the circuit, the problem is in the chime or transformer.

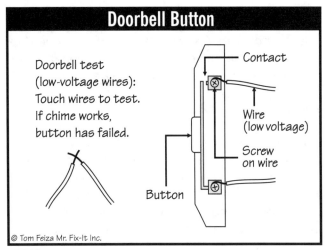

Doorbell Button

Doorbell test (low-voltage wires): Touch wires to test. If chime works, button has failed.

Contact

Wire (low voltage)

Screw on wire

Button

© Tom Feiza Mr. Fix-It Inc.

E010

Check the chime: remove the cover, and take a peek at the chime. Make sure it is level. Vacuum away any dust. You will see a round plunger that needs to move freely in the magnet surrounding it. Look for broken parts or damaged brackets.

After you have checked these items, the next step would be to use a voltmeter to analyze the transformer and wiring. This is a task you may wish to leave to a professional because it involves working with 110-volt power.

Or, for about $20, you can buy a new battery-operated chime/button set that needs no wires. The button is mounted anywhere within 100 feet of the chime. This is a great option when wires are damaged.

Removing Broken Light Bulbs

Sometimes, especially on exterior light fixtures, the glass bulb breaks away from the metal base. There is no best way to remove the base from the fixture, but here are several options.

Before replacing an exterior light, purchase a higher quality bulb with a brass-plated or copper-plated base that will not rust. You could coat the threads with a special dielectric grease available at automotive stores. Dry lubricant, Permatex Anti-Seize, and Vaseline will also work.

To remove the broken base, first make sure the power is off. Wear eye protection. Protect the immediate area from broken glass that may remain on the base. I like to use a needle nose pliers to grab the metal rim of the bulb and twist it. You can also jam the nose of the pliers into the base of the bulb to get a grip. Sometimes opening the pliers inside the metal threads will give you a grip.

If all else fails, use the needle nose pliers to collapse the metal threads until you can remove them.

Folks have phoned my radio show with the following suggestions for removal:

- Use your fingers, protected by heavy gloves.

- Use a fuse puller the same way I use a needle nose pliers.

- Jam into the broken base and turn with:

  – a large cork.

  – a wooden ruler.

  – a wad of white bread (perhaps you need some really heavy Italian bread).

  – a potato.

  – a trimmed paint-stirring stick.

Patio Screen Door Sticks and Rubs

Almost every sliding patio screen door in the world sticks, because few homeowners know they can adjust the rollers that run in the track. You still need to keep the track clean, but adjusting the rollers is the key.

Look at the base of the door; you will see two small Phillips screw heads. They will be above the frame or in the side of the door, near the bottom. Tightening these screws lowers the rollers and lifts the door so the door rolls on the rollers without rubbing the frame.

Most doors have a similar roller adjustment for the top rollers. If the door is tight or bound in the frame, loosen these top screws to allow the door to be raised when lowering rollers and screws. Don't adjust the door to the point that it's squeezed between the top and bottom frame.

When you adjust the rollers, clean the track. Then spray a light lubricant on the frame and track.

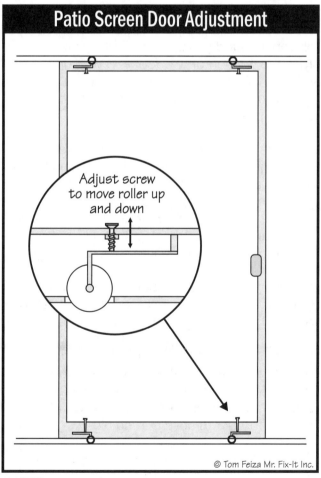

Patio Screen Door Adjustment

Adjust screw to move roller up and down

© Tom Feiza Mr. Fix-It Inc.

M003

Bathroom Paint and Mildew Problems

If your bathroom has problems with moisture, mildew and peeling paint, an exhaust fan is the best solution. You could have a fan installed in the ceiling or, if that's not practical, perhaps you can put a fan directly in an exterior wall.

Reduce bathroom moisture problems by wiping down wet surfaces after a shower and removing wet towels. Keep the bathroom door open after a shower. Consider using a small fan to circulate air into the hall.

You can also use a special paint that resists mildew and peeling. First, kill existing mildew with laundry bleach and water. Scrape away any loose paint, and sand the surfaces smooth. Spackle as needed. Then paint with Zinsser brand Perma-White Bathroom Wall and Ceiling Paint. This is a self-priming paint, so apply two coats.

Zinsser Perma-White is a white semi-gloss paint that can also be tinted. I have used it for several years with great success. It is guaranteed to resist mildew and peeling.

For information on how to contact the manufacturer of Zinsser Perma-White, see the References section.

Proper Venting of a Fireplace

The draft problem with most fireplaces in tightly-built homes is that the fire lacks sufficient air for combustion unless a window is open. Sometimes this produces smoke indoors. Fireplaces in older homes didn't have this problem because leaks around windows, doors and framing provided plenty of air for combustion.

A fireplace with an inadequate air supply can be dangerous. As a fire is starting or going out, it may back up dangerous carbon monoxide into your home. A fire with a strong draft can also interfere with the natural venting of a gas-fired water heater or furnace, causing a backdraft of combustion fumes into the home. Any gas-burning appliance vented by gravity up a chimney can have such a problem.

One good solution is to install small fresh-air vents that bring outside air directly in the firebox. A qualified brickmason, fireplace contractor, or chimney sweep must install such a system; it is definitely not a do-it-yourself project. The vent must penetrate an outside wall and the side or front of the fireplace. The vent may also need to be combined with fireplace doors.

Remember that most natural fireplaces are heat losers when operated in cold weather. Most of the heat goes up the chimney. Fireplaces do work well at removing excessive moisture levels in the winter because they draw lots of air into your home for ventilation (provided a window is open!)

Gutter Leak—a Quick Patch

For quick repair of small holes in the rain gutters, try gutter repair or flashing tape. It's available in most hardware stores and is manufactured by several companies. This thick aluminum foil tape uses a mastic-type adhesive that's almost like thick tar. The tape comes in short rolls either 2" or 3" wide and costs just a few dollars.

To repair the gutter, clean away debris with a wire brush. Wash the area. Once it's dry, apply the tape, rubbing it well into the hole. The aluminum facing

on the back side allows you to rub the tape securely onto the gutter. The foil also protects the patch from sunlight. The adhesive of the tape is thick enough to fill small holes and seams. This repair can easily last several years.

Black Stuff Growing on the Roof

If your roof has light-colored shingles, you may see black streaks on them, especially on the north side. The problem is caused by mildew or fungus growth. There is less sunlight on the north side, so the roof stays damp. Mildew loves a damp surface.

The best way to prevent this algae growth is to provide sunlight and natural ventilation to dry the roof. Obviously, this is not always possible. At least keep all tree branches and leaves about 4 feet away from the roof.

Short of replacing the roof, there is no good quick fix. You could try killing the mildew with a strong solution of laundry bleach and water. Spray or brush the solution on the roof and wait until the areas turn lighter. Then rinse well. You could also use a mildew wash that is sold in paint stores for washing painted wood siding.

Several cautions about using bleach: protect yourself, the gutters, and plant materials. Spilled bleach solution can kill grass and bushes. Use eye and skin protection. Do not walk on the roof while cleaning; it will be slippery and dangerous. Work from a ladder or use other special equipment. Flush the gutters and metal flashing well to prevent damage.

I suggest you hire a professional roofer for the cleaning. You can also purchase a product called Shingle Shield, which consists of zinc strips that are placed under the shingles near the peak of the roof. The zinc reacts with rainwater to produce a chemical that prevents the growth of fungus and mildew. Again, consult a professional roofer. Although the product inhibits the growth of new algae, it may not remove existing algae.

If you ever plan to replace the roof or build a new house, keep in mind that several shingle manufacturers offer shingles with a built-in mildew-resistant chemical.

Masonry Fireplace - Outside Air Supply

Flue tile
Damper
Smoke shelf
Air Supply
Ash door
Basement
Smoke chamber
Mantel
Throat
Firebox
Hearth extension
Ash pit
Chimney cleanout

© Tom Feiza Mr. Fix-It Inc.

F009

Peeling Varnish on Front Door

Many homes feature a beautiful wood front door that is stained and varnished. In time, though, the varnish begins flaking and peeling, especially if there's no storm door.

Sunlight is the culprit. Ultraviolet (UV) rays attack the cellular structure of the wood under the varnish, giving it a "sunburn." Varnish can't stick to damaged wood. UV rays also damage the clear finish.

The best solution is to paint the door. Paint has coloring pigment that blocks UV rays and protects the wood. But if you really like that stained and varnished look, it requires a little work.

First you must sand, scrape or strip the damaged finish. Where the finish is in good condition, you must sand and roughen the surface. If the color of the wood has changed, you will need to stain the door before varnishing.

How far you go with the refinishing depends on the condition of the door. If more than 25% of the finish is damaged, your best bet is to chemically strip the door and start with bare wood.

For a final clear finish, look for a UV-resistant varnish (often called spar varnish or marine finish). This finish is expensive and may only be available in a gloss formula. Follow the specific instructions for your varnish, and don't forget to finish all six areas of the door (front, back, top, bottom and sides).

A final option would be to install a storm door to protect the wood door. There are attractive storm doors available that are mostly glass so your wood door can still show through.

Opening the Garage Door During a Power Outage

Let's say you've got an automatic garage door opener. It's a great convenience, one you take for granted…until the power goes out. Now what do you do?

Your door opener came with an emergency release. This allows you to disconnect the door from the automatic opener unit and open the door manually. The release is a lever attached to the track and door arm connection.

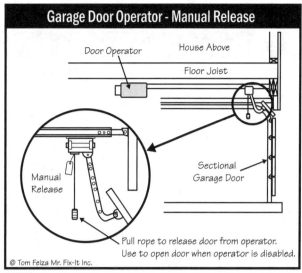

Garage Door Operator - Manual Release

Door Operator · House Above · Floor Joist · Manual Release · Sectional Garage Door

Pull rope to release door from operator. Use to open door when operator is disabled.

© Tom Feiza Mr. Fix-It Inc.

M015

It's a good idea to test this emergency release before you need it, just to make sure it works properly. If you are confused by the procedure even after reading the following instructions, have someone show you how the release operates.

Start with the door closed. This is very, very important. If the springs are not adjusted properly, a door released in the up position may crash to the ground. Open the door manually. You should only need to apply a few pounds of lift, and the door should almost balance at any point as you raise and lower it. If you must use excessive force to open the door or if it closes very quickly, the balancing springs need to be adjusted.

These springs have a tremendous amount of force, so have any necessary adjustment done by a professional. Sometimes the cable and pulley mechanisms also need adjustment or replacement.

If you have a detached garage without a service door (an ordinary-size door that provides alternate access without using the overhead door), you will be locked out of the garage when the power is off and the garage door is down. You need to find the special lock that releases the door from the outside. Hopefully, your door will have this feature–if not, you should add the release.

Find a circular lock at the top panel of the garage door, near the center, where the door connects to the operator track. Open this lock and pull the attached cable through the opening. The cable attaches to the release that detaches the opener. You can now open the door manually.

Clean and Polish Brass Hardware

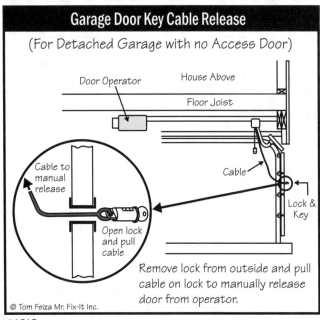

Garage Door Key Cable Release

(For Detached Garage with no Access Door)

Door Operator

House Above

Floor Joist

Cable to manual release

Cable

Lock & Key

Open lock and pull cable

Remove lock from outside and pull cable on lock to manually release door from operator.

© Tom Feiza Mr. Fix-It Inc.

M018

Real polished brass finishes on hardware and plumbing fixtures are preserved by the factory with a coat of clear lacquer finish. The lacquer prevents oxidation and tarnishing. Most of the shiny brass or antique brass finishes we see today feature a plated or painted finish, not real polished brass. You will find real polished brass only on very expensive hardware and old hardware.

If your fixtures have real polished brass, you can preserve the finish. First you must meticulously clean the surface with a cleaner or buffing compound. You can also clean and polish brass with 0000-grade steel wool and a paint stripper.

Once the brass is polished, apply a high-quality, non-abrasive, polymer-based car wax. If you prefer a more durable finish, apply lacquer or exterior polyurethane sealer. Wipe down the surface with lacquer thinner, and handle the surface only with clean cloths. Fingerprints contain skin oils that can damage the finish. After the surface is clean, apply the clear coating.

If your fixture has a brass finish with a polished, clear finish, don't use strong or abrasive cleaners. Instead, apply a coat of paste wax or automotive wax or a product like Faucet Bright to polish and protect the surface.

For information on how to contact the manufacturer of Faucet Bright (T.R. Industries), see the References section.

Chapter 11 – Plumbing Mysteries and Secret Solutions

Garbage Disposal Out to Lunch

Two problems commonly occur with garbage disposals: (1) they make no noise and don't run at all, or (2) they "hum" without spinning. You can perform simple service on the unit yourself.

If the unit no longer "hums," the overload probably is tripped. First, switch the unit off. Then look under the sink and locate a small red button on the base of the unit. This is the electrical reset. Push this button to reset the thermal overload/reset.

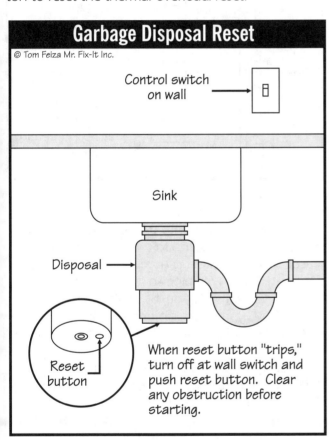

© Tom Feiza Mr. Fix-It Inc.

Garbage Disposal Reset

Control switch on wall

Sink

Disposal

Reset button

When reset button "trips," turn off at wall switch and push reset button. Clear any obstruction before starting.

P013

Switch the unit on. If it "hums" but will not run, turn it off immediately—this indicates a jam in the disposal that needs to be cleared. The jam is what tripped the overload.

Look under the sink for a small L-shaped service wrench that looks like an Allen wrench with a bend on each end. It may be in a small plastic pouch stapled to the side of the cabinet. The bent end of

this tool is a hex wrench. Insert it into the hole you'll find under the disposal, at the center bottom. Work the wrench back and forth for several revolutions until the unit moves freely. As you move the wrench, you are moving the shaft of the disposal and clearing the jam.

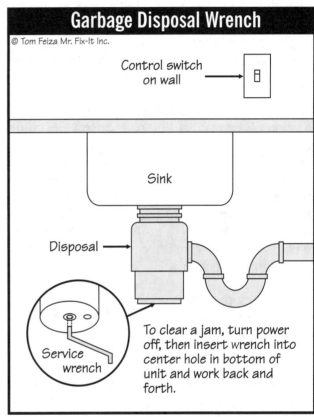

© Tom Feiza Mr. Fix-It Inc.

Garbage Disposal Wrench

Control switch on wall

Sink

Disposal

Service wrench

To clear a jam, turn power off, then insert wrench into center hole in bottom of unit and work back and forth.

P014

If you don't find a service wrench in your cabinet, you can buy one at any hardware store. You can also free the disposal by working from above with a socket on the end of a long extension. The socket lets you turn a hex nut atop the shaft in the disposal.

Now look inside the disposal from above for any foreign objects and remove them with tongs. Run water and start the unit.

Frozen Pipes at the Kitchen Sink

A kitchen sink on an outside wall may be vulnerable to freezing during cold, windy conditions. The water supply and drain lines routed through the exterior wall can easily freeze when exposed to a small cold-air leak.

If the pipes are frozen, turn off the water supply, because when the ice begins to melt there may be a major leak. Thaw the pipes by opening the sink cabinet doors and directing a fan or a small space heater into the cabinet. In the basement or crawl space below the sink, place a small heater or heat lamp to warm the pipes.

You can also warm the pipes with a hair dryer or heat gun, but don't ever use a tool with an open flame. Take your time, and warm the pipes slowly. Periodically turn on the water supply to check for flow. Once the pipes are thawed, turn on the water and check for leaks. Remember that a small leak could be hidden in the wall.

You should also seek a permanent solution to the situation by looking for tiny holes that allow cold air to blow in and freeze a pipe. Start in the basement on a sunny day. Keep the basement lights turned off. See if sunlight leaks through the basement wall, sill area, foundation overhangs, or lower edge of the house siding. Caulk and fill any gaps; some may need to be filled from the outside. Remove existing insulation to expose the wood framing for inspection.

Next, make sure there is good insulation in the sill area above the foundation wall. Fill the area with tight-fitting fiberglass. Pack all areas between the outside framing and the top of the basement wall.

Insulate the supply pipe with plastic foam insulation (available at most building supply centers). Trim the insulation for a tight fit, and tape all joints.

If the problem persists, you may need to open kitchen sink cabinet doors during cold weather to allow for warm air circulation. You could also place a fan or small heater in the basement to help move and warm the air around the pipes.

As a last resort during very cold weather, leave the water running in a trickle at the fixture that freezes. The water circulation will warm the pipe and prevent freezing. This is a desperate measure, though, because it wastes a natural resource and puts an unnecessary load on sewage treatment facilities.

Frozen Sump Pump Lines

If your sump pump discharges through a 1-1/4" plastic pipe exposed to the weather, it could be vulnerable to freezing. A frozen pipe prompts the sump pump to run continuously until it fails, and then you can get water in the basement.

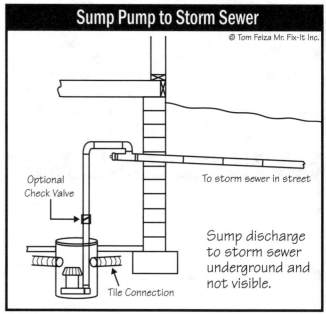

Sump Pump to Storm Sewer

© Tom Feiza Mr. Fix-It Inc.

Optional Check Valve

To storm sewer in street

Sump discharge to storm sewer underground and not visible.

Tile Connection

B056

The best alternative is to have a storm sewer line installed underground into the basement and then connect the sump pump to this line, but this is not practical with an existing home. Your next best bet is to route the 1-1/4" pipe so it exits the basement at about 12" above grade if possible. Extend the pipe 12" away from your home and connect it to a 4"- to 6"-wide plastic drain tile, plastic pipe, or large downspout. Extend this large pipe at a steep pitch so it discharges 6 to 8 feet away from your house. Water will drain through this large pipe with little chance of plugging and freezing.

It's important to pitch the exposed 1-1/4" pipe in the right direction as it exits the house. The "right" pitch depends on whether your sump pump has a check valve. If there is a check valve, it will be on the vertical discharge pipe just above the pump. The check valve is slightly larger than the pipe. If the pipe is steel, the check valve is screwed in; if the pipe is plastic, the check valve is attached with rubber hose connections When the pump turns off, the check valve is the part that "clunks" shut.

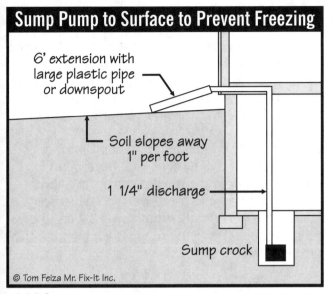

Sump Pump to Surface to Prevent Freezing

6' extension with large plastic pipe or downspout

Soil slopes away 1" per foot

1 1/4" discharge

Sump crock

© Tom Feiza Mr. Fix-It Inc.

B006

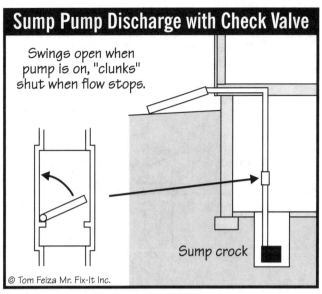

Sump Pump Discharge with Check Valve

Swings open when pump is on, "clunks" shut when flow stops.

Sump crock

© Tom Feiza Mr. Fix-It Inc.

B007

If your sump pump has a check valve, pitch the pipe away from your home; otherwise the check valve will trap water in the pipe, where it could freeze. If your pump doesn't have a check valve, pitch the pipe slightly toward the inside, allowing water to siphon back into the crock when the pump turns off.

Thumping from the Sump Pump

The check valve is the culprit when you hear a loud noise as the sump pump shuts off. Every time the pump runs, it pushes open the check valve. When the pump stops, the valve slams shut with a thump. This can be annoying at times.

Some clunking is normal as the check valve stops water from siphoning back down the discharge pipe into the crock. If there is a long pipe run, this siphoning water could fill the crock. The pump would start up again to remove the same water. This could happen over and over. So—the check valve is important.

On a short pipe run that goes directly up and out of the basement with no horizontal section more than 5 feet long, it's less likely that water will flow back into the crock. In this case, you could remove the check valve. You could also experiment with adding a small hole or vent pipe at the top of the pipe run outside your home. This small hole will allow air into the top of the pipe and break the siphoning. The water below the vent will still flow back into the crock.

Or, consider installing a newer check valve that may be quieter.

Finally, try to isolate the piping from the wood framing of your home. If the piping is firmly attached to the wood framing or wedged against the framing, the wood amplifies sounds and vibrations. Hang the piping with wire or metal straps and add foam insulation between the piping and the straps.

If Your Sump Pump Never Runs...

In some houses, the sump pump never seems to run. Is this a problem?

If your basement walls and floor are always dry, even during heavy rains, you don't need to do anything. Natural drainage around your home must be preventing water from reaching the drain tile system and sump crock. Test the pump several times a year by filling the crock with a hose until the pump turns on. That way, you know the pump will work if water ever does enter the system.

However, if there is dampness in your basement and your sump crock remains dry, there may be a problem with the tile system. Water around the foundation should reach the crock and get pumped out. This situation should be checked by a consultant or contractor because of the potential for excessive pressure that can cause extensive basement wall problems.

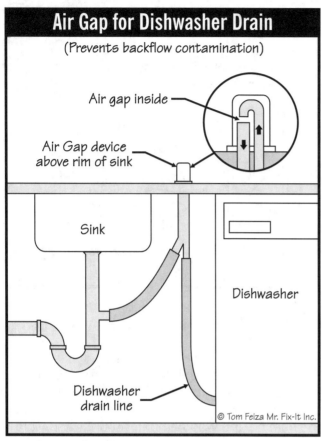

Air Gap for Dishwasher Drain
(Prevents backflow contamination)

Air gap inside

Air Gap device above rim of sink

Sink

Dishwasher

Dishwasher drain line

© Tom Feiza Mr. Fix-It Inc.

PO23

Leaking Air Gap ("Chrome Mushroom") on the Sink

The "chrome mushroom" next to the kitchen faucet is an air gap for the dishwasher drain line. When the dishwasher pumps out the dirty water, it flows up to this air gap, makes a U-turn, and is routed down a drain line. This "air gap" provides a physical break that keeps dirty water from flowing back into the dishwasher.

Without an air gap, the drain line from the dishwasher would be connected directly to the garbage disposal or the side of the drain line below the sink. If the sink or disposal ever backs up with dirty water, this line could carry contaminated water into the dishwasher.

If the air gap leaks, remove the chrome or plastic cover and clean the plastic parts. The cover simply lifts off. You will find a plastic U-shaped tube that routes water back down a drain line. At the opening in the U, look for deposits that need to be removed.

Toilet Running at Night

Ah, yes! The mysterious toilet that runs in the night. If you hear this happening and want to check what's going on, place a few drops of food coloring in the tank, and soon color will appear in the bowl. This indicates a slight leak in the flush valve.

Water is slowly draining from the tank into the bowl, then down the sewer line. Because the excessive water in the bowl automatically flows through the trap into the sewer, you never see a leak. As the water in the tank slowly lowers, the float goes down and the fill valve automatically fills the tank.

Check the fit of the flush valve to its seat. There may be a flapper valve or a ball valve. Dirt or rust that accumulates on the mating surfaces can cause a small leak; wipe the parts with a coarse cloth. Also, the parts may be out of alignment, or the rubber of the flush valve may be cracked and leaking. Replace the valve if it is damaged.

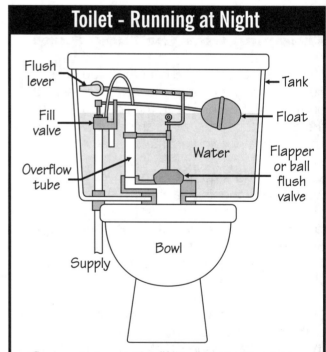

Toilet – Running at Night

Flush lever

Tank

Fill valve

Float

Water

Flapper or ball flush valve

Overflow tube

Supply

Bowl

The mysterious toilet "filling" during the night: There is a leak at the flush valve and water flows into bowl and down to sewer. Then tank mysteriously refills.

© Tom Feiza Mr. Fix-It Inc.

PO24

Toilet with Poor Flush

You could try several things on a stubborn toilet:

1. Pour 2 or 3 gallons of water from a pail directly into the bowl. If it flushes well, the drain and vent are probably clear. If it does not flush, clear the trap with a plunger or snake. As a last resort, remove the toilet to clear the trap, or have a plumber clear the blockage.

2. Make sure that the water level in the tank is at the water mark or just below the overflow tube.

3. If there are rocks or bottles in the tank, throw them at the former homeowner. (Just joking!) Remove them, because they displace some of the water needed for a good flush.

4. Check the operation of the flush valve. Is it opening fully and staying open until all the water is out of the tank? Some valve balls or flappers become waterlogged and close too early. Hold the valve open and check the flush.

5. Check for a jet flush hole—a 3/4" opening in the front edge of the toilet trap. Water flows from the jet to aid the flow down the trap. If there is a jet flush hole, it should be free of deposits. If necessary, use acid cleaner (available at plumbing supply stores) and a stick to clear the opening.

6. On an old toilet, the holes around the rim and the chamber leading to the holes may be blocked. Use acid cleaner to clean this chamber and the holes. Follow specific instructions on the product you buy. The usual procedure is to plug the holes with plumber's putty, pour acid into the overflow tube, and allow the acid to sit for a while to dissolve deposits.

7. Calling a plumber or installing a new toilet is my last suggestion.

Banging Pipes (Water Hammer)

Why do water pipes bang?

You might hear thumping or banging when water stops filling the toilet tank...or when you turn water off quickly at certain faucets...or after the washing machine draws water.

You may need a plumber to fix this problem, but first you can try a simple trick. Your plumbing system probably has air cushions. These cushions or shock absorber chambers, located near the laundry, the kitchen, or the main valve, were initially filled with air so that when a valve closed quickly, the force of the water movement bounced against the air cushion. This prevented the hammering.

Now these air cushions are probably filled with water. To solve the problem, you need to drain your plumbing system. Start by turning off the main water supply. Then open all the faucets in your home. Air will be drawn into the upper faucets. Water will drain from the lower faucets.

When water stops flowing, slowly fill the system by opening the main valve slightly. Walk through your home, closing each valve as air is eliminated and a solid stream of water flows through that faucet. After you have closed all the faucets, open the main valve fully.

Now you should have an air cushion in the shock absorber chambers. If this does not do the trick, call a plumber. Remember that sediment and air may come out of the faucets for a short time after you've performed this procedure.

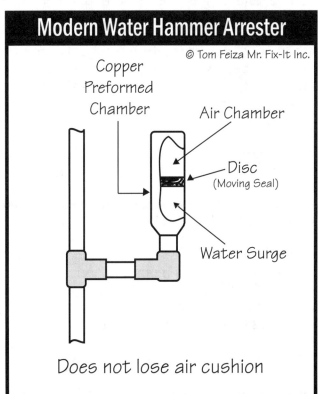

Modern Water Hammer Arrester

© Tom Feiza Mr. Fix-It Inc.

Copper Preformed Chamber

Air Chamber

Disc (Moving Seal)

Water Surge

Does not lose air cushion

P032

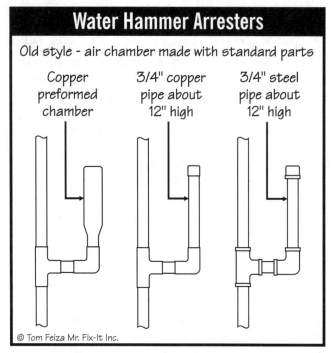

Water Hammer Arresters

Old style - air chamber made with standard parts

Copper preformed chamber

3/4" copper pipe about 12" high

3/4" steel pipe about 12" high

© Tom Feiza Mr. Fix-It Inc.

PO15

The water-hammer effect can be especially severe with automatic washing machines that have electrically operated water valves which may close very quickly. If your washer doesn't have shock absorber chambers, a plumber can install them. To check whether yours does, look for a 12" tube or a 4" chamber extending above the hose bib connections for the water.

Also, check that piping to the washer is properly supported, because the banging can be compounded when pipes move around and hit wood framing or other objects. Adding a support may help correct the problem.

Don't ignore the problem. Eventually, water hammer can cause a break. Have a qualified plumber modify your system.

Two Sump Pumps?

Homeowners sometimes wonder whether their basement has two sump pumps. That's not really the case. The answer involves understanding the two types of water that must be removed from the home: wastewater and groundwater.

Your home's sanitary waste system routes wastewater from toilets, sinks, tubs and drains to a septic system or a sewage treatment plant. In homes with a private septic system, the main line to the septic

tank usually exits the basement about 4 feet up from the basement floor.

Most wastewater flows by gravity through pipes to this main exit. However, water from the basement floor drain and any basement laundry tubs flows into a crock and must be pumped up to the main line. This is accomplished by a small pump called a lift pump or a gray water sewage ejector that looks like a sump pump.

In older homes, this lift pump may have a loose-fitting cover, just like a sump pump. It may be a pedestal pump with the motor above the water level or a submersible pump with the pump and motor below the water. Newer homes will have a tightly sealed crock and a submersible pump.

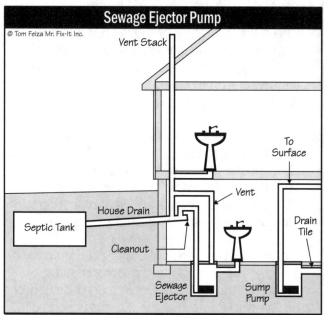

Sewage Ejector Pump

© Tom Feiza Mr. Fix-It Inc.

Vent Stack

To Surface

Vent

House Drain

Septic Tank

Drain Tile

Cleanout

Sewage Ejector

Sump Pump

PO21

The other pump in your basement is a sump pump. Groundwater flows through a drain tile system below the basement floor and near the footings. As this groundwater collects in the sump pump crock, the sump pump ejects it up to the surface or to a storm sewer line. Eventually, storm sewers discharge to rivers and streams, not to the septic system or the municipal sewer treatment plant.

So, you may have two pumps—a lift pump removing sanitary sewer water, and a sump pump removing clear water. I suggest you check these pumps periodically to make sure they are moving water. The newer type of lift pump in a covered sump pit should be tightly sealed with cover gaskets and screws.

One word of caution: there is always an exception. In a very large basement, or a remodeled or repaired basement, you may find two sump pumps. The key to determining the type of pump is the source or type of wastewater and the final destination of the water.

"Slippery" Water

If you are accustomed to unsoftened water and move into a home with a water softener, you might find that softened water feels slippery, especially in the shower. This can take a little adjustment on your part. However, with softened water, clothes will be easier to wash and dishes will have fewer water spots. There is no method that allows you to partially soften water and make it less slippery.

Dripping Water Heater

On the side of the water heater is a temperature/pressure valve with a handle. This valve is designed as a safety measure—it will open if the water heater overheats and creates excessive pressure.

When the valve develops a leak, though, water runs down the tube and drips on the floor. A leaky valve should be replaced. The leak can get worse at any time. More seriously, the constant flow of water may corrode or seal shut the valve with hard water scale, and that creates a potential danger. A new valve costs about $20 and takes less than 30 minutes to install.

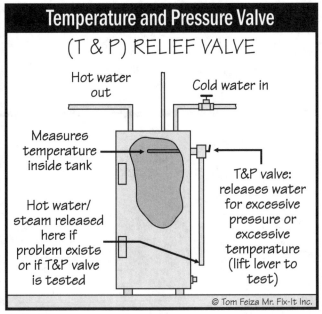

Temperature and Pressure Valve
(T & P) RELIEF VALVE

Hot water out

Cold water in

Measures temperature inside tank

Hot water/ steam released here if problem exists or if T&P valve is tested

T&P valve: releases water for excessive pressure or excessive temperature (lift lever to test)

© Tom Feiza Mr. Fix-It Inc.

W001

Dripping Valves—Interior

Sometimes an indoor valve—for example, a basement valve for an outside water connection—develops a slow drip. How can you fix the leak?

Examine the valve and you'll see that the handle is mounted on a round brass stem or shaft. The shaft enters the body of the valve through a hole in a hex nut. If you tighten this hex nut (packing nut), the leak should stop. You only need to tighten this packing nut slightly to stop the drip.

If you overtighten the packing nut, the valve will be hard to operate and you may not be able to turn the handle at all. If the valve is hard to operate, just loosen the nut.

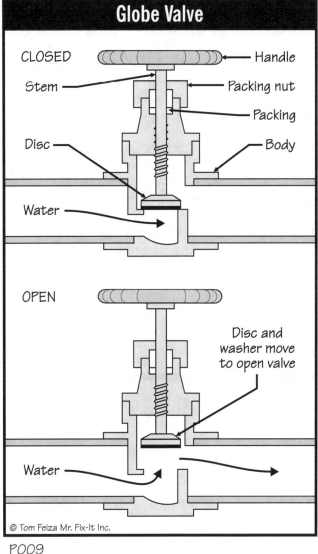

Globe Valve

CLOSED — Handle

Stem

Packing nut

Packing

Disc

Body

Water

OPEN

Disc and washer move to open valve

Water

© Tom Feiza Mr. Fix-It Inc.

P009

Caution

> If the valve has a buildup of corrosion and hard water scale inside, tightening the nut may not solve the problem. You may need to dismantle the valve and replace a packing ring or washer below the nut. To rebuild the valve, you may need to clean the stem and/or replace parts.

Dripping Garden Hoses

Many of us have problems with garden hoses that leak at the fittings. This is easy to fix with the new products on the market. By paying attention to leaks and spending a few bucks and a few minutes, we can conserve water—a precious resource.

The most common problem is a missing or hardened washer. Open the fitting and look for the washer inside the female end of the fitting. If the washer is hard or damaged, replace it with a new washer.

While you have the fitting open, look at the male end of the fitting. It should have a relatively flat surface to contact the washer. Both of the threaded ends should be relatively round.

If the threaded ends are out of round, or if they're bent or cracked, replace them. You can buy great replacement ends at the hardware store. Cut off the old fitting with a sharp knife and take it to the hardware store to match the inside hose diameter with the new fitting. The best fittings are plastic with small plastic clamps. You slip the fitting into the hose and tighten down the clamp. If you have trouble slipping the hose over the fitting, warm it with hot water.

If there's a break or split in the hose, cut out the bad area and buy a fitting to connect the hose sections.

The Name Game: Hose Bib

"Hose bib" is a plumbing term for an exterior hose faucet or hose connection. I don't know where the term orginated, but a hose bib is just a faucet.

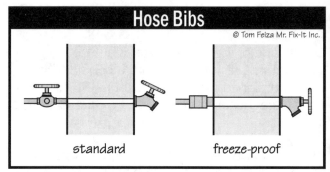

Hose Bibs
© Tom Feiza Mr. Fix-It Inc.

standard   freeze-proof

P010

Numerous plumbing leak problems are addressed at the end of Chapter 9 – Emergencies and Simple Solutions.

Chapter 12 – Electric Mysteries & Secret Solutions

Dishwasher Will Not Run

Let's say you've just moved into your home. You load the dishwasher for the first time, and it won't run.

Before you complain to the former homeowner or call a repair technician, try this:

There may be a switch on the wall above the kitchen counter. It looks like a light switch, but it turns electricity to the dishwasher on and off to prevent the dishwasher from being turned on when you don't want it on (for instance, when a toddler starts playing with the controls).

Every homeowner should know about this mystery switch. Even I had to learn about it from somebody else—and I'm "Mr. Fix-It."

Fuses or Breakers: Which Is Better?

An older fuse system that is working well need not be replaced merely to convert to modern circuit breakers; it is a safe system. However, replacing it with circuit breakers will increase the value of your home and may be needed for increased capacity.

Both systems have pros and cons. A fuse is the best protection for an overload—it will trip every time. A circuit breaker, on the other hand, is an electro-mechanical device that has a very slight chance of failure to trip.

On some fuse systems, a fuse can be replaced with a fuse that's too large, creating a potential overload of wiring.

Dishwasher - Water & Electrical Supply

From Under Sink
Electrical disconnect above counter
Dishwasher
Valve
Hot Water Pipe
Water Hammer Arrester
© Tom Feiza Mr. Fix-It Inc.

From Basement or Crawl
Electrical disconnect
Water Hammer Arrester
Dishwasher
Hot Water Pipe
Valve
Flexible Pipe

PO61

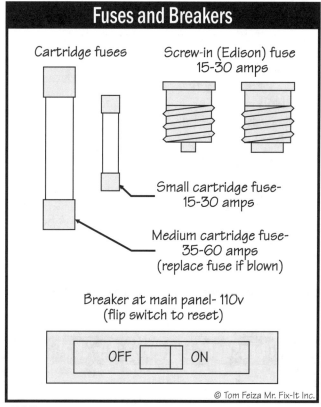

Fuses and Breakers

Cartridge fuses

Screw-in (Edison) fuse 15-30 amps

Small cartridge fuse- 15-30 amps

Medium cartridge fuse- 35-60 amps (replace fuse if blown)

Breaker at main panel- 110v (flip switch to reset)

OFF | ON

© Tom Feiza Mr. Fix-It Inc.

EO11

If you are concerned about your system, hire an electrician or home inspector to do an inspection that includes:

- checking the wiring for signs of overheating.

- tightening of connections.

- inspecting the main feed and ground.

- checking that all fuses and breakers are matched to the wire size they feed.

- inspecting feeds and grounds to subpanels.

- checking several typical outlets for proper wiring.

After this inspection, you can decide whether a new system is warranted. Systems are usually replaced when increased electrical service is required; 60-amp fuse systems have limited capacity.

Problems with Fluorescent Lights

Always switch off the fixture before you remove lamps (bulbs) from a fluorescent light.

Humming

Humming or buzzing in a fluorescent light fixture is usually caused by a ballast that's poorly built or improperly mounted. The hum occurs as electrical current moves through metal plates in the ballast.

With the power off, open the fixture. The ballast is a metal box with wires leading to it. (In a 4'-long fixture, the ballast measures about 2" by 3" by 10".) Make sure that the mounting screws are tight. If there are vibration-isolation spacers, check them. Identify the problem by comparing this bad fixture to any similar quiet fixtures you may have. It may be necessary to replace the ballast.

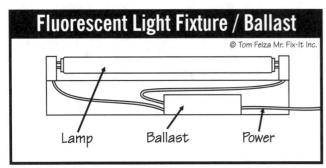

Fluorescent Light Fixture / Ballast

© Tom Feiza Mr. Fix-It Inc.

Lamp   Ballast   Power

EO12

Also check to make sure that the metal housing of the fixture is not amplifying the sound. You may need to change the mounting.

Flashes and Intermittent Light

When a fluorescent fixture flashes and glows but don't fully light, or if one bulb works and the other doesn't, try these steps.

The electrical connections at the end of the bulbs (technically called lamps or tubes) may be dirty. Remove the lamps and inspect the the metal connectors at either end. If they are dirty, rub with a coarse cloth. If there is visible corrosion, lightly sand the metal until it is clean and shiny. Re-install the lamps and test the fixture.

If they still don't light, try replacing them. Worn lamps will have black marks inside, near the ends. Some of the white coating inside the lamps may be falling off. When a fixture has more than one lamp, replace all the lamps at once. Note the identification numbers on the ends of the lamps so you can buy matching lamps.

Also, inspect the lamps' mounting brackets. They may be loose or corroded; the metal parts may be damaged. Make sure that the metal conductors inside the brackets securely contact the metal tips of the lamps.

If the light still does not work, it may have a faulty ballast or starter. This type of replacement is best left to a professional, and often it's not worth the time and effort on a cheap shop-type fixture.

Humming Ceiling Fan

That humming may be due to a light dimmer switch rather than a motor control rheostat for the fan's motor. Replace the light dimmer with a motor control rheostat recommended or provided by the fan manufacturer. And don't let Uncle Joe add the dimmer next time.

Dryer or Range Plug Will Not Fit

Electrical codes are changing related to 240-volt cords and outlets for large appliances like ranges and electric clothes dryers. The 240-volt outlets are the big clunky ones at the stove and clothes dryer. Around the year 2002, the national code for 240-volt outlets began requiring a grounded outlet; the new outlets and cords have a four-prong connection. Older systems had a non-grounded three-prong connection. The new requirements provide an additional level of safety because now the appliance is grounded—a good thing.

If you move older equipment or purchase new equipment, you may encounter a compatibility problem. Most municipalities now require the four-prong plug, and any compatibility issues should be corrected by installing a four-prong plug or a four-prong outlet. An electrician should do this work.

240 Volt Outlet - With and Without Ground

30 amp Non-Grounded	30 amp Grounded

- Older system
- 3 wire

- Newer system
- 4 wire
- Required around 2002

© Tom Feiza Mr. Fix-It Inc.

E021

It will take several years to achieve consistency as homeowners replace appliances and municipalities adopt the new code requirements.

Electrical Outlets Not Working

It's a mystery—the exterior outlets worked the last time you tried them. Today they don't work. The breaker is not tripped, and everything else seems to be working fine.

It's the ground fault circuit interrupter (GFCI) mystery, a common problem. GFCI outlets are often used to protect additional outlets wired downstream from the GFCI. This allows one device to protect several outlets but can create confusion in locating the reset. You will find the situation in most newer homes.

Often, two GFCI outlets protect all the kitchen outlets. A GFCI in the garage may protect all the exterior outlets. A bath GFCI may protect all the bathrooms, the garage and the exterior. In newer homes, numerous GFCI outlets are used, and in older homes you never know where to look, so start in the bathroom, which is the most likely location.

In older homes, you will often find a GFCI breaker in the main electrical panel, so don't forget to look there. At times you may find a GFCI outlet in the basement ceiling framing or near the main electrical panel.

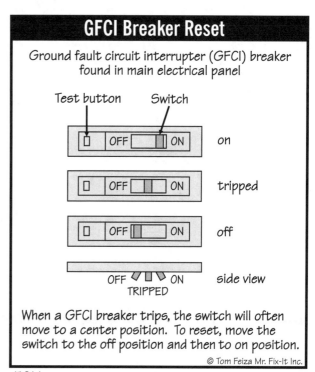

GFCI Breaker Reset

Ground fault circuit interrupter (GFCI) breaker found in main electrical panel

Test button   Switch

on

tripped

off

side view

When a GFCI breaker trips, the switch will often move to a center position. To reset, move the switch to the off position and then to on position.

© Tom Feiza Mr. Fix-It Inc.

E014

The GFCI protects you from electrical shock. It is a sensitive electrical device that quickly detects low-level current leakage. If there is leakage, the current could flow through you and give you an electric shock. The GFCI trips before a significant shock occurs. By the way, a 15-amp or 20-amp breaker or fuse protects the circuit from overheating and fire—it does not protect you from a shock.

GFCI Protects Outlets Downstream

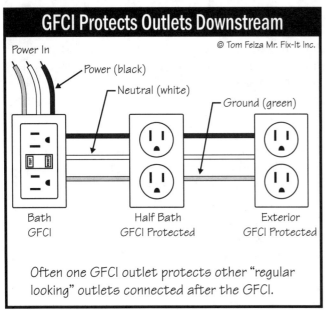

Power In

© Tom Feiza Mr. Fix-It Inc.

Power (black)

Neutral (white)

Ground (green)

Bath
GFCI

Half Bath
GFCI Protected

Exterior
GFCI Protected

Often one GFCI outlet protects other "regular looking" outlets connected after the GFCI.

EO22

Bath Outlets Not Working

Often one ground fault circuit interrupter (GFCI) outlet protects outlets downstream on the same electrical circuit. Check all the bathroom outlets and the main electrical panel for a tripped GFCI. If the GFCI trips a second time, have an electrician check the problem or stop using the electrical device that is causing the problem.

(See also Electrical Outlets Not Working.)

Chapter 13 – Heating, Air Conditioning & Ventilation

Attic Fan

On hot days during the summer, you might hear a faint noise coming from the attic. It's not your imagination—it's the attic ventilation fan.

This fan is designed to remove excessive heat from the attic during hot summer days. The fan unit includes an electric box with a commercial-type thermostat that must be set with a screwdriver. It will be set at about 100 degrees F.

The sun's rays can easily heat the attic to 100 degrees. At that point, the fan turns on, drawing cooler air through the attic vents. When the attic temperature drops below 100 degrees, the fan turns off.

Cooling the attic in this way limits the buildup of heat that would otherwise flow through the ceiling into your home's living spaces.

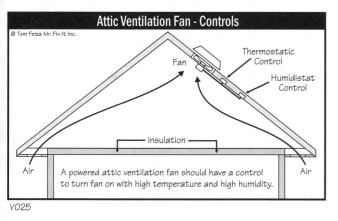

Attic Ventilation Fan - Controls

© Tom Feiza Mr. Fix-It Inc.

Fan

Thermostatic Control

Humidistat Control

Insulation

Air   Air

A powered attic ventilation fan should have a control to turn fan on with high temperature and high humidity.

V025

Cool Air from the Furnace

If you were accustomed to an older furnace and now have a high-efficiency gas furnace, the air coming from the grills might feel cool and drafty.

Modern energy-efficient furnaces convert as much as 95% of gas energy into heat. Very old furnaces converted as little as 60% of the energy into heat.

This increase in efficiency means that newer furnaces can't heat the air to a high temperature the way the old furnaces did. To further increase efficiency, newer furnaces must also move more air across the heat exchanger surfaces. You may feel a

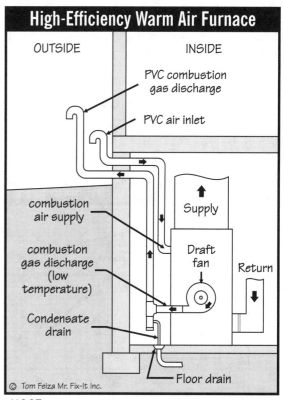

High-Efficiency Warm Air Furnace

OUTSIDE   INSIDE

PVC combustion gas discharge

PVC air inlet

combustion air supply

Supply

combustion gas discharge (low temperature)

Draft fan

Return

Condensate drain

Floor drain

© Tom Feiza Mr. Fix-It Inc.

H003

draft as this cooler air discharges at a greater speed from the supply duct grills.

You could install plastic deflectors on the grills to redirect the air flow. When the air is not blowing across your skin, you will not feel the draft.

If you are still uncomfortable, ask your contractor to check whether the furnace was set up properly and that the fan speed is set correctly. If you notice a draft at one particular register, ask the contractor to lower the flow to that register.

Some top-of-the-line furnaces also have variable speed fans (variable air flow) and variable heating rates to adjust for this "draft" problem. Have the contractor check that all settings are correct.

Most people don't find the new furnaces objectionable once they understand the operating principles. You may just need to get used to the cooler air discharge while you enjoy the 35% energy savings. And because this furnace uses less energy, now you can afford to set the thermostat higher for greater comfort.

One Cold Room

Suppose you notice, during your first heating season in a home, that one of the rooms is always cold and that there is little air flow through the heating duct even when the grill is fully open. The previous owner may have closed the heating supply duct to this room.

In the basement, look at the main warm-air supply duct. This duct originates directly above the furnace. Often it is a rectangular duct running down the center of the basement.

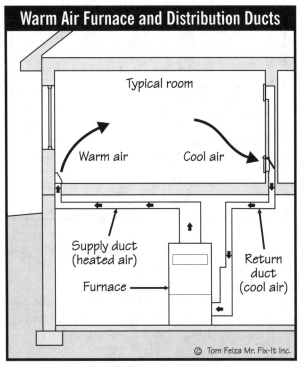

Warm Air Furnace and Distribution Ducts

Typical room

Warm air   Cool air

Supply duct (heated air)

Furnace

Return duct (cool air)

© Tom Feiza Mr. Fix-It Inc.

H004

This rectangular duct may branch off into smaller circular ducts serving individual room registers. Where the round duct is attached to the rectangular main, look for evidence of a duct damper—a wing nut around the end of a 1/4" threaded rod. There will be a screwdriver slot in the end of the rod.

If the slot is perpendicular to the small round duct, the damper is closed. If the slot is parallel to the duct, the damper is open. You can loosen the wing nut and change the position of the damper. Then secure it by retightening the wing nut.

The threaded rod might have a lever that indicates whether the damper is open or closed. Some rods have flat sides parallel to the duct damper.

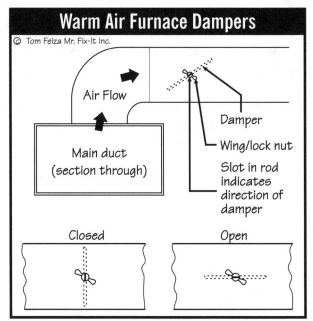

Warm Air Furnace Dampers

© Tom Feiza Mr. Fix-It Inc.

Air Flow

Damper

Wing/lock nut

Slot in rod indicates direction of damper

Main duct (section through)

Closed   Open

H020

Some room ducts may be rectangular rather than round, but they will have similar rods and controls.

If opening the damper solves the problem, great. If the room is still cold, you may need to partially close other dampers to direct more air to the cold room. Often, dampers fit loosely, and even when fully closed, they can leak substantial amounts of air.

Close Storm Windows with Air Conditioning

If possible, close storm windows when running your air conditioner. For some homes, this is impossible, because the storms are replaced with screens for the summer.

Adding that one pane of glass to a standard window increases the R value (insulation value) from 1 to 2, doubling the resistance to heat loss. The storm also helps stop infiltration of hot, moist air into your home. Closing blinds to block out the sun also greatly reduces heat gain.

Using storms in the summer is less important than using them in the winter because of temperature differentials. In the winter we can experience temperature differences between the inside air and outside air of 70 degrees or more. During the summer, the difference is rarely more than 20 degrees. However, storms are still important in summer, because running the air conditioner is more expensive per energy unit than running the furnace.

Clean the Heating Ducts

Cleaning the ductwork is not necessary in a newer home unless someone in the family has a respiratory problem. But in homes that are more than 25 years old, cleaning the ducts is a good idea, especially if you are considering a new furnace.

New energy-efficient furnaces move more air through the ductwork, stirring up old dust. Also, cleaning the ductwork helps keep the furnace clean, which prolongs its life and produces greater energy efficiency. You could clean the ductwork before you install the furnace or as the furnace is installed, when the ducts will be opened.

For a free booklet about cleaning ducts, contact the Environmental Protection Agency (see EPA listing under Government Agencies in the References chapter).

Dehumidifier Freeze-Up

Many homeowners run a dehumidifier in the basement. Sometimes the dehumidifier will freeze up and stop running. There are several causes to investigate.

The humidifier could have a dirty coil. Dirt slows air flow and limits heat transfer, causing the coil to ice up.

After disconnecting the power, clean the coils with a vacuum. Remember that there are two sets of coils to clean. Inspect the fan (you might need to remove a cover to reach it), because the fan blades may also need to be washed.

It may be too cold in the basement. You can raise the temperature by providing heat to the basement. You can also keep the dehumidifier far above the floor so it operates in warmer air.

Finally, the unit may have a refrigeration or control problem that needs to be evaluated by a professional.

Leaks at the Air Conditioner

A leak can occur at the air conditioner cooling coil (evaporator coil) for several reasons. The condensate drain pan may be damaged or tipped, the drain line may be blocked, or the drain line may be disconnected. This type of leak occurs silently, and a significant amount of water can cause extensive rot and mold problems as materials near the leak remain wet over a long period of time.

When an air conditioner operates, interior air cools as it flows across the cold coil. As the air is cooled, moisture condenses on the coil, drips into a pan and is drained with tubing or piping to a sewer connection or to the exterior.

If the air conditioning system is part of a forced air heating system, the leak can cause extensive damage to the heating system. The leak often starts at the top of the furnace, near the condensate pan. Water will rust the housing. It can damage the heat

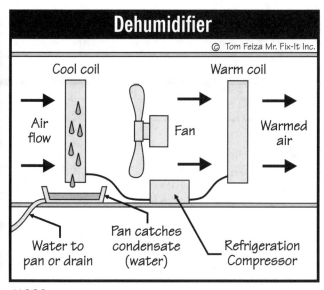

Dehumidifier

© Tom Feiza Mr. Fix-It Inc.

Cool coil

Warm coil

Air flow

Fan

Warmed air

Water to pan or drain

Pan catches condensate (water)

Refrigeration Compressor

HO22

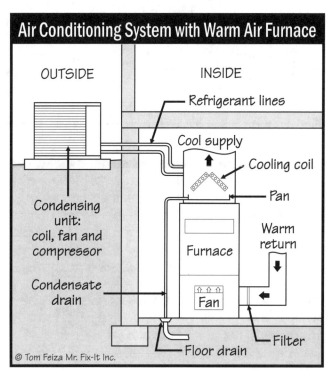

Air Conditioning System with Warm Air Furnace

OUTSIDE

INSIDE

Refrigerant lines

Cool supply

Cooling coil

Pan

Condensing unit: coil, fan and compressor

Furnace

Warm return

Condensate drain

Fan

Floor drain

Filter

© Tom Feiza Mr. Fix-It Inc.

A001

exchanger, controls and electronic circuit boards. A wet circuit board will disable the air conditioner and require an expensive repair. When a leak occurs, it will appear on the concrete floor and run toward the floor drain.

If the air conditioning system is located in the attic, significant damage can occur to drywall and wood framing below the unit. Water can follow tubing, framing and piping; it may soak hidden areas of framing and the floor structure. Water can wet the concrete slab below the framing, and the damage might only become visible once rot has occurred and the carpet is wet.

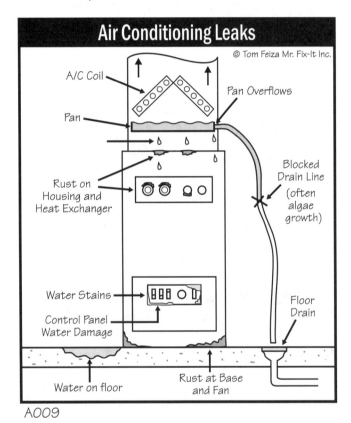

A009

For air conditioners located in the attic, it is always wise to have a second drain pan with a separate drain line under the entire unit. If the normal condensate pan and drain line leak, the second pan will catch and remove the water. If you have such a system, keep an eye on the second drain line; water will only drain from this line if there is a problem.

You should understand how the condensate water flows in your home and where the piping or tubing drains. If the unit is operating and there is no water draining from the tubing, you know you have a problem.

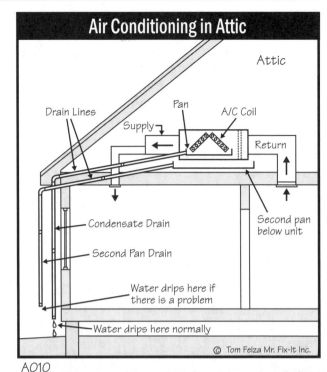

A010

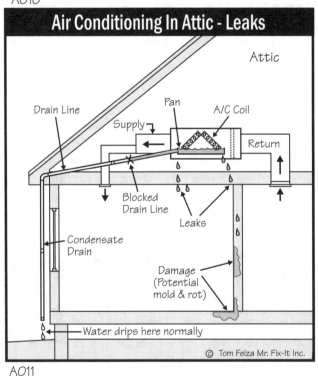

A011

Condensate drain lines are often just flexible tubing that can easily be blocked by algae and debris. This is a big problem in warmer climates where the tubing is warmer and algae can form quickly in the line.

The fix for a blocked condensate drain line is simple: replace it or flush it so it drains properly. In warm climates it may be wise to flush the line with a bleach and water solution to help control algae.

Chapter 14 – Water, Ice and Steam Everywhere

Snow and Water in the Attic

Heavy wind during snowstorms or rain storms can carry snow or rain through attic vents at times. This is normal. Often, the moisture will evaporate before you notice it. However, if there are water stains on the insulation or ceilings, you should have a roofer move or modify the vent.

Placing a pan below the vent is a good option for an occasional small leak. The water in the pan will evaporate without damage to your home. Don't try to get by using a pan for a large leak, though—it could lead to a large problem.

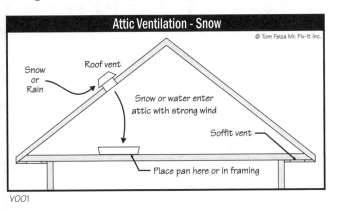

Attic Ventilation - Snow
© Tom Feiza Mr. Fix-It Inc.

Snow or Rain

Roof vent

Snow or water enter attic with strong wind

Soffit vent

Place pan here or in framing

V001

Ice Blocking the Gutters

In winter, ice can build up in the gutters, forming a condition called an ice dam.

The process is triggered by excessive heat in the attic. The heat warms the roof deck, causing rooftop snow to melt. The slushy melted snow flows down the roof and into the gutters. Since gutters aren't warmed by the escaping heat, they remain cold, and the slush refreezes there. As the process continues, the ice gets thicker, forming a dam.

Eventually, water ponds behind the ice (the same way water pools behind a river dam), and this water can leak through an asphalt shingle roof. Roof shingles are designed to shed water but will not resist ponding water. The leaks will occur just above the ice dams, penetrating the overhangs.

Your best defense against ice dams is to keep the attic cool with good ventilation and adequate insu-

lation. The attic should have about R-40 (about 15") of insulation. Close all air leaks into the attic, and insulate and seal all access doors.

Check ventilation openings. There should be about one square foot of ventilation per 150 square feet of attic floor space. Half the ventilation openings should be high in the attic and half should be in the overhangs. For homes with a vapor barrier below the insulation, the ventilation ratio is 1 per 300.

If ice dams persist even when there are no obvious problems with attic insulation and ventilation, you may need the help of a professional insulation contractor. Ventilation can be tricky with complicated roof designs. Air leaks from the heated space to the attic are a common cause of attic problems, but often they are hard to find.

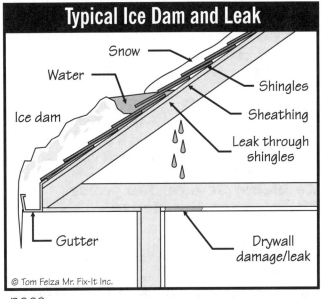

Typical Ice Dam and Leak

Snow

Water

Ice dam

Shingles

Sheathing

Leak through shingles

Gutter

Drywall damage/leak

© Tom Feiza Mr. Fix-It Inc.

R002

Moisture on the Windows

See Chapter 28–All Fogged Up: Solving Window Condensation Problems for more information on solving window moisture problems.

Often, moisture ("steam") condenses on windows in the fall with the start of the winter heating season. As long as moisture condenses only occasionally and disappears after several weeks, you don't need to do anything.

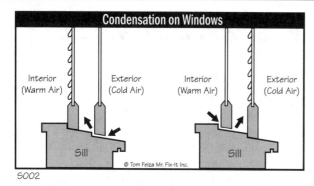

Condensation on Windows

Interior (Warm Air)   Exterior (Cold Air)   Interior (Warm Air)   Exterior (Cold Air)

Sill   Sill

© Tom Feiza Mr. Fix-It Inc.

S002

Condensation requires a cool surface and moisture in the air. Inside your home, when the temperature of the glass drops below the dew point of the inside air, invisible water vapor in the air condenses on the cool glass. More condensation occurs when there is more water vapor in the air and/or when glass surfaces become colder.

Over the summer, moisture slowly accumulates in furniture, walls, woodwork, cloth and other surfaces. In the fall, as the exterior temperature drops for the first time, some of this moisture condenses on cold window glass. Most moisture leaks out of your home as your furnace runs and vent fans are used. Eventually, all the materials in your home dry out, and moisture stops condensing on the windows. This normally takes a few weeks.

If condensation continues to form on windows after several weeks, your home may have excessive moisture. Most moisture problems can be solved by limiting sources of moisture and improving ventilation.

Reducing Severe Dampness Throughout the House

Some homes have problems with excessive moisture. It's most noticeable as condensation on windows. If moisture is excessive and stays on your windows for several days...if water runs off windows and damages wood surfaces...if ice forms on windows and frames...or if storm windows remained fogged up and icy all winter, you need to reduce the humidity level inside your home.

Condensation requires a cool surface and moisture in the air. Inside your home, when the temperature of the glass drops below the dew point of the inside air, invisible water vapor in the air condenses as water on the cool glass. More condensation occurs when there is more water vapor in the air and/or when glass surfaces become colder.

Evaluate changes you have made to your home—any effort to tighten up a home and reduce air infiltration will increase humidity levels. A high-efficiency furnace vented with two plastic pipes draws combustion air from outside and reduces ventilation. Weatherstripping, better windows, caulking, and any other measures you have taken to reduce air leaks will increase the amount of moisture retained inside your home.

Try to increase ventilation by running kitchen and bath exhaust fans whenever steam is produced by cooking or bathing/showering. In the bathroom, keep the fan running until the bathroom is dry. Add timer switches to the fans if necessary.

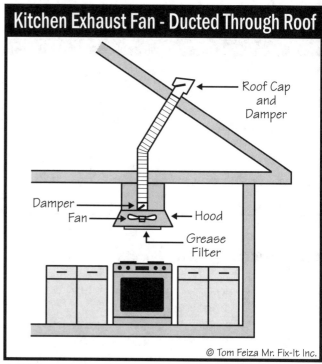

Kitchen Exhaust Fan - Ducted Through Roof

Roof Cap and Damper

Damper

Fan   Hood

Grease Filter

© Tom Feiza Mr. Fix-It Inc.

V013

Limit the number of plants in your home. Look for plumbing leaks or damp areas in the basement. If basement crawl spaces have bare soil, cover the soil with a vapor barrier.

There are many other sources of moisture and ways to eliminate excess moisture. Often your local natural gas utility company can provide information on moisture problems. University extensions often have good booklets on solving moisture problems.

Bath Exhaust Fan Through Roof

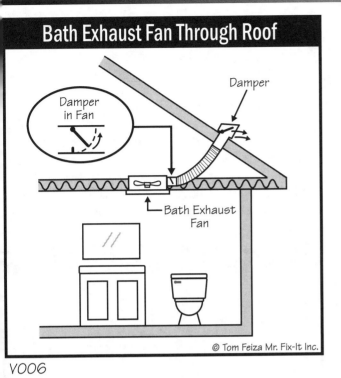

V006

Excessive Winter Dryness Indoors

Humidification of air inside the home has been the subject of many articles and investigations. Manufacturers of humidifiers have claimed that humidified air would protect us from health hazards, but there are no firm facts that humidified air is better for us. In fact, humidifiers can cause problems with excessive moisture and even mold or bacteria.

To decide on the need for a humidifier, evaluate the comfort of your home during the dead of winter. Many of today's tighter, energy-efficient homes don't need additional moisture. Condensation on windows indicates excessive humidity; in that case, you don't need a humidifier. However, if your nose and skin are dry, and static electricity is a problem, you may need a humidifier.

The best type is a central humidifier that mounts on a forced-air furnace. Look for one that flushes water over a panel and drains away excess water as it operates. It should be mounted on the return duct to prevent water leaks into the furnace, and it should have a humidistat control that automatically turns the unit on as needed.

Aprilaire is a quality brand of furnace-mounted humidifier. Its newer models have a removable plastic cover that makes the unit easy to maintain. This

Humidifier System and Controls

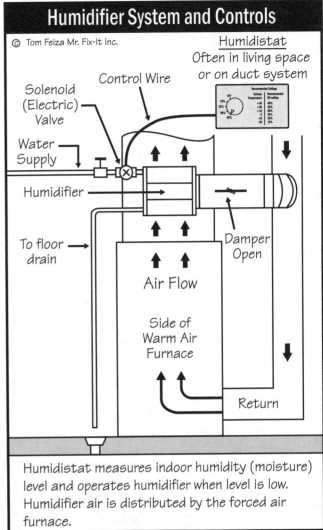

Humidistat measures indoor humidity (moisture) level and operates humidifier when level is low. Humidifier air is distributed by the forced air furnace.

H034

type flushes water over a panel and doesn't require a water reservoir.

Portable humidifiers can operate with a reservoir and evaporative panel. To create mist, some use ultrasound, others use a spinning wheel (for a cool mist), and others use heat (making steam). I consider all of these types hard to maintain and difficult to control. Any unit with a water reservoir is a potential source of mold or bacteria and must be meticulously cleaned and disinfected on a routine basis.

Water in the Basement

See Chapter 25: Keep Your Basement Dry for a complete analysis of basement water problems.

In a home with a basement, water entry will occur eventually. I like to say that a basement is a hole in the ground just waiting to fill with water. The most

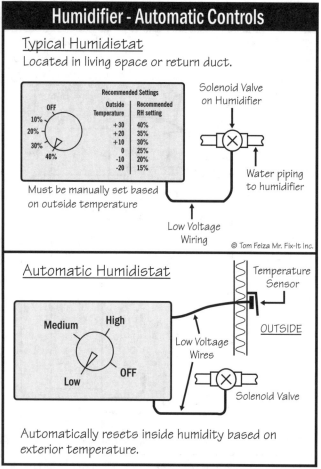

Humidifier - Automatic Controls

Typical Humidistat
Located in living space or return duct.

	Recommended Settings	
	Outside Temperature	Recommended RH setting
OFF		
10%	+30	40%
20%	+20	35%
30%	+10	30%
40%	0	25%
	-10	20%
	-20	15%

Must be manually set based on outside temperature

Solenoid Valve on Humidifier

Water piping to humidifier

Low Voltage Wiring

© Tom Feiza Mr. Fix-It Inc.

Automatic Humidistat

Medium   High
Low   OFF

Temperature Sensor

OUTSIDE

Low Voltage Wires

Solenoid Valve

Automatically resets inside humidity based on exterior temperature.

H035

Humidifier - Fan Powered

© Tom Feiza Mr. Fix-It Inc.

Water In

Solenoid (electrically - operated valve)

Furnace Duct

Fan

Water Panel

Pan

Drain

Fan draws air from warm air duct through the wet water panel and returns humidified air to duct.
Humidistat opens solenoid valve and water wets panel. Excess water is drained away.

H037

common reason for water entry into the basement is problems with grading, gutters or downspouts. If surface water is allowed to collect near the basement walls, it will enter the basement.

Keep your gutters clean, and extend the downspouts away from the basement. Keep soil and all hard surfaces around the basement pitched away from the basement. If you want to check for potential water problems, walk around your home during or just after a heavy rainfall; you will see where surface water may be collecting or flowing.

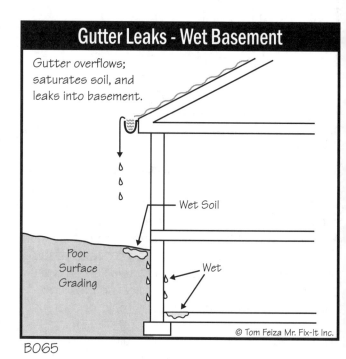

Gutter Leaks - Wet Basement

Gutter overflows; saturates soil, and leaks into basement.

Wet Soil

Poor Surface Grading

Wet

© Tom Feiza Mr. Fix-It Inc.

B065

Moisture in the Attic

With tighter homes and less airflow through the structure, we have reduced heating and cooling costs, but we have also increased the potential for moisture problems. Air moving through a home literally vents moisture to the outside. Drafty old homes were always dry and cold because of air leaks.

We need to be diligent about maintaining moisture balance in our modern homes. You may want to review Chapter 28–All Fogged Up: Solving Window Condensation Problems for detailed information about moisture in a home.

In cold climates, excessive moisture can result in condensation in the attic. I suggest you periodically check your attic during the winter for condensation, frost and any other signs of moisture. If you find a problem, have an expert review the situation and suggest possible solutions.

Ventilation - Two Basic Types

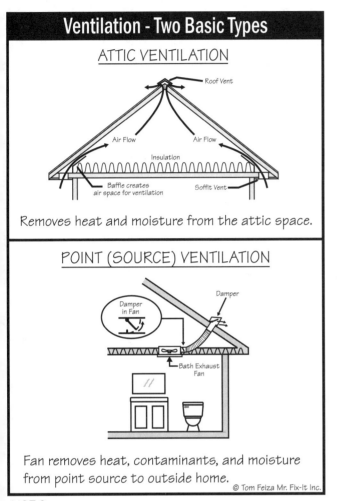

ATTIC VENTILATION

Removes heat and moisture from the attic space.

POINT (SOURCE) VENTILATION

Fan removes heat, contaminants, and moisture from point source to outside home.

© Tom Feiza Mr. Fix-It Inc.

V030

Until recently, most experts suggested that attic moisture problems are the result of inadequate attic ventilation. The standards for attic ventilation have been around a long time and were originally based on larger buildings with damp crawl space problems. The standards really don't have a scientific basis; they were just repeated over the years.

Recently, controlled experiments have found that most attic moisture problems result from excessive moisture in a home and air leaks into the attic. Sealing the leaks from the heated space into the attic dramatically reduces heating costs and limits the amount of moisture seeping into the attic. Some experts even recommend tightly sealing the attic's connection to the living space. We need to wait and see what develops with this.

Attic Ventilation Requirements - Typical

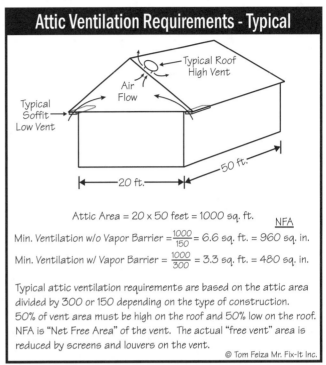

Attic Area = 20 x 50 feet = 1000 sq. ft.

$$\text{Min. Ventilation w/o Vapor Barrier} = \frac{1000}{150} = 6.6 \text{ sq. ft.} = 960 \text{ sq. in.}$$

$$\text{Min. Ventilation w/ Vapor Barrier} = \frac{1000}{300} = 3.3 \text{ sq. ft.} = 480 \text{ sq. in.}$$

Typical attic ventilation requirements are based on the attic area divided by 300 or 150 depending on the type of construction. 50% of vent area must be high on the roof and 50% low on the roof. NFA is "Net Free Area" of the vent. The actual "free vent" area is reduced by screens and louvers on the vent.

© Tom Feiza Mr. Fix-It Inc.

V042

Attic - Air Bypass

COMMON AIR LEAKS INTO AN ATTIC

Warm and moist interior air pushes into the attic through any opening.

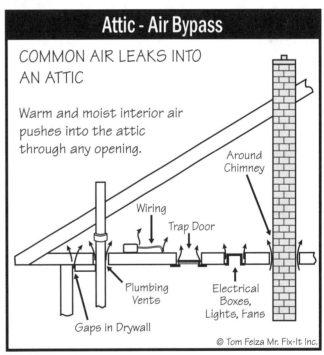

© Tom Feiza Mr. Fix-It Inc.

1005

Chapter 15 – Mysterious Sounds & Simple Solutions

Strange Sounds Throughout the House

During the night, you may hear creaking, cracking and other strange sounds in various parts of your house. You might also hear sounds during the day when other noises have quieted. What causes the sounds?

Our homes are "breathing" and reacting to moisture and temperature changes.

Most of the noises you hear are natural, and you need not worry unless walls are leaning, doors are sticking, and floors are sagging. The noises are caused by the normal expansion and contraction of wood and manmade materials.

Some of the biggest offenders are wood framing, vinyl and metal siding, plumbing, and heating ducts. Wood can shrink 1/4" or more across 6" of wood grain as its moisture content changes with the seasons. This movement makes floors creak, move and crack.

As the drywall or plaster attached to the wood framing attempts to move, you can hear cracks and pops. You will often see drywall nails popping from the drywall surface as the wood shrinks or expands.

Masonry chimneys, tile chimney liners and the wood framing attached to them move at different rates, and this also creates noises. Imagine how hot that chimney liner can get and how much it may move in that cold masonry chimney.

Your basement has metal heating ducts and metal piping attached to wood framing. When you run hot water in the bathroom, the cool pipe becomes hot and expands significantly. This expanding pipe is attached to the wood frame of your home, and it must bounce and slide along the framing or hangers until the expansion is accommodated.

Outside your home, vinyl siding is often a culprit for clicks and thumps. Vinyl siding must be installed so it can move horizontally. As outdoor temperatures change, or when bright sunlight hits the siding on a cold day, you will hear movement noises. Aluminum siding, metal gutters, and metal flashing all move with temperature changes.

Balloon Frame / Platform Frame

© Tom Feiza Mr. Fix-It Inc.

- Sole plate
- 2nd floor joist
- Firestop
- Ribbon
- Stud
- Sill
- Double top plate
- Stud
- Header
- 1st floor joist
- Sill
- Foundation wall

S006

Home Cross Section

© Tom Feiza Mr. Fix-It Inc.

S003

And boy, those water pipes pound, slush, and gurgle as water flows and drains. Pipes can pound loudly if the air cushion has been lost in the water hammer arresters—air chambers that absorb the energy when water changes direction. See the Plumbing Mysteries chapter for more detail.

Does your toilet run at night when no one is using the bathroom? There's a solution to this problem, too, in Plumbing Mysteries.

Don't forget that the water softener and sump pump can run at almost any time with a spurt, whoosh or clunk as a valve closes.

Did I miss anything? Sure. Everything in your home that is hot, cool, dry or moist or that moves water or air can cause noises. Don't worry about the sounds. Just chalk them up to the personality of your living, breathing home.

Water Heater Popping and Pounding

If your gas water heater makes a popping and pounding sound when heating water, this indicates that sediment has built up on the bottom of the tank. When the gas flame is on, the water boils, just like water in a metal pan on the stovetop. The sediment at the tank bottom hinders heat transfer and releases steam bubbles, and when the bubbles rise into colder water in the upper part of the tank, they collapse as the steam turns back into water. Their collapsing makes the popping and pounding sounds.

Often there is little you can do to remove the sediment from the bottom of the tank. Usually it consists of hard water scale that is literally bonded to the tank. This same scale sticks to the plumbing fixtures in your home. You could try draining several gallons of water from the drain valve near the bottom of the tank, which removes any loose sediment. To do this, attach a hose to the valve on the bottom of the tank and let 5 or 10 gallons of water drain out. Be careful—the water will be hot. If the drain water is full of sediment, you are having some success and you should repeat the procedure several times over several days. Often, though, little or no sediment will be removed.

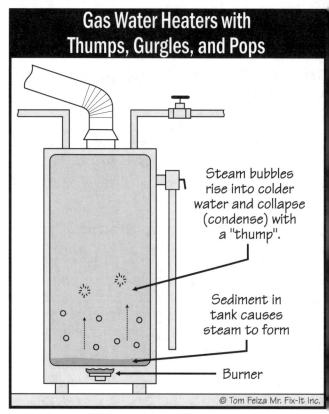

Gas Water Heaters with Thumps, Gurgles, and Pops

Steam bubbles rise into colder water and collapse (condense) with a "thump".

Sediment in tank causes steam to form

Burner

© Tom Feiza Mr. Fix-It Inc.

W002

Since the drain probably hasn't been operated for years, be prepared for leaks in the stem or valve. You can use a garden hose cap with a rubber washer to stop a drip from the valve. You can also tighten the valve stem to stop a leak at the stem. If there is excessive leaking, you will need to replace the valve.

The popping and pounding does little harm to the water heater or the piping. When a water heater gets to be about 10 or 20 years old, it has exceeded its normal lifespan, and you should plan for a replacement.

Banging / Clicking Heat Ducts

You might notice two distinct sounds coming from your warm air furnace and central air conditioner. When the air conditioning starts, the ductwork may produce a loud bang; this does not occur when the heat turns on. On the other hand, when the heating system starts and runs for a few minutes, you might hear clicking and slight pounding in the ductwork at the far end of the basement. Both problems have simple solutions.

When the air conditioner runs, the furnace fan must move more air through the system than when the unit is used for heating. Often the fan will automatically run at a higher speed for greater volume and pressure.

Because air is moving through the system with greater speed, volume, and pressure, it is more likely that the ductwork will "pop" outward. Isolate the problem by listening for the sound and watching the ductwork when the air conditioner starts. You will probably find the sound coming from large, flat pieces of sheet metal near the furnace. Screw a lightweight angle iron over the part of the duct that is moving.

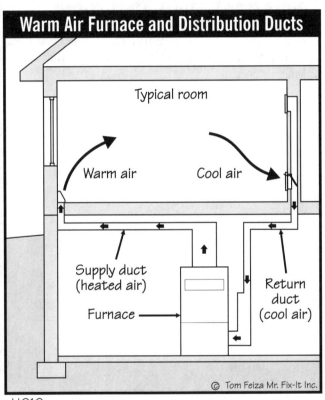

Warm Air Furnace and Distribution Ducts

Typical room

Warm air

Cool air

Supply duct (heated air)

Return duct (cool air)

Furnace

© Tom Feiza Mr. Fix-It Inc.

H010

In the case of heating noises, the problem occurs as the metal ductwork heats up. Metal expands as it heats, so it needs room to move. If the ductwork is trapped within the wood framing in the basement, or if it's too tightly secured to the framing, this creates friction that causes the noise. Watch the ductwork and listen for the sounds as the furnace runs. You may need to loosen some mounting brackets or adjust ductwork that's forced against wood framing.

Floor Squeaks

Floor squeaks are caused by loose floorboards and framing that move and rub as you walk on the floor. It could be wood rubbing on wood or wood rubbing on nails. Most often this occurs in the winter, because our homes dry out during the heating season. As wood dries, it shrinks, and gaps open up. A common 1 by 6 could shrink as much as 1/4" across its 6" width when going from damp summer conditions to dry winter/heating conditions.

See Chapter 29 – Floor Squeaks for complete details on solving floor squeaks.

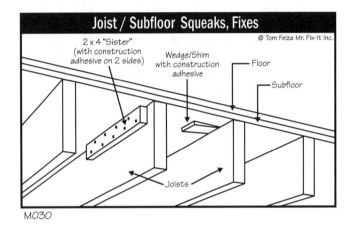

Joist / Subfloor Squeaks, Fixes

2 x 4 "Sister" (with construction adhesive on 2 sides)

Wedge/Shim with construction adhesive

Floor

Subfloor

© Tom Feiza Mr. Fix-It Inc.

Joists

M030

If the squeaks occur on the first floor and you can reach this area from the basement, try the following measures. (If you can't get underneath the squeaking floor, see the information below about a product called Squeeeeek No More.)

Have someone walk on the offending floor while you listen for squeaks and watch for movement in the basement. Mark the problem areas.

If you can reach the joists and subflooring in the squeaking area, your best fix is to "sister" a 2 by 4 or 2 by 6 to the side of the joist and tight against the subfloor. "Sister" is a carpentry term meaning that the 2 by 4 is parallel to the joist with the wide, flat surfaces together.

Use a short length—18" to 36"—and liberally apply construction adhesive to two adjacent 90-degree sides. Construction adhesive is dispensed from a caulking gun and has a caulk-like consistency. You then attach this board to the joist and the subflooring with several screws or nails driven into the joist at an angle.

The construction adhesive will effectively weld the wood to the joist and the subfloor, preventing movement. The adhesive fills voids and will not release as the wood shrinks and moves. Construction adhesive is the key—it will not shrink as it cures. Use as many short lengths as you need to stop the movement and squeaks.

Although many home improvement books recommend driving small shims between the joists and floorboards, I think this can complicate the problem. How far do you drive the shims into the gap? If you drive them in too far, you can loosen the subfloor.

Two products on the market work well to eliminate floor squeaks. Squeak-Relief from ATCI Consumer Products provides a small aluminum bracket and specially sized screws. The bracket takes the place of the 2 by 4. It effectively secures the floor to the bracket and the joist.

Squeeeeek No More from ATCI Consumer Products works from above the squeak through carpeting or hardwood flooring. It is a special bracket that holds and drives a long notched screw. Once driven into the offending area, the screw disappears. The bracket ensures that the screw is driven to the right depth. Then you use the bracket to break off the head and shank of the screw just below the wood. If you use this on a finished wood floor, it will create a tiny hole that should be patched with wood putty.

For information on how to contact ATCI Consumer Products, see the "Fasteners" section of the References chapter.

Fluorescent Light That Hums

For solutions to a loudly humming fluorescent light, see Chapter 12–Electric Mysteries and Secret Solutions.

Chapter 16 – Smelly Mysteries & Simple Solutions

Sewer Smell in Home

When you detect a sewer smell in your home, there may be a dry trap in the drainage system. Often the smell comes from a seldom-used floor drain in the basement.

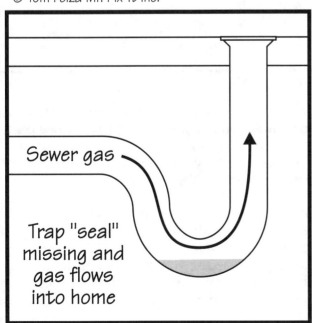

Floor Drain Trap

Sewer gas

Water in trap: "traps" sewer gas

Water

© Tom Feiza Mr. Fix-It Inc.

Sewer gas

Trap "seal" missing and gas flows into home

All drains to a sewer system have a P-shaped trap which is usually filled with water. The trap provides a seal to keep out sewer gas. If your basement floor drain is rarely used, water evaporates from the trap over time. Eventually the seal is eliminated, allowing sewer gas (and smell) into your house. The solution is easy: pour water into the drain.

If the trap is okay and the smell is noticeable mainly around a sink, try flushing a strong cleaner and bleach down the sink's overflow—the small hole(s) inside the bowl near the rim. This area may have an odor because when the sink fills to near overflowing, water is routed through an inner chamber to the drain. Debris can collect inside the inner chamber, causing odor.

S Trap - Not Allowed

Water draining through the "S" trap will siphon out the water seal and allow sewer gas and vermin into home.

Will drain with a "glug - glug."

© Tom Feiza Mr. Fix-It Inc.

P037

If neither of these measures solves the problem, there may be a small leak in one of the vent lines of the plumbing system, or a small leak around the base of a toilet or other fixture. You may need the help of a plumber. Check for loose fittings, corrosion, or holes in vent piping. Also, check the top side of horizontal drain pipes. If the top is rusted, it may never leak liquid, but it will leak sewer gas. Drain lines made of copper, steel or cast iron may all exhibit this problem.

Sewer Smell from Toilet

When urine and sewer smells persist near a toilet despite careful cleaning, identify the source of the smell. Is it from the hot water? Is it from the floor around the toilet? Is it from the sink or tub?

Smells from the hot water may be caused by bacteria in the water heater and the anode rod. Smells from the floor area may indicate that the toilet is leaking, wetting the subfloor. Traps in sinks and tubs also can give off odors from time to time. Once you know the source, you can track down a solution.

If the smell comes from the area around the toilet, there may be an air leak at the wax ring of the toilet or in the vent pipe. Check to see if the toilet is tightly sealed to the floor. Grab the bowl of the toilet and try to slide it from side to side. It should resist a few pounds of pressure. If the toilet rocks from side to side, the wax ring has failed.

To replace the wax ring, hire a professional plumber. It's necessary to check the spacing between the pipe flange and the toilet base, and it is difficult to properly secure a toilet in place.

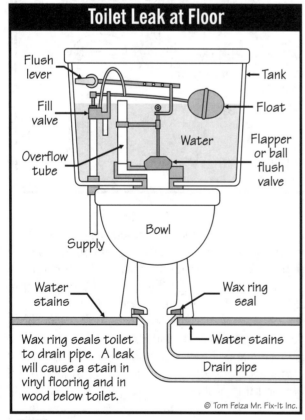

Toilet Leak at Floor

Flush lever

Tank

Fill valve

Float

Water

Overflow tube

Flapper or ball flush valve

Bowl

Supply

Water stains

Wax ring seal

Water stains

Drain pipe

Wax ring seals toilet to drain pipe. A leak will cause a stain in vinyl flooring and in wood below toilet.

© Tom Feiza Mr. Fix-It Inc.

P027

Water Supply Smells Like Rotten Eggs

Some homeowners have recurring problems with bad odor in the water supply—especially the "rotten egg" smell of sulfur. Water odors are a tough problem to solve, but I suggest you follow up on these ideas.

First, check whether your neighbors are experiencing similar problems. If your water comes from a municipal well, maybe your local water utility can help.

If your home has its own well, the smell may originate in the well system. There could be sulfate-reducing bacteria in the water supply. While the smell is bad, it usually is not a health risk. However, excessive sulfur bacteria can damage your water system.

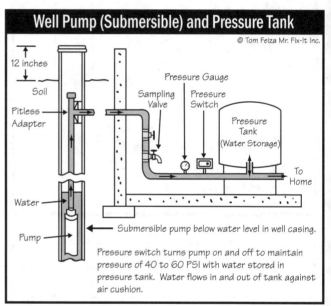

Well Pump (Submersible) and Pressure Tank

© Tom Feiza Mr. Fix-It Inc.

12 inches

Soil

Pressure Gauge

Sampling Valve

Pressure Switch

Pitless Adapter

Pressure Tank (Water Storage)

To Home

Water

Pump

Submersible pump below water level in well casing.

Pressure switch turns pump on and off to maintain pressure of 40 to 60 PSI with water stored in pressure tank. Water flows in and out of tank against air cushion.

P055

It is relatively common to have this rotten egg odor in hot water only. In that case, the water heater's "sacrificial" anode rod is to blame. This rod, made of magnesium, helps protect the tank lining from corrosion; instead, the rod itself corrodes.

Unfortunately, as it does, the magnesium gives off electrons that nourish sulfate-reducing bacteria. Removing this rod may eliminate the problem (although it may also void the warranty for the water heater). The anode rod may be replaced with an aluminum rod.

Typical Water Heater Parts - Electric

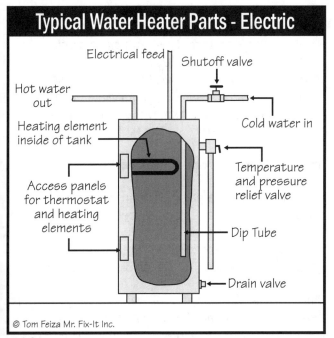

© Tom Feiza Mr. Fix-It Inc.

P081

If odor exists in both hot and cold water systems, you may need to treat the well with a shock chlorination. I suggest you use a contractor for this service. The contractor will add a strong chlorine solution to your well and circulate it through the system. The solution must remain in the well and piping for at least 24 hours and then be flushed out. The chlorine solution must be removed carefully because it will kill grass and shrubs and should not run into a lake or stream. This process may need to be repeated more than once. Equipment is available for automatic and routine addition of chlorine to the well if needed.

If you are concerned whether your water is safe to drink, have it tested. Often your city or county's health department or building inspection department or your state's department of natural resources will perform tests and explain the results. A local well service company can also test your water.

Also, most local water treatment contractors or the local health department will know about the common problems with water in your area. Your neighbors probably have the same water problems and can share their solutions or the names of good resources.

One final tip—the water holding/pressure tank can be a source of odor problems. Most modern tanks have a rubber bladder that holds the water

away from the air cushion in the tank. This bladder may increase odor. An air-over-water tank with an air release system can help. In this system, the pump adds air to the tank each time it runs, and a float in the tank releases excess air. There is no rubber bladder.

Does this all sound complicated? It is. I suggest you consult a professional who has experience in your specific area. If you choose this route, interview several water specialists. Make sure the one you choose will investigate your problem fully and isn't just selling you a standard package of expensive water treatment equipment. Find out how your neighbors solve the problem.

Smoke Smells from the Fireplace— Without a Fire

A smoky smell coming from a fireplace that's not in use is probably caused by negative pressure that draws air down the chimney, past the stinky ashes, and into your home.

First, check that the damper is in good condition and is tightly closed. If there are fireplace glass doors, close them. Close any outside air supply to the fireplace.

Backdrafting Fireplace, Kitchen Fan = SMELL

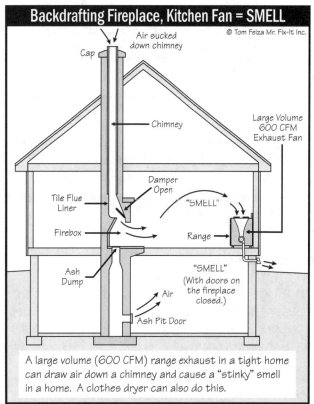

A large volume (600 CFM) range exhaust in a tight home can draw air down a chimney and cause a "stinky" smell in a home. A clothes dryer can also do this.

V031

197

Now think about what may be causing the pressure that draws air down the chimney. Clothes dryers and kitchen exhaust fans are notorious for this. Bathroom fans and other ventilation fans also remove air. A whole-house ventilation fan is another likely culprit. A naturally drafted gas appliance like a water heater or furnace also removes air from your home and sends it up a different chimney along with combustion gas. Some high-efficiency furnaces and water heaters have a draft fan that draws air.

Analyze this problem carefully, because the negative pressure could also cause a gas furnace or water heater to backdraft, sending combustion gas into your home. Backdrafting is a serious safety concern. You may need to have a heating contractor or an engineer analyze the problem.

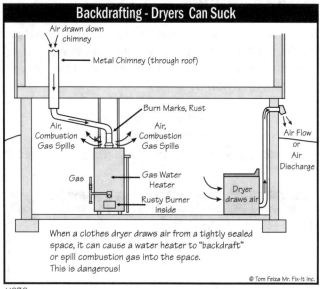

V032

The solution may also be simple: open a window slightly when running the clothes dryer or kitchen exhaust fan to provide another air source so air won't be drawn down the fireplace chimney.

Removing Smoke Smells from Home or Car

Cigarette Smoke

Once cigarette smoke smell has penetrated finish materials in a home or car, it is difficult to remove. Professional cleaners or scents to cover the smell don't always work.

Have the carpets and furniture or car seats professionally cleaned. Also, scrub all washable surfaces.

One great way to remove or cover smoke smells is with Pine-Sol cleaner. Place several small bowls of Pine-Sol in the problem area and close it off overnight or for several days. Pine-Sol's detergent smell is very strong and will cover the smoke smell. Afterward, open the area and ventilate with outdoor air. As fresh air removes the detergent scent, most or all of the smoke odor will be gone, too.

Smoke Smells from a House Fire

If part of the house has been damaged by fire, obviously you'll need to replace carpeting and drapes in affected areas. Standard repainting may not be sufficient to seal the smoke/burn smell; many times a special primer/sealer like Kilz or Bin is required.

Before replacing carpeting, clean the wood underneath, then seal with Bin or Kilz. Even though wood may not look damaged, it may still retain a smoke smell. You might also need to clean the ductwork and the furnace.

Finally, check the attic above the fire area. Is there a smoke smell or damage in the insulation, ceiling or roof? You may need to seal these surfaces and remove damaged materials.

See the References chapter for information about the manufacturers of Bin (Zinsser Co.) and Kilz (Masterchem Industries).

Burning Odor from Light Fixture

If a light fixture gives off a burning smell, disconnect the fixture until you have determined the source of the odor. Overheating electrical wires and devices often emit a burning smell. Don't use the fixture again until it has been repaired by a professional.

A fluorescent fixture may have a ballast that has failed and is spilling tar.

For typical incandescent light fixtures, the burning smell may occur if you're using an oversized bulb. Check the rating of the fixture and the wattage of the bulb. Never exceed the wattage recommended.

There might also be a loose electrical connection at the splice or in the outlet box, or a loose screw or lamp base. A loose connection creates excessive resistance to electrical flow, and the resistance builds up heat. Excessive heat makes metal connections expand and contract, loosening them further. This heat can damage insulation and even start a fire. Sometimes, when such excessive heat melts plastic, the problem area emits a misleading "dead animal" smell.

If you notice any strong smells near outlets, electrical boxes, or light fixtures, they may be due to an electrical problem. Call an electrician to evaluate and fix the problem. In the meantime, do not use electrical power in that area.

Stinky Garbage Disposal

A smell at a garbage disposal can have several sources. There may be food particles and general muck collected in the disposal, the trap or the flaps that cover the disposal opening. I suggest you run a trayful of ice cubes through the disposal to dislodge any particles and then follow with boiling water and some disinfectant cleaner.

If an odor is still noticeable, use a coarse rag or a scrubbing pad to scrub the underside of the rubber flappers, where food particles may stick. Be very careful, and make sure the disposal remains off while you clean the flaps.

Smelly Sink

Odors in a bathroom sink can be hard to trace. Your first step should be to remove the stopper and clean debris from it. Then remove any debris from

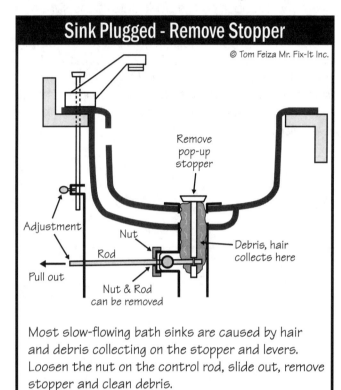

Sink Plugged - Remove Stopper

© Tom Feiza Mr. Fix-It Inc.

Remove pop-up stopper

Adjustment

Nut

Rod

Debris, hair collects here

Pull out

Nut & Rod can be removed

Most slow-flowing bath sinks are caused by hair and debris collecting on the stopper and levers. Loosen the nut on the control rod, slide out, remove stopper and clean debris.

P099

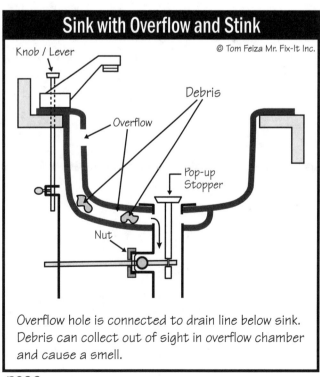

Sink with Overflow and Stink

© Tom Feiza Mr. Fix-It Inc.

Knob / Lever

Debris

Overflow

Pop-up Stopper

Nut

Overflow hole is connected to drain line below sink. Debris can collect out of sight in overflow chamber and cause a smell.

P096

Disposal Smell

Control Switch

Rubber flaps must be cleaned to prevent smell.

Sink

Disposal

To Sewer

Power Feed

Trap

© Tom Feiza Mr. Fix-It Inc.

P060

the trap and flush the trap with hot water and a disinfectant cleaner. Wear rubber gloves—this is a dirty job.

If you still detect odors, there could be debris in the overflow chamber on the underside of the sink. The overflow is not readily visible; it looks like a hole or slot on the side of the sink, just below the rim. If water flows down the overflow chamber, it ends up in the drain below the sink. Debris can build up in this chamber and cause a smell. Flush the chamber with hot water and disinfectant if you think this is causing an odor.

Chapter 17 – When To Call a Professional

When To Call a Professional

Many of us successfully complete home repair and improvement projects with a feeling of great accomplishment. Some of us approach a project out of necessity: we just can't afford to hire a contractor or we can't find a contractor for a small job. Some of us love the challenge. Some of us love the diversion from our day-to-day work. Whatever the reason, home repairs and remodeling can be a great source of satisfaction and pride.

Most of us will start with simple projects like painting, wallpapering and related decorating. We may attempt simple carpentry and refinishing furniture or woodwork. Eventually we get involved in building a deck or installing a garage door operator.

How do you know when to hire a professional and when you can do it yourself? This question comes up all the time on my radio show. And the answer depends on your skill level, your level of interest and how willing you are to seek professional help. The answer varies for each person.

You can't get into much trouble with painting, decorating and simple carpentry. But what about electrical, plumbing, heating and structural work? Where should we draw the line?

I think you should consider the complexity of the project and ask your local municipal building inspector if a permit is required for the work. When a permit is required, this often means a professional trade person would normally do the work. Once a permit is "pulled," the work is subject to local building codes and controls. You must conform to codes and safety requirements. A code official will check your work.

I suggest that most average handy-people stay away from electrical, plumbing, roofing and structural work because of the complexity. If you must try this type of work, I suggest you ask yourself the following questions. If you can't pass the test, don't attempt the work.

Can You Handle Advanced Projects? Take This Quiz and Find Out!

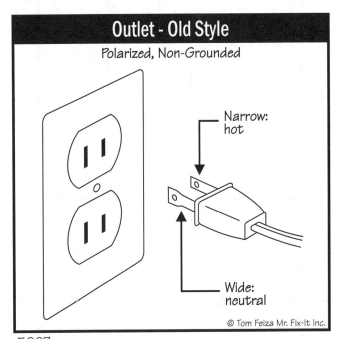

E007

Electrical

1. Explain polarity.

2. On a lamp cord, how is the neutral wire marked?

3. In a main electrical panel, what two colors are ground wires?

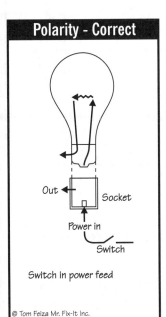

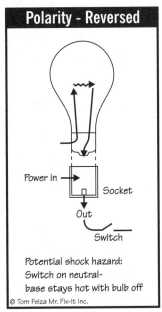

E008

4. Can a white neutral wire give you a shock?

5. What size wire is used for a 30-amp line for a clothes dryer?

Plumbing

1. Explain how a trap works.

2. What does the T and P valve on the water heater or boiler do?

3. How many fixtures can be served by a 1/2-inch copper line?

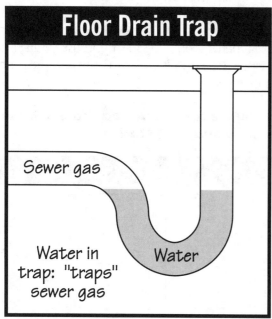

Floor Drain Trap

Sewer gas

Water in trap: "traps" sewer gas

Water

© Tom Feiza Mr. Fix-It Inc.

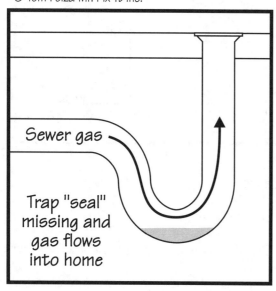

Sewer gas

Trap "seal" missing and gas flows into home

P026

4. What type of solder must be used today for copper pipes?

5. Explain water hammer and how to eliminate it.

Roofing

1. How many layers of shingles will you find in one layer of a three-tap asphalt shingle?

2. What is the lowest slope roof for a standard asphalt shingle application?

3. Describe roof slope and define the terms used.

4. Why must an attic be ventilated?

5. What is a step flashing?...counter flashing?

Structural

1. What is the normal span for 2 by 10 on 16 centers?

2. Explain "16 on center."

3. How does a cap flashing work at a window?

4. Why are joist hangers used on a deck?

5. How deep must deck posts go into the soil?

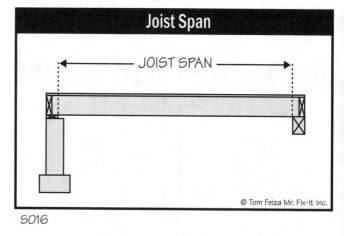

Joist Span

JOIST SPAN

© Tom Feiza Mr. Fix-It Inc.

S016

Mechanical

1. Explain a condensing, high efficiency warm air furnace.

2. Why can a "orphaned" gas water heater create a problem in a masonry chimney?

Flashing Over Window

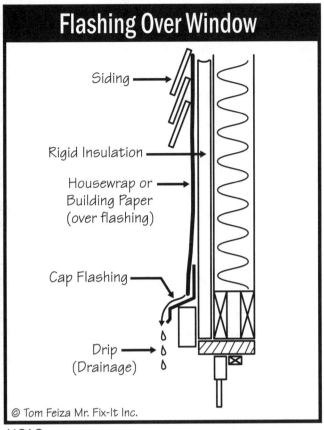

Siding

Rigid Insulation

Housewrap or Building Paper (over flashing)

Cap Flashing

Drip (Drainage)

© Tom Feiza Mr. Fix-It Inc.

X010

High-Efficiency Warm Air Furnace

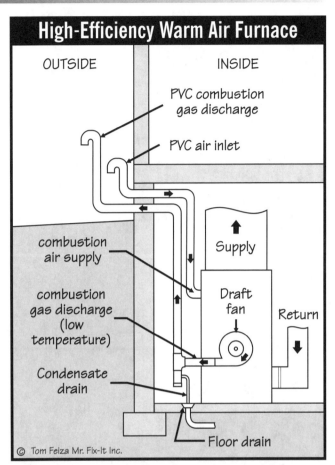

OUTSIDE   INSIDE

PVC combustion gas discharge

PVC air inlet

combustion air supply

Supply

combustion gas discharge (low temperature)

Draft fan

Return

Condensate drain

Floor drain

© Tom Feiza Mr. Fix-It Inc.

H003

Air Conditioning System with Warm Air Furnace

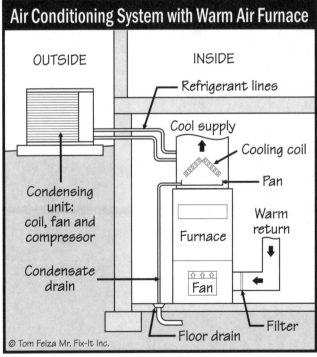

OUTSIDE   INSIDE

Refrigerant lines

Cool supply

Cooling coil

Pan

Condensing unit: coil, fan and compressor

Furnace

Warm return

Condensate drain

Fan

Floor drain

Filter

© Tom Feiza Mr. Fix-It Inc.

A001

3. Do you need a check valve on a sump pump?

4. What are the symptoms of a waterlogged pressure tank on a private well system?

5. Where is the evaporator coil in a central air conditioning system?

If you can pass the test, perhaps you can try your hand at more complicated repairs. Some of the answers are in this book, but others are beyond the scope of this book and the knowledge of most homeowners. You need to know all the answers before you attempt extensive home repairs.

Remember to follow all safety precautions and manufacturers' instructions. Take out a building permit and follow the advice of the local building inspector. Have your work inspected. Consult a professional as needed or whenever you have any questions.

Good luck!

Chapter 18 – Vacations: Closing Your Home

Short Trips

It's good to think ahead if you're going to leave your home unoccupied for a while. Most people don't think about what could happen to their home during vacation until they come home to a disaster.

For a short (3- to 5-day) absence during the summer, turn off the main water supply valve. (If you've asked a neighbor to come in and water your house plants, fill the bathtub with water first to provide water for the task.) Also, turn the water heater and water softener to a "vacation" setting if there is one.

Any minor plumbing leak can cause a major disaster. One of my friends came home to a $20,000 problem because a second-story toilet supply line had sprung a leak; by the time the family came home, the kitchen cabinets were on the floor.

One caution: inspect and test the main water valve long before you plan to shut it off. Because the valve is rarely used, it may be corroded and can even be stuck in the open position. If the valve looks clean and is easy to operate, turn it off as a

test. If the valve is corroded and the handle seems hard to turn, don't force it; get a plumber to replace or repair the valve. Once you move the handle, the valve may leak, and it could become impossible to shut it off all the way. Don't use a wrench or pliers on the handle or stem, and don't test the valve on a Sunday or holiday when you can't get help or parts.

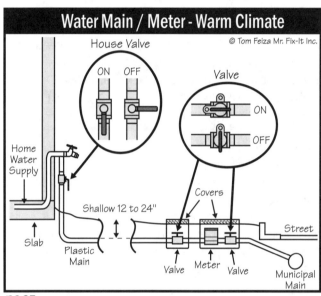

P063

If you have central air conditioning, set it to a high temperature (85 degrees or above), or just turn it off. If there is a sump pump in the basement, test it before you leave. (For instructions, see "Sump Pump Maintenance" in Chapter 19.)

For a short trip during the summer, leave the rest of the utilities on. Set up timers on some interior lights. Ask a neighbor or friend to check on the house. Don't forget to have someone pick up your mail and newspaper to make the house look "lived in."

For short winter absences, set the heating temperature to 55 or 60 degrees but no lower. Don't risk frozen pipes in your home. Also, make sure that all widows and doors are tightly closed—even a small draft can freeze a pipe.

Water Supply System in a Cold Climate
TWO TYPICAL OPTIONS

Street

Curb Valve

Meter

THROUGH FOUNDATION WALL

Valves

Water main below street

Supply Line

Valve

Meter

Valve

THROUGH BASE-MENT FLOOR

© Tom Feiza Mr. Fix-It Inc.

P005

Shutting Down for a Whole Winter

The chief risks associated with leaving a home unheated over a cold winter season involve freezing water and the movement of framing, drywall, plaster and flooring.

Properly securing the water system involves much more than turning off the water. You must also secure anything that may contain water, including drain traps, all piping, water heater, dishwashers, and clothes washers. You must actually open up the piping at several locations to drain water. Then you must fill drain traps and toilets with antifreeze to keep sewer gas from entering your home. It's important to use a special type of antifreeze, designed for use in motor homes, to prevent damage to the sewage system.

Turn off the washing machine supply lines and remove and drain them. To clear water from the washing machine pump, run the washer on the fill part of its cycle, set to warm water. For a dishwasher, remove the inlet hose and open the supply valve after you have turned off the water supply to the house. Operate the dishwasher to clear the valve; remove the drain hose.

Unplug all electrical appliances to prevent any damage from power surges or lightning strikes.

Another serious potential problem is expansion and contraction of the structure of your home from changes in temperature and humidity. Expansion and contraction may cause cracks in plaster, tile, flooring, wood trim and other components that would be expensive to repair. Keep the heat turned on, at a low setting. The risk of structural damage isn't worth the relatively small amount you would save by turning off the heat altogether.

Damage from animals and insects is another potential problem. With no people around, pests can have free run of the house.

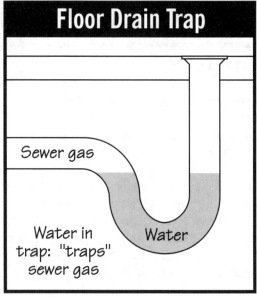

Floor Drain Trap

Sewer gas

Water in trap: "traps" sewer gas

Water

© Tom Feiza Mr. Fix-It Inc.

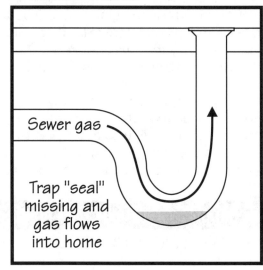

Sewer gas

Trap "seal" missing and gas flows into home

P026

Rain gutters, downspouts, sump pumps, and appliances can malfunction during a long winter absence. Security is also a major concern—someone could break in, or that beautiful oak tree could fall on the roof or the picture window.

In short, if you plan to leave your home for the winter, turn the water off, secure the plumbing, and leave the heat on at a low setting. Also, find someone to check on the house weekly.

Chapter 19 – Little Problems That Become Big Problems

Floor Stains Around the Toilet

A small leak can seriously damage floor covering and framing if not repaired promptly.

The most likely source of water or water stains around the base of a toilet is a leaky seal between the toilet outlet and the toilet drain flange. Grab the toilet and gently try to move it slightly from side to side or rock it back and forth. If there is any movement, the toilet needs to be reset to the drain line.

When the toilet was installed, a wax ring was placed between the base of the toilet and the drain pipe. Eventually, the toilet and piping can move, and this seal can be broken, allowing a small leak every time someone flushes the toilet. If the floor framing is visible in the floor below (for instance, in the basement), you will also see stains and dampness below the toilet.

Toilet Leak at Floor

Flush lever

Tank

Fill valve

Float

Water

Overflow tube

Flapper or ball flush valve

Bowl

Supply

Water stains

Wax ring seal

Water stains

Drain pipe

Wax ring seals toilet to drain pipe. A leak will cause a stain in vinyl flooring and in wood below toilet.

© Tom Feiza Mr. Fix-It Inc.

Replacing the wax ring requires removing the toilet. In most cases, I suggest you hire a plumber to do this, because many problems can occur and most households can't afford losing the use of a toilet for too long.

Here is what's involved in the repair. You will need to obtain a new wax ring and probably new bolts, too.

First, disconnect the water supply and drain all water from the tank and bowl. Remove the bolts on either side of the toilet, and lift the toilet from the floor. Because the old bolts may be almost impossible to remove, often they're just cut off. The new replacement bolts should be cut to the required length.

Clean away the old wax ring and place a new one on the base. Carefully set the toilet in place over the bolts. Gently tighten the bolts until the toilet is secure.

Rusted Metal Lintels (Beams) at Windows

Rusted lintels can create serious cracks and masonry failure.

A brick or stone home may have steel angles over windows and doors. These angles, called lintels, hold up the brick and stone over the openings.

Most people don't realize that the lintels are there, and they allow them to rust away. When the lintel eventually fails, the wall may split apart at the mortar joints. Over large openings, the brick and rusted lintel can sag into the opening, requiring a major repair.

Treat this steel lintel like any exterior metal. Remove the rust down to bare metal, prime with a metal primer, and paint with an exterior metal paint.

An option to cleaning down to bare metal is to remove most of the rust, then paint/prime the remaining solid rust with a product like Rust-Oleum Rust Reformer or a rusty-metal primer. Reformer transforms the existing rust to stop the rusting action and provides a primer for the finish coat.

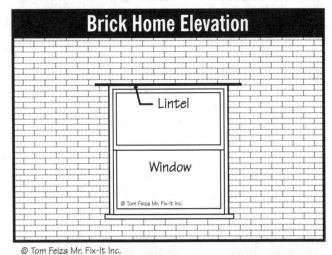

Brick Home Elevation

Lintel

Window

© Tom Feiza Mr. Fix-It Inc.

© Tom Feiza Mr. Fix-It Inc.

Masonry Lintel Section

Brick

Wallboard

Lintel
(steel beam
or angle)
supports
brick above
windows
and doors

Headers

Window

S009

Often, latex exterior house paint is mistakenly applied to the metal lintels when the wood siding and trim are painted. Latex paint will not hold up over the long run and can allow the metal to rust.

There may also be small openings between the top of the lintel and the brick. These openings allow condensation (water) in the wall to drain away. Do not seal these openings, and don't caulk this joint. Sealing the openings will cause excessive rust and wall damage.

Garage Door—Paint It to Save It

If you don't paint all sides of a wood garage door, it will fail.

When your wood or wood-product garage door needs painting, your first step is to clean the door with detergent and a scrub brush. Rinse well, then allow the door to dry for several days.

Wipe the cleaned surface with your finger. If the paint leaves a chalky deposit on your finger, you need to prime the surface.

To determine if the paint is loose, try this cellophane tape test. Cut a shallow "X" in the surface and rub tape over the X. Lift the tape quickly. If paint comes off in chunks, it's loose. Loose paint must be removed and primed, or at least primed. Sand the door first if necessary.

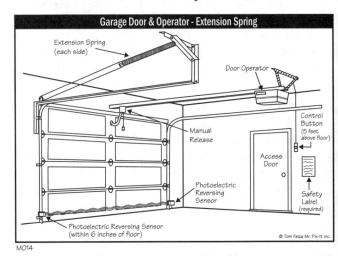

Garage Door & Operator - Extension Spring

Extension Spring
(each side)

Door Operator

Manual
Release

Control
Button
(5 feet
above floor)

Access
Door

Photoelectric
Reversing
Sensor

Safety
Label
(required)

Photoelectric Reversing Sensor
(within 6 inches of floor)

© Tom Feiza Mr. Fix-It Inc.

M014

Prime the surface with an exterior oil-based primer. If you wish to change the door to a lighter color, prime with a special stain blocker/primer such as Bin or Kilz. (For more information about the manufacturers of Bin and Kilz, see the References chapter.)

If the existing paint surface is solid and not too "chalky," paint directly over it with a high-quality 100% acrylic latex paint.

When painting a garage door, remember that each door panel has six sides that need painting. To reach areas between panels at the hinges, you must paint with the door partially open. The most common mistake people make when painting a garage door is to skip the other five sides of the panels.

Drainage Problems

Ignoring improper drainage allows serious basement leaks to create structural problems. See Chapter 25 – Keep Your Basement Dry for complete details.

Most basements have a drainage system designed to remove groundwater near the floor and walls. There are exterior tiles at the base of the wall and interior tiles just beneath the concrete floor. These systems are connected under the foundation wall by bleeder tiles through the footings. Bleeder tiles direct the water to a sump pump, which pumps the water out.

If the gutters or the sump pump discharge their water near the foundation wall, the soil can become saturated, pushing inward on the foundation. Water seeps into the block or concrete and eventually flows inside at the top or midpoint of the basement wall.

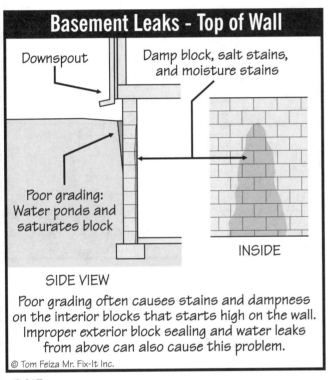

B013

It's essential to direct surface water at least 6 feet from the foundation to a point where the water naturally flows away from your home.

Drainage problems are compounded in the spring when there is a large snow meltdown and most of the ground is still frozen. Ice and snow piles may also trap water against your home. The soil next to your home thaws before the rest of the soil because of heat from your basement, and this thawed soil accepts water while the frozen soil rejects water.

Monitor these conditions, and correct problems at the surface of the soil. If leaks continue or cracks develop in basement walls, contact a basement specialist.

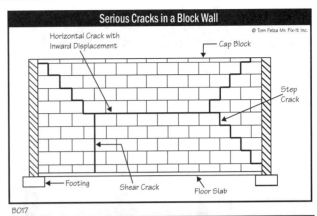

B017

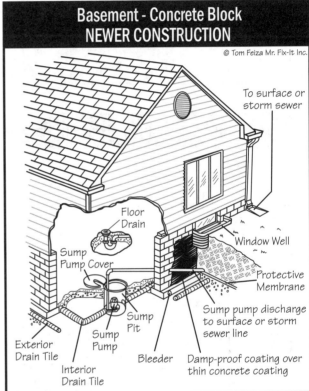

B005

Grading Soil and Hard Surfaces

Improper grading contributes to basement leaks and serious structural problems.

More than 90% of basement dampness and seepage problems are caused by poor grading or poor maintenance of gutters and downspouts.

When your home was built, the excavation was dug larger than the basement to allow space for workers to construct the walls. Often, the hole is backfilled with native soil that settles quickly for up to 5 years and then more slowly after that. If the fill contains debris or organic materials, settling is even more pronounced.

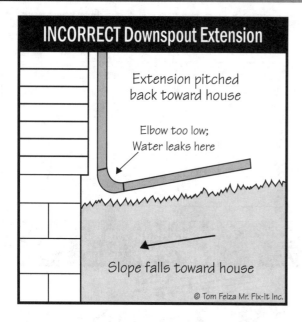

INCORRECT Downspout Extension

Extension pitched back toward house

Elbow too low; Water leaks here

Slope falls toward house

© Tom Feiza Mr. Fix-It Inc.

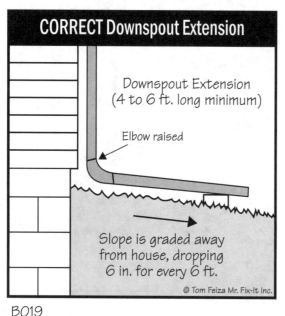

CORRECT Downspout Extension

Downspout Extension (4 to 6 ft. long minimum)

Elbow raised

Slope is graded away from house, dropping 6 in. for every 6 ft.

© Tom Feiza Mr. Fix-It Inc.

B019

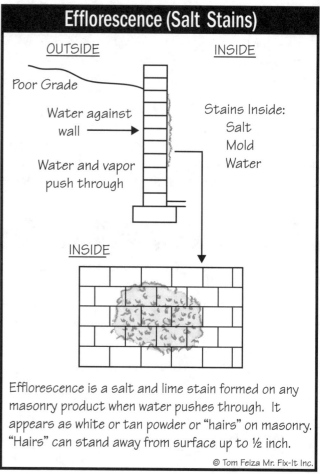

Efflorescence (Salt Stains)

OUTSIDE   INSIDE

Poor Grade

Water against wall

Water and vapor push through

Stains Inside:
Salt
Mold
Water

INSIDE

Efflorescence is a salt and lime stain formed on any masonry product when water pushes through. It appears as white or tan powder or "hairs" on masonry. "Hairs" can stand away from surface up to ½ inch.

© Tom Feiza Mr. Fix-It Inc.

B033

Soil and soft surfaces such as grass should always be pitched away from the foundation with a minimum 5% slope—about 1/2" of drop for every 12 linear inches. A better slope would be 1" to 2" every 12". This slope should extend at least 6 feet from the basement wall to an area where water will naturally flow away from your home.

When regrading your landscaping, it is a good idea to exceed the minimum requirements, because the soil will continue to settle for a long time afterward.

Hard surfaces such as concrete need less slope than soft surfaces, because water runs freely on the hard surfaces, but they still need a minimum slope of 1% to 2%. That is about 1/8" to 1/4" of drop for every foot of horizontal run—so in 4 feet, the patio should slope 1/2" to 1" away from your foundation. These hard surfaces should route water to a location that will naturally drain it away.

Sagging Patio or Sidewalk

Improper surface-water flow can damage the basement or crawl space.

Any hard surfaces pitched toward your home present a problem. They allow water to pond next to the foundation wall. Water will flow to the lowest level—into your basement or crawl space, or below the patio slab.

As noted above, saturated soil exerts excessive horizontal pressure that can crack basement walls and move them inward. Water collecting below a patio slab makes the soil move and heave until the slab breaks.

Patio Slab Settlement

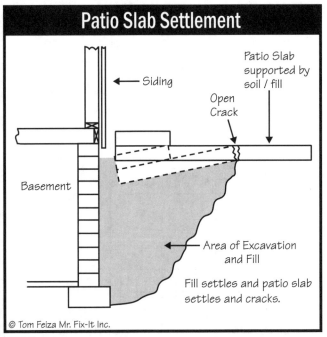

B058

Grading - Negative, Problem

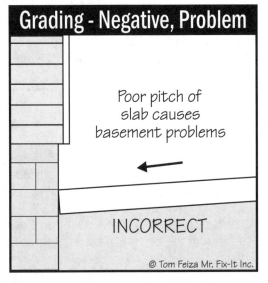

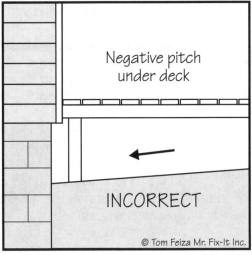

B008

If the patio or sidewalk is poorly pitched but otherwise in good condition with few cracks, mudjacking can help. Mudjacking involves drilling several holes, about 2" in diameter, in the low end of the slab. You probably have seen similar holes or patches on commercial properties. "Mud" (actually a mixture of ground stone, water and a little Portland cement) is forced into the hole under pressure by a pump. The pressure raises or levels the slab.

This repair will not be permanent, because the slab will continue to settle. However, mudjacking is much less expensive than replacing the concrete and allows you to "recycle" an otherwise good concrete slab.

Mudjacking is desirable only if the slab is in good condition with little cracking. If not, the concrete should be replaced.

How Important Is Furnace Servicing?

Neglecting routine service ignores safety and efficiency measures.

Generally, forced air furnaces will run for many years without a dramatic breakdown or loss of heat. However, for safety, energy efficiency and extended life of the furnace, you should have it serviced every year.

Proper service includes cleaning the burner and heat exchanger and inspecting for cracks or other damage. A dirty or mis-adjusted burner can produce carbon monoxide, a dangerous gas that you can't see or smell. Carbon monoxide inside your home can make you sick and can even kill you.

When a burner is tuned properly, it works with maximum efficiency. This will save you money. And a properly tuned burner is less likely to produce dangerous carbon monoxide.

Good servicing also includes testing of all safety controls; lubrication; belt maintenance; and inspection of the combustion flue pipe or discharge piping. Other areas to check include gas piping and electrical components. The service technician should also check the humidifier, air conditioning coil, drain pan, and all drain lines.

Mudjacking

1. Typical broken concrete slab as a result of settling:

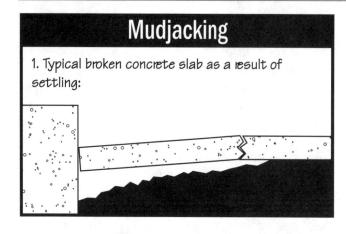

2. Pressure lifts the slab above a cone of "mud" forced through a drilled hole:

© Tom Feiza Mr. Fix-It Inc.

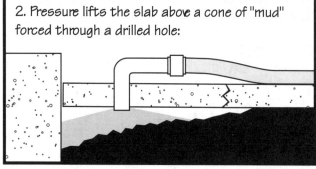

3. Additional holes are drilled to fill voids as needed to support the slab:

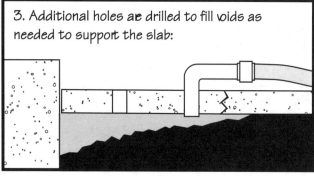

M001

Have a professional service the furnace yearly. A good time for service is in the spring—you can have both the furnace and the air conditionioner serviced at a reduced cost.

For more detailed information, see the Service Checklists chapter.

Deteriorating Ceramic Tile at Tub or Shower

Damaged or loose ceramic tile or grout can lead to extensive damage to tiles and walls.

If ceramic wall tile around a tub or shower starts coming loose, don't delay the repair. Once water

Humidifier Problems

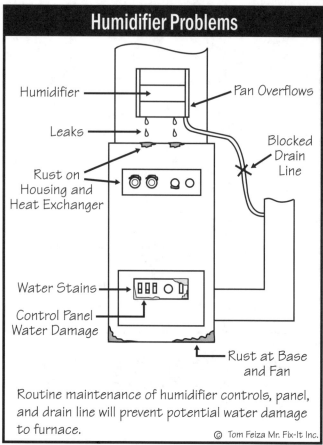

Routine maintenance of humidifier controls, panel, and drain line will prevent potential water damage to furnace.

© Tom Feiza Mr. Fix-It Inc.

H031

finds its way behind the tile, the drywall or plaster will start to deteriorate. If drywall is the backing material, large chunks of the wall can be damaged, and tile and drywall will fall off the wall. In addition, water will leak into the surrounding wall and floor.

Even a small break needs immediate repair. Replace the loose grout. If the break is near a spout or faucet, caulk around it, creating a tight seal. If tile is loose, remove it from the wall and then re-secure it with tile adhesive or waterproof construction adhesive.

If the wall is damaged behind the tile, remove the soft material and patch with plaster, wood bracing and/or cement board. You may need to cut out enough material to reach the wood studs to support the patch.

What if you can't fix the break immediately? Cover the area with plastic sheeting taped or caulked tightly to the good tile around the damaged area. This little "umbrella" over the damage will keep the water out until you can do a total repair.

Cleaning Fireplace and Flue

Failing to clean the fireplace and flue can lead to a serious chimney fire.

A fireplace requires routine maintenance to prevent safety problems and expensive repairs. The frequency and type of maintenance depends on the type of fireplace and how often you use it. There are two basic types of fireplaces: metal fabricated and masonry (brick).

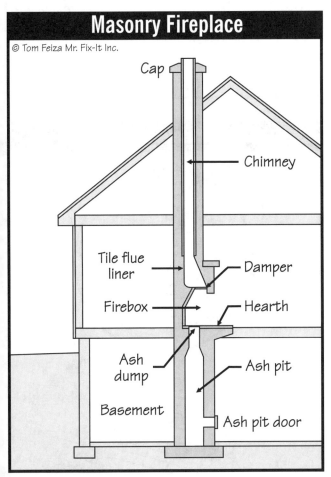

Masonry Fireplace

© Tom Feiza Mr. Fix-It Inc.

Cap

Chimney

Tile flue liner

Damper

Firebox

Hearth

Ash dump

Ash pit

Basement

Ash pit door

F005

Even if you never use the fireplace, have the exposed chimney inspected and maintained to prevent weather damage.

If you just purchased your home, have a professional clean and evaluate the fireplace before you use it. The professional should check the damper and flue for proper construction, look for any creosote or soot buildup, make sure the fireplace operates properly, and evaluate clearances to combustibles. Outside, the inspector should evaluate the cap, screen, flue, flashings, and chimney structure.

If you hire a professional chimney sweep, he or she should take the time to explain the basic construction and operation of the fireplace. A thorough sweep will also give you information on building a safe fire and maintaining your chimney. Consider hiring a chimney sweep who is a member of the Chimney Safety Institute of America (CSIA).

The CSIA has great brochures on fireplace maintenance and operation, and will also provide a list of certified chimney sweeps in your area.

See the References section for information on how to contact the CSIA.

Inspecting a Masonry Chimney

Failing to maintain the exposed parts of a masonry chimney can lead to expensive damage.

You can, if you wish, inspect your own chimney. A masonry chimney should be inspected every year. Outside, masonry surfaces take a beating from the weather. Inside, we often start with cold chimney surfaces and heat them with a roaring fire in the fireplace—pretty tough on the materials. Chimneys are also subjected to moisture and acid from the combustion of natural gas or fossil fuels.

You can inspect the chimney from the ground (with binoculars) or from the roof if you can safely reach the roof area around the chimney. Don't go on a roof that is steep or slippery. If there is a question of safe access or potential damage to roofing surfaces, leave the inspection to a professional.

Start your inspection with the top of the chimney. The clay tile should be solid with no major cracks, gaps, or broken sections. The tile should extend above the top cap. Use a flashlight to peer down into the tile. You can also view the inside of the tile from the fireplace or the cleanout door in the basement. Look up at the tile with a bright light and a mirror. There should be no obstructions inside the tile.

Around the clay tile, on the top of the chimney, there will be a cap made of stone, cast concrete or mortar. The cap seals against the tile and covers the top of the masonry surfaces, keeping moisture out. If you see minor cracks in the cap or the joint, caulk them with masonry or silicone caulk. Major cracks or broken sections dictate replacing the cap.

Chimney Parts - Good Design

(Solid, thick cap)

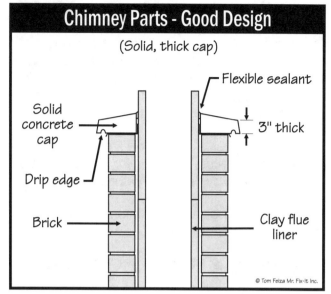

- Flexible sealant
- Solid concrete cap
- 3" thick
- Drip edge
- Brick
- Clay flue liner

F008

Chimney Parts - Poor Design

(Damaged cap causes brick and mortar damage)

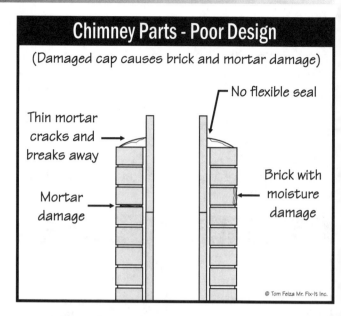

- Thin mortar cracks and breaks away
- No flexible seal
- Mortar damage
- Brick with moisture damage

The cap is essential. Fixing a minor cap problem will prevent a major failure down the road. Any moisture that bypasses the cap will destroy the masonry surfaces in time as freeze-and-thaw cycles ruin the brick and mortar.

Inspect the brick or stone and mortar. Minor cracks can be caulked; monitor them thereafter to make sure they don't grow. Major cracks, spalling (flaking) brick surfaces or loose bricks require the attention of a professional. See below for more information on how to recognize and repair spalling brick.

Simple maintenance can prevent huge repair bills. Rebuilding the top of a small chimney will cost about $200 per linear foot—which can add up to over $1,000 for a small chimney.

Check the metal flashing where the brick meets the roofing material. The top flashing or counter flashing should be sealed tightly into the mortar joints. Often this joint "steps" down the mortar joint and is actually cut into the mortar. To prevent water penetration, seal any gaps at this joint with either caulk or mortar, depending on the existing conditions.

Some flashings will be sealed with tar or roofing cement. If there are gaps or cracks in the roofing cement, re-seal the surface. With this type of coating, it is often impossible to see the type or condition of the actual flashing, so sealing any open areas is often the only alternative.

Chimney Flashing

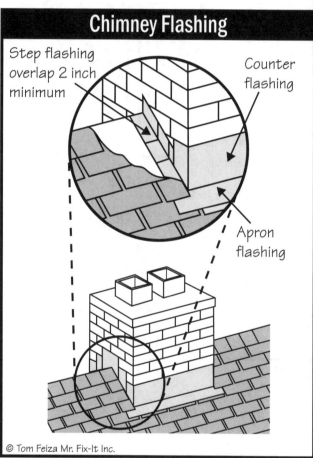

- Step flashing overlap 2 inch minimum
- Counter flashing
- Apron flashing

R009

If the chimney has a metal cap, make sure it is securely fastened and not blocked by debris. Normally a metal chimney cap is a good idea because it deflects rain and snow away from the clay tile. The cap also keeps animals out of the chimney.

Finally, your inspection should include all connections to the chimney. Metal fittings should be tightly mortared and sealed to the chimney. Minor cracks and openings can be filled with fireplace mortar or with furnace and fireplace cement. You can purchase this material in caulking tubes or in small tubs to be applied with a putty knife. Follow the instructions for the material you purchase.

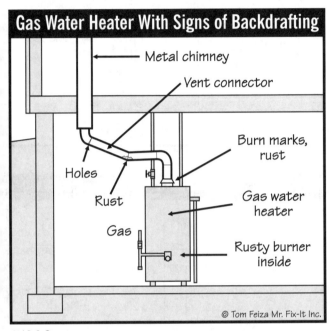

Gas Water Heater With Signs of Backdrafting

Metal chimney
Vent connector
Burn marks, rust
Holes
Gas water heater
Rust
Gas
Rusty burner inside

© Tom Feiza Mr. Fix-It Inc.

W006

Any rusted or loose flue pipes leading to the chimney should be repaired and securely supported. This includes the flue pipe from the water heater and the furnace. A chimney flue used for natural-gas-fired appliances should not be shared with a fossil fuel burner such as a wood stove or an incinerator.

Inspecting a fireplace chimney should include a check inside the fireplace with a bright light. Open the damper and look up the flue. The brick and mortar should be sound, without gaps. There should be very little buildup of shiny creosote or fluffy soot. If the buildup exceeds 1/4", the chimney needs cleaning. The damper should open fully and latch securely in the open position.

If any of this is confusing, or if you suspect a problem, contact a professional chimney sweep, heating contractor, or roofing contractor. Chimney and flue connections are designed to safely remove the products of combustion from your home. Don't risk any chance of smoke, fire or carbon monoxide entering your home.

Spalling (Flaking) Chimney Brick

Flaking bricks that aren't repaired promptly can lead to structural failure.

When the face of a brick breaks away, the brick is said to be "spalling." Usually, this happens when water penetrates the brick and the freeze/thaw cycle separates the surface from the brick. Moisture problems can also lead to mortar cracking around the brick.

Inspect the cap of the chimney. Moisture problems are most often caused by a failing cap. The cap is supposed to seal the flue, covering the top of the brick and protecting the structure below from water. Many caps are a "mortar wash" type that provide only a thin coat of mortar; the mortar is higher and thicker near the flue and tapers to a thin covering near the edge of the chimney. A better cap is made of pre-cast concrete or cast-in-place concrete that is about 3" thick with a tapered top surface.

If there is any damage to the cap or the flue, or any source of water leakage above the brick, you have found the problem. Eliminate the source of the moisture as soon as possible to prevent serious damage to the chimney. Once deterioration starts, it can progress rapidly.

Chimney sweeps and brickmasons will perform chimney repair. If your chimney has one of those cheap mortar wash caps, consider having it replaced. It is common for caps to deteriorate after 10 years or less.

Sump Pump Maintenance

A failed sump pump = water in the basement.

To understand why it's important to maintain your sump pump, first you should know what the sump pump does. Groundwater flows through drain tiles around and below the basement floor. After the water collects in the sump pump crock, the pump lifts it to the surface outside or into an underground storm sewer pipe draining away from your home. This system is separate from the sanitary sewer system that drains wastewater from toilets, sinks, the washing machine, and so on, routing it to the sanitary sewer treatment plant.

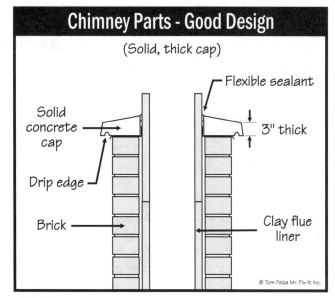

Chimney Parts - Good Design

(Solid, thick cap)

- Flexible sealant
- Solid concrete cap
- 3" thick
- Drip edge
- Brick
- Clay flue liner

© Tom Feiza Mr. Fix-It Inc.

F008

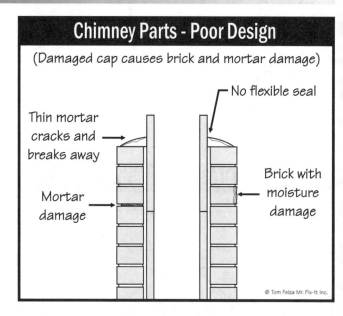

Chimney Parts - Poor Design

(Damaged cap causes brick and mortar damage)

- No flexible seal
- Thin mortar cracks and breaks away
- Brick with moisture damage
- Mortar damage

© Tom Feiza Mr. Fix-It Inc.

Test your sump pump every few months. Add water to the crock; the pump should switch on when the water is 8" to 12" below the top of the concrete floor. You could also start the pump by lifting the float. Watch to make sure the pump removes water from the crock. If groundwater has collected in the crock, the water should be clear. The crock should be free of roots or debris.

If the pump has a float on a metal rod, check that the float operates easily and doesn't rub against the crock or the cover. If a float sticks, the pump will not run, and your basement could flood.

The pump should be securely mounted in the crock. Its plug should be securely fastened in an outlet, not an extension cord. Replace the pump if it is old and worn, rusty, or noisy.

If the pump runs more than several times per day and runs often during heavy rain, purchase a spare pump, or mount a second pump in the crock. The second pump could have its float set for a higher water level so it will run only if the first pump fails.

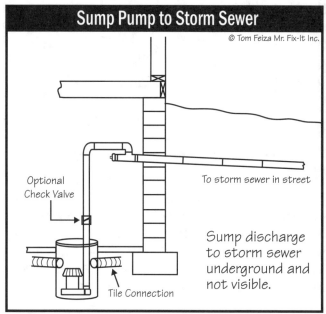

Sump Pump to Storm Sewer

© Tom Feiza Mr. Fix-It Inc.

- Optional Check Valve
- To storm sewer in street
- Tile Connection

Sump discharge to storm sewer underground and not visible.

B056

Leaks at the Air Conditioner

A leak can occur at the air conditioner cooling coil and cause rot, mold and structural damage. See Chapter 13 for the solution.

Chapter 20 – My Top Energy-Saving And Comfort Tips

General Philosophy

Energy efficiency with comfort is a goal I learned from my energy buddy Clyde Rymer more than 20 years ago when we were trying to save energy at a large college facility. No one gets excited about simply saving energy, but if you can combine energy conservation with comfort improvements, everyone is happy.

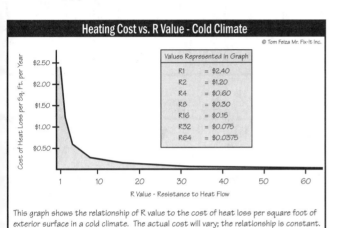

Heating Cost vs. R Value - Cold Climate

© Tom Feiza Mr. Fix-It Inc.

Values Represented in Graph	
R1	= $2.40
R2	= $1.20
R4	= $0.60
R8	= $0.30
R16	= $0.15
R32	= $0.075
R64	= $0.0375

Cost of Heat Loss per Sq. Ft. per Year
R Value - Resistance to Heat Flow

This graph shows the relationship of R value to the cost of heat loss per square foot of exterior surface in a cold climate. The actual cost will vary; the relationship is constant.

I003

Insulation vs. Heat Loss

Typical cost of heat loss through 1 square foot of exterior surface.

Material	R Value	Heat Cost / Sq. Ft.
Single Glass	R1	$2.40
Double Glass	R2	$1.20
4" of Wood	R4	$0.60
Basement w/ 1" Foam	R8	$0.30
Typical Wall	R20	$0.12
Attic Insulation	R40	$0.06

Double the R value and cut the heat loss (cost) in half. Actual cost will change based on climate and heat source. The relationship is constant.

© Tom Feiza Mr. Fix-It Inc.

I004

These are my top tips on saving energy and improving comfort in your home. (By the way, at the college we reduced energy bills every year for 14 years straight and saved over $10 million during a period when energy costs were increasing!)

1. Insulate the Attic Trap Door

Insulating and weatherstripping the trap door to the attic is one of the best energy-saving measures you can take. It costs little and will eliminate a large heat loss and potential attic moisture problems.

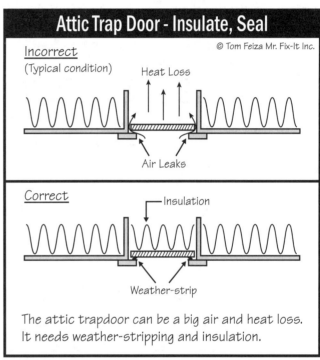

Attic Trap Door - Insulate, Seal

© Tom Feiza Mr. Fix-It Inc.

Incorrect
(Typical condition) Heat Loss

Air Leaks

Correct — Insulation

Weather-strip

The attic trapdoor can be a big air and heat loss. It needs weather-stripping and insulation.

I006

You don't feel cold air at the trap door because warm house air pushes up through cracks and gaps into the cold attic. Weatherstripping will stop these air leaks, and a few layers of insulation will prevent heat transfer through the door.

2. Water Heater Temperature

Lower the water heater temperature to the lowest setting you find comfortable. This saves energy by reducing the continuous heat loss that occurs when storing a tank of hot water. It will also reduce the chance that anyone may be scalded by hot water.

How low can you set the water temperature? Normally 120 degrees is the recommended temperature for energy savings. Water feels hot at 105 degrees. At 115 degrees, water can cause first-degree burns. Gas water heaters will not have an actual temperature indicated on the dial, so set the heater to the lowest or "warm" setting and check the temperature at a hot water faucet the next day. It will take some time for the water in the tank to cool.

Electric water heaters may have a setting that indicates the actual temperature. Sometimes the dial is exposed on the side of the heater, but most often it is under the top cover. Be careful when you open the cover, since there may be some "hot" exposed wires beneath. Check the actual water temperature after you reset the unit. If the water feels too cold, you can always increase the temperature.

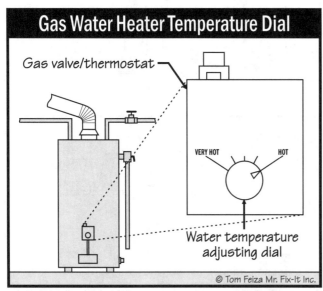

W004

Note: some dishwashers require 140-degree water. Check the directions for the dishwasher and for the detergent you are using. Consider switching to a detergent that works better at a lower temperature.

Also, try to conserve hot water. Wash clothes in cool, cold or warm water. Take a quick shower and use a low flow showerhead.

3. Thermostat Settings

You can save a substantial amount of energy by lowering the temperature setting for your heating system in the winter and raising the temperature for the air conditioning in the summer. By dialing back your heating system 1 degree, you can save up to 3% on your heating bills.

In the winter, try to live with the thermostat set at 68 degrees. This may require wearing a sweater if

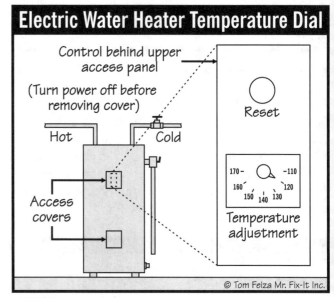

W003

you are older or don't move around much. In the summer, try setting the thermostat at 78 degrees for cooling.

During a period of hot weather, leave your air conditioning system on throughout. Don't turn it on and off from day to day. The air conditioning system removes moisture from the interior air, and this helps you feel comfortable. If you open the windows for a few hours to air out your home, you will immediately lose all that dry air.

Consider installing a setback (programmable) thermostat to control your heating and cooling systems. Programmable thermostats have come a long way in the last 20 years. Now they are electronic wonders – easy to install, easy to program and very inexpensive (about $50 to $100). Properly used, these thermostats can save you 10% of your heating and cooling bill.

Programmable thermostats allow you to set back the heating temperature during the evening when you are sleeping or during the day when no one is home. You program the unit to increase the temperature before you wake up or before you come home from work. This results in substantial energy savings with no loss in comfort. You can also program the temperature setting for your air conditioning.

Programmable thermostats come with complete installation instructions, and most handy people can install them. The only wiring involved is low-voltage control wiring, and you just need to match the wire colors. When looking for a thermostat, remember that there are heating-only units and combination heating-cooling units.

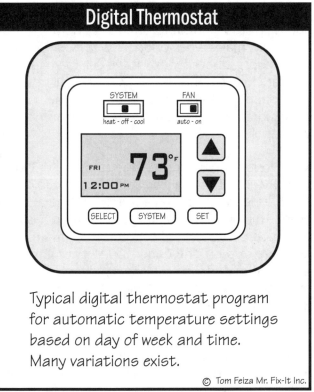

Typical digital thermostat program for automatic temperature settings based on day of week and time. Many variations exist.

© Tom Feiza Mr. Fix-It Inc.

H025

4. Band Joist (Sill Plate) Insulation

You may have one large bare area around your home that allows a huge heat loss—the area at the band joist or sill plate. This is the area just above the basement wall, between the joists of the first floor of your home. On the outside, this area is near the ground but still exposed to weather.

In this area, you may have no insulation, just the wood frame (a 1-1/2"-thick band joist) and the siding. An area like this has less insulation value than a common insulated glass window.

To insulate this area, first look for any gaps or cracks. Study the area when the sun is bright outside; keep the basement lights low. The gaps will be obvious. Seal them with caulk or a foam sealant.

Insulate with 6"-thick unfaced fiberglass insulation. Buy insulation that is designed to fit between the spacing of the joists—normally between 16"-on-center joists. (The actual space is 14-1/2" wide once

you subtract for the 1-1/2"-thick lumber.) Cut the insulation by compressing it against a board with a straightedge. It will slice easily with a utility knife. Cut the insulation slightly larger than the opening so that friction will hold it in place.

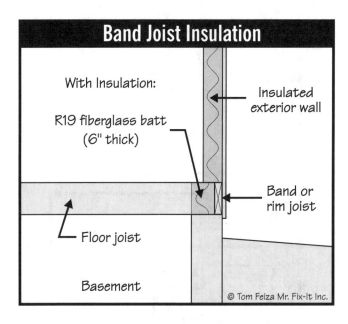

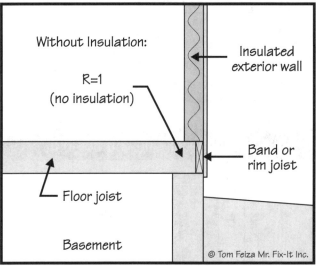

S001

5. Weatherstripping and Caulking

In general, it makes a lot of sense to seal up the exterior envelope of your home. This eliminates heating and cooling losses and seals your home against potential pests. Every year you should check caulking and sealant used around any penetration through the exterior wall of your home.

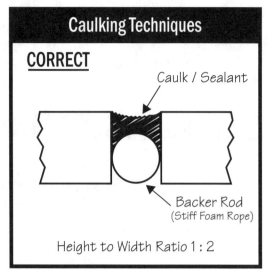

Caulking Techniques

CORRECT

Caulk / Sealant

Backer Rod
(Stiff Foam Rope)

Height to Width Ratio 1 : 2

© Tom Feiza Mr. Fix-It Inc.

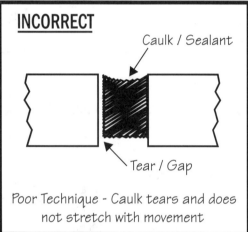

INCORRECT

Caulk / Sealant

Tear / Gap

Poor Technique - Caulk tears and does not stretch with movement

M009

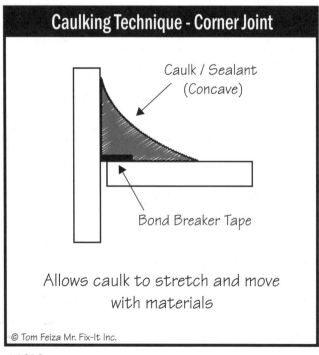

Caulking Technique - Corner Joint

Caulk / Sealant
(Concave)

Bond Breaker Tape

Allows caulk to stretch and move with materials

© Tom Feiza Mr. Fix-It Inc.

M010

Check window and door caulking. An investment of a few dollars and a few hours can eliminate drafts and make your home more comfortable.

Weatherstripping around windows and doors can also help stop cold drafts and save energy. There are many, many types of door sweeps, strips, foam strips, rubber tapes, closed-cell foam tape, tubular vinyl, felt, bronze strips, open-cell tape, vinyl clad foam—the list goes on. Visit the hardware store and choose the product that is right for your application.

My favorite product for weatherstripping is 3-M brand V-Seal. This is a very thin vinyl that folds along its length to form a V, similar to the age-old bronze metal strips. The key to this product is its size, ease of use, and effectiveness. It has an adhesive strip on one edge. You just cut it to the length you need with a scissors, peel off the backing tape and place the V-Seal in the opening. Because the product is so thin, it fits easily around doors and windows.

I actually used V-Seal to "double weatherstrip" all my doors. It is easy to use and inexpensive, and it will last a long, long time. You can find it at all hardware stores.

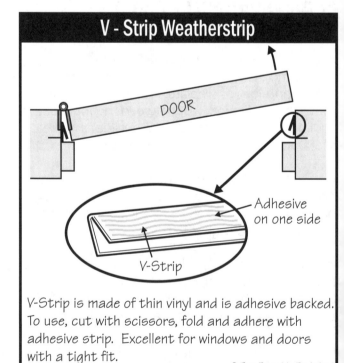

V - Strip Weatherstrip

DOOR

Adhesive on one side

V-Strip

V-Strip is made of thin vinyl and is adhesive backed. To use, cut with scissors, fold and adhere with adhesive strip. Excellent for windows and doors with a tight fit.

© Tom Feiza Mr. Fix-It Inc.

D006

6. Temporary Caulking and Storms

If you need a quick fix for air leaks, consider removable caulks and sealant. You can place these around offending windows to effectively seal them in place for the winter. In the spring, remove the caulk. These work great on drafty old windows you don't plan on opening for a season or two.

Also consider temporary inside or outside storms. These are great products first introduced by the 3-M Company. You place two-sided tape around the inside of the offending window or door, then place clear plastic on the tape. When you heat the plastic with a hair dryer, it stretches to become an invisible storm window. A similar product can also be used outside.

I have saved my kids several times in their old, drafty, dumpy, awful college rentals with these sealers and inside storms.

7. Showerheads

A low flow showerhead can give a good shower while saving a substantial amount of water as well as energy used to heat the water. I understand that this technology was perfected in submarines, where conserving water was an absolute necessity. Low flow heads have suffered a bad reputation for several years, but now many options and good showerheads are available.

You can also add a flow control valve at the showerhead. This allows everyone to adjust the flow to his or her preference.

If you want to test your showerhead, put a bucket below the showerhead and turn the water on full force. After 30 seconds, measure the amount of water in the bucket. Double that amount to determine the flow per minute. A good low-flow showerhead uses well below 2.5 gallons per minute. (You can also measure the flow for a full minute if you have a large bucket and a strong arm.)

A low flow showerhead will cost from $5 to $20 and can easily save more than that amount each year in reduced energy, water and sewer costs.

8. Lighting Controls

Teens or younger children seldom remember to turn lights off. From personal experience, I know that the best way to keep the lights off in a home shared with teenagers is to send them away to college. If that is not practical, here are several aids I have used successfully.

For walk-in closets or storage areas, replace the switch with a 15-minute timer. The maximum the light can be on is 15 minutes, and often the kids will switch the timer off because of its annoying ticking. This also works in bathrooms and bedrooms, but there you will need a longer (1- or 2-hour) timer.

For exterior lights, I always use fixtures with a built-in photo-eye control so the light only operates after dark. Fluorescent and sodium lights are also big energy savers for outdoor fixtures.

For bathroom and bedrooms, I have had mixed results with motion sensor switches. They can be hard to adjust and may turn off at inappropriate times. Ask yourself: would waving your hands in the dark while taking a shower be fun or frustrating? Despite some problems with adjustment, though, I think motion sensors generally work well.

9. Stop All Water Leaks

Any small drip or water leak will waste a huge amount of water and energy. Energy is required to pump the water and heat it. Once the water is in the sewer, it must be treated by the sewer system.

A small drip that fills a coffee cup in a 10-minute period wastes about 3,280 gallons of water per year. A drip rate of one per second can waste up to 200 gallons of water per month or 2,400 gallons per year.

Repair any leaking faucet or fixture to save energy and our precious resources.

10. Switch to Fluorescent Lamps

Now here is where I get in trouble. I love fluorescent light fixtures and the small fluorescent bulbs that can be used in standard lamps. I love the energy they save, but I get in trouble because my wife and kids have complained about these fixtures in our home for the last 20 years.

I will admit that 20 years ago, these fluorescent lights produced a poor, harsh color, and they often failed prematurely. But they have come a long way in 20 years, and come to think about it, I have not had a complaint at home for about 5 years. Perhaps my family has adjusted to my favorite lights, maybe because the lights have improved greatly.

I started using fluorescent and compact fluorescent bulbs in my commercial building projects 20 years ago and often brought home a few trial fixtures. I also consistently bought and received fixtures through utility company programs designed to save energy.

Today the fluorescent fixtures are great! You can buy color-corrected lamps that give off a warm light that is close to the color of natural sunlight. You can buy fluorescent bulbs that will fit in most lamps and fixtures. These fluorescent bulbs typically last 10 times as long as standard incandescent bulbs and produce the same amount of light for one-quarter the cost. Give them a try—at least in fixtures you use a lot or in your security lights.

11. Maintain Heating and Cooling Equipment–Yourself

Basic maintenance of heating and cooling equipment can easily save you up to 5% of your heating and cooling bill and will help avoid a potentially expensive outage.

What can you do? What must you do? Read the recommendations elsewhere in this book for the specific type of equipment in your home. Remember: change filters, keep coils clean, and keep plants away from air conditioners and heat pumps. Simple steps can save lots of money.

12. Maintain Heating and Cooling Equipment–Professionals

Don't forget to schedule professional service for your home's main heating and cooling equipment. Professionals can keep your equipment in top shape and can tune the equipment for energy efficiency. Have them follow the guidelines provided in this book.

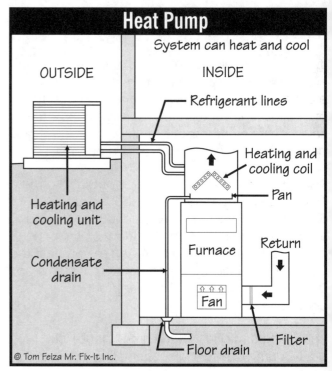

A003

For more information, see the References section and Chapter 23 – Service Checklists.

13. Seal Heating and Cooling Ducts

Recent studies have confirmed that there is a huge potential for energy savings by sealing heating and cooling ducts in unconditioned spaces. These studies and airflow evaluations have found energy losses and comfort problems due to losses from distribution ducts.

These problems typically occur when heating and cooling ducts are run in unheated attics or crawl spaces. Any hole or crack in a heating/cooling duct will dump energy to the outside, reducing comfort inside your home. Leaks are often found at joints that are not sealed or those sealed with duct tape that has failed. Duct tape is only a temporary fix; it will eventually dry out.

I have performed thousands of home inspections over the years and have often found damaged, uninsulated, disconnected ductwork in attics and crawl spaces. Why? Well, whoever looks in the attic or the crawl space?

Ductwork inspection and sealing is not easy but can produce great savings. Hire a professional

Filter Maintenance - Warm Air Furnace

(upflow type)

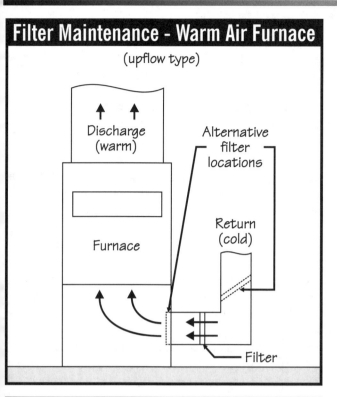

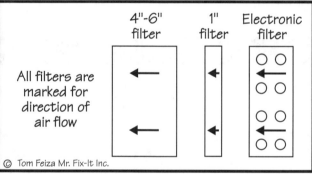

H009

home inspector or heating contractor to inspect your system, and plan on corrective work based on the inspection. Use special duct sealant to seal small cracks. Repair larger openings or gaps with special sealing mesh and duct sealant and a putty knife. Repair disconnected ducts.

14. Seal Openings Into the Attic

This is another tough problem. Many homes were built with poor sealing between the conditioned living space and the attic. This results in extensive air leaks and loss of heat and moisture. There may even be moisture damage in the attic due to leaks around pipes, electrical wiring, and vents routed through the ceilings.

Attic - Air Bypass

COMMON AIR LEAKS INTO AN ATTIC

Warm and moist interior air pushes into the attic through any opening.

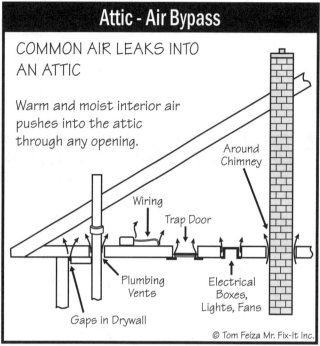

I005

Warm Air Furnace and Distribution Ducts

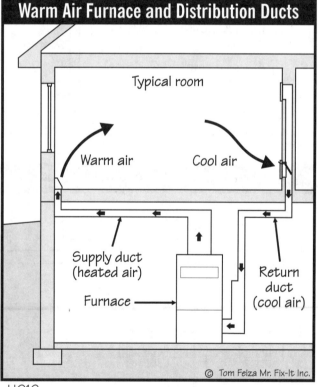

H010

Spotting this type of problem requires a throrough inspection of the attic—perhaps a task best left to an insulation firm or a professional home inspector. A professional will look for gaps around any penetration through the ceiling envelope of your home. Gaps may occur around piping, wiring, fans, chimneys and other penetrations. Often an air leak will

223

leave telltale signs such as mildew, moisture stains or dirt stains from air movement.

All of these gaps and holes can be filled with caulk, foam sealant or sheet metal caulked in place. Often a professional should do this work because of the hazards of working in an attic.

One word of caution: don't seal around standard recessed light fixtures. They need air movement to dissipate heat. Special sealed light fixtures can be installed to prevent air movement and heat loss.

15. Fireplaces: Warm and Romantic, But...

I hate to tell you this, but I have to: your standard masonry fireplace is a big, big heat loser. When you build a fire, a tremendous amount of air that was heated by your furnace goes up the chimney.

You can help this situation by using glass fireplace doors and having a contractor install an outside air supply for the fireplace. You can also help by closing the damper and doors when the fire is completely out.

Notice that I have been talking about standard masonry fireplaces. Modern metal-framed fireplaces with an outside air supply and the ability to heat some of the room air are much more efficient.

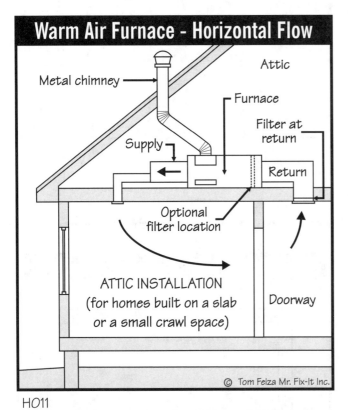

HO11

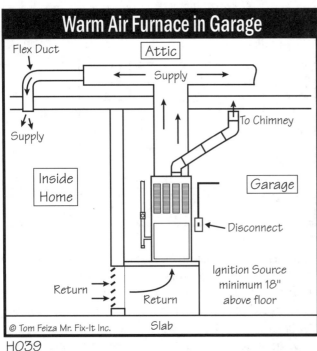

HO39

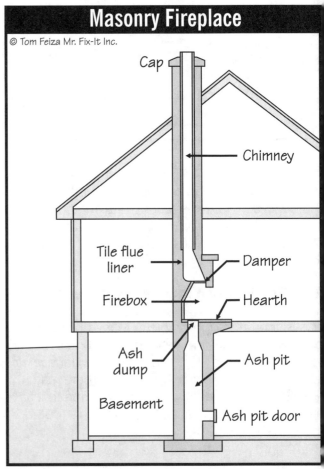

FOO5

Modern gas-fired, sealed-combustion, direct-vented fireplaces are great! Consider one of these if you are building or remodeling. Their efficiency rivals that of furnaces, and they can heat a room or a portion of your home.

Energy: A Quick Summary

You will notice that I have not addressed replacing furnaces, replacing windows, or insulating attics as my top energy-saving and comfort tips. While these are all fine approaches to saving energy, most of us complete these projects because of other concerns: the furnace is failing, the windows don't work, or there is no insulation in the attic.

I have addressed simple energy-saving ideas that you can easily work into your everyday routine and budget—things that work and provide substantial savings compared to the cost involved, and things that improve the comfort of your home.

Don't get hung up on big, expensive projects like a furnace replacement or insulation project until you have addressed the simple fixes. Also, consider contacting your local utility, which may offer a free or low-cost professional energy evaluation of your home.

Chapter 21 – Recommended Books and Magazines

For Most Homeowners

I have collected almost all the available books on home repair, and I do have several favorites. The best books provide accurate information on how systems work, give repair information, and offer lots of pictures or sketches.

One of the best home repair books is *The New Complete Do-It-Yourself Manual* from Reader's Digest. A great review of systems in a home is *How A House Works* by Duane Johnson (which is a series of articles from The Family Handyman magazine, reprinted in book format by Reader's Digest). Other good books include *The Stanley Complete Step-By-Step Book of Home Repair and Improvement, Ortho's Home Improvement Encyclopedia*, and the home repair and improvement book series published by Time-Life Books. Another of my favorites—no surprise here—is my own *Just Fix It*, which provides hundreds of answers to common home problems; ordering information appears at the end of this book.

Look for a reference work that focuses on the type of work you plan to perform. Some books are strong in painting and refinishing, others in mechanical and electrical repairs. Don't start with big, complicated home repairs and improvements if you've never done small jobs. You need to experience success on small projects and build from there.

My favorite magazines for the typical homeowner include The Family Handyman, Consumer Reports, Home Mechanics, Today's Homeowner and Practical Homeowner.

For Restoration

Folks involved in restoration of older homes can certainly use the books listed above, and should add the following:

Magazines

Old-House Journal

Books

The Old-House Journal Guide to Restoration (Dutton)

The Old-House Journal Restoration Directory (an annual sourcebook of suppliers)

Caring for Your Historic House, edited by Charles E. Fisher (Harry N. Abrams)

Directory of Building Preservation by Ward Butcher (Wiley)

For Experts

Here are sources of info for experts and for amateurs with a special interest in residential construction:

Magazines

Fine Homebuilding

Fine Woodworking

The Journal of Light Construction

Books

Residential & Light Commercial Construction Standards (Robert S. Means Co.)

Builder's Guide to Cold Climates by Joseph Lstiburek (Taunton)

Builder's Guide to Mixed Climates by Joseph Lstiburek (Taunton)

Troubleshooting Guide to Residential Construction (from the editors of The Journal of Light Construction)

Chapter 22 – References

Quick Index for Categories Listed:

Home related associations and manufacturers with addresses, 800 numbers and website information.

Adhesives

DAP

2400 Boston St.
Suite 200
Baltimore, MD 21224
800-543-3840
www.dap.com

Elmer's Products

180 E. Broad St.
Columbus, OH 43215
www.elmers.com
888-543-6377

Franklin Int'l Titebond

800-347-4583
www.titebond.com

Gorilla Glue

800-966-3458
www.gorillaglue.com

Loctite Corp.

1001 Trout Brook Crossing
Rocky Hill, CT 06067
800-LOCTITE
www.loctite.com

Macco Adhesives

Liquid Nails

15885 West Sprague Rd.
Strongville, OH 44136
800-634-0015
www.liquidnail.com

Ohio Sealants

PL and Quickbond
7405 Production
Mentor, OH 44060
800-321-3578
www.osisealants.com

Air Conditioning (See Heating)

Air Quality

Allergy and Asthma Network

2751 Prosperity Ave.
Suite 150
Fairfax, VA 22031
800-878-4403
www.aanma.org

American Lung Association

61 Broadway, 6th Floor
New York, NY 10006
800-548-8285
www.lungusa.org

Asthma and Allergy Foundation of America

800-727-8462
www.aafa.org

Building Air Quality

U.S. Environmental Protection Agency
Washington, DC 20460
202-233-9030

U.S. Environmental Protection Agency

Indoor Air Quality
202-343-9370
www.epa.gov/iaq

Appliances

Amana Refrigeration

www.amana.com

American Whirlpool

800-327-1394
www.americanwhirlpool.com

Association of Home Appliance Manufacturers

Suite 402
1111 19th St. NW
Washington, DC 20036
202-872-5955
www.aham.org

Black & Decker

Consumer Service Center
626 Hanover Pike
Hampstead, MD 21074
800-54-HOW-TO
www.blackanddecker.com

Electrolux Home Products

800-458-1445
www.electrolux.com

Eureka

www.eureka.com

Frigidaire

Electrolux Home Products
P.O. Box 212378
Martinez, GA 30917
800-374-4432
www.frigidaire.com

GE Appliances

800-626-2005
www.geappliances.com

Gibson

www.electrolux.com

Hamilton Beach/Proctor-Silex

www.hamiltonbeach.com

HotPoint Appliances

www.hotpoint.com

In-Sink-Erator Division

Emerson Electric Co.
4700 21st Street
Racine, WI 53406
800-558-5700
www.insinkerator.com

Kelvinator

www.electrolux.com

Kenmore/Sears

800-349-4358
www.sears.com

KitchenAid

P.O. Box 218
St. Joseph, MI 49085
800-422-1230
www.kitchenaid.com

Maytag Corporation

240 Edwards St.
Cleveland, TN 37311
800-688-9900
www.maytag.com

Sanyo Corporation

800-421-5013
www.sanyo.com

Sears / Kenmore

3333 Beverly Rd.
Hoffman Estates, IL 60179
800-349-4358
www.sears.com

Sub-Zero Freezer

P.O. Box 44130
Madison, WI 53744-4130
800-222-7820
www.sub-zerofreezer.com

Tappan

www.electrolux.com

U-Line Corp.

P.O. Box 245040
Milwaukee, WI 53224-3540
414-354-0300
www.u-line.com

Whirlpool Corporation

800-253-1301
www.whirlpool.com

White Westinghouse

www.electrolux.com

Associations: Contractor, Supplier, and Builder

ACI International
(American Concrete Institute)

P.O. Box 9094
38800 Country Club Dr.
Farmington Hills, MI 48333
248-848-3700
www.aci-int.net

Acoustical Society of America

2 Huntington Quadrangle
Suite 1N01
Melville, NY 11747
516-576-2360
asa.aip.org

Adhesive and Sealant Council

7979 Old Georgetown Rd.
Suite 500
Bethesda, MD 20814
301-986-9700
www.ascouncil.org

American Forest and
Paper Association
American Wood Council

1111 Nineteenth St.
Suite 800
Washington, DC 20036
202-463-2766
www.awc.org

American Gas Association

202-824-7000
www.aga.org

American Hardboard Assoc.

1210 W. Northwest Highway
Palatine, IL 60067
847-934-8800

American Hardware
Manufacturers Association

801 N. Plaza Drive
Schaumburg, IL 60173-4977
847-605-1025
www.ahma.org

American Homeowners
Association

800-470-2242
www.ahahome.com

American Industrial
Hygiene Association

2700 Prosperity Ave.
Suite 250
Fairfax, VA 22031
www.aiha.org

American Institute of Architects

1735 New York Ave., NW
Washington, DC 20006
202-626-7300
www.aiaonline.com

American Insurance Association

1130 Connecticut Ave., NW
Washington, DC 20036
202-828-7100
www.aiadc.org

American Iron and Steel Institute

1101 17th St., NW
Washington, DC 20036
202-452-7100
www.steel.org

American Lighting Association

P.O. Box 420288
Dallas, TX 75342-0288
800-274-4484
www.americanlightingassoc.com

American National
Standards Institute

11 W. 42nd Street, 13th Floor
New York, NY 10036
212-642-4900
www.ansi.org

American Red Cross

www.redcross.org

American Society for
Testing & Materials (ASTM)

100 Barr Harbor Dr.
West Conshocken, PA 19428
610-832-9585
www.astm.org

American Society of Heating,
Refrigerating and Air
Conditioning Engineers, Inc.

1791 Tullie Circle, NE
Atlanta, GA 30329
800-527-4723
www.ashrae.org

American Society of
Home Inspectors

932 Lee St. Suite 101
Des Plaines, IL 60016
800-743-2744
www.ashi.org

American Society of
Safety Engineers

1800 E. Oakton St.
Des Plaines, IL 60018
800-380-7101
www.asse.org

American Wood
Preservers Institute

2750 Prosperity Ave.
Suite 550
Fairfax, VA 22031
800-356-AWPI
www.awpi.org

APA – The Engineered
Wood Association

7011 S. 19th
Tacoma, WA 98466
253-565-6600
www.apawood.org

Architectural Landscape Lighting

800-854-8277
www.alllighting.com

Asphalt Roofing
Manufacturers Assoc.

Public Information Dept.
1156 15th St. NW, Suite 900
Washington, DC 20005
202-207-0917
www.asphaltroofing.org

Associated General Contractors
of America

333 John Carlyle Street
Alexandria, VA 22314
703-548-31118
www.agc.org

Association of Home
Appliance Manufacturers

Suite 402
1111 19th St. NW
Washington, DC 20036
202-872-5955
www.aham.org

Association of Pools and Spas

602-252-4664

Association of the Wall & Ceiling
Industries International

803 West Broad St.
Suite 600
Falls Church, VA 22046
703-534-8300
www.awci.org.

Bat Conservation Int'l

P.O. Box 162603
Austin, TX 78716
512-327-9721
www.batcon.org

BOCA International

(Building Officials and Code
Administrators)
4051 West Flossmoor Rd.
Country Club Hills, IL 60478
www.bocai.org

Brick Industry Association

11490 Commerce Park Drive
Reston, VA 20191-1525
703-620-0010
www.bia.org

California Redwood Association

405 Enfrente Dr., Suite 200
Novato, CA 94949
888-225-7339
www.calredwood.org

The Carpet & Rug Institute

P.O. Box 2048
Dalton, GA 30722
800-882-8846
www.carpet-rug.com

Cedar Shake & Shingle Bureau

P.O. Box 1178
Sumas, WA 98295-1178
604-820-7700
www.cedarbureau.org

Cedar Shingles

www.cedarbureau.org

Ceiling and Interior Systems
Construction Association

1500 Lincoln Hwy.
Suite 202
St. Charles, IL 60174
630-584-1919
www.cisca.org.

Chimney Safety Institute
of America

2155 Commercial Dr.
Plainfield, IN 46168
317-837-5392
www.csia.org

Construction
Specification Institute

99 Canal Center Plaza
Suite 300
Alexandria, VA 22314
800-689-2900

Department of Housing &
Urban Development

451 Seventh St, SW
Washington, DC 20410
202-708-0417
www.hud.gov

Drywall Finishing Council

345 West Meats Ave.
Orange, CA 92865
714-637-2770

EFIS Industry
Members Association

3000 Corporate Center Dr.
Suite 270
Morrow, GA 30260
770-968-7945

Garage Door
Hardware Association

2850 S. Ocean Blvd.
Suite 311
Palm Beach, FL 33480
407-533-0991

Gas Research Institute

8600 W. Bryn Mawr
Chicago, IL 60631
773-399-8100

General Services
Administration (U.S.)

1800 F Street, NW
Suite 6137
Washington, DC 20405
202-501-0800
www.gsa.gov

Gypsum Association

810 First St. NE
Suite 510
Washington, DC 20002
202-289-5440
www.gypsum.org

Hardwood Council

800-373-WOOD
www.hardwoodcouncil.com

Hardwood
Manufacturers Association

400 Penn Center Blvd.
Suite 530
Pittsburgh, PA 15235
412-829-0770
www.hmamembers.org

Hardwood Plywood &
Veneer Association

P.O. Box 2789
Reston, VA 20195
703-435-2900
www.hpva.org

Home Ventilating Institute

1000 N. Rand Rd.
Suite 214
Wauconda, IL 60084
847-526-2010
www.hvi.org

Interlocking Concrete
Pavement Institute

1444 "I" St. NW
Suite 700
Washington, DC 20005
202-712-9036

International Association of
Lighting Designers (IALD)

312-527-3677
www.iald.org

International Conference of
Building Officials

5360 Workman Mill Rd.
Whittier, CA 90601
800-284-4406
www.icbo.org

International Code Council

5203 Leesburg Pike
Suite 708
Falls Church, VA 22041
703-931-4533
www.intlcode.org.

International Staple, Nail, and
Tool Association (ISANTA)

512 W. Burlington Ave.
Suite 203
LaGrange, IL 60525
708-482-8138
www.isanta.org

Maple Flooring
Manufacturers Association

60 Revere Dr. Suite 500
Northbrook, IL 60062
847-480-9138
www.maplefloor.org

The Marble Institute of America

28901 Clemens Rd. Suite 100
Westlake OH, 44145
440-250-9222
www.marble-institute.com

National Association of
Architectural Metal Manufacturers

8 South Michigan Ave.
Suite 1000
Chicago, IL 60603
312-332-0405
www.naamm.org

National Association of
Brick Distributors

1600 Spring Hill Rd.
Suite 305
Vienna, VA 22182
703-749-6223

National Association of
Home Builders

1201 15th Street NW
Washington, DC 20005
800-368-5242
www.nahb.com

National Association of
Home Inspectors

4248 Park Glen Rd.
Minneapolis, MN 55416
800-448-3942
www.nahi.org

National Association of the
Remodeling Industry

780 Lee St. Suite 200
Des Plaines, IL 60016
800-298-9200
www.nari.org

National Concrete
Masonry Association

13750 Sunrise Valley Dr.
Herndon, VA 20171-4462
703-713-1900
www.ncma.org

National Conference of States on
Building Codes and Standards

505 Huntmar Park Dr.
Suite 210
Herndon, VA 20170
703-437-0100
www.ncsbcs.org

National Electrical
Manufacturers Association

1300 North 17th St.
Suite 1847
Rosslyn, VA 22209
703-841-3200
www.nema.org

National Fire Prevention
Association (NFPA)

1 Batterymarch Park
Quincy, MA 02169-7471
617-770-3000
www.nfpa.org

National Institute of
Building Sciences

1090 Vermont Ave. NW
Suite 700
Washinton, DC 20005
202-289-7800
www.nibs.org

National Lime Association

200 North Glebe Rd.
Suite 800
Arlington, VA 22203
703-243-5463
www.lime.org

National Oak Flooring
Manufacturers Association

P.O. Box 3009
Memphis, TN 38173
901-526-5016
www.nofma.org

National Paint &
Coatings Association.

1500 Rhode Island Ave. NW
Washington, DC 20005
202-462-6272
www.paint.org

National Pest
Management Association

9300 Lee Highway, Suite 301
Fairfax, VA 22031
703-352-6762
www.pestworld.org

National Propane
Gas Association

1150 17th St. NW
Suite 310
Washington, DC 20036-4623
202-466-7200
www.npga.org

National Safety Council

1121 Spring Drive
Itasca, IL 60143
800-621-7619

National Technical
Information Center

U.S. Dept. of Commerce
5295 Port Royal Rd.
Springfield, VA 22161
703-487-4650
www.ntis.gov

National Wood
Flooring Association

111 Chesterfield Industrial Blvd.
Chesterfield, MO 63005
800-422-4556

National Wooden Pallet and
Container Association

1800 N. Kent St., Suite 911
Arlington, VA 22209
703-527-7667

Painting & Decorating
Contractors of America

11960 Westline Industrial Dr.
Suite 201
St. Louis, MO 63146
800-332-7322
www.pdca.com

Plumbing Heating
Cooling Contractors –
National Association

P.O. Box 6806
Falls Church, VA 22040
800-533-7694
www.phccweb.org

Portland Cement Association

5420 Old Orchard Road
Skokie, IL 60077-4321
847-966-6200
www.cement.org

Red Cedar Shingle and Handsplit
Shake Bureau

515 – 116th Avenue NE
Suite 275
Bellevue, WA 98004

Resilient Floor Covering Institute

401 E. Jefferson St.
Rockville, MD 20850
301-340-8580
www.rfci.com

Riverbank Acoustical Laboratories

1512 S. Batavia Ave.
Geneva, IL 60134
630-232-0104
riverbank.alionscience.com

Southern Building Code

Congress International
900 Montclair Rd.
Birmingham, AL 35213
205-591-1853
www.sbcci.org

Southern Forest
Products Association

Box 641700
Kenner, LA 70064
504-443-4464
www.southernpine.com

Southern Pine Council

Box 641700
Kenner, LA 70064
504-443-4464
www.southernpine.com

Structural Insulated
Panel Association

3413 56th St. NW Suite A
Gig Harbor, WA 98335
253-858-7472
www.sips.org

Tile Council of America

100 Clemson Research Blvd.
Anderson, SC 29625
864-646-8453
www.tileusa.com

Truss Plate Institute

583 D'Onofrio Dr. Suite 200
Madison, WI 53719
608-833-5900

Underwriters Laboratories

333 Pfingsten Road
Northbrook, IL 60062
847-272-8800
www.ul.com

U.S. Department of Labor
Occupational Safety &
Health Administration

200 Constitution Ave.
Washington, DC 20210
800-321-OSHA
www.osha.gov

Vinyl Siding Institute

www.vinylsiding.org

Warnock Hersey International

Intertek Testing Services
530 Garcia Ave.
Pittsburg, CA 94565
925-432-7344
www.warnockhersey.com

Western Wood
Products Association

522 S.W. Fifth Avenue
Portland, OR 97204-2122
503-224-3930
www.wwpa.org

World Floor Covering Assn.

2211 E.Howell Ave.
Anaheim, CA 92806
800-624-6880
www.wfca.org

Brick

Brick Industry Association

11490 Commerce Park Drive
Reston, VA 20191-1525
703-620-0010
www.bia.org

National Association of
Brick Distributors

1600 Spring Hill Rd.
Suite 305
Vienna, VA 22182
703-749-6223

National Concrete
Masonry Association

2302 Horse Pen Rd.
Herndon, VA 20171
703-713-1900
www.ncma.org

Building Codes

ICC International
Code Council

5203 Leesburg Pike
Suite 600
Falls Church, VA 22041
888-422-7233
www.iccsafe.org

Building Products

Alcoa Home Exteriors

Omega Corporate Center
1590 Omega Dr.
Pittsburgh, PA 15205
800-962-6973
www.alcoahomes.com

California Closets

1000 Fourth St. Suite 800
San Rafael, CA 94901
415-256-8500
www.calclostets.com

Cemplank

26300 La Alameda
Suite 250
Mission Viejo, CA 92691
877-CEMPLANK
www.cemplank.com

Certainteed

800-233-8990
www.certainteed.com

DOW Chemical USA

2040 W H Dow Center
Midland, MI 48674
800-441-4369
www.oikos.com

Gentek Building Products

P.O. Box 110
Akron, OH 44309
www.gentekinc.com
800-548-4542

Georgia-Pacific

133 Peachtree St.
Atlanta, GA 30303
404-652-4000
www.gp.com

Gutter Helmet

888-4-HELMET

Homasote Co.

P.O. Box 7240
West Trenton, NJ 08628-0240
800-257-9491
www.homasote.com

James Hardie Industries

26300 La Alameda
Suite 250
Mission Viejo, CA 92691
888-J-HARDIE
www.jameshardie.com

Johns Manville

JM Headquarters

P.O. Box 5108
Denver, CO 80217-5108
800-654-3103
www.jm.com

L P Building Products

414 Union St. Suite 2000
Nashville, TN 37219
877-744-5600
www.lpcorp.com

Masonite

1 North Dale Mabry
Suite 950
Tampa, FL 33609
800-895-2723
www.masonite.com

Norandex-Reynolds

8450 S. Bedford Rd.
Macedonia, OH 44056
800-528-0942
www.norandex.com

Owens Corning

800-GET-PINK
www.owenscorning.com

Simpson Strong-Tie

800-999-5099
www.strongtie.com

Swan Secure Systems

7525 Perryman Ct.
Baltimore, MD 21226-1752
800-966-2801
www.swansecure.com

Tyvek

www.tyvek.com

Weyerhaeuser Co.

P.O. Box 9777
Federal Way, WA 98063-9777
800-525-5440
www.weyerhaeuser.com

Carpet

3M

800-626-8578

ANSO

www.anso.com

BASF

800-652-9964

The Carpet & Rug Institute

P.O. Box 2048
Dalton, GA 30722
800-882-8846
www.carpet-rug.com

DuPont

Chestnut Run Plaza
705/GS38
Wilmington, DE 19880-0705
800-441-7515
www.dupont.com

Honeywell International Inc.

101 Colombia Road
Morristown, NJ 07962
800-328-5111
www.honeywell.com

Carpet Cleaning

Host Products

800-558-9439
www.hostcarpetcleaning.com

Caulks and Sealants

Adhesive and Sealant Council

7979 Old Georgetown Rd.
Suite 500
Bethesda, MD 20814
301-986-9700

DAP Inc.

2400 Boston St.
Suite 200
Baltimore, MD 21224
www.dap.com

Dow Corning Corp.

P.O. Box 994
Midland, MI 48686-0994
989-496-4400
www.dowcorning.com

Elmer's Products Inc.

www.elmers.com

Franklin Int'l Titebond

800-347-4583
www.titebond.com

Geocel Corp

P.O. Box 398
Elkhart, IN 46515
800-348-7615

PL - Adhesives and Sealants

800-999-8920

Ceiling Fans

Casablanca Fan Co.

761 Corporate Center Dr.,
Pomoa, CA 91768
888-227-2178
www.casablancafanco.com

Emerson

P.O. Box 4100
8000 West Florissant Ave.
St. Louis, MO 63136-8506
314-553-2000
www.emersonfans.com

Hunter Fan Company

888-830-1326
www.hunterfan.com

Cement, Concrete

National Concrete
Masonry Association

13750 Sunrise Valley Dr.
Herndon, VA 20171-4462
703-713-1900
www.ncma.org

Portland Cement Association

5420 Old Orchard Road
Skokie, IL 60077-4321
708-966-6200
www.cement.org

Chimneys

Chimney Safety Institute
of America

2155 Commercial Dr.
Plainfield, IN 46168
317-837-5392
www.csia.org

Countertops

AGCO

2782 Simpson Circle
Norcross, GA 30071
770-447-6990
www.worldpanel.com/dia-
monite.htm

Avonite

1945 Highway 304
Belen, NM 87002
800-866-8324
www.avonite.com

Barton Enterprises Inc.

329 W. Lone Cactus, Suite 8
Phoenix, AZ 85027
623-581-9965
www.bartonenterprises.com

Centura Solid Surfacing

3525 State Rd. 32 West
Westfield, IN 46074
888-398-8896
www.centurasolidsurface.com

DuPont Corian

Chestnut Run Plaza
705/GS38
Wilmington, DE 19880-0705
800-441-7515
www.dupont.com

Formica Corporation

255 E. 5th Street
Suite 200
Cincinnati, OH 45202
800- FORMICA
www.formica.com

Halstead International

15 Oakwood Ave.
Norwalk, CT 06850
800-699-9324
www.halsteadintl.com

Hartson-Kennedy

P.O. Box 3095
Marion, IN 46953
800-388-8144
www.hartsonkennedy.com

International Solid Surfaces
Fabricators Association (ISSFA)

975 American Pacific Dr.
Suite 102
Henderson, NV 89014
888-679-2970
www.issfa.net

LG Chemical of America

1000 Sylvan Ave.
Englewood Cliffs, NJ 07632
201-816-2311
www.lgchem.com

Lippert

P.O. Box 1030
Menomonee Falls, WI 53052
800-869-8775
www.lippertcorp.com

Pionite Plastics Corp.

1 Pionite Road
Auburn, ME 04211
800-746-6483

Ralph Wilson Plastics

P.O. Box 6110
2400 Wilson Place
Temple, TX 76503
800-433-3222

Royal Stone Industries

2949 North 31st Ave.
Phoenix, AZ 85017
888-633-4537
www.royalstoneind.com

Samsung/Cheil Industries

14251 E. Firestone Blvd.
La Mirada, CA 90638
562-926-5520
www.staron.com

Solid Surface Magazine

P.O. Box 460
Fort Atkinson, WI 53538
800-547-7377
www.solidsurfacemagazine.com

Stone Creations Enterprises

50 W. Third St.
Holland, MI 49423
616-395-5467
www.nu-ance.com

The Swan Corp.

One City Centre, Suite 2300
St. Louis, MO 63101
800-325-7008
www.theswancorp.com

Talon Surfaces

32031 Howard St.
Madison Heights, MI 48071
877-567-7866
www.talonllc.com

Transolid

2533 Charlotte Hwy.
Morresville, NC 28115
800-766-2452
www.transolid.com

Vassallo Unlimited

787-848-0612
www.lassica.com

Wilsonart International

P.O. Box 6110
2400 Wilson Place
Temple, TX 76503-6110
800-433-3222
www.wilsonart.com

Designers

American Institute of Architects

1735 New York Ave. NW
Washington, DC 20006
202-626-7310
www.aia.org.

American Institute of
Certified Planners

1776 Massachusetts Ave. NW
#400
Washington, DC 20036
202-872-0611
www.planning.org

Construction
Specifications Institute

601 Madison St.
Alexandria, VA 22314
800-689-2900
www.csinet.org

Doors (See Windows)

Electrical

AMP

800-468-2023
www.amp.com

General Electric

580-634-0151
www.ge.com

Siemens Energy

800-548-6405

Square D

888-778-2733
www.squared.com

Westinghouse

866-442-7873
www.westinghouse.com

Energy, Energy Conservation

Advanced Energy Corp.

P.O. Box 12699
Research Triangle Park, NC 27709
919-361-8000
www.aec.ncsu.edu

Alliance to Save Energy

www.ase.org

American Council for an
Energy-Efficient Economy

1001 Connecticut Ave. NW
Suite 801
Washington, DC 20036
202-429-8873
www.aceee.org

American Gas Association

202-824-7000
www.aga.org

Energy Efficiency and
Renewable Energy

(U.S. Dept. of Energy)
877-EERE-INF
www.eere.energy.gov

Energy Efficient
Building Association

2950 Metro Dr. Suite 108
Minneapolis, MN 55425
612-851-9940
www.eeba.org

Energy Guide

www.energyguide.com

Florida Solar Energy Center

University of Central Florida
1679 Clearlake Rd.
Cocoa, FL 32992
407-638-1000
www.fsec.ucf.edu

Home Energy

2124 Kitredge St. # 95
Berkeley, CA 94704
510-524-5405
www.homeenergy.org

Gas Research Institute

www.gri.com

Honeywell

101 Colombia Road
Morristown, NJ 07962
800-328-5111
www.honeywell.com

National Center for
Appropriate Technology

(NCAT)
P.O. Box 3838
Butte, MT 59702
800-ASK-NCAT
www.ncat.org

Residential Energy
Services Network

12350 Industry Way #208
Anchorage, AK 99508
907-345-1930
www.natresnet.org

Rocky Mountain Institute

1739 Snowmass Creek Rd.
Snowmass, CO 81654
303-927-3851
www.rmi.org

Southface Energy Institute

241 Pine Street
Atlanta, GA 30308
404-872-3549
www.southface.org

U.S. Department of Energy
U.S Environmental
Protection Agency

www.HomeEnergySaver.lbl.gov

U.S. EPA Energy Star
Buildings Program

401 M Street, SW
Washington, DC 20460
888-STAR-YES
http://www.energystar.gov

Epoxy Repair Products

Abatron Inc.

5501 95th Ave.
Kenosha, WI 53144
800-445-1754
www.abatron.com

Advanced Repair Tech

607-264-9040
www.advancedrepair.com

Bondo Corporation

3700 Atlanta Industrial Pkwy NW
Atlanta, GA 30331
800-622-8754
www.bondo-online.com

Cabot

800-US-STAIN
www.cabotstain.com

Minwax Company

10 Mountainview Rd.
Upper Saddle River, NJ 07458
800-523-9299
www.minwax.com

Mr. Mac's Concrete Products

800-654-8454

Exhaust Fans

Broan

P.O. Box 140
Hartford, WI 53027
800-558-1711
www.broan.com

NuTone Inc.

4820 Red Banks Rd.
Cincinnati, OH 45227-1599
888-336-3948
www.nutone.com

Therma-Stor

2001 S. Stoughton Rd.
P.O. Box 8050
Madison, WI 53708
800-533-7533
www.thermastor.com

Fasteners

Arrow Fastener

www.arrowfastener.com

ATCI Consumer Products

800-343-6129
www.worksavers.com

McFeely's

800-443-7937
www.mcfeelys.com

PrimeSource

800-676-7777
www.primesourcebp.com

Senco

800-543-4596
www.senco.com

Simpson Strong-Tie

800-999-5099
www.strongtie.com

Stanley Bostitch

800-556-6696
www.bostitch.com

USP Structural Connectors

800-328-5934
www.uspconnectors.com

Fireplaces

Chimney Safety Institute
of America

2155 Commercial Dr.
Plainfield, IN 46168
317-837-5392
www.csia.org

Heat-N-Glo

20802 Kensington Blvd.
Lakeville, MN 55044
888-427-3973
www.heatnglo.com

Heatilator

1915 W. Saunders Street
Mt. Pleasant, IA 52641
800-927-6841
www.heatilator.com

Kozy Heat

800-253-4904
www.kozyheat.com

Majestic Products

905-670-7777
www.vermontcastings.com

Temco Fireplace Products

905-670-7777
www.temcofireplaces.com

Vermont Castings

905-670-7777
www.vermontcastings.com

Flashing Material

Davis Wire Co.

5555 Irwindale Ave.
Irwindale, CA 91706
800-350-7851, ext. 217

Dupont

P.O. Box 70805
Wilmington, DE 19880-0705
800-448-9835
www.dupont.com

Fortfiber Company

300 Industrial Dr.
Fernley, NV 89408
800-773-4777
www.fortfiber.com

Grace Construction Products

62 Whittemore Ave.
Cambridge, MA 02140
617-876-1400
www.na.graceconstruction.com

Hal Industries

9681 187th Street
Surrey, B.C. Canada
V4N 3N3
604-888-0777
www.halind.com

Leatherback Industries

P.O. Box 594
Hollister, CA 95023
800-538-5950

MFM Building Products Corp.

P.O. Box 340
Coshocton, OH 43812
800-882-7663
www.mfmbp.com

Floor Covering-See Carpet, Laminate, Vinyl, Wood

Garage Doors and Openers

Chamberlain Lift Master

800-528-5880
www.liftmaster.com

Garage Door
Hardware Association

2850 S. Ocean Blvd.
Suite 311
Palm Beach, FL 33480
407-533-0991

Genie Industries

18340 NE 76th St.
P.O. Box 97030
Redmond, WA 98073-9730
800-536-1800
www.genielift.com

Overhead Door Corporation

1900 Crown Drive
Farmers Branch, TX 75234
800-929-DOOR
www.overheaddoor.com

Stanley

1000 Stanley Dr.
New Britain, CT 06053
860-225-5111
www.stanleyworks.com

Wayne Dalton

One Door Drive
P.O. Box 67
Mt. Hope, OH 44660
800-827-DOOR
www.wayne-dalton.com

Windsor Door

P.O. Box 8915
Little Rock, AR 72219-8915
501-562-1872
www.windsordoor.com

American Geothermal

800-766-8039
www.amgeo.com

ECR Technologies

866-211-6102
www.ecrtech.com

International Ground Source
Heat Pump Association

www.igshpa.okstate.edu

Geothermal Heat Pump
Consortium

www.geoexchange.org

Government Agencies

Building Research Council

University of Illinois at Urbana –
Champaign
One East Saint Mary's Rd.
Champaign, IL 61820
800-336-0616
www.arch.uiuc.edu

Chemical Referral Center

800-CMA-8200

Environmental Protection Agency

US EPA Region 5 (Midwest)
77 W. Jackson Blvd.
Chicago, IL 60604
800-621-8431
www.epa.gov

FEMA National Flood Insurance

800-745-0243
www.fema.gov

Forest Products Laboratory

(USDA Forest Service)
One Gifford Pinchot Drive
Madison, WI 53705
608-231-9200
www.fpl.fs.fed.us

Lead Safety

www.leadsafeusa.com
www.epa.gov/lead

National Park Service

www.nps.gov

National Small
Flows Clearinghouse

(Septic Information)
West Virginia University
P.O. Box 6064
Morgantown, WV 26506-6064
800-624-8301
www.nesc.wvu.edu

National Technical
Information Service

(Energy Related Information)
5285 Port Royal Road
Springfield, VA 22161
703-605-6585
www.ntis.gov

U.S. Government Printing
Office (GPO)

732 N. Capitol St. NW
Washington, DC 20401
202-512-0000
www.gpo.gov

U.S. Consumer Product
Safety Commission

Washington, DC 20207-0001
800-638-2772
www.cpsc.gov

Hardware Specialties

Acorn Manufacturing

800-835-0121
www.acornmfg.com

American Hardware
Manufacturers Association

801 N. Plaza Drive
Schaumburg, IL 60173-4977
847-605-1025
www.ahma.org

Baldwin Hardware

841 E. Wyomissing Blvd.
P.O. Box 15048
Reading, PA 19612
800-566-1986
www.baldwinhardware.com

Blaine Window Hardware

(Replacement Hardware)
17319 Blaine Dr.
Hagerstown, MD 21740
800-678-1919
www.blainewindow.com

Johnson Products, Inc.

(Pocket Door Hardware)
2100 Sterling Ave.
Elkhart, IN 46516
800-837-5664
www.johnsonhardware.com

Kwikset Corporation

Consumer Service
19701 DaVinci
Lake Forest, CA 92610
800-327-LOCK
www.kwikset.com

Larsen Products

8264 Preston Ct.
Jessup, MD 20794
800-633-6668
www.larsenproducts.com

Mag Security

714-891-5100
www.magsecurity.com

Master Lock

414-444-2800
www.masterlock.com

Medeco Security Locks

800-675-7558
www.medeco.com

Omnia Industries

800-310-7960
www.omniaindustries.com

Renovators Supply
(Reproduction Hardware)

800-659-2211
www.rensup.com

Schlage Lock Co.

 1010 Santa Fe
 Olathe, KS 66051
 800-847-1864
 www.schlagelock.com

Security Door Controls

 800-413-8783
 www.sdsecurity.com

Stanley Tools

 1000 Stanley Dr.
 New Britain, CT 06053
 860-225-5111
 www.stanleyworks.com

Weiser Lock

 19701 Da Vinci
 Lake Forest, CA 92610
 800-677-LOCK
 www.weiserlock.com

Yale Commercial Locks
and Hardware

 1902 Airport Rd.
 Monro, NC 28110
 800-438-1951
 www.yalelocks.com

Heating and Air Conditioning

Air-Conditioning &
Refrigeration Institute (ARI)

 4100 N Fairfax Dr.
 Suite 200
 Arlington, VA 22203
 703-524-8800
 www.ari.org

American Standard Heating and
Air Conditioning

 6200 Troup Highway
 Tyler, TX 75711
 800-752-6292
 www.amstd-comfort.com

Arcoaire

 800-315-4370
 www.arcoaire.com

Armstrong Air Conditioning

 419-483-4840
 www.armstrongair.com

Bard Manufacturing Co.

 419-636-1194
 www.bardhvac.com

Bryant

 800-428-4326
 www.bryant.com

Carrier

 One Carrier Place
 Farminton, CT 06034-4015
 800-4-CARRIER
 www.carrier.com

Century

 517-787-2100
 www.heatcontroller.com

ClimateMaster

 405-745-6000 ext. 347
 www.climatemaster.com

Coleman

 405-419-6541
 www.colemanac.com

Comfort-Aire

 517-787-2100
 www.heatcontroller.com

Comfortmaker

 800-315-4370
 www.comfortmaker.com

Concord

 419-483-4840
 www.concord-air.com

Dectron

 888-332-8766 ext. 260
 www.dry-o-tron.com

Ducane

 803-284-5371
 www.ducanehvac.com

EMI

 315-336-3716
 www.enviromaster.com

Enstar HVAC and Supplies

 206-575-8808
 www.enstar-hvac.com

Fedders

 908-604-8686
 www.fedders.com

Friedrich

 210-357-4400
 www.friedrich.com

Frigidare

 636-561-7477
 www.fridgidare.net

Fujitsu General America

 973-575-0380
 www.fujitsugeneral.com

Gas Research Institute

 8600 W. Bryn Mawr
 Chicago, IL 60631
 312-399-8100

Gibson

 636-561-7477
 www.nordyne.com

Goodman Mfg. Co.

 7401 Security Way
 Houston, TX 77040
 888-593-9988
 www.goodmanmfg.com

Heil Heating & Cooling Products

www.heil-hvac.com

Honeywell Inc.

101 Colombia Rd.
Morristown, NJ 07962
800-328-5111
www.honeywell.com

Hydronics Institute

P.O. Box 218
Berkeley Heights, NJ 07922
908-464-8200

Kelvinator

636-561-7477
www.nordyne.com

LG Electronics USA

201-816-2981
www.lge.com

Lennox

P.O. Box 799900
Dallas, TX 75379-9900
800-9-LENNOX
www.davelennox.com

Luxaire

5005 York Dr.
Norman, OK 73069
877-874-7378
www.luxaire.com

Luxaire-Fraser-Johnston

P.O. Box 1592
York, PA 17405-1592
717-771-6130

McQuay International

800-432-1342
www.mcquay.com

Maytag

636-561-7477
www.maytagvac.com

Payne

888-41-PAYNE
www.payne.com

Philco

636-561-7477
www.nordyne.com

Plumbing Heating
Cooling Contractors –
National Association

P.O. Box 6806
Falls Church, VA 22040
800-533-7694
www.phccweb.org

Rheem

Air Conditioning Division
P.O. Box 17010
Fort Smith, AR 72917-7010
479-648-4900
www.rheem.com

Robertshaw

800-445-8299
www.robertshaw.com

Ruud Air Conditioning

P.O. Box 17010
Fort Smith, AR 72917
479-648-4900
www.ruudac.com

Sanyo Fisher Co.

818-998-7322
www.sanyovac.com

Slant/Fin Corp.

100 Forest Dr.
Greenvale, NY 11548
800-775-4552
www.slantfin.com

Tappan

636-561-7365
www.tappan.net

Tempstar Heating and
Cooling Products

www.tempstar.com

Therma-Stor

2001 S. Stoughton Rd.
P.O. Box 8050
Madison, WI 53708
800-533-7533

Thermo Pride

574-869-2133
www.thermopride.com

Trane

www.trane.com

Weil-McLain

500 Blaine St.
Michigan City, IN 46360-2388
219-879-6561
www.weil-mclain.com

Westinghouse

636-561-7477
Westinghousehvac.com

Winia USA

201-727-0009
www.winiausa.com

WIRSBO

5925 148th St. W
Apple Valley, MN 55124
800-321-4739
www.wirsbo.com

Xpediair

405-917-7690
www.xpediair.com

York International

P.O. Box 1592
York, PA 17405-1592
717-771-6225
www.york.com

Insulation

Certainteed

800-782-8777
www.certainteed.com

Johns Manville

800-654-3103
www.jm.com

Owens Corning

800-GET-PINK
www.owenscorning.com

Irrigation

DIG Irrigation Products

800-322-9146
www.digcorp.com

DripWorks

800-522-3747
www.dripworks.com

The Drip Store

866-682-1580
www.dripirrigation.com

Raindrip

877-237-3747
www.raindrip.com

Laminate Flooring

Alloc

877-362-5562
www.alloc.com

American Olean Tile Co.

1000 Cannon Ave.
Lansdale, PA 19446
www.americanolean.com

Armstrong

800-233-3823
www.armstrong.com

BHK of America

800-663-4176
www.bhkuniclic.com

Colombia Flooring

800-654-8796
www.colombiaflooring.com

Congoleum Corp.

P.O. Box 3127
Mercerville, NJ 08619
800-274-3266
www.congoleum.com

Formica Corp.

10155 Reading Rd.
Cincinnati, OH 45241
www.formica.com

Kronotex

678-513-5699
www.kronotexusa.com

Mannington Mills

800-356-6787
www.mannington.com

Mohawk Laminate Flooring

800-266-4295
www.mohawklaminateflooring.com

North American Laminate
Flooring Association (NALFA)

202-785-9500
www.nalfa.com

Pergo

800-337-3746
www.pergo.com

Quick-Step

866-220-5933
www.quick-step.com

Quickstyle

800-387-8953
www.quickstyle.net

Shaw Laminates

800-441-7429
www.shawfloors.com

Uniboard Surfaces

800-978-9448
www.uniboardsurfaces.com

Wilsonart

800-710-8846
www.wilsonartflooring.com

Witex Flooring

800-948-3987
www.witexusa.com

Landscaping

Allied Landscape Industry

1250 "I" St. NW Suite 500
Washington, DC 20037
202-457-8437

American Fence Association

2890 Gant Quarters
Circle Marietta, GA 30068
770-578-9765
www.americanfenceassoc.org

American Landscape
Maintenance Association

737 Hollywood Blvd.
Hollywood, FL 33019
954-927-3100

American Nursery and
Landscape Association

1250 "I" St. NW Suite 500
Washington, DC 20005
202-789-2900
www.anla.org

American Society of Consulting Arborists

15245 Shady Grove Rd
Suite 130
Rockville, MD 20850
301-947-0483
www.asca-consultants.org

American Society of Irrigation Consultants

P.O. Box 426
Byron, CA 94514
925-516-1124

American Society of Landscape Architects

636 Eye St. NW
Washington, DC 20001
202-216-2339
www.asla.org/asla

Associated Landscape Contractors of America

12200 Sunrise Valley Dr.
Suite 150
Reston, VA 22091
703-620-6363
www.alca.org

Associated Professional Landscape Designers

1924 North Second St.
Harrisburg, PA 17102
717-238-9780
www.apld.org

International Erosion Control Association

P.O. Box 774904
Steamboat Springs, CO 80477
800-455-4322
www.ieca.org

Irrigation Association

8260 Willow Oaks Corp. Dr.
Suite 120
Fairfax, VA 22031
703-573-3551
www.irrigation.org.

Landscape Contractors Association

9053 Shady Grove Ct.
Gaithersburg, MD 20877
301-948-0810
www.lcamddcva.org

Landscape Maintenance Association

41 Lake Morton Dr. #26
Lakeland, FL 33801
813-680-4008

National Arborist Association

P.O. Box 1094
Amherst, NH 03031
603-673-3311
www.natlarb.com

National Gardening Association

180 Flynn Ave.
Burlington, VT 05401
802-863-1308
www.nationalgardening.com

Lighting

Allscape Architectural Landscape Lighting

2930 S. Fairview St.
Santa Anna, CA 92704
800-854-8277
www.alllighting.com

American Lighting Association

Box 420288
Dallas, TX 75342-0288
800-274-1184
www.americanlightingassoc.com

Catalina Industries

18191 NW 68 Avenue
Miami, FL 33015
800-966-7074
www.catalinaltg.com

Cooper Lighting

www.cooperlighting.com

GE Lightning

800-626-2000
www.gelighting.com

Greenlee Lighting

1300 Hutton Dr.
Suite 110
Carrollton, TX 75006
www.greenleelighting.com
972-466-1133

Intermatic Inc.

Intermatic Plaza
Spring Grove, IL 60081
www.intermatic.com

International Association of Lighting Designers (IALD)

IALD Headquarters Office
Merchandise Mart
Suite 9-104
200 World Trade Center
Chicago, IL 60654
www.iald.org

Lights of America

800-321-8100
www.lightsofamerica.com

Philips

200 Franklin Square Dr.
Somerset, NJ 08875
800-555-0050
www.lighting.philips.com

Sylvania

100 Endicott St.
Danvers, MA 01923
978-777-1900
www.sylvania.com

Lubricants

WD 40

Customer Relations
P.O. Box 80607
San Diego, CA 92138
888-324-7596
www.wd40.com

Marble, Synthetic Marble

Avonite

7350 Empire Drive
Florence, KY 41042
800-354-9858
www.avonitesurfaces.com

Cultured Marble Institute

435 E. Ohio St.
Suite 400
Chicago, IL 60611
312-644-0828

Dupont Corian

800-4-CORIAN
www.corian.com

The Formica Corp.

10155 Reading Rd.
Cincinnati, OH 45241
800-367-6422
www.formica.com

The Marble Institute of America

28901 Clemens Road
Suite 100
Westlake, OH 44145
440-250-9222
www.marble-institute.com

Nails (Fasteners)

Jamestown Distributors

500 Wood Street
Building #15
Bristol, RI 02809
www.jamestowndistributors.
com

Independent Nails

30 Mozzone Blvd.
Taunton, MA 02780
800-443-0030
www.mazenails.com

Maze Nails

100 Church St.
Peru, IL 61354
800-435-5949
www.mazenails.com

Swan Secure Products Inc.

7525 Perryman Ct.
Baltimore, MD 21226-1752
800-966-2801
www.swansecure.com

Tremont Nail Co.

8 Elm Street
Wareham, MA 02751
800-842-0560
www.mazenails.com

USP Structural Connectors

800-328-5934
www.uspconnectors.com

Paints and Related Products

3M Consumer Relations

800-842-4946

Ace Hardware

866-290-5334
www.acehardware.com

AKZO Nobel

www.akzonobelusa.com

American Wood Preservers Institute

2750 Prosperity Ave.
Suite 550
Fairfax, VA 22031
800-356-AWPI www.awpi.org

Behr

800-854-0133
www.behrpaint.com

Benjamin Moore & Co.

51 Chestnut Ridge Road
Montvale, NJ 07645
800-826-2623
www.benjaminmoore.com

Bondex

www.bondex.com.au

Cabot

800-US-STAIN
www.cabotstain.com

Citristrip

Consumer Products Group
P.O. Box 1879
Memphis, TN 38101
800-398-3892
www.citristrip.com

Color Putty Co., Inc.

P.O. Box 738
Monroe, WI 53566
608-325-6033
www.colorputty.com

Coronado Paint Company

308 Old County Rd.
Edgewater, FL 32132
800-883-4193
www.coronadopaint.com

Daubert Coated Products

www.daubert.com

DAP Products Inc.

2400 Boston St.
Suite 200
Baltimore, MD 21224
www.dap.com

Dutch Boy

800-828-5669
www.dutchboy.com

Flecto

11 Hawthorn Pkwy.
Vernon Hills, IL 60061
800-553-8444
www.flecto.com

The Flood Company

P.O. Box 2535
Hudson, OH 44236-0035
800-321-3444
www.floodco.com

Formby's Company

10 Mountainview Rd.
Upper Saddle River, NJ 07458
800-290-1105
www.formbys.com

Fuller O'Brien

www.fullerpaint.com

General Finishes

P.O. Box 510567
New Berlin, WI 53151
800-783-6050
www.generalfinishes.com

Glidden

800-GLIDDEN
www.gliddenpaint.com

Home Right Paint Tools

1661 94th Lane N.E.
Minneapolis, MN 55449
800-264-5442
www.homeright.com

Insl-X

50 Holt Drive
P.O. Box 694
Stony Point, NY 10980
845-786-5000
www.insl-x.com

Klean-Strip

Box 1879
Memphis, TN 38101
800-235-3546
www.kleanstrip.com

Krylon

800-4-KRYLON
www.krylon.com

Martin Senour Paints

101 Prospect Ave. NW
Attn. Customer Affairs
Cleveland, OH 44115
800-677-5270
www.martinsenour.com

Masterchem Industries LLC

866-774-6371
www.kilz.com

Minwax Company Inc.

10 Mountainview Road
Upper Saddle River, NJ 07458
800-523-9299
www.minwax.com

National Paint & Coatings Assoc.

1500 Rhode Island Ave. NW
Washington, DC 20005
202-462-6272
www.paint.org

Olympic

800-235-5020
www.olympic.com

Painting & Decorating
Contractors of America

11960 Westline Industrial Dr.
Suite 201
St. Louis, MO 63146-3209
800-332-PDCA
www.pdca.com

Parks Corporation

One West Street
Fall River, MA 02720
800-225-8543
www.newparks.com

Pittsburgh Paints (PPG)

800-441-9695
www.pittsburghpaints.com

Pratt & Lambert

800-BUY-PRATT
www.prattandlambert.com

The Rohm & Haas Paint
Quality Institute

P.O. Box 904
Spring House, PA 19477
www.paintquality.com

Rustoleum

11 Hawthorn Parkway
Vernon Hills, IL 60061
800-553-8444
www.rustoleum.com

Savogran

259 Lennox St.
P.O. Box 130
Norwood, MA 02062
800-225-9872
www.savogran.com

Sears Paints

www.sears.com/paint

Sherwin Williams

www.sherwin-williams.com

UGL – United
Gilsonite Laboratories

570-344-1202
www.ugl.com

Valspar Corp.

> 1191 Wheeling Rd.
> Wheeling, IL 60090
> 800-845-9061
> www.valspar.com

Wagner

> 1770 Fernbrook Lane
> Minneapolis, MN 55447
> 763-519-3555
> www.wagnerspraytech.com

Zar (See UGL)

Zinsser Co.

> 173 Belmont Dr.
> Somerset, NJ 08875
> www.zinsser.com

Pests

Bat Conservation International

> www.batcon.org
> 512-327-9721

Pest Facts

> 202-872-3860
> www.pestfacts.org

National Pest
Management Association

> www.pestworld.org

Plastic Laminate (See Countertops)

Plumbing

American Standard

> P.O. Box 6820
> One Centennial Plaza
> Piscataway, NJ 08855
> 800-524-9797
> www.americanstandard-us.com

Association of Pool and
Spa Professionals

> 703-838-0083
> www.dheapsp.org

Bemis Manufacturing Company

> 300 Mill Street
> Sheboygan Falls, WI 53085
> 800-558-7651
> www.bemismfg.com

Chicago Faucets

> 2100 Clearwater Dr.
> Des Plaines, Il 60018
> 847-803-5000
> www.chicagofaucets.com

Consolidated Plumbing Industries

> 865-690-1558
> www.durapex.com

Delta Faucet Co.

> 55 E. 111th St.
> P.O. Box 40980
> Indianapolis, IN 46280
> 800-345-3358
> www.deltafaucet.com

DuPont Corian

> P.O. Box 08721
> 721 Maple Run
> Wilmington, DE 19880
> 800-426-7426
> www.corian.com

Eljer Plumbingware Inc.

> 14801 Quorum Dr.
> Dallas, TX 57254
> 800-423-5537
> www.eljer.com

Elkay Mfg. Co.

> 2222 Camden Court
> Oak Brook, IL 60523
> 630-574-8484
> www.elkay.com

Formica Corp.

> 10155 Reading Rd.
> Cincinnati, OH 45241
> 800-FORMICA
> www.formica.com

Franklin Brass

> 800-421-3375

Gerber Plumbing Fixtures Corp.

> 4600 W. Touhy Ave.
> Lincolnwood, IL 60712
> 847-675-6570
> www.gerberonline.com

Grohe America Inc.

> 241 Covington Dr.
> Bloomingdale, IL 60108
> www.groheamerica.com
> Hubbard Enterprises
> 800-321-0316
> www.holdrite.com

In-Sink-Erator

> (Garbage Disposals)
> 800-558-5700
> www.insinkerator.com

Jacuzzi Whirlpool Bath

> 14081 Quorum Drive
> Suite 550
> Dallas, TX 75254
> 866-440-1931
> www.jacuzzi.com

Kitchenaid

> 800-422-1230
> www.kitchenaid.com

Kohler Co.

> 444 Highland Drive
> Kohler, WI 53044
> 800-4-KOHLER
> www.kohlerco.com

KraftMaid

> 800-571-1990

Moen Faucet

> 800-BUY-MOEN
> www.moen.com

Nevermar Corp.

8339 Telegraph Rd.
Odenton, MD 21113
800-638-4380
www.nevermar.com

The Onyx Collection

202 Anderson Ave.
Belvue, KS 66407
www.onyxcollection.com

Peerless Products Inc.

2403 South Main St.
P.O. Box 431
Fort Scott, KS 66701
866-420-4000
www.peerlessproducts.com

Plastic Pipe and
Fittings Association

630-858-6540
www.ppfahome.org

Plumbing Heating
Cooling Contractors –
National Association

800-533-7694
www.phccweb.org

Price Pfister Inc.

19701 Da Vinci
Foothill Ranch, CA 92610
800-PFAUCET
www.pricepfister.com

RTI Systems

800-784-0234
www.rtisystems.com

Sloan Flushmate

800-553-3460
www.flushmate.com

Stadler-Viega

800-370-3122
www.stadlerviega.com

Sterling

888-STERLING
www.sterlingplumbing.com

Swan Corp.

1 City Centre, Suite 2300
St. Louis, MO 63101
800-325-7008
www.theswancorp.com

Universal Rundle Corp.

303 North Ave.
New Castle, PA 16103
800-955-0316
www.craneplumbing.com

Vanguard Piping Systems

800-775-5039
www.vanguardpipe.com

Watts Radiant

800-276-2419
www.wattsradiant.com

Wilsonart International

P.O. Box 6110
Temple, TX 76503
800-433-3222
www.wilsonart.com

Wirsbo

800-321-4739
www.wirsbo.com

Zurn Plumbing Products

903-886-2580
www.zurn.com

Pumps

Flotec

293 Wright St.
Delavan, WI 53115
800-365-6832
www.flotecpump.com

Little Giant Pump Co.

P.O. Box 12010
Oklahoma City, OK 73157
405-947-2511
www.littlegiant.com

Sta-Rite Industries

293 Wright St.
Delavan, WI 53115
800-472-0884
www.starite.com

Zoeller Pump

800-928-PUMP
www.zoeller.com

Remodeling

National Association of the
Remodeling Industry (NARI)

800-611-NARI
www.nari.org

Roofing

Air Vent

3000 W. Commerce St.
Dallas, TX 75212
800-247-8368
www.airvent.com

Alcoa Building Products

800-962-6973
www.alcoa.com

American Slate Co.

1243 Alpine Rd.
Walnut Creek, CA 94596
800-553-5611
www.americanslate.com

Asphalt Roofing
Manufacturers Assoc.

1156 15th St. NW
Suite 900
Washington, DC 20005
www.asphaltroofing.org

ATAS International Inc.

6612 Snowdrift Rd.
Allentown, PA 18106
800-468-1441
www.atas.com

Atlas Roofing Corp.

2322 Valley Rd.
Meridian, MS 39302
800-933-2721
www.atlasroofing.com

Cedar Shake & Shingle Bureau

P.O. Box 1178
Sumas, WA 98295
604-820-7700
www.cedarbureau.org

CertainTeed Corp

800-782-8777
www.certainteed.com

Classic Products

8510 Industry Park Dr.
Piqua, OH 45356
800-543-8938
www.classicroof.com

Dura-Loc Roofing Systems Ltd.

800-265-9357
www.duraloc.com

ELK Corp

www.elkcorp.com

Everlast Roofing Inc.

239 N. Fifth Ave.
Lebanon, PA 17046
888-339-0059
www.everlastroofing.com

GAF Materials Corp.

1361 Alps Road
Wayne, NJ 07470
973-628-3000
www.gaf.com

Georgia Pacific

133 Peachtree Street N.E.
Atlanta, GA 30303
404-652-4000
www.gp.com

National Roofing
Contractors Association

10255 W. Higgins Rd.
Suite 600
Rosemont, IL 60018
847-299-9070
www.nrca.net

National Tile Roof
Manufacturers Association

P.O. Box 40337
Eugene, OR 97404
541-689-0366
www.ntrma.org

Revere Copper Products Inc.

1 Revere Park
Rome, NY 13440
800-448-1776
www.reverecopper.com

Roofing People

9949 Valley View Rd.
Eden Prairie, MN 55344
866-849-ROOF
www.roofingpeople.com

The Tile Man Inc.

520 Vaiden Rd.
Louisburg, NC 27549
www.thetileman.com

US Tile

909 W. Railroad St.
Corona, CA 92882
www.ustile.com

Vande Hey-Raleigh
Manufacturing Inc.

1665 Bohm Drive
Little Chute, WI 54140
800-236-8453
www.vhr-roof-tile.com

Welsh Mountain Slate Inc.

800-865-8784
www.welshmountainslate.
com

Safety

National Lead Information Center

800-424-LEAD
www.epa.gov/lead

Screen Material

Phifer Wire Products Inc.

P.O. Box 1700
Tuscaloosa, AL 35403-1700
205-345-2120
www.phifer.com

Screen Tight

One Better Way
Georgetown, SC 29440
800-768-7325
www.screentight.com

Sealers (See Paints)

Septic Information

National Small Flows
Clearinghouse

P.O. Box 6064
West Virginia University
Morgantown, WV 26505
800-624-8301
www.nsfc.wvu.edu

Small Scale Waste
Project Management

UW Environmental Resources
Center
1545 Observatory Dr.
Madison, WI 53706
608-262-3799
www.uwex.edu/erc

Siding

Alcoa Building Products

800-962-6973
www.alcoa.com

Alside Inc.

www.alside.com

American Hardboard Association

www.hardboard.org

American Society for Testing & Materials

www.astm.org

Brick Industry Association

www.bia.org

Cedar Shake & Shingle Bureau

P.O. Box 1178
Sumas, WA 98295
604-820-7700
www.cedarbureau.org

Cemplank

26300 La Alameda
Suite 250
Mission Viejo, CA 92691
877-CEMPLANK
www.cemplank.com

Certainteed

www.certainteed.com
800-233-8990

Dryvit Systems, Inc.

One Energy Way
P.O. Box 1014
West Warwick, RI 02893
800-556-7752
www.dryvit.com

EIFS Industry Members Association

800-294-3462
www.eima.com

GAF Materials Corp.

1361 Alps Road
Wayne, NJ 07470
973-628-3000
www.gaf.com

Georgia-Pacific

133 Peachtree St.
Atlanta, GA 30303
404-652-4000
www.gp.com

Gypsum Association

810 First St., NE #510
Washington DC, 20002
202-289-5440
www.gypsum.com

James Hardie Industries

26300 La Alameda
Suite 250
Mission Viejo, CA 92691
888-J-HARDIE
www.jameshardie.com

LP Building Products

414 Union St, Suite 2000
Nashville, TN 37219
877-744-5600
www.lpcorp.com

Marshall & Swift

Residential Cost Handbook
www.marshallswift.com

Masonite

1 North Dale Mabry
Suite 950
Tampa, FL 33609
800-895-2723
www.masonite.com

Master Craftsman Education & Deveopment Program

www.certainteed.com/
mastercraftsman

Mastic Cedar Discovery

www.mastic.com

Nichiha USA

www.nichiha.com

Norandex

www.norandex.com

Owens Corning

www.owenscorning.com

Pactiv Corp.

www.pactiv.com

Paint Quality Institute

www.paintquality.com

Progressive Foam Technologies Fullback

www.fullback.com

Match

www.sidingmatch.com

Sto Corporation

3800 Camp Creek Pkwy.
Building 1400, Suite 120
Atlanta, GA 30331
800-221-2397
www.stocorp.com

Vinyl Siding Institute

www.vinylsiding.org

U.S. Consumer Product Safety Commission

www.cpsc.gov

Weyerhaeuser Co.

P.O. Box 9777
Federal Way, WA 98063
800-525-5440
www.weyerhaeuser.com

Millenium

www.siding.com

Skylights

Solatube International Inc.

2210 Oak Ridge Way
Vista, CA 92081
800-966-7652
www.solatube.com

Velux Skylights

www.veluxusa.com

Small Engine

Briggs and Stratton Corp.

P.O. Box 702
Milwaukee, WI 53201
414-259-5333
www.briggsandstratton.com

Stains (See Paints)

Tools

American Tool

92 Grant St.
Wilmington, OH 45177
www.americantool.com
800-866-5740

Arrow Fastener

www.arrowfastener.com

Black & Decker

800-54-HOW-TO
www.blackanddecker.com

Bosch

www.bosch.com

Cooper Hand Tools

919-781-7200
www.cooperhandtools.com

Craftsman

800-349-4358
www.sears.com/craftsman

Delta Machinery

4825 Hwy. 45 North
P.O. Box 2468
Jackson, TN 38302
www.deltawoodworking.com

DeWalt

626 Hanover Pike
Hampstead, MD 21074
800-4-DEWALT
www.dewalt.com

Dirt Devil

800-321-1134
www.dirtdevil.com

Dremel Tools

4915 21st Street
Racine, WI 53406
800-437-3635
www.dremel.com

Erwin Industrial Tool Co.

800-866-5740
www.erwin.com

Grizzly Industrial

570-546-9663
www.grizzlyindustrial.com

Hitachi

www.hitachi.com

ITW/Paslode

888 Forest Edge Dr.
Vernon Hills, IL 60061
800-682-3428
www.paslode.com

Klein Tools Inc.

P.O. Box 599033
Chicago, IL 60659
800-553-4676
www.klein-tools.com

Leatherman

P.O. Box 20595
Portland, OR 97294
800-847-8665
www.leatherman.com

Makita

www.makita.com

Milwaukee Electric Tool

13135 W. Lisbon Rd.
Brookfield, WI 53005
800-SAWDUST
www.milwaukeetool.com

Panasonic

www.panasonic.com

Porter Cable Corp.

4825 Hwy. 45 North
P.O. Box 2468
Jackson, TN 38302
800-321-9443
www.porter-cable.com

Powermatic

WMH Tool Group, Inc.
2420 Vantage Dr.
Elgin, IL 60123
800-274-6848
www.powermatic.com

Ridgid

800-4-RIDGID
www.ridgid.com

Ryobi

www.ryobitools.com

Sears-Craftsman

800-349-4358
www.sears.com

Senco Products

8485 Broadwell Rd.
Cincinnati, OH 45244
800-543-4596
www.senco.com

SK Hand Tool Corp.

6500 W. 55th St., Suite B
McCook, IL 60525
800-U-CALL-SK
www.skhandtool.com

Stanley Tools

1000 Stanley Drive
New Britain, CT 06053
860-225-5111
www.stanleyworks.com

Starrett

978-249-3551
www.starrett.com

Vermont American

www.vermontamerican.com

Wagner Tools

www.wagnertools.com

Ventilation

American Aldes Ventilation Corp.

800-255-7749
www.americanaldes.com

Broan-NuTone

P.O. Box 140
Hartford, WI 53027
800-558-1711
www.broan.com

Bryant Heating and
Cooling Systems

800-428-4826
www.bryant.com

Carrier Corporation

800-227-7437
www.carrier.com

Des Champs Laboratories

800-265-6921
www.deschamps.com

Home Ventilating Institute

1000 N. Rand Rd., Suite 214
Wauconda, IL 60084
847-526-2010
www.hvi.org

Honeywell Inc.

800-328-5111
www.honeywell.com

Kanalflakt Inc.

800-565-3548
www.kanalflakt.com

Lennox International

972-497-5000
www.lennoxinternational.
com

New Age Ventilation

902-865-2284

Nu-Air Ventilation Systems

902-757-1910
www.nu-airventilation.com

Nutech Energy Systems

519-457-1904
www.lifebreath.com

Nutone Inc.

888-336-3948
www.nutone.com

Raydot Inc.

800-328-3813
www.raydot.com

RenewAire

800-627-4499
www.renewaire.com

Research Products Corp.

800-334-6011
www.aprilaire.com

Rheem Air Conditioning Division

501-646-4311
www.rheemac.com

Ruud

800-848-7883
www.ruudac.com

Stirling Technology Inc.

800-535-3448
www.lychonia.com

Trent Metals Limited
Summeraire Division

705-745-4736
www.summeraire.com

United Air Specialists Inc.

800-551-5401
www.uasinc.com

Venmar Ventilation Inc.

800-567-3855
www.venmar-ventilation.com

Vinyl Flooring

Armstrong World Industries

2500 Colombia Ave.
P.O. Box 3001
Lancaster, PA 17604
717-397-0611
www.armstrong.com

Congoleum Corporation

Department C
P.O. Box 3127
Mercerville, NJ 08619
800-274-3266
www.congoleum.com

Mannington Flooring

75 Mannington Mills Road
Salem, NJ 08079
856-935-3000
www.mannington.com

Resilient Floor Covering Institute

966 Hungerford Drive
Suite 12-B
Rockville, MD 20850
301-340-8580

Tarkett

888-639-8275
www.tarkett.com

Wilsonart Flooring

3301 Center St.
P.O. Box 6110
Temple, TX 76503
800-710-8846
www.wilsonart.com

Water Heaters

American Water Heater Co.

500 Princeton Rd.
Johnson City, TN 37601
423-283-8000
www.americanwaterheater.com

A.O. Smith Corporation

11270 West Park Place
Milwaukee, WI 53224
414-359-4000
www.aosmith.com

Bradford-White

www.bradfordwhite.com

Rheem

www.rheem.com

State Industries

500 Lindahll Parkway
Ashland City, TN 37015
www.stateind.com

Water Softeners

Bruner Corp.

3637 Lacon Rd.
Hilliard, OH 43026
614-334-9000
www.brunercorp.com

Culligan

One Culligan Pkwy.
Northbrook, IL 60062
800-CULLIGAN
www.culligan.com

Rainsoft Water Treatment Systems

www.rainsoft.com

Windows and Doors

Adams Architectural
Wood Products

888-285-8120
www.adamsarch.com

Allegheny Restoration

904-594-2570
www.alleghnyrestoration.com

Allied Windows Inc.

11111 Canal Rd.
Cincinnati, OH 45241
800-445-5411
www.invisiblestorms.com

Anderson

100 Fourth Ave. North
Bayport, MN 55003
888-888-7020
www.andersonwindows.com

Architectural Components

413-367-9441

The Bilco Company

P.O. Box 1203
New Haven, CT 06505
203-934-6363
www.bilco.com

Blaine Window Hardware

17139 Blaine Drive
Hagerstown, MD 21740
800-678-1919
www.blainewindow.com

Certainteed

800-233-8990
www.certainteed.com

Clopay

800-225-6729
www.clopaydoor.com

Crestline

www.crestlinewindows.com

Four Seasons Sunrooms

5005 Veterans Memorial Highway
Holbrook, NY 11741
800-FOUR-SEASONS
www.fourseasonssunrooms.com

Hull Historical Restoration

817-332-1495
www.hullhistorical.com

Hurd Millwork Co.

575 South Whelen Ave.
Medford, WI 54451
800-2BE-HURD
www.hurd.com

Jeld-Wen Inc.

800-JELD-WEN
www.jeld-wen.com

Kolbe Vinyl Windows and Doors

550 S.W. Industrial Way
1211 Depot St.
Manawa, WI 54949
920-596-2501
www.kolbe-kolbe.com

Lincoln Windows

1400 W. Taylor
P.O. Box 375
Merrill, WI 54452
715-536-2461
www.lincolnwindows.com

Marvin Windows & Doors

P.O. Box 100
Warroad, MN 56763
888-537-7828
www.marvin.com

Masonite Corporation

800-663-DOOR
www.masonite.com

Mauer & Shepherd Joyners

860-633-2383

Norco Windows, Inc.

715-585-6311

Pella Windows & Doors

102 Main Street
Pella, IA 50219
800-242-6212
www.pella.com

Pozzi Wood Windows

800-257-9663
www.pozzi.com

Premdor

800-663-DOOR
www.premdor.com

Simpson Door Co.

400 Simpson Ave.
McCleary, WA 98557
800-952-4057
www.simpsondoor.com

Stanley Door Systems

1000 Stanley Drive
New Britain, CT 06053
860-225-5111
www.stanleyworks.com

Velux Skylights

www.veluxusa.com

Vetter Windows and Patio Doors

www.vetterwindows.com

Weather Shield Windows
and Doors

One Weather Shield Plaza
P.O. Box 309
Medford, WI 54451
800-477-6808
www.weathershield.com

The Woodstone Co.

802-722-9217
www.woodstone.com

Zeluck Architectural Wood
Windows and Doors

800-233-0101
www.zeluck.com

**Wood, Wood Products, and
Wood Flooring**

Alloc Inc.

3441 S. Memorial Dr.
Racine, WI 53403
877-362-5562
www.alloc.com

American Hardboard Assoc.

1210 W. Northwest Highway
Palatine, IL 60067
847-934-8800

American Wood
Preservers' Association

334-874-9800
www.awpa.com

American Wood
Preservers Institute

2750 Prosperity Ave.
Suite 550
Fairfax, VA 22031
703-204-0500

APA-The Engineered
Wood Association

P.O. Box 11700
Tacoma, WA 98411
www.apawood.org

Armstrong

2500 Colombia Ave.
P.O. Box 3001
Lancaster, PA 17604
717-397-0611
www.armstrong.com

Bruce Hardwood Floors

Armstrong World Industries
P.O. Box 3001
Lancaster, PA 17604
800-233-3823
www.bruce.com

California Redwood Association

888-225-7339
www.calredwood.org

Canadian Wood Council

613-747-5544

Engineered Wood
Association – Help Line

253-620-7400
www.apawood.org

Environmental Protection Agency

202-272-0167
www.epa.gov

Forest Products Laboratory
USDA Forest Service

One Gifford Pinchot Drive
Madison, WI 53726
608-231-9200
www.fpl.fs.fed.us

Forest Products Society

2801 Marshall Ct.
Madison, WI 53705
608-231-1361

Hardwood Council

800-373-WOOD
www.hardwoodcouncil.com

Hardwood Information Center

400 Penn Center Blvd.
Suite 530
Pittsburgh, PA 15235
800-373-WOOD
www.hardwood.org

Hardwood
Manufacturers Association

400 Penn Center Blvd.
Suite 530
Pittsburgh, PA 15235
412-829-0770
www.hmamembers.org

Hardwood Plywood &
Veneer Association

P.O. Box 2789
Reston, VA 20195
703-435-2900
www.hpva.org

Hartco Hardwood Floors

P.O. Box 4009
Onieda, TN 37841
800-769-8528
www.hartcoflooring.com

Kahrs International Inc.

940 Centre Circle, No. 1000
Altamonte Springs, FL 32714
800-800-KAHR
www.kahrs.com

Kraftmaid Cabinetry

P.O. Box 1055
15535 South State Ave.
Middlefield, OH 44062
440-632-5333
www.kraftmaid.com

Mannington Mills Inc.

75 Mannington Mills
Salem, NJ 08079
856-935-3000
www.mannington.com

Minwax Company

10 Mountainview Rd.
Upper Saddle River, NJ
07458
800-523-9299
www.minwax.com

National Forest
Products Association

1111 Nineteenth St. NW
Suite 700
Washington, DC 20036
202-463-2700

National Oak Flooring
Manufacturers Association

P.O. Box 3009
Memphis, TN 38173
901-526-5016
www.nofma.org

National Wood
Flooring Association

111 Chesterfield Industrial Blvd.
Chesterfield, MO 63005
800-422-4556

NOFMA: The Wood Flooring
Manufacturers Association

P.O. Box 3009
Memphis, TN 38173
www.nofma.com

Northeastern Lumber
Manufacturer's Association

272 Tuttle Rd.
Cumberland Center, ME 04021
207-829-6901

Robbins Hardwood Floors

16803 Dallas Pkwy.
Addison, TX 75001
800-733-3309
www.robbins.com

Southern Forest
Products Association

Box 641700
Kenner, LA 70064
504-443-4464
www.southernpine.com

Southern Pine Council

Box 641700
Kenner, LA 70064
504-443-4464
www.southernpine.com

Western Wood
Products Association

522 S.W. Fifth Avenue
Portland, OR 97204-2122
503-224-3930
www.wwpa.org

Weyerhaeuser Co.

P.O. Box 9777
Federal Way, WA 98063
800-525-5440
www.weyerhaeuser.com

Wolman Wood Care Products

800-556-7737
www.wolman.com

Chapter 23 – Service Checklists

Whether you're doing it yourself or hiring professionals to service your home, these checklists help ensure that all important points are covered.

Tear out applicable checklists and make photocopies. You can send a copy to the service company when you arrange service, and/or review the list with the technician at the beginning of the service call.

Warm Air Furnace – Homeowner Service Checklist

Note: Turn off power to the unit before inspection or maintenance.

❑ Maintain records. Have a professional service the unit yearly. Proper maintenance keeps equipment operating efficiently and ensures safety. Contact the manufacturer of your furnace for specific maintenance requirements.

❑ Change the filter as required—often every other month.

❑ Switch high/low returns at the start and end of the heating season. For complete instructions, see "High and Low Returns" in Chapter 3.

❑ Check all flue pipes and vents for rust, water leaks, and loose connections.

❑ Lubricate the fan motor and fan bearing with a few drops of oil twice per year. (This is only required on certain units.)

❑ Check the belt to make sure it's not cracked or loose. (This is only required with belt-driven fans.)

❑ Listen to the furnace operate and follow up on any strange sounds.

❑ Check drain lines to make sure they are clear and draining properly.

❑ Look for water leaks or changes in the system.

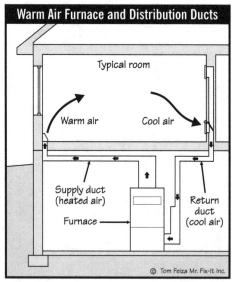

Warm Air Furnace and Distribution Ducts

Typical room

Warm air   Cool air

Supply duct (heated air)

Return duct (cool air)

Furnace

© Tom Feiza Mr. Fix-It Inc.

HO04

Warm Air Furnace – Professional Service Checklist

During a routine service call, the service technician should perform the following general maintenance measures. The technician may perform other checks, too, depending on the type of furnace.

❏ Check and clean burner.

❏ Check flue pipes, draft diverter, heat exchanger, and chimney.

❏ Remove burners to clean burners and heat exchanger if necessary.

❏ Check electrical wiring and connections.

❏ Check and clean circulating fan. Lubricate fan and motor if necessary.

❏ For belt-driven fans: check for tension, wear and alignment.

❏ Check supply and return ducts for air leakage, water stains, rust.

❏ Check and maintain filter.

❏ Perform an operational check of furnace and safety controls.

❏ Test for carbon monoxide in the flue gas and in the air around the furnace.

❏ Check for gas leaks.

❏ Check, clean, and (if necessary) adjust pilot light.

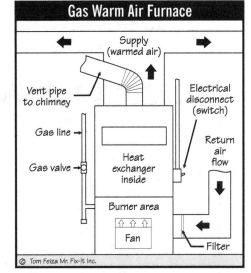

H001

❏ Check the water heater. For a gas water heater, check flue gas for carbon monoxide.

For a high-efficiency furnace, the technician should also:

❏ Check for water leaks (condensation from combustion).

❏ Check flue pipes and connections.

❏ Check for condensation on metal pipes and parts.

❏ Check for a clean condensate drain line.

❏ Check operation and condition of draft fan.

Hydronic Heating – Homeowner Service Checklist

Note: Turn off power to the unit before inspection or maintenance.

❐ Maintain records, and have a professional service the unit yearly.

❐ Check all flue pipes and vents for rust, water leaks, loose connections.

❐ Listen to the boiler operate, and follow up on any strange noises.

❐ Check drain lines to make sure they are clear and draining properly. (This is required only for high efficiency condensing units.)

❐ Look for water leaks or changes in the system.

❐ Oil the circulating pump twice per year. (Use just a few drops.)

❐ Check that the temperature/pressure gauge is in the operating range identified by a professional service technician. Mark the proper range on the gauge.

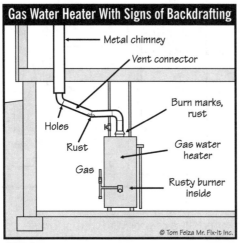

Gas Water Heater With Signs of Backdrafting

Metal chimney
Vent connector
Burn marks, rust
Holes
Rust
Gas water heater
Gas
Rusty burner inside

© Tom Feiza Mr. Fix-It Inc.

W006

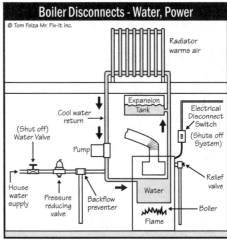

Boiler Disconnects - Water, Power

© Tom Feiza Mr. Fix-It Inc.

Radiator warms air
Expansion Tank
Cool water return
Electrical Disconnect Switch
(Shut off) Water Valve
(Shuts off System)
Pump
Relief valve
House water supply
Pressure reducing valve
Backflow preventer
Water
Boiler
Flame

H038

Hydronic Heating – Professional Service Checklist

A service technician should perform the following general maintenance measures. The service technician may also perform additional checks, depending on the type of furnace.

- ☐ Check and clean burner.

- ☐ Vent the system at the high points as necessary.

- ☐ Check all flue pipes, draft diverter, boiler housing, and chimney.

- ☐ Remove burners to clean burners and heat exchanger if necessary.

- ☐ Check electrical wiring and connections.

- ☐ Check and lubricate circulating pump(s).

- ☐ Check for water leaks.

- ☐ Check temperature and pressure relief valve.

- ☐ Check water supply system and backflow preventer.

- ☐ Add backflow preventer if none is present.

- ☐ Check expansion tank for proper water level.

- ☐ Check for gas leaks.

Hydronic (Hot Water) Boiler and Distribution
© Tom Feiza Mr. Fix-It Inc.

H005

- ☐ Test for carbon monoxide in the flue gas and in the air around the furnace.

- ☐ Perform an operational check of controls for temperature, pressure and safety.

- ☐ Check, clean, and (if necessary) adjust pilot light.

- ☐ Check the water heater. For a gas water heater, check flue gas for carbon monoxide.

Additional checks for a high-efficiency boiler with a draft fan:

- ☐ Check draft fan for condensation and rust.

- ☐ Check flue pipe for condensation.

- ☐ Check condensate drain lines.

Oil Heating – Homeowner Service Checklist

Note: Turn off all power to the unit before attempting inspection or maintenance.

❏ Follow the maintenance requirements listed on previous pages for warm air or hydronic boiler systems.

❏ Schedule routine maintenance yearly.

❏ Lubricate the burner motor if it has oil ports.
(Ask your service technician.)

❏ Make sure the system never, never runs out of fuel oil.

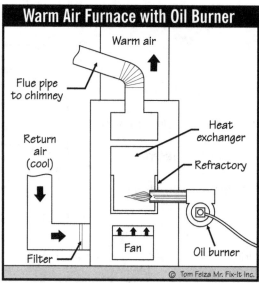

H013

Oil Heating – Professional Service Checklist

A service technician should perform the following general maintenance measures. The service technician may also perform additional checks, depending on the type of furnace.

Note: The first item on this checklist refers to general maintenance requirements found in the checklist for a warm-air furnace, so photocopy the warm air furnace checklist, too, and give both lists to your service technician.

❑   Follow applicable maintenance requirements listed for a warm air furnace.

❑   Remove and clean burner, clean blower blades, replace or clean filter and/or strainer, replace the nozzle, clean flame and heat sensors, check and clean or replace electrodes.

❑   Lubricate the burner motor.

❑   Check flue and barometric damper.

❑   Check for oil leaks.

❑   Check and clean oil pump.

❑   Clean and test stack control.

❑   Check and adjust draft regulator.

❑   Test for efficiency and make proper adjustments.

❑   Check the water heater. For a gas water heater, check flue gas for carbon monoxide.

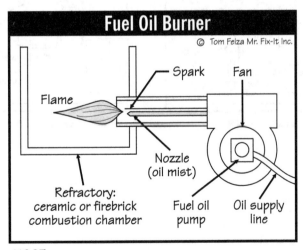

H007

Steam Heating – Homeowner Service Checklist

Note: Turn off power to the unit before inspection or maintenance.

☐ Maintain records.

☐ Check all flue pipes and vents for leaks, rust, and loose connections.

☐ Check the system for any leaks.

☐ Check the steam gauge. Have your contractor mark the normal range.

☐ Check the water level every month. The normal range should be marked on a sight glass.

☐ Make sure the radiators slope slightly toward the steam inlet pipe. This will help keep the pipe from knocking or pounding.

☐ Make sure the vents on the radiators are operating; otherwise, radiators may be cold.

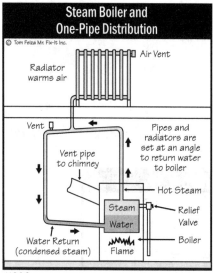

Steam Boiler and One-Pipe Distribution

© Tom Feiza Mr. Fix-It Inc.

Air Vent
Radiator warms air
Vent
Vent pipe to chimney
Pipes and radiators are set at an angle to return water to boiler
Hot Steam
Steam
Water
Relief Valve
Water Return (condensed steam)
Flame
Boiler

H006

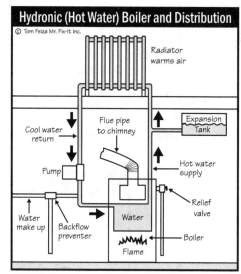

Hydronic (Hot Water) Boiler and Distribution

© Tom Feiza Mr. Fix-It Inc.

Radiator warms air
Cool water return
Flue pipe to chimney
Expansion Tank
Pump
Hot water supply
Water make up
Backflow preventer
Water
Relief valve
Flame
Boiler

H005

Steam Heating – Professional Service Checklist

A service technician should perform the following general maintenance measures. The service technician may also perform additional checks, depending on the type of boiler. For an oil fired system, see the information on oil burners, which require additional checks.

❑ Check and clean the burner.

❑ Check all vents on radiators and piping.

❑ Check all flue pipes, draft diverter, boiler housing and chimney.

❑ Remove burners to clean them and the heat exchanger if necessary.

❑ Check electrical wiring and connections.

❑ Check for water or steam leaks.

❑ Check the temperature and pressure relief valve.

❑ Add a backflow preventer if none is present.

❑ Perform an operational check of controls for temperature, pressure and safety.

❑ Test for carbon monoxide in the flue gas and the air around the boiler.

❑ Check for gas leaks.

❑ Check, clean, and (if necessary) adjust the pilot light.

❑ Check the water heater. For a gas water heater, check flue gas for carbon monoxide.

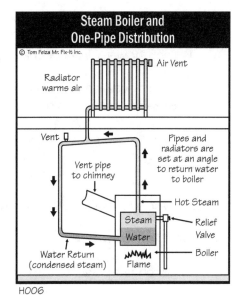

Steam Boiler and One-Pipe Distribution

© Tom Feiza Mr. Fix-It Inc.

Radiator warms air — Air Vent

Vent

Vent pipe to chimney

Pipes and radiators are set at an angle to return water to boiler

Hot Steam

Steam
Water

Relief Valve

Boiler

Water Return (condensed steam) — Flame

H006

Central Air Conditioning – Homeowner Service Checklist

Note: Turn off all power and disconnect switches before performing inspections/maintenance.

❏ Maintain records, and have a professional service the unit yearly.

❏ Change the filter as often as required (in some cases, every month).

❏ Switch high/low returns (and adjust ductwork if necessary) at the start and end of the cooling season. For complete instructions, check the section on "Heating and Cooling Distribution" in Chapter 3.

❏ Listen to the air conditioner operate, and follow up on any strange noises.

❏ Check drain lines from the furnace to make sure they are clear and draining properly.

❏ Look for water leaks or changes in the system.

❏ Keep plants and obstructions away from the exterior coil and fan. Allow 3 feet of clearance at the air discharge and 1 foot all around the unit.

❏ Keep the exterior coil clean.

❏ Keep the exterior unit level and away from soil or landscape materials.

❏ Make sure that supply and return registers inside your home are not blocked.

Fall Maintenance

❏ Disconnect power to the unit to prevent accidental use.

❏ (Optional)—Cover the top of the unit.

Spring Maintenance

❏ Uncover the unit.

❏ Turn the power on 24 hours before operation. Keep the thermostat off.

❏ Perform the maintenance listed above and arrange for professional service.

Central Air Conditioning – Professional Service Checklist

A service technician should perform the following procedures during a routine service call. The technician may perform additional checks, depending on the type of air conditioner you have.

❒ Check filter and replace as needed.

❒ Check exterior unit for level conditions, a clean coil, clearances, and adequate air flow.

❒ Check interior temperature drop across the cooling coil (15 to 22 degrees F).

❒ Check the condensate drain pan and line.

❒ Check secondary pan and line if unit is located in an attic.

❒ Look for signs of water leaks or excessive air leaks.

❒ Lubricate the fan motor and check the belt if required.

❒ Inspect electrical connections.

❒ Inspect refrigerant lines for signs of leaks.

❒ If performance problems exist, the technician may check for amp draw, clean the coils, check the refrigerant charge, and/or complete general performance tests.

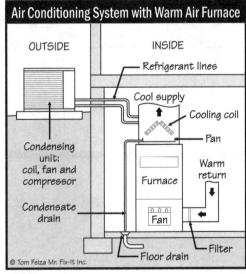

Air Conditioning System with Warm Air Furnace

OUTSIDE   INSIDE

Refrigerant lines

Cool supply

Cooling coil

Pan

Condensing unit: coil, fan and compressor

Warm return

Furnace

Condensate drain

Fan

Filter

Floor drain

© Tom Feiza Mr. Fix-It Inc.

A001

Heat Pump – Homeowner Service Checklist

Note: Turn off all power and disconnect switches before performing inspections/maintenance.

☐ Schedule professional service yearly.

☐ Watch for ice forming on the exterior unit. This is a serious problem indicating that the unit needs service.

☐ Follow all the maintenance recommendations for central air conditioning.

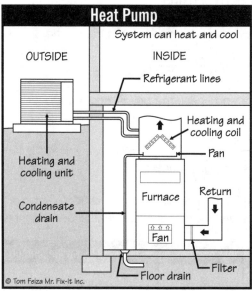

A003

Heat Pump – Professional Service Checklist

A service technician should perform the following procedures during a routine service call. The technician may perform additional checks, depending on the type of heat pump you have.

❑ Check filter and replace as needed.

❑ Check exterior unit for level conditions, a clean coil, clearances, and adequate air flow.

❑ Check interior temperature drop across the cooling coil (15 to 22 degrees F).

❑ Check the condensate drain pan and line.

❑ Check secondary pan and line if unit is located in an attic.

❑ Look for signs of water leaks or excessive air leaks.

❑ Lubricate the fan motor and check the belt if required.

❑ Inspect electrical connections.

❑ Inspect refrigerant lines for signs of leaks.

❑ If performance problems exist, the technician may check for amp draw, clean the coils, check the refrigerant charge, and/or complete general performance tests.

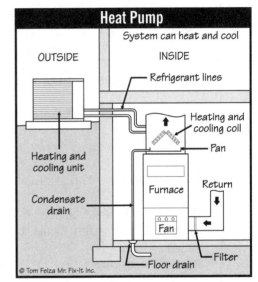

A003

❑ Follow any specific recommendations made by the heat pump manufacturer.

❑ Check the water heater. For a gas water heater, check flue gas for carbon monoxide.

Evaporative Cooler – Homeowner Service Checklist

Note: Turn off all power and disconnect switches before performing inspections/maintenance.

☐ Maintain records. Have a professional service the unit yearly. Proper maintenance keeps the equipment operating efficiently and eliminates contaminants from the system. Maintenance will help prevent water leaks. Contact the manufacturer of the unit for the specific maintenance requirements.

☐ In the winter, drain the reservoir and supply piping. Clean the pan. Close the duct and cover the unit.

☐ In the spring, clean the reservoir and activate the supply piping.

☐ Routinely inspect the unit and the area around it for leaks.

☐ Inspect and test the drain piping.

☐ Clean the pads and reservoir on a routine basis.

☐ Paint rusted areas as needed.

☐ Clean louvers in the cabinet as needed.

☐ If the unit has a belt drive, check the belt condition and belt tension. The belt should not shimmy and should not have cracks on its edges.

☐ Open windows when the unit is in operation.

☐ If you have central air conditioning and an evaporative cooler, do not run the units at the same time. This wastes energy.

☐ If you operate central air conditioning, close the windows that you have opened while operating the evaporative cooler.

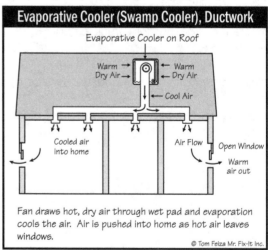

Evaporative Cooler (Swamp Cooler), Ductwork

Evaporative Cooler on Roof

Warm → Dry Air →   ← Warm Dry Air

← Cool Air

Cooled air into home   Air Flow   Open Window

Warm air out

Fan draws hot, dry air through wet pad and evaporation cools the air. Air is pushed into home as hot air leaves windows.

© Tom Feiza Mr. Fix-It Inc.

V048

Evaporative Cooler – Professional Service Checklist

A service technician should perform the following procedures during a routine service call. The technician may perform additional checks, depending on the type of evaporative cooler and related equipment.

- ❏ Check and lubricate motors.

- ❏ Check belt and replace if necessary. Check tension of the belt.

- ❏ Clean fan as required.

- ❏ Clean or replace evaporative pads as needed. Clean pad frames, and paint as needed.

- ❏ Clean the evaporative water pan.

- ❏ Test and clean the drain lines.

- ❏ Test and operate the fill system, valve, and float. Check for valve leaks, and check the float level. Adjust float to maintain proper water level in the pan.

- ❏ Test the pump to ensure that the proper amount of water is being delivered to the evaporative pads and that the pads are fully wetted.

- ❏ Clean the water distribution system as needed. Tubes can become clogged with mineral deposits from the water. Replace any damaged tubing.

- ❏ Lubricate the pump if needed.

- ❏ Inspect electrical wiring and controls for damage and to ensure proper operation.

- ❏ Check the overall unit for proper operation.

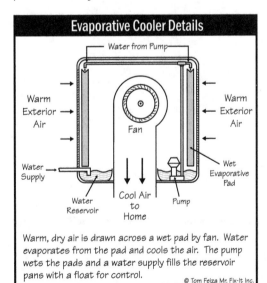

Evaporative Cooler Details

Warm, dry air is drawn across a wet pad by fan. Water evaporates from the pad and cools the air. The pump wets the pads and a water supply fills the reservoir pans with a float for control.

© Tom Feiza Mr. Fix-It Inc.

V049

Chapter 24 – In Case of Emergency: Things Everyone in the Household Should Know

In Case of Emergency: Things Everyone in the Household Should Know

It's a great idea for every homeowner to set up an emergency plan and create a list of things everybody in the household should know. Your safety plan could involve maintaining a list of emergency shutoffs, compiling information sources, and gathering basic tools.

You may need to find an expert to help locate, repair or maintain some of these valves and switches. Locating and tagging them is a helpful exercise for homeowners. Use the tags provided in this journal. After tagging each item, take a tour with all family members explaining what these items do and how to operate the controls. In addition, develop a list of emergency numbers and an escape plan.

Here is a checklist to help you get started:

☐ Main electrical disconnect. This will be located at the main fuse box or breaker panel. Usually there is one main switch or fuse block, but older systems may have multiple disconnects.

☐ Water main valve. This valve turns off all the water to your home. If the valve looks old, worn or rusty, have a plumber check it for proper

operation. If you use a municipal water supply, the valve will be located in the basement on the "street side" of your home near the water meter. If your house has its own well, the valve will be near the pressure tank. In this case, to disable the system you must turn off the main valve and the electrical switch for the well pump.

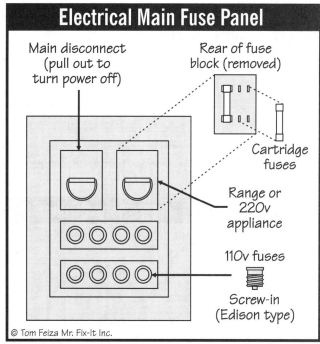

Electrical Main Fuse Panel

Main disconnect (pull out to turn power off)

Rear of fuse block (removed)

Cartridge fuses

Range or 220v appliance

110v fuses

Screw-in (Edison type)

© Tom Feiza Mr. Fix-It Inc.

E003

Electrical Main Circuit Breaker Panel

Main breaker (turns off all power)

Double breaker (220v)

Single breaker (110v)

Blanks

© Tom Feiza Mr. Fix-It Inc.

E002

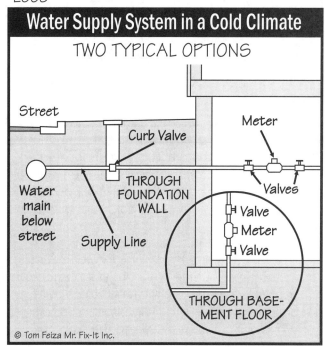

Water Supply System in a Cold Climate

TWO TYPICAL OPTIONS

Street

Curb Valve

Meter

Water main below street

THROUGH FOUNDATION WALL

Supply Line

Valves

Valve
Meter
Valve

THROUGH BASEMENT FLOOR

© Tom Feiza Mr. Fix-It Inc.

P005

Well - Main Water Disconnects

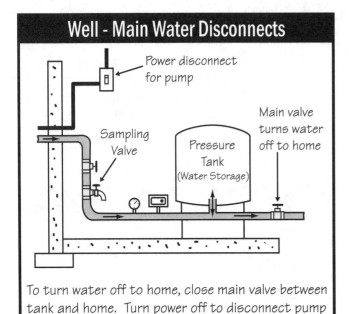

To turn water off to home, close main valve between tank and home. Turn power off to disconnect pump and stop pump operation.

© Tom Feiza Mr. Fix-It Inc.

P056

Water Heater Valves / Disconnects

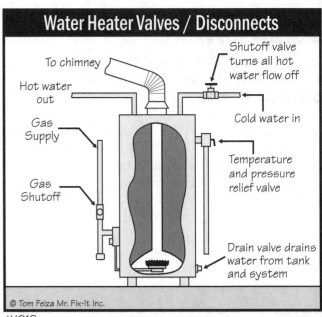

© Tom Feiza Mr. Fix-It Inc.

W012

Water Main / Meter - Warm Climate

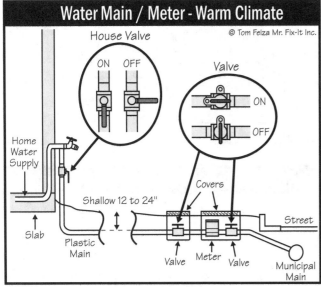

P063

Exterior Gas Meter and Shutoff

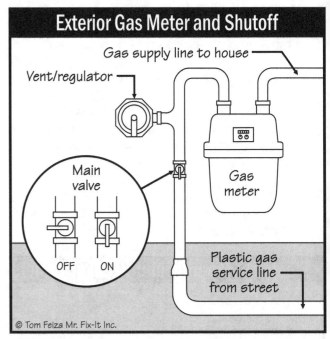

© Tom Feiza Mr. Fix-It Inc.

P002

☐ Water heater shutoff. This valve is located on the cold-water inlet at the top of the water heater. It turns off the hot water supply to your home by closing the cold supply to the water heater.

☐ Natural gas main. This will be located near the meter, either outside or inside your home. Many of these valves require a wrench to operate; a quarter-turn moves the valve from on to off. When the handle is parallel to the pipe, the valve is open.

☐ Local gas valves. These should be located at each gas appliance; they, too, close with a quarter-turn.

☐ Air conditioning disconnect. This switch, near the exterior air conditioning unit, turns off the 240-volt electrical supply.

Gas Shutoff Valve - Typical

© Tom Feiza Mr. Fix-It Inc.

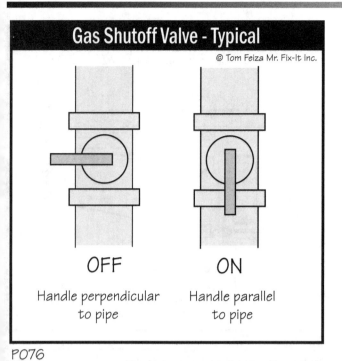

OFF

ON

Handle perpendicular
to pipe

Handle parallel
to pipe

P076

Air Conditioning - Exterior Electrical Disconnect

(To turn off electrical power to unit)

Electrical switch
on wall outside

Air conditioning
compressor and coil

© Tom Feiza Mr. Fix-It Inc.

Types of Exterior Disconnects

Switch
(switch on/off)

Breaker
(switch on/off)

Pull-out fuse block
(pull out: off)

Pull-out plug
(pull out: off)

(A second disconnect will be located
inside at the main electrical panel)

A004

□ Furnace and air conditioning main switch. This is usually mounted on the furnace. In a modern system, it will look like a light switch. It turns off the central heating and cooling system.

□ Emergency release for garage door. The automatic garage door opener has an emergency release so you can open the door when there is a power failure. Show everyone how it operates. Do this with the door down, because a poorly balanced door may crash to the ground. The release is located where the door attaches to the opener track. Pull the handle to release it—remember, do this with the door down—and then lift the door.

Furnace Utility Disconnects

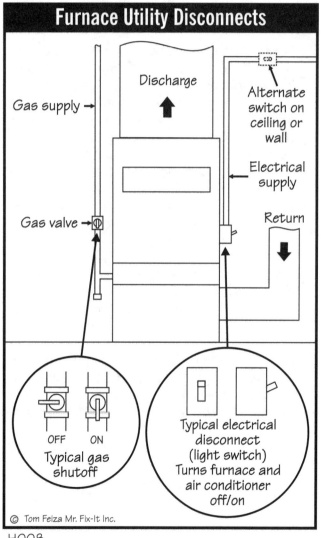

Gas supply →

Discharge

Alternate
switch on
ceiling or
wall

Electrical
supply

Gas valve →

Return

OFF   ON
Typical gas
shutoff

Typical electrical
disconnect
(light switch)
Turns furnace and
air conditioner
off/on

© Tom Feiza Mr. Fix-It Inc.

H008

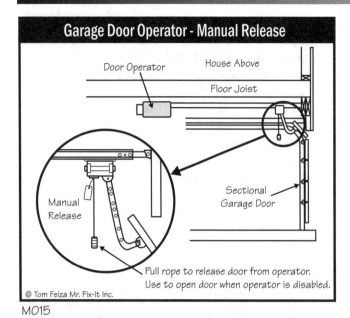

Garage Door Operator - Manual Release

Door Operator House Above

Floor Joist

Manual Release

Sectional Garage Door

Pull rope to release door from operator.
Use to open door when operator is disabled.

© Tom Feiza Mr. Fix-It Inc.

M015

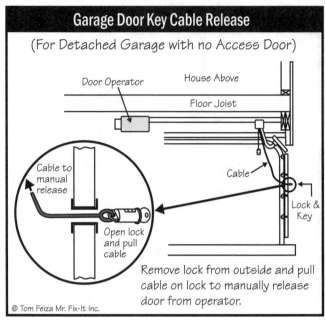

Garage Door Key Cable Release

(For Detached Garage with no Access Door)

Door Operator House Above

Floor Joist

Cable to manual release

Cable

Lock & Key

Open lock and pull cable

Remove lock from outside and pull cable on lock to manually release door from operator.

© Tom Feiza Mr. Fix-It Inc.

M018

❏ Emergency release for garage door—with a key (when there is no service door to the garage). In this situation, to release the garage door opener when the power is out, you must open a special lock and remove a cable. You'll find a circular lock near the top center of the garage door. Open this lock and pull the attached cable out through the opening. Doing this will release the opener from the garage door so you can open the door manually. Always remember that the door should be down before you test the release.

❏ Emergency phone numbers. Keep a list of how to reach the fire department, ambulance/ rescue, police, Mom, Dad, relatives, workplace(s), and others appropriate to your household.

❏ Fire extinguishers. Place fire extinguishers in your kitchen, garage, and basement. Make sure everyone knows how to use them.

❏ Escape plan. Have a plan for how to get out fast in case of emergency. Establish a specific location where everyone can meet just outside the house. Practice your plan.

❏ Emergency toolbox. Have a flashlight and basic tools set aside for emergencies. The flash- light should be rechargeable; keep it mounted on its charger.

This is a basic list. For more detailed information, contact your local utilities, police, and fire depart- ment. It is very important to know how to react to an emergency and to know that emergency shut- offs will work when needed.

This chapter provides a set of tags you may attach to various utilities in your home.

Water main valve, cold climate (Municipal water system)
Usually located on street side of home

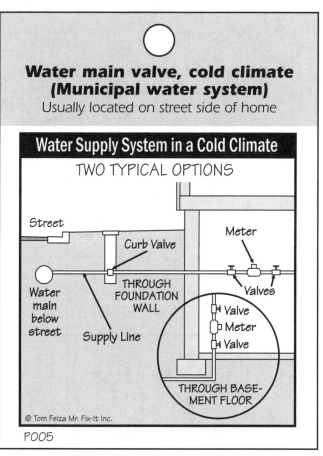

Water Supply System in a Cold Climate

TWO TYPICAL OPTIONS

Street

Curb Valve

Meter

THROUGH FOUNDATION WALL

Valves

Water main below street

Supply Line

Valve
Meter
Valve

THROUGH BASEMENT FLOOR

© Tom Feiza Mr. Fix-It Inc.

P005

Main valve for water (Well-water system)
Located near well pressure tank

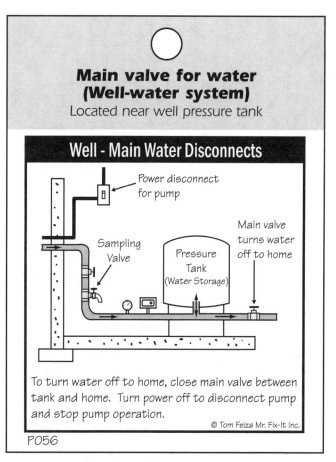

Well - Main Water Disconnects

Power disconnect for pump

Sampling Valve

Pressure Tank (Water Storage)

Main valve turns water off to home

To turn water off to home, close main valve between tank and home. Turn power off to disconnect pump and stop pump operation.

© Tom Feiza Mr. Fix-It Inc.

P056

Main disconnect for power (Well-water system)
Located near well pressure tank

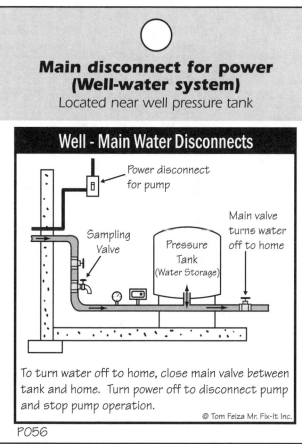

Well - Main Water Disconnects

Power disconnect for pump

Sampling Valve

Pressure Tank (Water Storage)

Main valve turns water off to home

To turn water off to home, close main valve between tank and home. Turn power off to disconnect pump and stop pump operation.

© Tom Feiza Mr. Fix-It Inc.

P056

Water main valve, warm climate
Located outside on street side

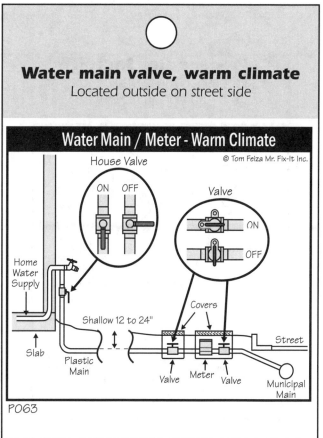

Water Main / Meter - Warm Climate

© Tom Feiza Mr. Fix-It Inc.

House Valve

ON   OFF

Valve

ON

OFF

Home Water Supply

Covers

Shallow 12 to 24"

Street

Slab

Plastic Main

Valve   Meter   Valve

Municipal Main

P063

Natural gas main valve
Located at gas meter

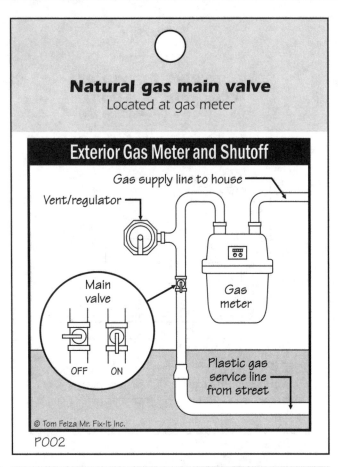

Exterior Gas Meter and Shutoff

Gas supply line to house

Vent/regulator

Main valve

OFF · ON

Gas meter

Plastic gas service line from street

© Tom Feiza Mr. Fix-It Inc.

P002

Furnace / Air Conditioner main switch
Located on or near furnace

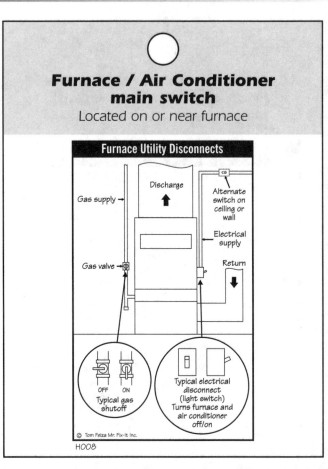

Furnace Utility Disconnects

Gas supply

Discharge

Alternate switch on ceiling or wall

Electrical supply

Gas valve

Return

OFF · ON
Typical gas shutoff

Typical electrical disconnect (light switch) Turns furnace and air conditioner off/on

© Tom Feiza Mr. Fix-It Inc.

H008

Propane Gas Shutoff
Located near entrance of pipe to home and/or on tank

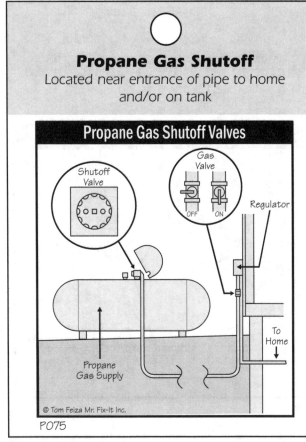

Propane Gas Shutoff Valves

Shutoff Valve

Gas Valve

OFF · ON

Regulator

To Home

Propane Gas Supply

© Tom Feiza Mr. Fix-It Inc.

P075

Oil Supply Valve
Located at lower end of tank on oil tubing

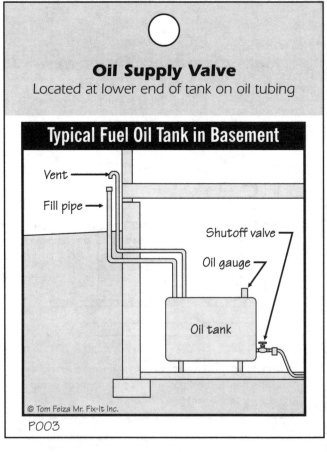

Typical Fuel Oil Tank in Basement

Vent

Fill pipe

Shutoff valve

Oil gauge

Oil tank

© Tom Feiza Mr. Fix-It Inc.

P003

Dishwasher Supply
Located below the sink or in the crawl space or basement below

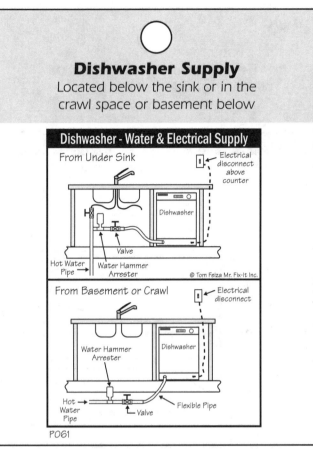

P061

Furnace – Outside Air Supply Damper
Located in duct to furnace return

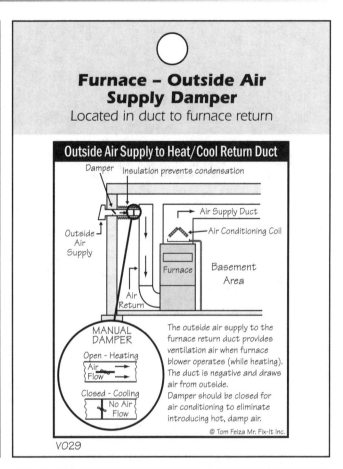

V029

Water heater shutoff
Cold-water valve located at top of water heater

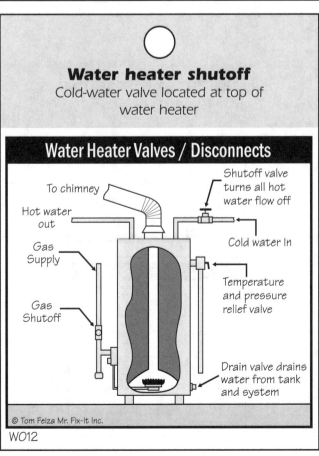

W012

Main electrical disconnect
Located at main fuse box or breaker

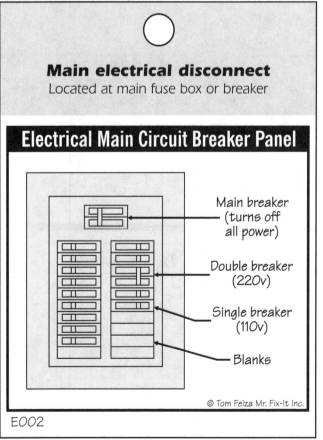

E002

Emergency release for garage door
Located where door connects to opener track

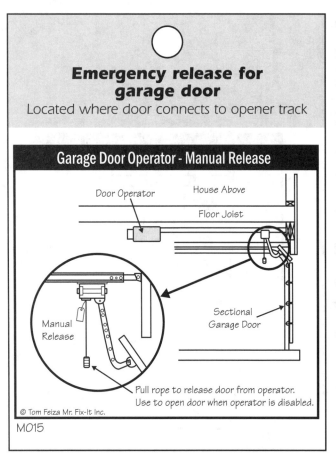

Garage Door Operator - Manual Release

Door Operator
House Above
Floor Joist

Manual Release

Sectional Garage Door

Pull rope to release door from operator.
Use to open door when operator is disabled.

© Tom Feiza Mr. Fix-It Inc.

M015

Emergency garage door cable release
Lock located in garage door

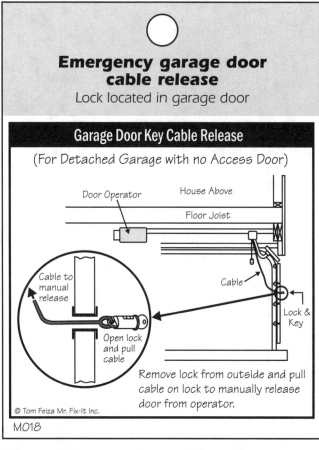

Garage Door Key Cable Release
(For Detached Garage with no Access Door)

Door Operator
House Above
Floor Joist

Cable to manual release

Cable

Open lock and pull cable

Lock & Key

Remove lock from outside and pull cable on lock to manually release door from operator.

© Tom Feiza Mr. Fix-It Inc.

M018

Air conditioner 240-volt disconnect
Located near exterior AC unit

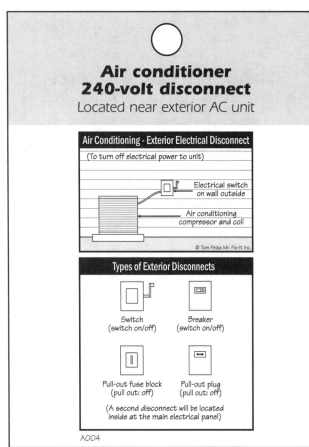

Air Conditioning - Exterior Electrical Disconnect
(To turn off electrical power to unit)

Electrical switch on wall outside

Air conditioning compressor and coil

© Tom Feiza Mr. Fix-It Inc.

Types of Exterior Disconnects

Switch (switch on/off)

Breaker (switch on/off)

Pull-out fuse block (pull out: off)

Pull-out plug (pull out: off)

(A second disconnect will be located inside at the main electrical panel)

A004

Heat Pump Disconnect
Located near exterior heat pump unit

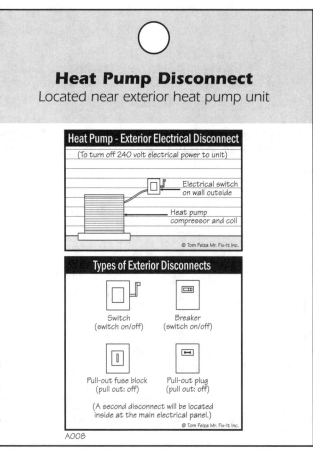

Heat Pump - Exterior Electrical Disconnect
(To turn off 240 volt electrical power to unit)

Electrical switch on wall outside

Heat pump compressor and coil

© Tom Feiza Mr. Fix-It Inc.

Types of Exterior Disconnects

Switch (switch on/off)

Breaker (switch on/off)

Pull-out fuse block (pull out: off)

Pull-out plug (pull out: off)

(A second disconnect will be located inside at the main electrical panel.)

© Tom Feiza Mr. Fix-It Inc.

A008

Steam Boiler Water Supply
Located near boiler on a water line

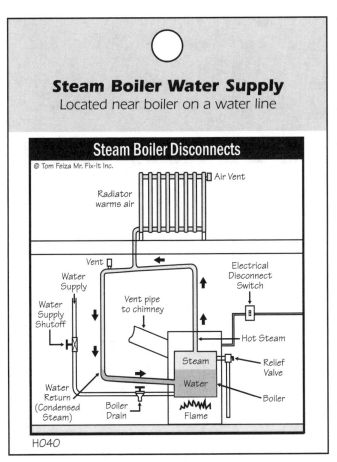

H040

Steam Boiler Electrical Disconnect
Located near boiler

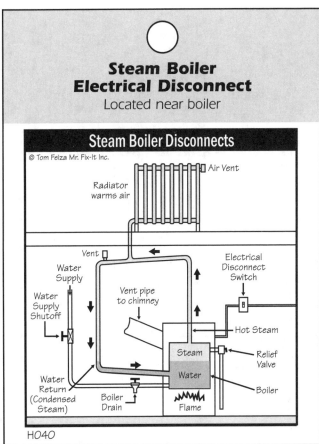

H040

Local gas valve
Located at all gas appliances: furnace, water heater, stove, fireplace

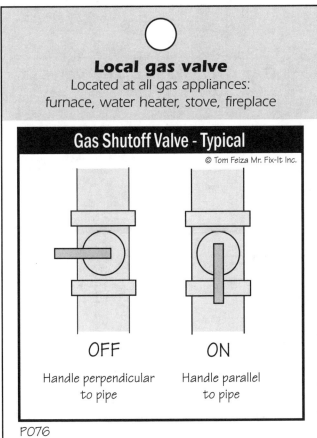

P076

Irrigation, Sprinkler Valve
Located in crawl space, in basement, or outside near irrigation system

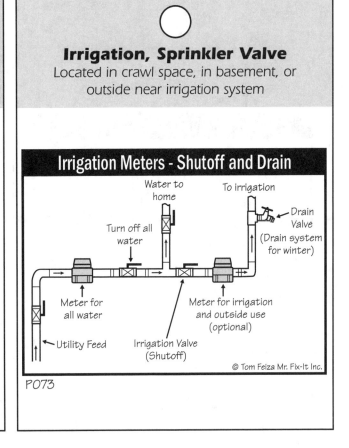

P073

Hard water
Located on pipe feeding water softener

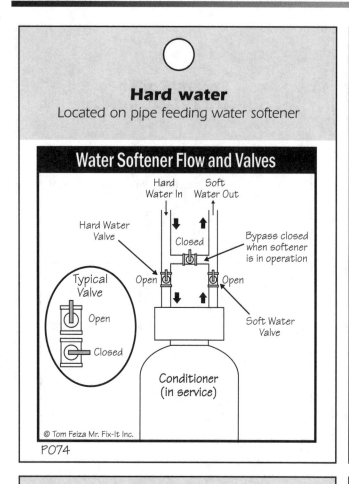

P074

Soft Water
Located on pipe leaving water softener

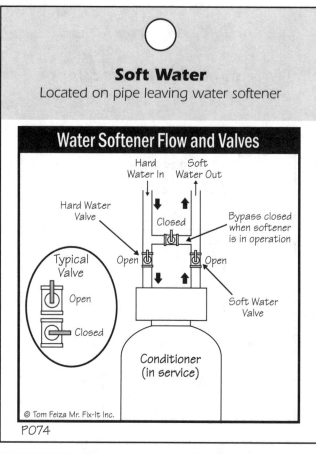

P074

Softener Bypass
Located between the hard and soft water pipes

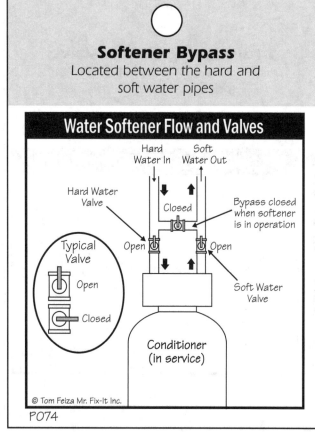

P074

Gas Grill, Gas Supply Valve
Located near the grill

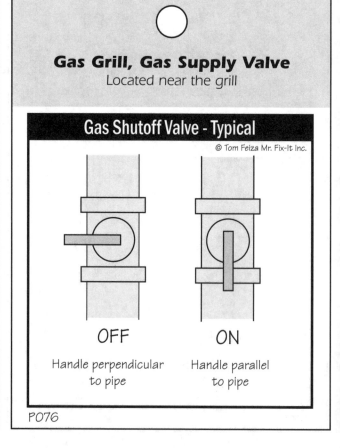

P076

Humidifier Water Supply
Located on water supply line near furnace

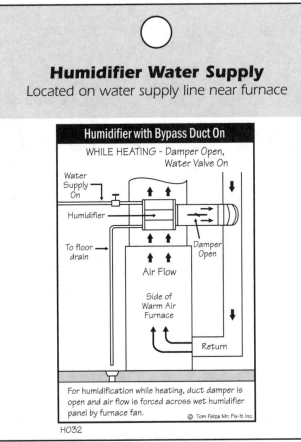

Humidifier with Bypass Duct On

WHILE HEATING - Damper Open, Water Valve On

Water Supply On

Humidifier

To floor drain

Damper Open

Air Flow

Side of Warm Air Furnace

Return

For humidification while heating, duct damper is open and air flow is forced across wet humidifier panel by furnace fan.

© Tom Feiza Mr. Fix-It Inc.

H032

Boiler Water Supply
Located on water pipe near boiler

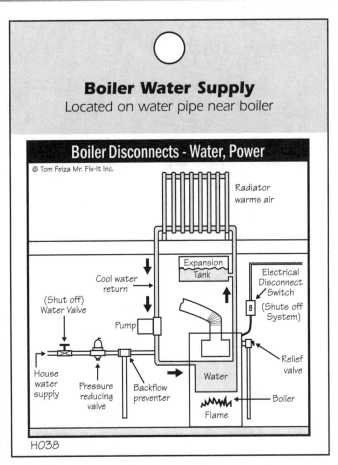

Boiler Disconnects - Water, Power

© Tom Feiza Mr. Fix-It Inc.

Radiator warms air

Cool water return

Expansion Tank

Electrical Disconnect Switch (Shuts off System)

(Shut off) Water Valve

Pump

House water supply

Pressure reducing valve

Backflow preventer

Water

Relief valve

Boiler

Flame

H038

Boiler Electrical Disconnect
Switch located near boiler

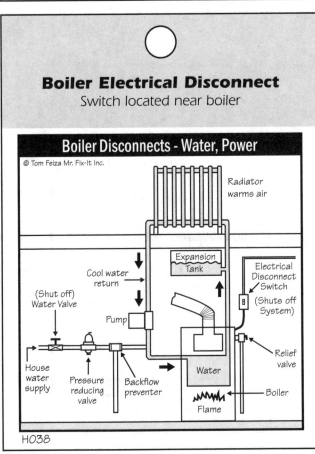

Boiler Disconnects - Water, Power

© Tom Feiza Mr. Fix-It Inc.

Radiator warms air

Cool water return

Expansion Tank

Electrical Disconnect Switch (Shuts off System)

(Shut off) Water Valve

Pump

House water supply

Pressure reducing valve

Backflow preventer

Water

Relief valve

Boiler

Flame

H038

Humidifier damper Winter/Summer
Located on humidifier or on duct to humidifier

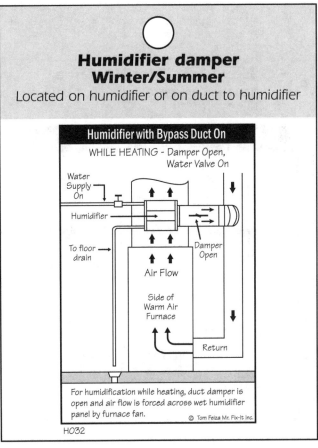

Humidifier with Bypass Duct On

WHILE HEATING - Damper Open, Water Valve On

Water Supply On

Humidifier

To floor drain

Damper Open

Air Flow

Side of Warm Air Furnace

Return

For humidification while heating, duct damper is open and air flow is forced across wet humidifier panel by furnace fan.

© Tom Feiza Mr. Fix-It Inc.

H032

283

Gas Fireplace
Located on gas line near fireplace

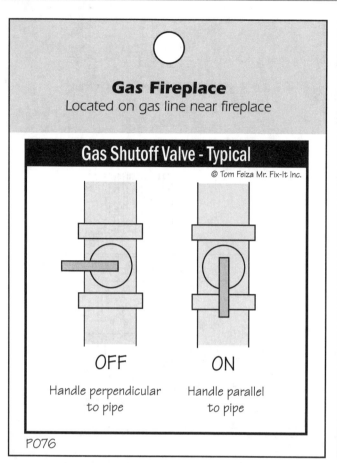

Gas Shutoff Valve - Typical
© Tom Feiza Mr. Fix-It Inc.

OFF
Handle perpendicular to pipe

ON
Handle parallel to pipe

P076

Gas Range
Located behind gas range

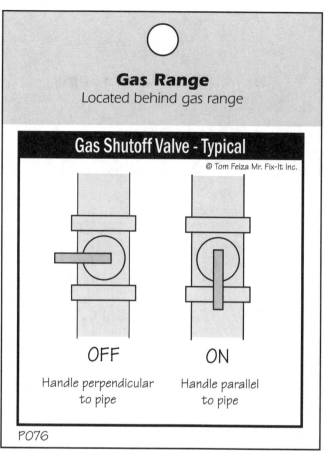

Gas Shutoff Valve - Typical
© Tom Feiza Mr. Fix-It Inc.

OFF
Handle perpendicular to pipe

ON
Handle parallel to pipe

P076

Hose Bib Interior Valve
Located in the basement, crawl space or home

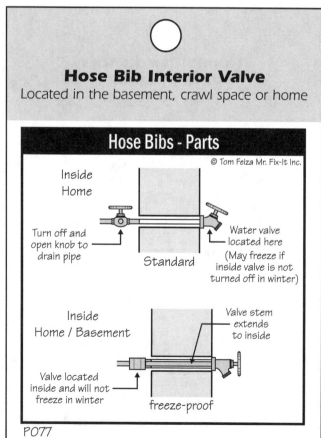

Hose Bibs - Parts
© Tom Feiza Mr. Fix-It Inc.

Inside Home

Turn off and open knob to drain pipe

Standard

Water valve located here (May freeze if inside valve is not turned off in winter)

Inside Home / Basement

Valve stem extends to inside

Valve located inside and will not freeze in winter

freeze-proof

P077

Ice Maker Supply
Located behind or below the refrigerator

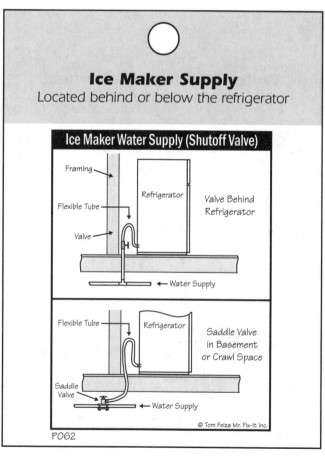

Ice Maker Water Supply (Shutoff Valve)

Framing

Refrigerator

Flexible Tube

Valve

Valve Behind Refrigerator

Water Supply

Flexible Tube

Refrigerator

Saddle Valve in Basement or Crawl Space

Saddle Valve

Water Supply

© Tom Feiza Mr. Fix-It Inc.

P062

Chapter 25 – Keep Your Basement Dry

Simple, routine maintenance can keep your basement dry and prevent damage that requires costly repairs. Since most basement damage occurs slowly, over many years, you may not notice a problem until there is a water leak or a major crack. Let's walk through the systems protecting your basement to see how they work and how to maintain them.

Sanitary and Storm Sewers

First, it helps to have a little background on the sewers that drain water away from your home. Most larger municipalities have two types of sewers, each built for a specific purpose. Sanitary sewers carry waste from sinks and bathroom fixtures to the sewage treatment plant. Storm sewers collect rain and surface water and carry it to lakes or rivers.

Your basement is connected to the sanitary sewer system at the floor drain or at basement plumbing fixtures. The system carries waste out of the house. As it reaches the street, the flow may travel downhill, aided by gravity, or it may be assisted by pumps. In either case, its final destination is the sewage treatment plant.

The storm sewer is connected to the sewer grates in the street and eventually dumps the clear water (rainwater) into rivers and streams. If your sump pump is connected to a sewer line, it should be rerouted to the storm sewer. Downspouts and rain gutters that are routed into underground sewer lines should also be rerouted to the storm sewer. Some sump pumps will be routed to the surface soil; eventually the water flows to the storm sewer.

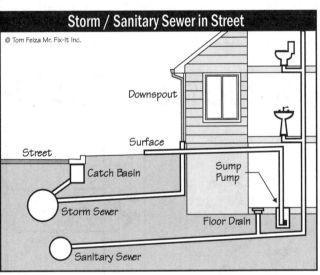

Storm / Sanitary Sewer in Street

© Tom Feiza Mr. Fix-It Inc.

Downspout

Surface

Street

Catch Basin

Sump Pump

Storm Sewer

Floor Drain

Sanitary Sewer

P017

You may have a foundation (basement) drain tile system that is connected to the storm sewer or to the combined sanitary sewer. Combined sewers? Yes, older systems may have "combined" sewers in which sanitary and storm sewers are combined in the street or below the house. Most of these systems are being renovated to keep surface water out of the sanitary sewers. We don't want to pay to treat rainwater, and we don't want it flooding our sewage plants. However, many combined systems still exist. The City of Milwaukee's deep tunnel system collects excess water from the combined sewers to help eliminate overflows into rivers and streams.

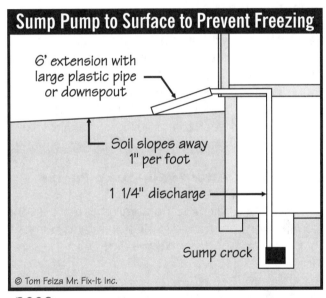

Sump Pump to Surface to Prevent Freezing

6' extension with large plastic pipe or downspout

Soil slopes away 1" per foot

1 1/4" discharge

Sump crock

© Tom Feiza Mr. Fix-It Inc.

B006

Protecting Your Basement: Drain Tile Systems

Older Homes: No Drain Tile System

Homes built around 1920 or earlier may not have drain tile systems. These homes were often built "high on the hill" with a shallow basement that simply depended on surface grading to divert water from the basement.

Drain Tiles, Bleeders, and Damp Proofing

Homes with drain tile systems share common components that collect and remove water. Exterior drain tiles are placed near or above the footings. These exterior tiles should be covered with at least 2 feet of gravel, allowing water to flow to the tiles. Older homes have concrete tiles; newer homes use perforated plastic pipe. Interior tiles receive water from exterior drain tiles via bleeders through the footings. Interior tiles route the water to a sump pump or palmer valve. (In the next section, we'll take a closer look at the palmer valve.) To keep water out of the rest of the basement, a thin coating of tar or damp proofing is applied to the outside of the foundation when the house is built. Block basement walls are "backplastered" with a thin concrete coating on the outside, under the damp proofing.

Homes Built from About 1920 to 1950— Palmer Valves

Early drain tile systems in municipal areas often were connected to the basement floor drain with a one-way check valve called a palmer valve. Some municipalities require that this connection be eliminated because it drains storm water into the sanitary sewer. You need to maintain this palmer valve by checking that it opens freely to discharge water.

Homes Built After 1950—Sump Pumps

Newer homes have a sump pump that removes the storm water from the drain tile system and pumps it to an underground storm sewer line or to the surface soil.

Rural Homes—Septic Systems, Basement Drainage

A home with a septic system simply has a private sewage treatment system. All the other principles of drainage are the same. Because the septic system's drain exits the basement near the midpoint of the wall, the house may have a second pump crock to lift sanitary sewage from the floor drain and laundry tubs up to the septic drain line. Homes in rural areas don't have storm sewers. All storm water is routed to the surface and to ditches.

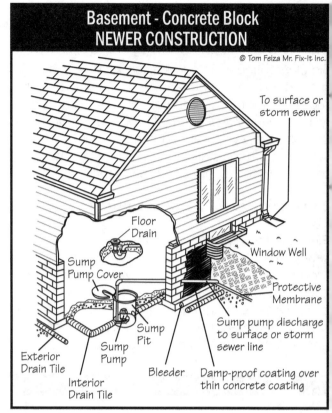

Basement - Concrete Block NEWER CONSTRUCTION

© Tom Feiza Mr. Fix-It Inc.

To surface or storm sewer

Floor Drain

Window Well

Sump Pump Cover

Protective Membrane

Sump pump discharge to surface or storm sewer line

Exterior Drain Tile

Sump Pit

Sump Pump

Bleeder

Damp-proof coating over thin concrete coating

Interior Drain Tile

B005

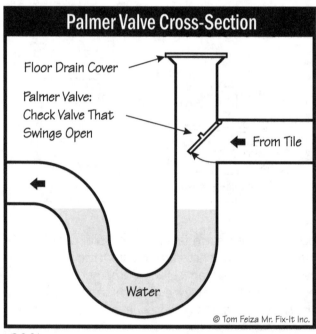

Palmer Valve Cross-Section

Floor Drain Cover

Palmer Valve: Check Valve That Swings Open

From Tile

Water

© Tom Feiza Mr. Fix-It Inc.

B001

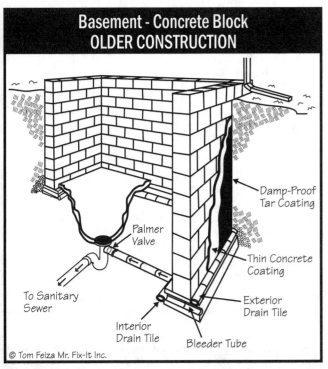

Basement - Concrete Block OLDER CONSTRUCTION

Damp-Proof Tar Coating

Palmer Valve

Thin Concrete Coating

To Sanitary Sewer

Interior Drain Tile

Bleeder Tube

Exterior Drain Tile

© Tom Feiza Mr. Fix-It Inc.

B002

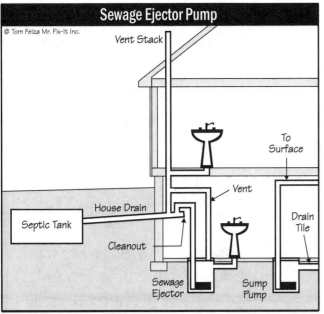

Sewage Ejector Pump

© Tom Feiza Mr. Fix-It Inc.

Vent Stack

To Surface

Vent

House Drain

Septic Tank

Cleanout

Drain Tile

Sewage Ejector

Sump Pump

P021

How Sewage Backs Up Into Your Basement

If the sanitary sewage system backs up, your basement could be affected. The sanitary system can back up because of a blocked pipe from your home or a blocked pipe in the street, or because the combined sewers are blocked or overflowing.

When the sanitary or combined sewage system backs up, sewage will enter your home through the floor drain or any plumbing fixture. When a whole neighborhood experiences a sanitary sewer backup, it's because a major sewage line is blocked or has more flow than it can handle. For instance, during a heavy rain, the combined sanitary and storm sewers may be unable to handle the sudden increased flow.

There is little you can do to prevent a neighborhood-wide sanitary sewer backup except to work with your local municipality to correct sewage system problems.

How Rainwater Backs Up Into Your Basement

If you have poor surface drainage or problems with gutters and downspouts, you are inviting rainwater into your basement. Drainage systems are not designed to handle excessive surface water. If water floods around your basement, water will come in.

Water from the Sump Pump

Your house may have a sump pump. A sump pump is designed to collect the water from your basement drain tile system. Water can back up from this sump pump if the electrical power goes out, the flow is too great, the discharge is blocked, or the pump malfunctions. This storm water may overflow the sump pump crock, run down the floor drain into the sanitary sewer, and/or flood your basement.

Water from the Walls, Window Well, Cracks, And Floors

Water may leak into your basement because of poor surface grading or problems with gutters, downspouts, and sump pump discharges. Leaks can also be caused by problems with the palmer valve, drain tile, storm sewer lines, or window wells.

Avoiding and Correcting Problems

You can avoid or solve most basement seepage problems by following these simple corrective steps, which are listed in order of priority.

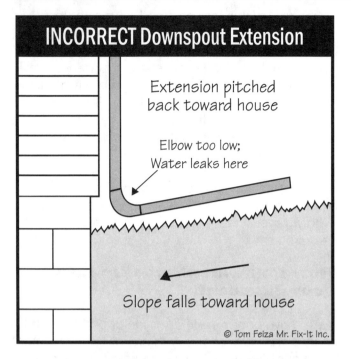

INCORRECT Downspout Extension

Extension pitched back toward house

Elbow too low; Water leaks here

Slope falls toward house

© Tom Feiza Mr. Fix-It Inc.

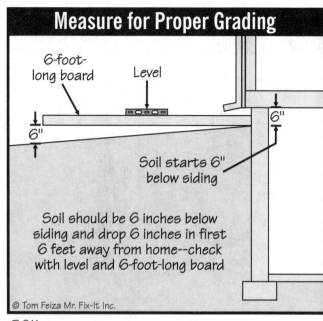

Measure for Proper Grading

6-foot-long board

Level

6"

6"

Soil starts 6" below siding

Soil should be 6 inches below siding and drop 6 inches in first 6 feet away from home--check with level and 6-foot-long board

© Tom Feiza Mr. Fix-It Inc.

B011

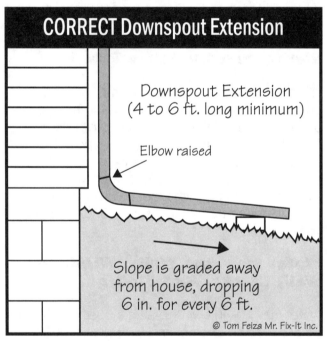

CORRECT Downspout Extension

Downspout Extension (4 to 6 ft. long minimum)

Elbow raised

Slope is graded away from house, dropping 6 in. for every 6 ft.

© Tom Feiza Mr. Fix-It Inc.

B019

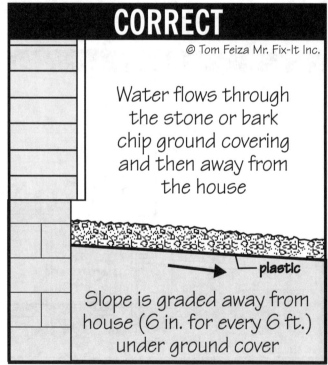

CORRECT

© Tom Feiza Mr. Fix-It Inc.

Water flows through the stone or bark chip ground covering and then away from the house

plastic

Slope is graded away from house (6 in. for every 6 ft.) under ground cover

B009

1. Keep gutters and downspouts clean, and direct them away from the basement. Downspouts must be routed to a storm sewer or at least 6 feet away from the foundation to an area where the water will flow away naturally.

2. Grade soft surfaces. All surface water must flow away from foundation walls. Soil should pitch away from the basement, dropping 6 inches for every 6 feet. The soil under any

bark or stone mulch around your home must pitch away; ideally, any plastic under the mulch will pitch away, too. Check under decks and porches. During a heavy rain, walk around your home to check for pooling water. No water should pool around or flow toward your basement walls.

Grading - Negative, Problem

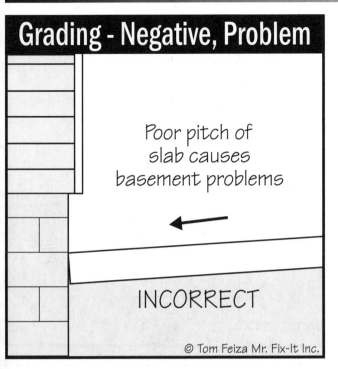

Poor pitch of slab causes basement problems

INCORRECT

© Tom Feiza Mr. Fix-It Inc.

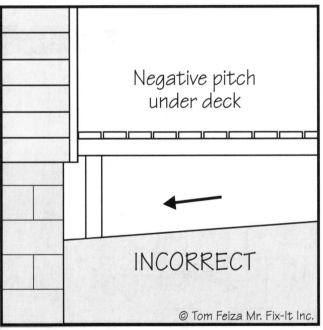

Negative pitch under deck

INCORRECT

© Tom Feiza Mr. Fix-It Inc.

B008

3. Grade hard surfaces. All concrete and asphalt surfaces must pitch away from the basement. Watch for slab concrete beneath decks. Check all stoops, drives, and walks.

4. Grade the soil around window wells to direct water away. Seal the window well tightly to the foundation, and keep the inside of the well clean. The inside of the window well should have a base of 6 to 18 inches of gravel—not

Window Well

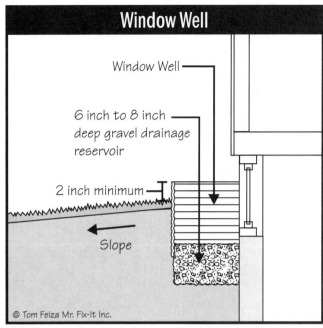

Window Well

6 inch to 8 inch deep gravel drainage reservoir

2 inch minimum

Slope

© Tom Feiza Mr. Fix-It Inc.

B010

mud. Also, the window well should either have its own drain or should flow into the exterior drain tile system through the gravel base.

5. Check the palmer valve. This check valve must swing open easily to drain water from the drain tile system. If it is stuck closed, water may back up in your basement, and eventually the drain tiles will become plugged with debris. Use a wire to hook the bottom of this round flap valve; it should swing upward on a hinge at the top of the disc. If the valve is stuck, free it with penetrating oil and a pry bar.

6. Check the sump pump. The float must easily move up and down to activate the pump. If the float sticks, you will have a flood. Make sure that the pump is secure and will not allow the float to stick to the sides of the crock or the cover. Lift the float to check that the pump will remove water from the crock; the pump should switch on when the float is 8 to 12 inches from the top of the crock. If the pump allows higher water levels than this, seepage near the floor may occur. Replace a sump pump that is old and worn. If your pump runs often, have a spare sump pump handy.

7. Look for gaps and cracks in joints. These can allow water to seep next to the basement. The gaps can be filled with a backer rod and concrete joint filler.

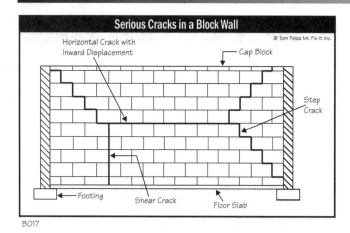

Serious Cracks in a Block Wall

© Tom Feiza Mr. Fix-It Inc.

Horizontal Crack with Inward Displacement

Cap Block

Step Crack

Footing

Shear Crack

Floor Slab

B017

8. Check for cracks in poured concrete walls or block walls. These should be evaluated and patched by a professional.

9. Check for problems with underground storm drain lines. If damp spots and seepage appear near a sump pump or downspout storm sewer line, the problem may be a broken or plugged underground line. You can test this line by running water into the pipe with a hose and watching for seepage in the basement. You can also temporarily abandon the underground line and route the sump pump or downspout to the surface, well away from your home. If seepage no longer appears in the basement, you'll know the problem is a broken drain line.

10. Investigate underground water supply lines. If seepage occurs near the water main into your home, suspect a broken underground water line.

11. Investigate all homeowner-installed underground drain lines. Often they are unable to withstand freezing because they are installed too near the surface and/or they're made of improper materials easily broken by frost. Also, many such lines can't effectively carry water away from the foundation because they have poor pitch or are undersized. Temporarily abandon these lines to test them. If you see water bubbling up from connections to these lines, you have a problem.

12. Watch for roots in the sump pump crock. Roots inside the crock mean there are roots in the bleeders and in the outside drain tiles. An expert should evaluate this problem.

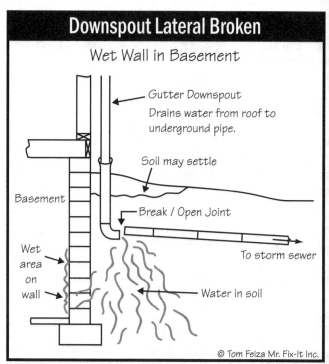

Downspout Lateral Broken

Wet Wall in Basement

Gutter Downspout Drains water from roof to underground pipe.

Soil may settle

Basement

Break / Open Joint

Wet area on wall

To storm sewer

Water in soil

© Tom Feiza Mr. Fix-It Inc.

B061

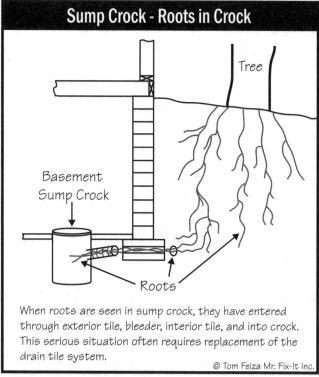

Sump Crock - Roots in Crock

Tree

Basement Sump Crock

Roots

When roots are seen in sump crock, they have entered through exterior tile, bleeder, interior tile, and into crock. This serious situation often requires replacement of the drain tile system.

© Tom Feiza Mr. Fix-It Inc.

B052

Before Major Repair, Test Drain Tiles

Continued seepage may indicate damaged or missing drain tiles, but don't ever start a major repair without first evaluating the interior and exterior drain tiles. These tests cost about $400.

An interior drain tile test involves cutting several holes in the basement floor to expose the interior drain tiles and bleeders in several areas so they can be inspected for debris and water flow.

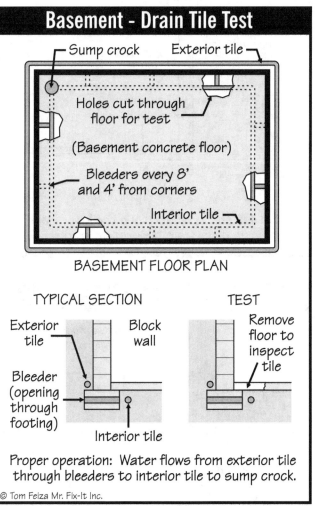

Basement - Drain Tile Test

Sump crock   Exterior tile

Holes cut through floor for test

(Basement concrete floor)

Bleeders every 8' and 4' from corners

Interior tile

BASEMENT FLOOR PLAN

TYPICAL SECTION   TEST

Exterior tile   Block wall   Remove floor to inspect tile

Bleeder (opening through footing)   Interior tile

Proper operation: Water flows from exterior tile through bleeders to interior tile to sump crock.

© Tom Feiza Mr. Fix-It Inc.

B014

Exterior drain tiles can be tested with a "water spud." This is a small-diameter pipe that looks like a tree root fertilizer tool. The pipe is inserted in the ground next to the foundation. Water is forced into the ground through the pipe, and the flow is traced into the drain tiles. If tiles are blocked, water will appear on the basement walls and at the wall/floor joint.

Knowing When You Need An Expert

If leakage continues after you complete all the simple maintenance steps, have your basement evaluated by an expert. You also need an expert if you discover wall and floor cracks associated with the leaks.

SYMPTOMS OF DRAINAGE PROBLEMS

- Active water leaks near the basement floor indicate problems with drain tile and surface drainage. (Drawing B012)

- Active water leaks higher on the wall usually indicate a surface water drainage problem or a broken drain or supply line. A problem with window or door flashing, windowsills, a roof leak, or brick veneer could also cause a leak on a basement wall. (Drawing B013)

- Efflorescence or salt stains indicate that water is pushing through the masonry surface and depositing these white or tan salt stains. (Drawing B033)

- Water stains, damp spots, mildew, and chipping/splintering of masonry indicate that water is pushing through the masonry.

- Dampness, odor, mold, mildew, and condensation indicate that water is pushing through surfaces or leaking into the structure. High levels of moisture in basement air can also cause these problems.

- Wood rot, wood movement, and stains on wood and drywall indicate leaks and moisture behind finishes.

- Cracks and wall movement may indicate an unstable foundation wall caused by drainage problems.

- Damp walls and floors with a dry sump pump crock indicate a drain tile or sump pump problem.

- Roots in the sump crock indicate a potentially serious drain tile blockage and drainage problem.

Efflorescence (Salt Stains)

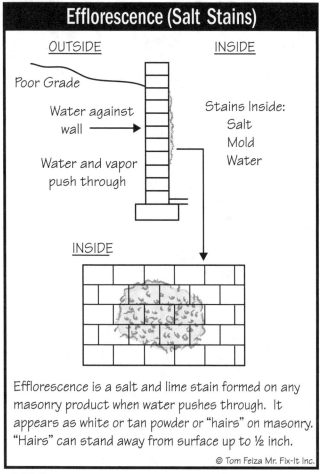

OUTSIDE   INSIDE

Poor Grade

Water against wall →

Water and vapor push through

Stains Inside:
Salt
Mold
Water

INSIDE

Efflorescence is a salt and lime stain formed on any masonry product when water pushes through. It appears as white or tan powder or "hairs" on masonry. "Hairs" can stand away from surface up to ½ inch.

© Tom Feiza Mr. Fix-It Inc.

B033

Find a consultant who is not connected with a basement repair company. You want someone who is selling consulting services, not basement repairs.

Don't make a quick decision on a basement repair contractor. Always check references and find a member of a professional contractor group. Don't buy a repair because it is "on sale today." Your basement will not fall apart overnight because of a leak.

Above all, maintain your basement. The maintenance steps are simple and can help prevent small problems from escalating into serious damage.

Basement Leaks at Lower Block

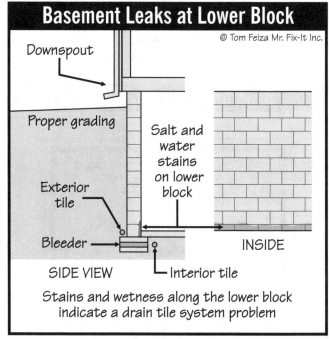

© Tom Feiza Mr. Fix-It Inc.

Downspout

Proper grading

Salt and water stains on lower block

Exterior tile

Bleeder →

INSIDE

SIDE VIEW   └ Interior tile

Stains and wetness along the lower block indicate a drain tile system problem

B012

Basement Leaks - Top of Wall

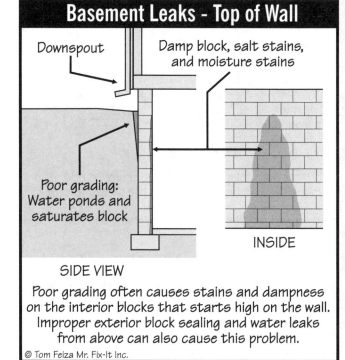

Downspout

Damp block, salt stains, and moisture stains

Poor grading: Water ponds and saturates block

INSIDE

SIDE VIEW

Poor grading often causes stains and dampness on the interior blocks that starts high on the wall. Improper exterior block sealing and water leaks from above can also cause this problem.

© Tom Feiza Mr. Fix-It Inc.

B013

Chapter 26 – Replace Your Furnace

When it's time to replace your furnace, you will be faced with many confusing questions and no clear answers. Contractors will be happy to give you options and recommendations, but you will be left to make the decisions. Do you know that you must consider the chimney? What about efficiency, Btu rating, condensation and ease of maintenance? What is a Btu?

This article will provide the basic information you need to evaluate furnace replacement options and make smart decisions for your home. The information is based on a forced air (warm air) furnace replacement in a northern region of the U.S.

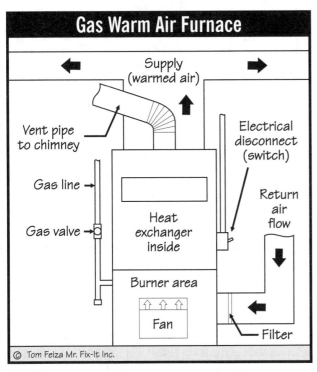

Gas Warm Air Furnace

Supply (warmed air)

Vent pipe to chimney

Electrical disconnect (switch)

Gas line

Return air flow

Heat exchanger inside

Gas valve

Burner area

Fan

Filter

© Tom Feiza Mr. Fix-It Inc.

H001

Understanding the Basics

Here are some basic terms used in the heating business:

Btu – British thermal unit – A unit of measurement for heat. A Btu is the amount of energy required to raise the temperature of one pound of water by one degree Fahrenheit. A Btu is approximately equal to the energy in one paper match burned end to end. A furnace rated 100,000 Btu input consumes 100,000 Btu per hour.

AFUE – Annual Fuel Utilization Efficiency – This percentage represents the average annual seasonal efficiency of a furnace or boiler. It shows how effectively the furnace converts gas into heating energy. An 80 percent efficient 100,000 Btu furnace provides approximately 80,000 Btu to your home.

Ductwork or ducts – This is a system of rectangular and circular metal tubes that carry heated or cooled air to the rooms of your home. Supply ducts move heated or cooled air into the rooms, and return ducts return air to the furnace.

Heat exchanger – A heat exchanger transfers heat from the furnace flame into a metal container and then into the air moving outside the metal container through the ductwork in your home. Products of combustion from the flame are never mixed with the air heating your home.

Blower / fan – Both terms are used for the fan that moves air through the furnace and through your home. The blower re-circulates air in your home.

Inducer – inducer fan – draft fan – These terms are used interchangeably for the motor and fan that move combustion products through a higher efficiency furnace and out a vent or chimney.

High and low returns – Many modern duct systems have a "high" and a "low" return. The high duct return is open when central air conditioning is in use, allowing the system to capture hot air near the ceiling. The low return grill is open during the heating season, returning cold air from the floor to the furnace.

Thermostat – A thermostat senses the room's temperature and turns the furnace on and off as needed to maintain the desired temperature.

How a Furnace Works

A typical forced air or warm air furnace burns a fossil fuel and distributes the warm air inside your home. The heat source is confined within a heat exchanger inside the furnace housing. Gas is burned below the heat exchanger. The hot products of combustion flow through the heat exchanger and up a chimney. Higher efficiency furnaces may use a draft fan to move the products of combustion, and the flame may be above or below the heat exchanger.

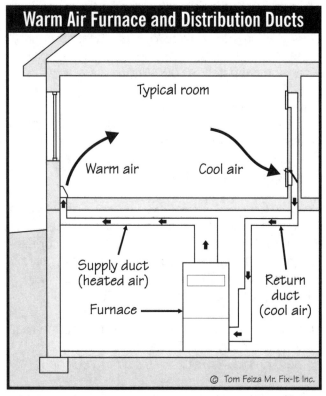

Warm Air Furnace and Distribution Ducts

Typical room

Warm air   Cool air

Supply duct (heated air)

Furnace

Return duct (cool air)

© Tom Feiza Mr. Fix-It Inc.

HO04

When a thermostat senses that heat is needed in the home, it signals the furnace to turn on. The hot products of combustion warm the metal of the heat exchanger. After a minute or so, when the heat exchanger's metal has warmed up, a limit switch or timer turns on the blower or circulating fan. The fan circulates air across the hot metal exterior of the heat exchanger.

The furnace re-circulates air in your home. It does not draw in outside air unless special provisions have been made for an outside air supply. The warm air flows through the supply ductwork to heat your home; cooler air returns to the furnace through return ductwork. Return air also passes through a filter in the ductwork before it reaches the furnace.

Duct systems for heated air circulation and ducting have changed through the years. An early "gravity" warm air furnace system (commonly called a octopus) did not use a blower fan. Warm air rose into the rooms.

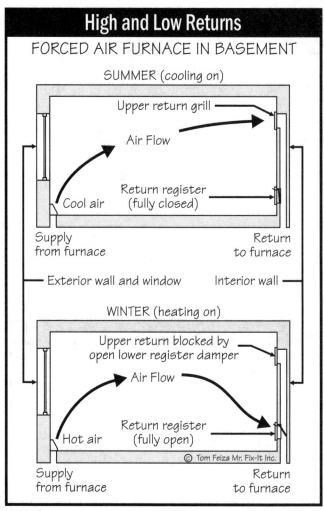

High and Low Returns

FORCED AIR FURNACE IN BASEMENT

SUMMER (cooling on)

Upper return grill

Air Flow

Return register (fully closed)

Cool air

Supply from furnace

Return to furnace

Exterior wall and window   Interior wall

WINTER (heating on)

Upper return blocked by open lower register damper

Air Flow

Return register (fully open)

Hot air

Supply from furnace

Return to furnace

© Tom Feiza Mr. Fix-It Inc.

HO19

In the 1950s, ductwork supplied air high on the inside walls using a blower. In the 1960s, ducts were moved low on the floor, below exterior windows.

Many forced air furnaces use natural gas. Other heat sources include oil, propane or even electrical resistance. This chapter will focus on natural gas furnaces because they are most common. Similar details pertain to propane and oil furnaces.

Types of Forced Air Furnaces

Standard Efficiency Furnace

Houses built around 1970 or earlier typically use standard efficiency furnaces. These furnaces vent combustion gas up a chimney and provide an efficiency ratio of about 60 percent. This means that about 40 percent of energy from the heat source is lost up the chimney. Since 1993, federal energy standards for new installations have required a minimum of 78 percent efficiency (AFUE).

These furnaces have a standing pilot light and must be vented up a masonry or metal chimney. Some of these furnaces were improved with spark ignition systems and combustion vent dampers for energy efficiency. They must keep the products of combustion warm enough to rise naturally up the chimney.

These furnaces use simple systems, but they waste a lot of heat up the chimney. Some of the older systems have very sturdy burners and heat exchangers and will operate for many years. However, many of these furnaces installed after 1970 have very thin metal heat exchangers that are subject to failure through cracks and corrosion.

Mid-Efficiency Furnace (80 Percent Furnace)

A mid-efficiency furnace utilizes about 80 percent of the energy from the fuel source. Actual efficiency may vary slightly but will usually average 80 percent.

This type of furnace requires a draft or inducer fan to move products of combustion through the heat exchanger and up the chimney. The heat exchanger is improved to utilize more heat from the products of combustion for heating your home. Typically, it has a hot surface or spark ignition device and does not have a standing pilot light.

Mid-Efficiency Warm Air Furnace

Metal flue pipe

Discharge

Combustion gas to chimney

Draft fan forces products of combustion up chimney

Draft fan

Return

© Tom Feiza Mr. Fix-It Inc.

H002

This type of furnace keeps the products of combustion warm enough to prevent condensation inside the furnace, but condensation can occur in the chimney if the chimney is not matched to the furnace.

High-Efficiency Furnace (90 Percent Furnace, Condensing Furnace, Sealed Combustion Furnace)

A high-efficiency furnace, also called a 90 percent, sealed combustion or condensing furnace, provides about 90 percent efficiency in converting fuel to heat. It condenses the steam from combustion into water.

Steam? That's right. Water in the form of steam is a product of combustion. The "smoke" you see going up a chimney from a standard furnace actually is steam. The secondary heat exchanger allows this type of furnace to reduce the temperature of the products of combustion below the point of condensation. The steam that would otherwise go up the chimney is converted into water. The products of combustion leave the furnace at about 120 degrees, and most (90 percent) of the fuel's heat energy goes into your home.

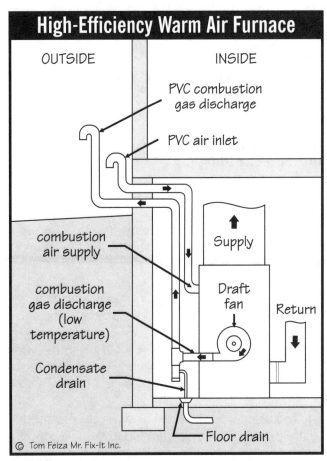

High-Efficiency Warm Air Furnace

OUTSIDE

INSIDE

PVC combustion gas discharge

PVC air inlet

combustion air supply

Supply

combustion gas discharge (low temperature)

Draft fan

Return

Condensate drain

Floor drain

© Tom Feiza Mr. Fix-It Inc.

H003

In the secondary heat exchanger, steam is condensed back into water and releases about 940 Btu per pound of water. That can amount to several gallons on a cold day. The secondary heat exchanger must be protected from this water with a special coating or with stainless steel.

Because the products of combustion are at such a low temperature when leaving the furnace, they can be vented with a plastic pipe; no chimney is required. The vent pipe may be routed through the side of the home.

Many high-efficiency furnaces also utilize outside air for combustion. This lets the furnace use clean outside air and avoids drawing combustion air from inside your home, providing additional energy savings. Drawing outside air eliminates the possibility of contaminating the combustion process with chemicals from the basement.

Because this is a "condensing" furnace, water must be drained from it. The water or condensate is corrosive, and heat exchangers made of stainless steel or with special coatings must be protected from it. Condensate is often collected at several points in the system.

This furnace also uses an inducer or draft fan that must be designed for a damp, corrosive environment. It utilizes a hot surface or spark ignition device and does not have a pilot light.

High-Efficiency Plus Furnace (90 Percent Plus)

I created the term "high-efficiency plus" because there is no standard, generic term for this type of furnace. It improves on the high-efficiency (90 percent) furnace by adding variable-speed fans and variable firing rates.

Some of these units fire or burn gas at two different rates, matching the performance of the furnace to the home's heating requirements. The lower rate is used most of the year. When it is very cold or when the home needs to be heated quickly, the furnace will fire at the higher rate.

The fan or blower circulates air at a rate matched to the burner. The lower fire and lower fan speed mean the furnace will be matched more closely to the needs of the home. The furnace runs longer, creating greater comfort, because air is more evenly distributed through the home. This type of fan is also quieter. Variable speed fans consume significantly less energy than single speed fans.

Furnace Sizing

The "size" of a furnace is rated in input Btu per hour. A typical furnace is rated at 100,000 or 80,000 Btu per hour. A residential furnace can be as small as 40,000 or as high as more than 200,000 Btu per hour.

Be aware that an old 100,000 Btu furnace running at 60 percent efficiency delivers about 60,000 Btu/hour of heat to your home. A new 90 percent high-efficiency furnace rated 60,000 Btu will deliver about 54,000 Btu/hour of heat to your home.

You should understand that most furnaces installed more than 20 years ago are oversized. In many cases, a smaller furnace (with a smaller Btu rating) can be installed, and the smaller, properly sized furnace will provide better comfort. A furnace should be sized so that it runs almost continuously when the weather is very cold and windy.

You can quickly evaluate your furnace by clocking its operation during very cold weather. If the furnace runs 15 minutes on and 15 minutes off during extreme weather, the furnace is about double the size needed. Remember that it is very common to have an oversized furnace if it was installed prior to 1980.

Trust your contractor to size the new furnace correctly. Contractors are responsible for selecting the correct type and size. They can check the existing furnace, and chances are they have already installed a replacement furnace in a home just like yours. They can also perform a heat loss calculation to determine the correct furnace size for a home with complicated heating needs.

The size of the furnace will depend on square footage, type of home, number of stories, windows, insulation, orientation, and exposure to the sun.

Chimney Issues

If your furnace vents through a masonry chimney, the chimney must be evaluated. Your contractor should automatically address the chimney; if not, you may face additional costs down the road or when the furnace is installed or damage to the chimney becomes evident.

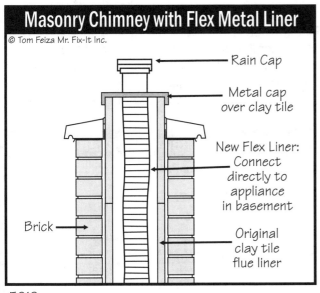

Masonry Chimney with Flex Metal Liner

© Tom Feiza Mr. Fix-It Inc.

- Rain Cap
- Metal cap over clay tile
- New Flex Liner: Connect directly to appliance in basement
- Brick
- Original clay tile flue liner

FO12

An 80 percent furnace puts much less heat up the chimney than does an older 60 percent furnace. When there is a lack of heat in a masonry chimney, combustion gas can condense in the chimney flue. This will ruin the liner and eventually ruin the structure of the chimney. In many cases, a thin metal liner must be installed inside a masonry chimney.

An 80 percent furnace venting up an existing metal chimney usually does not represent a problem, but it still needs to be evaluated. If the original masonry chimney is inside the structure of your home and the clay tile is very small, there is a chance the chimney can be used. In this case, the structure of the home surrounds the chimney and helps keeps the chimney warm.

For a 90 percent furnace, combustion gases are vented with a plastic pipe and no gases are vented up the chimney. If the chimney is used only by the furnace, no problem—cap the flue tile. If the chimney liner was shared by the original furnace and an existing gas water heater, you have a problem. The water heater will not warm the chimney, so you must have a small flexible liner installed.

If there is a significant chimney problem and the chimney needs to be rebuilt, consider installing a high-efficiency furnace and a direct vent water

heater that does not need a chimney. That will eliminate the use of the chimney and avoid the possibililiity of a major rebuild. Simply remove the chimney to the roofline.

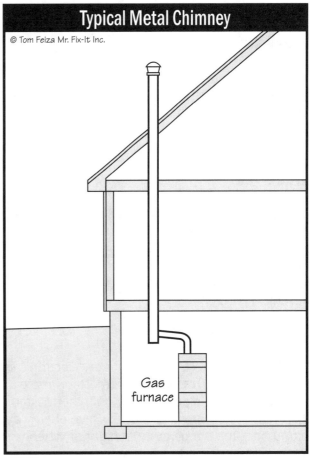

Typical Metal Chimney

© Tom Feiza Mr. Fix-It Inc.

Gas furnace

FO03

Selecting a Contractor

Many good furnace brands exist. The key to a successful furnace replacement is to work with a good contractor. How do you find one? Ask neighbors and friends, and check with the local builders' or remodelers' group. Consider the contractor who services your furnace. Don't depend on those who place big advertisements. Ask for several references and check them out. The contractor should make a visit to evaluate your home and establish the requirement for the new furnace.

Make sure your contractor is covered by workers' compensation and liability insurance. The contractor should automatically offer this information. Find a contractor who has been in the business for several years and who works with a quality furnace brand. Check out the salesperson's approach to the project. Will the salesperson automatically check the chimney, the thermostat, local permits, electrical and ductwork, and listen to your concerns?

Because this is a large and important purchase, you should check out two or three contractors.

Permits

Call your local municipal building inspection department and ask whether you need a permit for furnace replacement and related electrical work. The department may also have requirements for the chimney and furnace venting.

Electrical

In most areas, electrical codes will require a separate circuit for the new furnace. This is not required by all municipalities, but it is common. The heating contractor should be able to do a basic evaluation and determine whether providing a separate circuit presents a problem.

Thermostat

As part of the project, consider a new electronic setback thermostat. This type of thermostat is more accurate than the older mercury bulb thermostat. It is also easy to program so you can save energy by setting back the temperature at night or when your home is not occupied.

Filter

Now is your chance to improve your furnace air filtering system, particularly if you are not happy with your current system. The standard arrangement will be a slot for a 1-inch-thick throwaway or washable filter. While this meets minimum requirements for the furnace, it doesn't remove small particulates from the air. You can improve on the standard 1-inch fiberglass filter by using a pleated paper filter.

A frame for a 4- or 6-inch-thick pleated paper filter is a great improvement over the basic filter and will remove much smaller particulate matter from the air. This type of filter has a very small opening spread over a very large surface area. Normally a replacement filter costs about $25, and the filter lasts about a year.

The best filtering system for removing smoke and pollen particles is an electronic filter. This type of filter uses electronically charged plates and wires to attract particulates. The filter plates must be washed every so often in the tub or the dishwasher.

Finally, there are 1-inch-thick electrostatic filters and ultraviolet light air cleaners. Neither of these is very common, and I don't believe in experimenting with most new products until they have been tested and proven in the marketplace for a significant time.

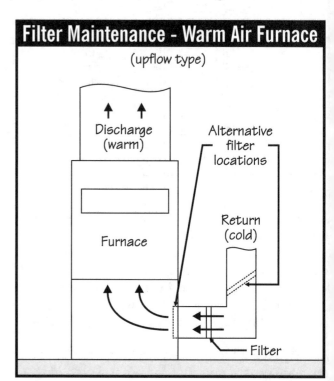

Filter Maintenance - Warm Air Furnace
(upflow type)

Discharge (warm)

Alternative filter locations

Return (cold)

Furnace

Filter

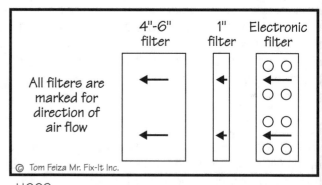

All filters are marked for direction of air flow

4"-6" filter

1" filter

Electronic filter

© Tom Feiza Mr. Fix-It Inc.

H009

Humidification–Not

In most cases, you should consider eliminating any humidification system. You can always add it later if needed. Newer furnaces draw less air from your home for combustion and do not create a constant flow up a chimney. The eliminates some of the ven-

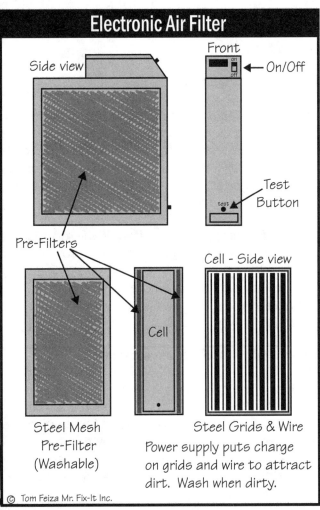

Electronic Air Filter

Side view

Front

On/Off

Test Button

Pre-Filters

Cell - Side view

Cell

Steel Mesh
Pre-Filter
(Washable)

Steel Grids & Wire
Power supply puts charge
on grids and wire to attract
dirt. Wash when dirty.

© Tom Feiza Mr. Fix-It Inc.

H029

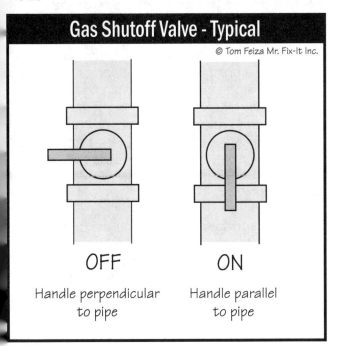

Gas Shutoff Valve - Typical

© Tom Feiza Mr. Fix-It Inc.

OFF

ON

Handle perpendicular
to pipe

Handle parallel
to pipe

P076

tilation or air leakage into your home. With less air loss, there is less air infiltration through leaks. With less infiltration, a newer furnace does not dry out your home.

Gas Valve

The gas valve should be updated with the new furnace.

Evaluating Ductwork

If your home was built before 1960, the ductwork needs a critical review. In some cases the ductwork and returns may be too small for a modern furnace and additional ductwork must be added. Some older systems have 4-inch round supply ducts that don't allow for proper flow. With an undersized duct system, the furnace will not operate properly and you will not have a comfortable home.

Cleaning Ductwork

Should your ductwork be cleaned as part of a furnace replacement? If you have a pre-1950 home, consider cleaning your ductwork. You should also consider cleaning if someone in your home is sensitive to dust and dirt.

Often, a new furnace moves more air through the duct system. When more air is moved, it flows at a faster speed. This may tend to dislodge and push additional dirt into your home.

Furnace Brands

All the furnace brands you recognize produce high-quality products. There was a period during the 1970s and '80s when some furnaces were poorly designed, but now all the major brand furnaces perform well. Consider the type of heat exchanger material and the warranty when making your replacement decision.

Bids / Quotes

You must receive a written quote that identifies at least the following items: brand, type, size, efficiency, Btu rating, and warranty information. The contract should state how venting and the chimney will be handled. The contractor should remove the old furnace and clean up afterward. Building permits and fee should be included.

Make sure the quotations give you all the information you need to compare apples to apples between the bids. They must quote the same type of furnace (same efficiency). Be careful of a very low quote; something may be left out. You can expect to pay a portion of the price when the furnace is ordered and to make the final payment when the furnace is installed and working properly.

Warranties

Because furnaces often are so similar to one another, consider choosing the furnace that provides the best warranty. Pay special attention to the warranty for the heat exchanger—it is the most expensive part of the furnace and is subject to heat and corrosive conditions.

How Much Can You Save?

You may ask the contractor to estimate the energy and cost savings for the replacement furnace.

You can also take an educated guess at the savings by evaluating your current heat costs. Gather up your gas bills for a one-year period. Total the costs for the six-month heating period. Then total the costs for the six-month spring and summer period. The summer bills will establish the base cost of gas service excluding heating cost; base cost includes the meter charge and gas used by the water heater, clothes dryer and stove. Subtract the summer total from the winter total, and you'll see your approximate heating cost.

Once you know your heating costs, look at the efficiency of your current furnace and of potential replacements. Increasing efficiency from 60 to 90 percent will save you about 30 percent in heating costs. This is not a precise calculation, but it will give you an idea of the savings.

You also need to consider the additional cost of moving from a 90 percent to a 90 percent plus furnace. You will save a little on gas and electricity. The payback may be minimal for the additional cost, but the comfort of your home will improve.

Noise

The only furnace that will have a significant difference in operating noise will be the 90 percent plus.

Its variable-speed, slow-start motors will be very quiet. When the furnace runs on low fire, there will be less fan noise.

Interior Comfort

All of the furnaces will provide excellent comfort, providing the duct system is adequate or improved. You will notice that the higher efficiency furnace moves more air—that is, more velocity at the grills. The discharge temperature will also be lower than that of a standard efficiency furnace.

When a furnace is properly sized, it will run more often and for a longer period of time, providing a more uniform temperature in your home. The 90 plus furnace can provide more comfort because it will often run at the lower fire rate and lower fan speed for longer periods.

Manuals and Instructions

Make sure the contractor walks you through the system and explains the operation of the system and the thermostat. The contractor should give you the detailed instructions provided by the manufacturer. Ask the contractor to identify emergency shut-offs for gas and for the furnace system and to walk you through filter maintenance.

Furnace Replacement With or Without Air Conditioning

Today, most forced air systems also function as central air conditioning with the addition of an exterior compressor and interior coil and piping. If your home has an older air conditioning system or you are considering adding air conditioning, do it when the new furnace is installed, or at least plan for coil installation in the ductwork above the furnace.

Summary

The key to a successful furnace replacement is finding a good contractor and understanding the basics of a furnace project. Focus on the quality of the contractor, not on the price. Review this article to ensure that all details are covered, and don't forget about the chimney for any furnace you buy.

Chapter 27 – Replace Your Roof

Asphalt shingles properly applied to a roof are extremely durable, but eventually they will need replacement. How do you select the type of shingle and the roofing contractor? Do you tear off the shingles or roof over them? What important details of the installation and the roof replacement contract should you know?

Things are pretty confusing when replacing a roof, and there aren't many resources to give you a quick or simple answer. Most people aren't familiar with roofs or roofing terms unless they've had a roof leak, have just replaced a roof, or have had a problem with a roofing contractor.

I have prepared this information to help you make sense of the many decisions involved in asphalt shingle roof replacements. This article will help you select a contractor, choose the roofing material, and establish a good contract for the replacement roof. By following through with the information in this article, you will have a better chance of completing a good roof replacement project.

Basic Terms

Knowing a few basic terms will help you communicate with roofing contractors and establish fair specifications for your new roof. Review the illustrations for details on the terms.

SQUARE – The amount of roofing material needed to cover 100 square feet. A roof that is 15 square has 1500 square feet of surface area.

FLASHING – Metal or roofing material that is used at starts, stops, penetrations, and changes in direction of the roof. This includes the intersection of the roof to chimneys, vents, valleys, and vertical surfaces. Step flashing is used at intersections to all vertical surfaces such as chimneys. Flashing is also installed around plumbing vents.

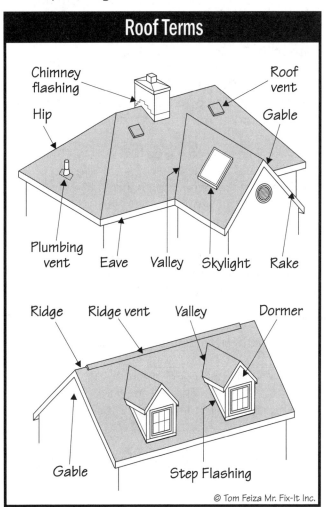

RO04

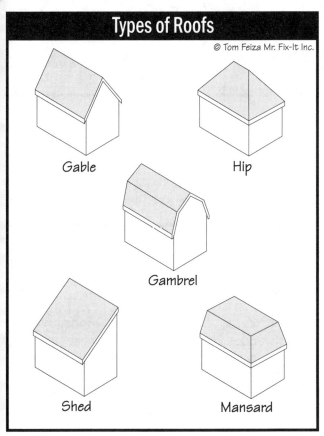

RO03

ROOF-OVER or RE-ROOF - Applying an additional layer of asphalt shingle roofing over an existing asphalt shingle roof. Normally, the maximum number of roofing layers is two.

SLOPE – Refers to the angle of the roof. A 4/12 slope refers to a roof that drops 4 feet (vertical) in a 12 foot run (horizontal). The 4/12 can be measured in feet or inches. A 12/12 roof is at a 45-degree angle.

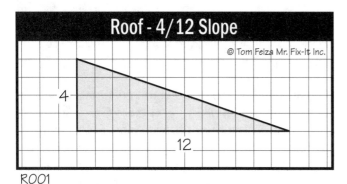

R001

THREE-TAB SHINGLE – This is the most common asphalt shingle. It is divided into three segments or tabs with a small vertical slot in the exposed lower edge of the shingle.

LAMINATED OR ARCHITECTURAL SHINGLE – An asphalt shingle composed of several layers of material to give the roof a wood-like or textured appearance.

ASPHALT, FIBERGLASS, ORGANIC, AND COMPOSITION SHINGLES – These terms are confusing because they are often interchanged. A composition shingle is an asphalt shingle. An asphalt shingle can be organic or fiberglass; asphalt bonds the shingle materials together. The base material for the shingle may be fiberglass (inorganic) or cellulose (organic) felt. About 80 percent of modern shingles have a fiberglass base material. In years past, organic base shingles were more common.

EAVE – The overhanging lower edge of a roof.

RAKE – The pitched edge of a roof that overhangs the wall of a home. This also refers to the board or molding placed along the sloping side of a gable roof end.

RIDGE – The top intersection of two roof planes; the peak.

VALLEY – The internal angle at the intersection of two roof planes. Can be an open metal valley or a valley formed of shingles or asphalt roofing material.

DRIP EDGE or GUTTER APRON – The metal strip that is installed along the edges of the roof to shed water away from the trim or into a gutter. It is often called a gutter apron or apron at the gutter. Usually, this is an L-shaped aluminum strip fitted under the edge of the shingles.

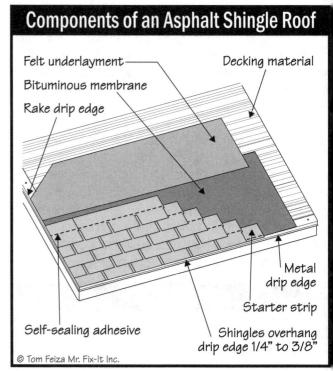

R005

DECK – The wooden board, plywood or oriented strand board (OSB) that supports the roof material and spans the framing joists or trusses.

FELT, TAR PAPER, BUILDING PAPER – Asphalt-saturated roll felt material used under roof shingles and siding. It can also be designated 15# or 30# felt. The 30# felt is thicker and heaver than the 15# felt.

Evaluate Your Roof

Asphalt roofs fail with age. A typical asphalt shingle roof lasts about 20 years. Sun is the main cause of natural aging, and you will find that southern exposures have the most wear and tear. Wind, hail, poor drainage, tree limbs, pollution, and climate extremes also affect the aging of a roof.

If your roof is 15 years old, you should start planning for replacement. If your roof is 20 to 25 years old, you need to have your roof evaluated for potential replacement.

When a roof ages, you will see the shingles shrinking and vertical gaps between the shingle tabs opening up on the typical three-tab shingle. On a new roof, the gap will be about 3/8 inch wide and the edges of the shingle will be square, smooth, and flat. On an older roof, the gap will open from 3/8 inch to 3/4 inch or even 1 inch, and the edges will curl and lift. Older roofs will also lose their granular coating, crack, cup, split, and thicken at the edges.

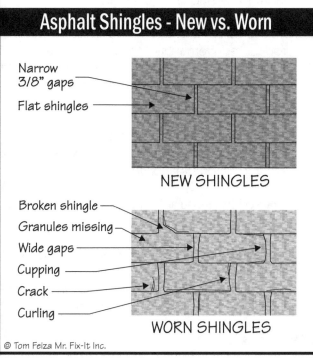

R006

Tear Off or Roof Over?

If you have a single layer of asphalt roofing material, adding a second layer of shingles ("roofing-over"/"re-roofing") is an option. This can be done if the old roof shingles are flat and in relatively good condition. A laminated or architectural single is a good option for a "roof-over" because the texture of the new shingle will cover imperfections. The roofing contractor must evaluate the roof before a roof-over is considered.

On a roof-over, you don't have the option of adding a special bituminous flashing material at the overhangs, valleys and penetrations. (Ice and Water

Shield is a popular brand. Also, the Grace Company makes bituminous flashing.) This flashing material will help prevent leaks from ice dams–an important consideration for cold climates and for homes that have experienced ice dams.

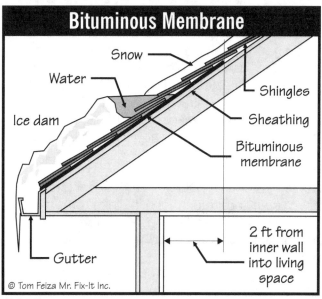

R007

If your roof has two or more layers of shingles or if the existing shingles are in poor condition, you must tear off the existing shingles down to the wood deck. In a tear-off, the wood deck and roof framing remains and all asphalt roofing materials and flashing materials are removed. Removing the old roofing materials also provides access to the roof deck so repairs can be made if necessary.

Adding a third layer of roofing material is never a good idea. It may not be allowed by local building codes, and it may violate the warranty for the new shingles. The third layer may also overload the roof structure.

What will it cost?

The cost depends on many variables. The material selection, the height of the home, the access to and slope of the roof have the biggest effect on cost. Flashings are also a major cost factor. If the home has chimneys and many changes in the roofline, the cost will be higher. Costs go up when roofing contractors are busy or if you are in a hurry to get the job done.

In general, a roof-over will cost about $2 per square foot, and a tear-off will cost about $4 per square foot. These estimates are based on 2003 prices for a simple low-slope roof with minimal penetrations or changes in direction and good access around the home.

Find a Good-Quality Professional Roofing Contractor

Finding a professional roofing contractor is the key to a successful roof replacement project. All manufacturers make good roofing materials, but only a knowledgeable contractor can properly design and install a replacement roof. The essentials are knowledge, experience, and attention to details during installation.

Ask friends and neighbors about contractors they have used. Local professional builders' or remodelers' organizations and roofing material suppliers can also provide names of good contractors. Start with two or three contractors.

Sit down with the contractor or contractor's salesperson and review the company's qualifications:

- Get a full name and street address. If the contractor has a permanent office, you know you'll be working with a larger, established business.

- Check on insurance: comprehensive liability and workers' compensation. Ask for a certificate of insurance; a quality contractor's carrier will provide this automatically.

- Is the contractor licensed by the state or the local municipality if required?

- How long has the company been in business? Established companies usually have greater experience and knowledge.

- Ask for references from local jobs. Take the time to call a few references and ask about appearance, cost, quality, promptness, cleanup, and problems.

- Ask about a performance guarantee. Normally, a roofer will guarantee workmanship, and the manufacturer will guarantee the roofing material.

- Will the contractor company perform the work with its own employees or use a subcontractor? Quality, knowledge, and performance are easier to control when the contractor uses its own employees.

- Will the contractor walk the roof and inspect the attic when preparing the quote? If not, how can the company give an accurate quote and address existing conditions? The contractor should check the attic to determine the condition of framing and roof deck to help prevent unpleasant surprises during the job. The contractor must also evaluate attic ventilation and plan for any necessary changes.

- Will the contractor follow the installation and product requirements of the material manufacturer? This is important to ensure a quality installation and to qualify for the manufacturer's material guarantee.

- Will the contractor provide on-site supervision during the job and complete a walk-through with you before final payment?

- How will the contractor protect your property during the project?

- The contractor should be a member of a professional group of builders or remodeling contractors. This ensures that the contractor is established and takes the time to invest in professional growth.

The Contract

A roof replacement requires a written contract to protect you and the contractor and to ensure that all terms, materials and conditions are identified. The contract should address all of the following.

- Material selections, described in detail; type of shingle and the specific name, color and manufacturer; valley, rake edge, and vent materials; and underlayment (tar paper) for the shingles. (The manufacturer's installation instructions must be followed.)

- A statement that all materials will be installed per the manufacturer's instructions. This will ensure that work is done correctly and the manufacturer's warranties will be honored.

- Details on initial deposit and progress payments. The contractor may want a partial payment when the job is started or materials are delivered. Some contractors ask for a small down payment when the contract is signed. Final payment should be made after the job is completed and inspected. A contractor should never be paid before work is completed and should never be given a substantial down payment.

- Construction start and finish date.

- Lien waver requirements. When bills are submitted, the contractor should submit a form that removes the ability of the contractor and suppliers to place a lien on your property. This means the contractor has paid the bills for work and material used on your property.

- Details on how flashings will be replaced–specify type of material and installation details for the chimney, valleys, plumbing vents, roof vents, and any interruption in the roofline.

- Specifications on the following: Will the shingles be removed? How will the home be protected from damage and debris? Will the site be cleaned up every day?

- Information on how any damage to your property or your neighbors' property will be handled.

- Details on how your property will be protected if a rainstorm or weather problems develop during the project.

- Working hours if this is important to you and your neighbors. Roofing is noisy and messy.

- Details on these issues: How will existing gutters and downspouts be protected, saved and re-used? Or, if the gutter and downspouts are to be replaced, what will be the size, color, and thickness of materials used?

- How additional work will be handled. Add a clause stating that deviations from the contract require a written change order before the work is done. The change order must specify the change and the cost.

- Details on costs of any additional roof deck plywood, OSB, or boards that will be required. This is a common situation and should be described as cost per lineal foot for lumber or per sheet for plywood or OSB decking.

- Specifications on how materials will be delivered and stored.

- Particulars on whether special bituminous flashing will be used at eaves, valley and gutter flashings. The contractor should describe the type of material that will be used. Such flashing should be use in cold climates, and it should extend at least 24 inches over the heated space. This may require two 36-inch-wide strips at the gutters if the home has wide overhangs.

- A description of insurance covering the job. The contract should also state that you will receive a certificate of insurance before work begins.

- Description of building permit requirements and a statement that the contractor will obtain the permit, pay for it, and ensure that a final inspection is completed.

- If subcontractors are to be used, the contract should identify them.

- Warranties and guarantees from the contractor and the material manufacturer.

- Details on type of fasteners and how they will be applied.

- Details on attic ventilation material and installation.

Insurance

An established contractor will automatically offer a certificate of insurance. The certificate, issued by an insurance company, will describe the type of insurance and the coverage. The contractor should carry comprehensive liability insurance and workers' compensation insurance.

The insurance certificate should be provided before the job is started. This requirement should be stated in the contract.

Lien Waivers

Contractors and suppliers for construction projects don't always get paid for work and materials. Filing a lien against the property for unpaid bills protects them. Owners are protected from liens by obtaining a lien waiver from the contractor when bills are paid.

Liens can become a sticky issue if you pay a contractor for a project but the contractor never pays for roofing materials used on your home. If the supplier files a lien against your home and you don't have a waiver, you are responsible for the cost of the materials. You could end up paying twice if the contractor has financial problems and takes a walk.

Subcontractors

Subcontractors—not a good idea? Unfortunately, some contractors sell roofing projects to homeowners and then turn around and hire a subcontractor to do the work. This is not bad if the contractor takes the time to supervise and communicate with the subs. It is bad if the contractor just turns the work over to the sub and then shows up to collect the check.

A contractor doing the roof project with its own employees usually employs better-qualified tradespeople who take more pride in their work. When the contractor buys materials, plans work, schedules workers, loads trucks, and so on, the contractor has a lot more ownership of the project and the results.

When you interview the contractor and establish the roof replacement contract, specifically address whether subcontractors will be used, and consider this in your selection process. Some states require contractors to identify subs in the contract.

Select the Shingle Material

Selecting an asphalt shingle for your roofing project is a major deal because of the many colors and texture variations. You can have a little fun with colors and appearance. Right now, architectural or laminated shingles are the most popular because they add some texture and color variation to the roof. You should review samples of the shingles and pictures of the shingles applied to a roof.

I believe you should purchase a 25-year or better shingle from a major manufacturer offering a good warranty. Your contractor can give you some advice on the products he or she prefers. You can purchase a shingle with more life, but don't buy a cheaper shingle.

The most common shingle style is a three-tab shingle with two thin slots that divide the exposed shingles into three parts or tabs. Almost all shingles today are "asphalt" shingles with a fiberglass (inorganic) mat. Asphalt shingles with an organic or cellulose fiber mat are less common but still used.

Shingles are rated by their weight per square. The heavier the weight, the longer the life of the shingle. The surface is coated with granules that protect the shingle from sunlight and provide color.

Manufacturer's Instructions

Shingles must be installed per the manufacturer's instructions to ensure a proper installation and comply with the warranty. These instructions are printed on the shingle package. You can also find them on the Internet or obtain them from the contractor or the material supplier.

The instructions include specific sketches and details on fastening, underlayment, spacing, valleys, flashing, and virtually any other detail required for the installation. Be sure to ask whether the contractor will follow the instructions. Add a clause in the contract stating that the instructions must be followed.

Warranties

Warranties will vary with contractors and material manufacturers, and you should take some time to review them. In general, the manufacturer warrants materials and the contractor warrants workmanship.

Contractors' warranties generally cover 1 to 5 years on workmanship. The important part of this warranty is the contractor's ability and intent to correct any workmanship problems. When you select an established contractor, there is a better chance that the contractor will be around to honor the warranty.

Manufacturers' warranties will cover materials and may cover some labor for the first few years for manufacturing defects. These warranties will require that materials are installed per the manufacturer's instructions. Warranties specify some type of proration based on age. They will also require that proper ventilation, fastening, flashing and installation details are used.

Fasteners

Most shingle manufacturers recommend using nails to fasten shingles to the roof deck. Nails can be driven by hand or with pneumatic nailers.

It is possible to get sloppy with pneumatic nailers, resulting in fasteners driven too deep, too shallow, at a slight angle, or beyond the proper nailing line location. This can cause problems down the road as shingles blow away from the surface. The old-fashioned hammer may just be the best tool for driving these fastening nails. Working by hand allows the installer to feel problems with the wood deck and quickly reset an offending nail. Discuss this with your contractor.

Ventilation

A good roofing contractor will always evaluate the ventilation of the attic below the roof. All roof material manufacturers' warranties require adequate attic ventilation. Ventilation removes moisture, limits heat build-up, and helps prevent ice dams.

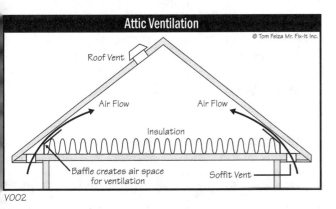

Attic Ventilation

© Tom Feiza Mr. Fix-It Inc.

Roof Vent

Air Flow   Air Flow

Insulation

Baffle creates air space for ventilation

Soffit Vent

V002

Most roof and attic systems that are 20 or more years old lack adequate ventilation. The general rule for ventilation is one square foot of net free ventilation area per 150 square feet of attic floor space. If there is a vapor barrier, ventilation can be reduced to one per 300. Half of the ventilation should be high on the roof and half should be low on the roof. Screens and grills on the vents reduce the "net free" area by about 50 percent.

Vents in the overhangs are often filled or covered with insulation as we add more insulation to our attics. A baffle should be installed under the roof sheathing at the eaves to provide a channel for air movement above and around the insulation.

Today, ridge vents are often utilized as a replacement for the standard roof vent that looks like a large metal mushroom near the top of the roof. A ridge vent runs along the peak or ridge of the roof. Most ridge vents are now covered with shingles to match the roof. From the ground, you will see a section along the ridge raised about 1 inch.

Cathedral ceilings present a special concern because it is hard to provide ventilation between all the rafter bays if there is limited air space below the roof deck. Most of these installations require a continuous ridge and soffit vent.

Ventilation: Bath and Kitchen Fans

When checking the attic ventilation, make sure that any bath and kitchen exhaust fans routed through the attic discharge to the outside. Before 1980, it was common practice to allow such fans to discharge into the attic, but this routes too much moisture into the attic. During roof replacement, the contractor should install special vents through the roof for these fan discharges.

Valley Flashings

Valley flashings can be installed with any of three methods, and all will work well. In northern climates, an open valley with a metal flashing is the most common. The metal extends up and under the shingles to form a joint between the planes of the roof. The metal carries the water to the edge of the roof.

A closed cut valley has one side of the roofing run up on the adjacent roof plane. The shingles from the other plane are then run up over the shingles into the valley and cut.

A woven valley uses shingles from both intersecting planes to "weave" a valley.

Discuss with your contractor the type of valley to be installed. Any type of valley will perform, and the contractor should install the preferred valley but must follow instructions for the specific shingle that will be used.

Attic Ventilation Requirements - Typical

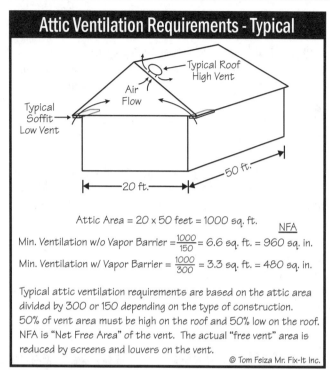

Attic Area = 20 x 50 feet = 1000 sq. ft.

$$\text{Min. Ventilation w/o Vapor Barrier} = \frac{1000}{150} = 6.6 \text{ sq. ft.} = 960 \text{ sq. in.}$$

$$\text{Min. Ventilation w/ Vapor Barrier} = \frac{1000}{300} = 3.3 \text{ sq. ft.} = 480 \text{ sq. in.}$$

Typical attic ventilation requirements are based on the attic area divided by 300 or 150 depending on the type of construction. 50% of vent area must be high on the roof and 50% low on the roof. NFA is "Net Free Area" of the vent. The actual "free vent" area is reduced by screens and louvers on the vent.

© Tom Feiza Mr. Fix-It Inc.

V042

Attic Ventilation: Ridge Vent

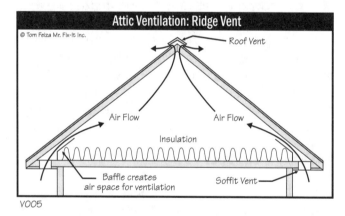

V005

Bathroom Fan Discharge Through Attic

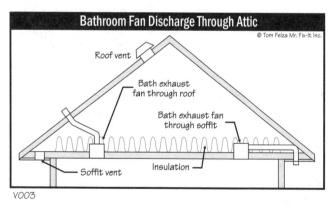

V003

Metal Valley Flashing (Open Valley)

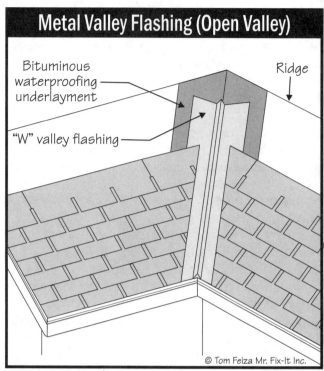

© Tom Feiza Mr. Fix-It Inc.

R008

Flashing Against a Vertical Sidewall

Flashing must be installed at all sidewall-to-roof connections. You will see this where the roof abuts a dormer or a second story. Where the roof angle intersects with a wall, a step flashing or tin must extend up and under the siding and building paper or house wrap. The siding and paper act as a counterflashing and cover the tin used for the step flashing.

Masonry (Brick or Stone) Chimneys

Chimneys present a special problem because they penetrate the roof and expand and move independently of the structure of the home. At the joint of the masonry chimney to the roof, there should be step flashing covered by counter flashing. The counter flashing should be cut into the masonry joints of the chimney.

Always require a metal step and counter flashing, and don't accept anything less. Watch out for contractors who quote a sealant or mastic flashing—these will not work.

Wide chimneys present special problems if water must flow around the chimney. The rule of thumb is that when a chimney is more than 3 feet wide it should have a cricket (saddle) to divert water.

Step Flashing - Sidewall / Building Paper

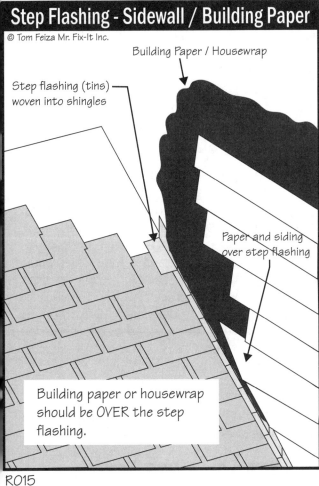

© Tom Feiza Mr. Fix-It Inc.

Building Paper / Housewrap

Step flashing (tins) woven into shingles

Paper and siding over step flashing

Building paper or housewrap should be OVER the step flashing.

R015

Chimney Flashing

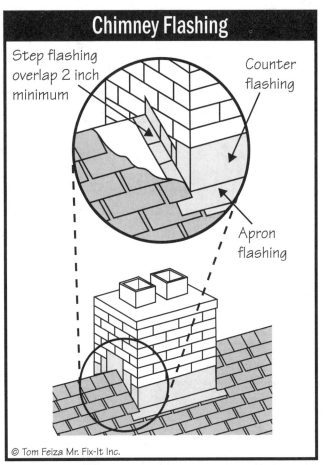

Step flashing overlap 2 inch minimum

Counter flashing

Apron flashing

© Tom Feiza Mr. Fix-It Inc.

R009

Chimney Saddle (Cricket)

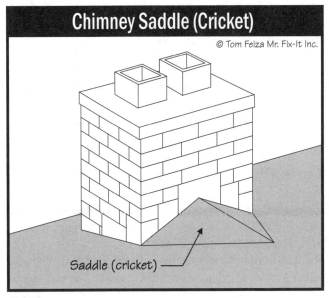

© Tom Feiza Mr. Fix-It Inc.

Saddle (cricket)

R010

Prevent Ice Dams

Ice dams occur when snow melts on a warm roof, slides to the cold edge of the roof, and re-freezes as ice in the gutter and overhang. This ice buildup creates a "dam" that blocks water on the roof. The water then leaks through the standard asphalt shingle assembly that is not designed to resist ponding water.

In northern climates, a bituminous membrane should be used on all roof replacements. The bituminous membrane is laid on the roof deck, under the shingles. The membrane seals around the nails as the shingles are applied. This membrane protects against ice dams by directing water to the edge of the roof even if the water has penetrated the asphalt shingles.

The bituminous membrane should be used at valleys and roof penetrations. At overhangs, the membrane should extend 24 inches over the heated space of your home.

Gutters and Downspouts

Gutters and downspouts must be considered when replacing roofing materials. If your home has newer gutters, you can ask the contractor to remove them and re-install them with the new roofing materials.

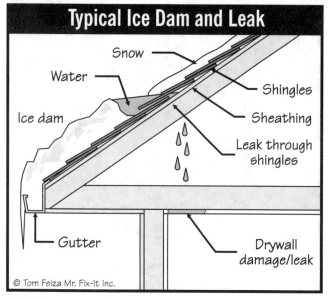

Typical Ice Dam and Leak

Snow

Water

Ice dam

Gutter

Shingles

Sheathing

Leak through shingles

Drywall damage/leak

© Tom Feiza Mr. Fix-It Inc.

R002

If the home needs new gutters and downspouts, the best time to replace them is during a roof replacement project. When done with a roof replacement, better performing "high back" gutters can be installed.

Skylights

Skylights that penetrate the roofing deck require a special step and counter flashing. These should be replaced. They are often purchased as a kit from the window manufacturer.

If your home has an inexpensive plastic skylight without step and counter flashing, consider replacing the skylight with a modern unit. Modern skylights will not leak, while the older plastic skylights will leak at some point.

Codes

Some municipalities require a permit for a roof replacement and will also inspect the project. Be sure the contractor handles the permit requirement and potential inspection coordination. Most municipalities have restrictions on the maximum number of roofing layers.

The Roof Deck

A "roof-over" adds asphalt shingles over existing shingles. Before the job, your contractor should inspect the roof deck to make sure it is in good condition. The deck must be sturdy enough to sup-

port the additional weight and provide sufficient grip for the shingle fasteners. Excessive rot or water damage are potential problems.

When a "tear-off" is completed, the roof deck must conform to the requirements of the shingle manufacturer. Shingles must be applied to a smooth, flat surface that will support the shingles and properly hold the fasteners.

A tear-off on a home built before 1950 or a roof that has old wood shingles as its lowest layer of shingles may reveal spaced roofing boards. These are generally a 1-by-6 nominal dimension with a space of 1/16 inch to 2 inches between boards. This spacing originally provided for air circulation and drying of the wood shingles. However, the arrangement will not properly support asphalt shingles. During the roof replacement, spaced boards are usually covered by plywood or oriented strand board (OSB) panels. This will add to the expense of the project, but it must be done.

In some cases, the contractor may propose adding strips of 1-inch-thick lumber in the gaps between the original deck boards.

Flat and Low-Slope Roofs

Information on replacing roof materials on flat or low-slope roofing could fill a whole new article. Low-slope roofs have a pitch of less than 4/12, and flat roofs are flat or close to flat. Asphalt shingles can't be used on low slope or flat roofs without special precautions. The most common roofing material for a flat roof is a rubber roof because it must be watertight. Rubber roofs are actually made of ethylene propylene diene monomer (EPDM).

Don't ever let a contractor place a standard asphalt shingle roof on a low-slope or flat roof. Without special construction details, it will leak. Every shingle manufacturer has specific instructions for low-slope roofs.

Unknowns

Expect some problems with a roof replacement project. Often, when the roof material is removed, problems are uncovered and need to be corrected.

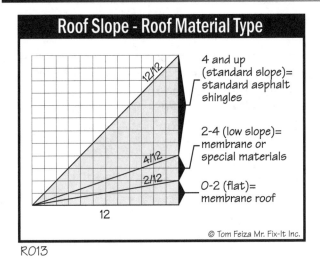

Roof Slope - Roof Material Type

12/12

4/12

2/12

4 and up (standard slope)= standard asphalt shingles

2-4 (low slope)= membrane or special materials

0-2 (flat)= membrane roof

12

© Tom Feiza Mr. Fix-It Inc.

R013

Low Bid or Best Bid?

Don't select your roofing contractor based on price. While you want a reasonable price, the quality of the roofing materials and the contractor's experience should be the most important criteria. Evaluate the contractor based on materials, roofer experience, completeness of the contract, references, and the overall feeling of confidence you have in the contractor.

Mildew and Algae Problems

Roofs that are shaded often show stains from the growth of algae or fungus. You can trim trees to help sunlight reach the roof and limit fungus problems.

If you select a darker shingle, staining will be less noticeable. If there is a severe staining problem, you can purchase special shingles that are algae resistant. These shingles use a metal oxide that prevents algae growth. You can also have zinc metal strips installed high on the roof under the edge of the top shingles. The zinc metal oxidizes, and the zinc oxide flows down with roof with rainwater to prevent algae growth.

When and How Long for Work To Be Done?

A small roofing project should be completed in a few days. A larger complex roof that includes a tear-off may require a week or more. Of course, the size of the roofing crew and the preparation of the contractor will affect the time required. Once the project is started, work should proceed uninterrupted. Gutters and downspouts may take a few extra days for completion.

The contractor should always provide protection from the elements if a roof is not completed at the end of the shift.

Protecting Your Home

The contractor should protect the siding of your home and your neighbors' homes. This may require tarps or plywood sheets to direct debris to the Dumpster or the ground. Discuss how your home will be protected and how debris will be removed.

How will your home be protected if a rainstorm occurs? Discuss this with the contractor and put some details in the contract. During a roof removal process, your home should never be left unprotected from weather problems. This often requires a contractor to remove roofing and finish those areas each day. A roof should never be left without some protection overnight.

Mess in the Attic

If a roof "tear-off" is part of the project, this can create a substantial mess in the attic. Homes built before 1950 usually have spaced wood deck boards. When roof material is removed down the decking, debris falls into the attic between the spaced boards. The debris consists of bits of shingles, tar paper, roof coating granules and nails.

Be prepared for the mess. Discuss options with your contractor. You may need to cover stored items in the attic or clean up the mess later.

During the Project

Cut the contractor a little slack during the project. Roofing projects are messy and noisy. Working conditions can be very hot. Keep your kids and cars clear of the project.

Check the shingle packages. Is this the product you selected? You can see the manufacturer's installation instructions on the package.

Take some time to talk to the contractor on the site and offer your help with details and coordination. Then stay out of the way. Provide the workers with refreshments and treats—a little help that can mean a lot to workers on the job.

Problems?

Address any concerns immediately with the contractor. Don't address the workers; talk to the office, the project manager, or the foreman. Most concerns can be solved easily if addressed early in the process. Don't keep a secret list of problem or concerns to spring on the contractor at the end of the project. Contractors are people, and they appreciate good communication that addresses issues as the project goes on.

The Finale

Try to establish a very good contract that establishes all the specifics of the roof replacement project. Compare prices based on the contract specifications, the materials, and the quality of the contractor. Base your selection on quality, not price.

Chapter 28 – All Fogged Up: Solving Window Condensation Problems

Each fall when we turn on our home heating systems, many of us experience condensation on windows: "steam" on the inside, or in extreme cases, water running down the glass. This condition may be only a temporary annoyance, but it could also signal serious moisture and window problems.

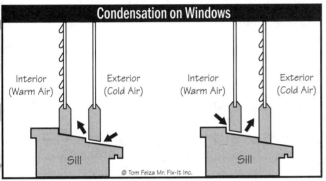

Condensation on Windows

Interior (Warm Air) Exterior (Cold Air) Interior (Warm Air) Exterior (Cold Air)

Sill Sill

© Tom Feiza Mr. Fix-It Inc.

S002

Where does all the water come from? Our parents' homes never had moisture problems, so why do we have them now? How can we solve the problems?

You can solve most condensation problems if you understand the basic principles of moisture and how it moves inside your home. Most likely, you'll just need to change a few daily routines. For serious problems, more extensive changes may be necessary: modifying windows, adding ventilation and improving heating equipment. The good news is that all moisture problems can be solved.

What Causes Condensation on Windows?

"Steam" (condensation) occurs when invisible water vapor in the air condenses on the cool glass. Windows and metal window frames tend to be the coolest surfaces in our homes, so moisture forms there first—just like condensation beads up on the outside of your ice-cold lemonade glass in the summertime.

Condensation requires a cool surface and moisture in the air. This moisture is measured as a percent of the total amount that the air will hold at a specific temperature, and the percentage is known as relative humidity. Warmer air holds more moisture. Cooler air holds less moisture.

Weather reports refer to relative humidity and dew point. The dew point is the temperature at which the air is fully saturated with invisible water vapor and the vapor starts to become visible water (dew). When the dew point is high, air feels damp and wet, and we have high relative humidity. When the outside air temperature drops below the dew point, rain or fog appears.

Inside your home, when the temperature of the glass drops below the dew point of the inside air, visible moisture forms on the glass. The combination of a high level of moisture in the air and a cool glass surface triggers the condensation process.

More condensation occurs when there is more water vapor in the air and/or when glass surfaces become colder.

Solving the Wet Window Problem

For some lucky homeowners, window condensation is just a temporary annoyance. A few weeks after the heating season begins, interior air dries and condensation stops forming on windows.

In other homes, though, condensation continues, becoming a serious problem. Water runs off the windows and damages wood surfaces. Ice may form on windows and frames. Storm windows remained fogged up and icy all winter as water ponds between the frames. This serious condition needs to be addressed before it rots wood, supports mildew growth and damages the home's structure.

To solve window condensation problems, you must reduce the invisible moisture in the air of your home and raise the surface temperature of the glass. Let's outline the steps you can take.

Reducing Moisture Levels–Limit Moisture Sources

Moisture, fog, steam, ice, water vapor—they are all water in different forms. The most important step in solving moisture problems is to limit moisture sources.

Showers, cooking, washing and similar activities add lots of moisture to the air. Studies have shown that a typical family of four releases over 2-1/2 gallons of water per day into the air of their home. Damp basements, plumbing leaks, pets and plants all compound the moisture generation problem. In fact, every time we exhale, we add moisture to the air.

Sources of Moisture

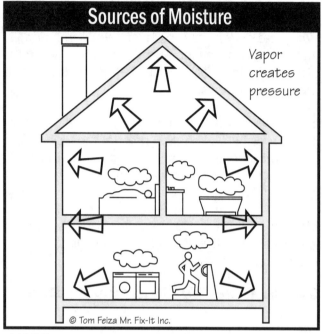

Vapor creates pressure

© Tom Feiza Mr. Fix-It Inc.

M006

Start limiting moisture sources as follows:

- Cure damp basement or crawl space problems. Cover any bare crawl space soil with a plastic vapor barrier. Correct grading and drainage problems. Seal basement walls and floors. Ensure that the sump pump keeps the water level 8 to 12 inches below the basement floor.

- If your furnace has a built-in humidifier, turn it off. Also, turn off the water supply to the humidifier. Try leaving this humidifier off year-round unless your home becomes extremely dry.

- Vent your clothes dryer to the outside. Don't air-dry clothes indoors.

- Eliminate plumbing leaks.

- Limit plants, aquariums and pets.

- Store firewood outside.

Humidifier Problems

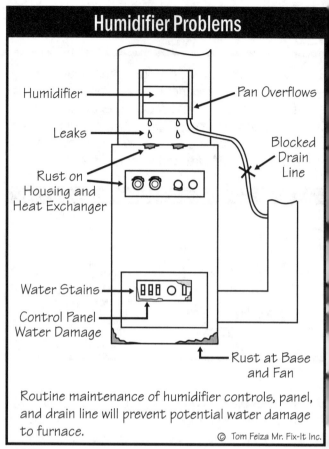

Humidifier

Pan Overflows

Leaks

Blocked Drain Line

Rust on Housing and Heat Exchanger

Water Stains

Control Panel Water Damage

Rust at Base and Fan

Routine maintenance of humidifier controls, panel, and drain line will prevent potential water damage to furnace.
© Tom Feiza Mr. Fix-It Inc.

H031

- Never use unvented fossil fuel burning devices like kerosene heaters indoors. Burning fossil fuels creates carbon dioxide and water vapor, introducing excessive moisture into your home. It can also create dangerous carbon monoxide.

- Check gas-fired appliances (furnaces and water heaters) to make sure they are drafting properly up the chimney. A backdraft would release carbon dioxide and water vapor into the home.

Reducing Moisture Levels—Ventilation

If reducing moisture sources does not solve the problem, you need to increase ventilation. Structural ventilation or attic ventilation removes moisture from the structure of your home. Because moisture flows with air leaks and can push through many materials, general structural ventilation is important. Point source ventilation removes moisture at specific sources.

Gas Water Heater With Signs of Backdrafting

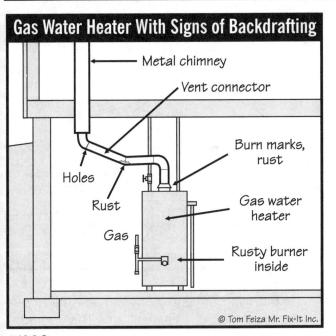

W006

Ventilation - Two Basic Types

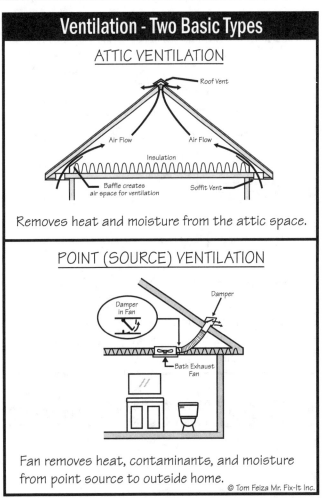

ATTIC VENTILATION

Removes heat and moisture from the attic space.

POINT (SOURCE) VENTILATION

Fan removes heat, contaminants, and moisture from point source to outside home.

V030

The following checklist addresses both methods of increasing ventilation:

- Use ventilation fans in bathrooms. Add fans if you don't have them, and route the exhaust outside your home. After a shower or bath, run the fan until the room is dry. This may require adding a timer switch in place of the regular fan switch.

- Be sure kitchen exhaust fans are routed outside, and use them when cooking.

- Evaluate attic ventilation. All bath and kitchen exhaust fans must exit the attic. There should be no hints of moisture (mildew or ice crystals) in the attic. In general, attics should have one square foot of free-air ventilation for each 150 square feet of attic floor space, or one square foot of ventilation per 300 square feet of attic space if there is a continuous vapor barrier. Half of the ventilation should be high on the roof and the other half in the overhangs. Make sure lower vents aren't blocked by insulation.

- When the outside air is dry, open windows to "air out" your home and remove moisture.

- Consider keeping a window slightly open all winter long or whenever condensation starts to occur. Pick a window on the downwind side of your home. Air will be drawn out of that win-

Bathroom Fan Discharge Through Attic

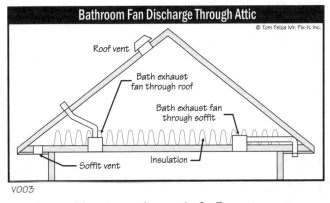

V003

dow without creating a draft. For a two-story home, select a second-floor downwind window instead of a first-floor window, because warm, moist air rises.

- Ventilate any sealed crawl spaces (except crawl spaces that open to the basement, which do not need ventilation to the exterior).

- Open the fireplace damper. Build a good fire to exhaust the stale, moist air in your home.

Kitchen Exhaust Fan - Ducted Through Sidewall

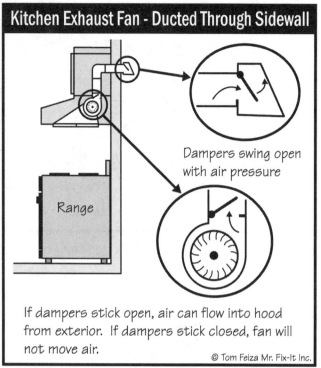

Dampers swing open with air pressure

Range

If dampers stick open, air can flow into hood from exterior. If dampers stick closed, fan will not move air.

© Tom Feiza Mr. Fix-It Inc.

V012

Attic Ventilation Requirements - Typical

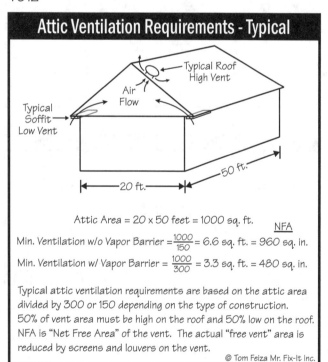

Typical Roof High Vent

Air Flow

Typical Soffit Low Vent

50 ft.

20 ft.

Attic Area = 20 x 50 feet = 1000 sq. ft.

NFA

Min. Ventilation w/o Vapor Barrier $= \frac{1000}{150} = 6.6$ sq. ft. $= 960$ sq. in.

Min. Ventilation w/ Vapor Barrier $= \frac{1000}{300} = 3.3$ sq. ft. $= 480$ sq. in.

Typical attic ventilation requirements are based on the attic area divided by 300 or 150 depending on the type of construction. 50% of vent area must be high on the roof and 50% low on the roof. NFA is "Net Free Area" of the vent. The actual "free vent" area is reduced by screens and louvers on the vent.

© Tom Feiza Mr. Fix-It Inc.

V042

- Consider adding an outside air supply to your furnace air return duct. Discuss this possibility with a heating contractor. When the furnace runs, this arrangement will draw dry outside air into the return duct of your furnace. The duct should be closed in the summer to prevent the entry of warm, moist air when the air conditioning is operating.

Wind Over Roof Creates Suction and Pressure

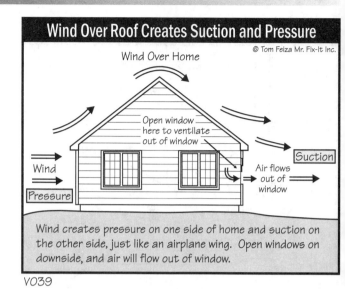

© Tom Feiza Mr. Fix-It Inc.

Wind Over Home

Open window here to ventilate out of window

Wind

Pressure

Air flows out of window

Suction

Wind creates pressure on one side of home and suction on the other side, just like an airplane wing. Open windows on downside, and air will flow out of window.

V039

- Consider forced ventilation with an exhaust system or a heat recovery ventilator. This upgrade is best left to professionals. It is only required when serious moisture problems can't be solved by any other method.

Mechanical Moisture Removal

Using a dehumidifier is an option, but you should only consider it if problems continue after you've increased ventilation. Dehumidifiers consume a lot of electricity, add heat to the space and are not very effective at temperatures below 65 degrees. They may also not be effective at the lower moisture levels found in most homes.

Reduce Condensation by Raising Surface Temperatures

You can also approach the condensation problem by raising the window glass surface temperature. Remember, if you raise the surface temperature above the dew point, you will not have condensation.

Try these tips:

- Open curtains and drapes to increase air circulation around windows

- Direct warm-air supply ducts toward windows or even use a fan for increased air circulation at windows. Operate ceiling fans.

Outside Air Supply to Heat/Cool Return Duct

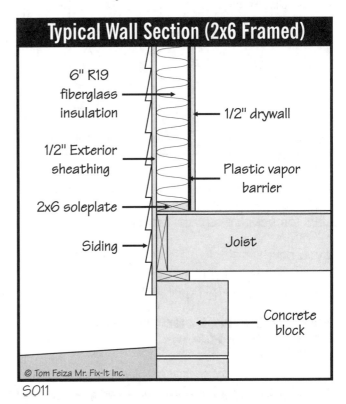

The outside air supply to the furnace return duct provides ventilation air when furnace blower operates (while heating). The duct is negative and draws air from outside.

Damper should be closed for air conditioning to eliminate introducing hot, damp air.

© Tom Feiza Mr. Fix-It Inc.

V029

Heat Recovery Ventilator (HRV)

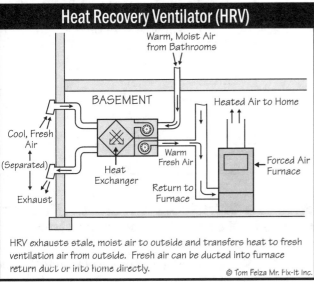

HRV exhausts stale, moist air to outside and transfers heat to fresh ventilation air from outside. Fresh air can be ducted into furnace return duct or into home directly.

© Tom Feiza Mr. Fix-It Inc.

V035

- Add interior or exterior storm windows to raise the insulation value and increase the interior glass temperature. Metal window frames, in particular, may need storm windows to create a thermal break that stops the transmission of heat or cold through the metal.

- Raise the room air temperature by turning up the thermostat.

Why Do Modern Homes Have This Moisture Problem?

As we tighten our homes for energy efficiency, we reduce air exchanges. Modern homes are also wrapped with a plastic vapor barrier to stop moisture and air leaks. Most moisture moves with air movement, and a tight home just doesn't exhaust air and moisture. Older homes, with many air leaks and drafts, were constantly dry in the winter because of excessive air exchange.

New windows and new furnaces are part of the ventilation picture. Tight windows limit air leaks. Furnaces that vent with two plastic pipes draw combustion air from the outside and don't exhaust air out a chimney flue.

Typical Wall Section (2x6 Framed)

6" R19 fiberglass insulation

1/2" Exterior sheathing

2x6 soleplate

Siding

1/2" drywall

Plastic vapor barrier

Joist

Concrete block

© Tom Feiza Mr. Fix-It Inc.

S011

But Don't Blame the Windows

Windows aren't the problem. They are just a cool surface delivering the message that excessive moisture is trapped inside a tight home. Your windows tell you when you need to reduce the moisture level.

Tighter modern windows do reduce air leaks, which limits ventilation and traps moisture. But tight windows also reduce heating costs, limit drafts and help keep our homes clean by stopping dirt

High-Efficiency Warm Air Furnace

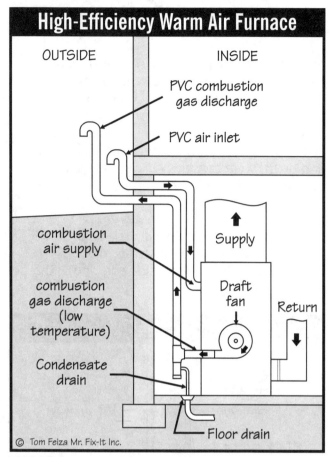

OUTSIDE | INSIDE

PVC combustion gas discharge

PVC air inlet

combustion air supply

combustion gas discharge (low temperature)

Condensate drain

Supply

Draft fan

Return

Floor drain

© Tom Feiza Mr. Fix-It Inc.

H003

infiltration. Modern windows with special glass may even reduce condensation problems because the glass temperature remains higher.

If you have old single glass windows or broken storms, shame on you. You deserve the condensation you get for wasting all that energy.

Expect Extra Condensation in Brand New Homes

New homes present special problems. In addition to being built very tight and allowing little air exchange, they trap construction moisture. When a home is built, much moisture is trapped in wood, drywall, concrete and other materials. It takes at least one full heating season to dry out a new home.

Why Is the Problem Really Bad in the Fall?

In the fall, we experience cold snaps. When exterior temperatures change quickly, window glass temperature also drops quickly, and condensation can form.

Also, when we first turn on our heating systems, all the higher summer moisture is trapped in wood, cloth, furniture and other porous surfaces. After a few weeks, most homes dry out and the problem disappears.

Why Do Bathroom Windows Fog Up So Readily?

Bathroom windows are subject to excessive moisture from showers and baths. This moisture condenses quickly on any cool surface, so the bathroom windows may fog while other windows remain clear. Use a bath exhaust fan to remove moisture.

Bath Exhaust Fan Through Roof

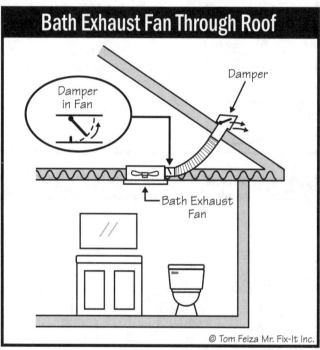

Damper in Fan

Damper

Bath Exhaust Fan

© Tom Feiza Mr. Fix-It Inc.

V006

Why Do Windows in Other Rooms Fog Up Mostly in the Morning?

Windows fog up in the early morning because lower overnight temperatures cool the glass below the dew point. Later, when the outside temperature rises, the glass warms and condensation disappears as visible moisture evaporates into invisible air vapor.

If you "set back" (lower) the temperature inside your home overnight, you compound the problem by increasing the relative humidity and lowering the dew point of the air inside your home.

Why Do Windows Fog on One Side of a Home?

This normally occurs on the inside of storm windows. Prevailing wind creates pressure on the side of your home facing the wind and creates a negative pressure on the downwind side. (The same principle causes high and low pressure around an airplane wing, creating lift.)

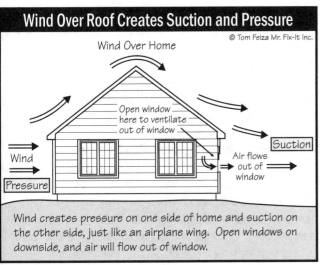

Wind Over Roof Creates Suction and Pressure

© Tom Feiza Mr. Fix-It Inc.

Wind Over Home

Open window here to ventilate out of window

Wind

Pressure

Suction

Air flows out of window

Wind creates pressure on one side of home and suction on the other side, just like an airplane wing. Open windows on downside, and air will flow out of window.

V039

Windows are not a perfect fit; they leak some air. Windows facing the wind tend to allow cold, dry exterior air to leak in. This keeps these storm windows dry.

On the downwind side, warm and moist interior air tends to leak from the inside window and can be trapped by the cold storm. The moist air condenses on inside of the storm. (This is the window you want to keep slightly open to ventilate your home, because the air will always push out without a draft.)

All storms should have "weep holes" at the lowest point of the window frames to allow condensation to drain from between the windows. These small weep holes can also ventilate the space and reduce condensation. Sealing the interior window will help eliminate condensation on the storm.)

Why Do Storm Windows Fog Up?

When an interior window leaks warm moist air, moisture condenses on the tighter, cooler storm.

Why Is Attic Ventilation Important?

Moisture moves through surfaces and follows air leaks. Vapor pressure pushes moisture to areas of lower moisture; warm air rises into your attic. All air leaks into an attic must be sealed.

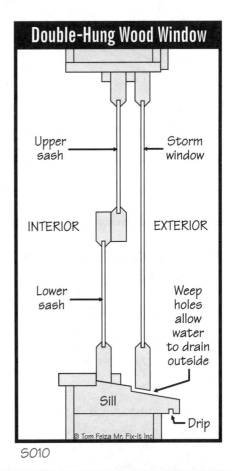

Double-Hung Wood Window

Upper sash

Storm window

INTERIOR

EXTERIOR

Lower sash

Weep holes allow water to drain outside

Sill

Drip

© Tom Feiza Mr. Fix-It Inc.

S010

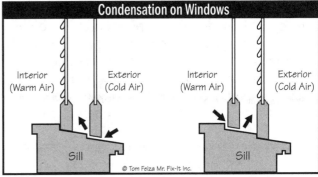

Condensation on Windows

Interior (Warm Air)

Exterior (Cold Air)

Interior (Warm Air)

Exterior (Cold Air)

Sill

Sill

© Tom Feiza Mr. Fix-It Inc.

S002

This means that your attic is a prime moisture-collector. Since the roof deck is cold, excessive condensation can occur inside the attic, leading to structural damage. Keeping the attic well ventilated bypasses these problems and reduces overall moisture levels inside your home.

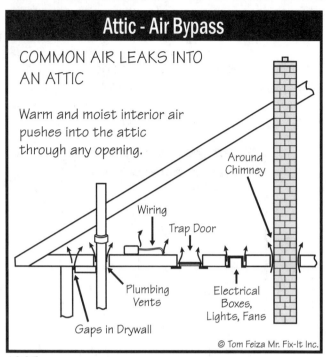

Attic - Air Bypass

COMMON AIR LEAKS INTO AN ATTIC

Warm and moist interior air pushes into the attic through any opening.

Around Chimney

Wiring

Trap Door

Plumbing Vents

Electrical Boxes, Lights, Fans

Gaps in Drywall

© Tom Feiza Mr. Fix-It Inc.

1005

How Do I Know the Correct Humidity Level?

Watch your windows to gauge the correct humidity level inside your home. If condensation occurs on the inside of interior windows, you have excessive moisture and should take steps to reduce moisture levels.

Don't rely on cheap humidity indicators. Generally, they're not accurate. If the humidity level is too high, your windows will tell you with constant fogging and water problems.

The correct humidity level depends on the type of window, the outside air temperature and the inside air temperature. These temperatures are important because they affect the interior glass temperature. When the glass is cold, the humidity level or dew point must be lower to prevent condensation.

For a home with double glazing (double glass) and an interior air temperature of 70 degrees, indoor humidity should not exceed the levels shown in the following guidelines. If humidity exceeds these levels, the windows will fog.

OUTSIDE AIR TEMPERATURE	MAXIMUM INTERIOR HUMIDITY
20 degrees F	40%
0	30%
-20	15%

If you have high-performance glazing or specially insulated glass, the interior glass temperature will be warmer because there is less heat loss. With a warmer glass temperature, you can raise the humidity level. If you have triple glazing, you can also raise the humidity level. With poor windows, you need to lower the humidity level.

Create a Moisture Balance

Every combination of home structure and family situation introduces an almost unlimited set of variables when evaluating condensation problems on windows. You need to try to understand the basics of moisture and condensation, limit moisture sources, and properly ventilate.

Watch those windows! They will tell you when you need to take action.

Don't worry about temporary or short-term fogging of windows. Do worry if you have constant moisture problems and you notice water damage, mildew or water stains. Follow the steps outlined here, and consult a professional if you have persistent problems.

And don't condemn modern building practices and windows. Modern products and building techniques have given us comfortable, energy efficient homes. While we enjoy our low energy bills, we simply need to understand how these homes react to moisture.

Chapter 29 – Floor Squeaks

Floor and stair squeaks might help you track the late-night arrival of your teenage daughter after a hot date, but most of us would like to eliminate annoying squeaks. Any home, whether it's old or new, can suffer the heartbreak of "the squeak." With a little knowledge, a few inexpensive materials, and some do-it-yourself effort, we can eliminate most squeaks in our homes.

We will focus on floor squeaks, since they are the most common and most annoying. The same principles and corrections apply to stairs.

What Makes the Noise?

Squeaks in homes occur when surfaces rub against each other. It could be a wood floorboard joint rubbing, a subfloor board rubbing on a nail, or movement between any two adjacent surfaces. The key here is movement. Eliminating the movement eliminates the squeak.

What Causes the Movement?

Most often, movement occurs at loose fits in a home caused by shrinkage of wood. Wood is a natural material, and as its moisture content changes, it expands or contracts. A two-story wood framed home can shrink 5/8 of an inch within a year of its completion. As wood dries and shrinks, gaps and cracks develop and fasteners become loose.

Some movement is caused by settling and loading of structural members. As wood is loaded, it can slightly compress and move. A load on a floor joist will actually cause a slight sag in the center of the floor.

Older homes are subject to more squeaks because their construction uses a greater percentage of natural wood materials. Natural wood is more prone to expansion and contraction compared to modern manufactured wood-based products. Older homes are subject to more air infiltration, which dries the wood and makes it more likely to move. Normal wear and tear also takes its toll on an older home.

Identify the Squeak and its Location

To squelch a squeak, creak or groan, we need to identify the cause of the movement. Often, wood movement is visible. You might pinpoint it by having one person walk or jump lightly on the offending floor while someone else looks and listens from below and marks the location of the noise and movement.

Work from Below— Movement at the Joists

You may find that floorboards have moved in relation to the joist framing; nails have loosened; and floorboards are rubbing against a nail fastener or another floorboard. You can correct this problem with either of two simple methods.

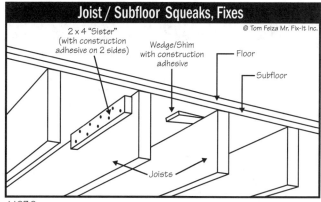

Joist / Subfloor Squeaks, Fixes
M030

Often the quickest and easiest fix is to "sister" a short length of 2 x 4 or 2 x 6 parallel to the loose floorboards and joist. Liberally coat the 2 x 4 on two sides with construction adhesive (such as Liquid Nails) applied with a caulk gun. Attach the board to the joist with a few long deck screws driven upward and angled into the joist. This pulls the patch up, into the floorboards.

The construction adhesive fills voids and laterally welds the lumber to the joist and subfloor. Construction adhesive does not shrink as it cures, so it creates a strong and solid bond.

In areas with gaps between the joists and subfloor, you can also gently tap wood shims coated with construction adhesive into the gaps. Don't drive too hard or you might separate the subfloor from the joists and complicate the problem.

You can try to squeeze construction adhesive into the joist/subfloor joint. Apply the material like caulk and try to force it into any opening or gap. This will only work if there is a minor amount of movement.

Work from Below— Movement Between the Joists

If the subfloor is cracked or shows movement between joists, you can correct the problem by installing bridging between the joists at the area of movement. Bridging is 2 inch wide framing lumber that is tightly installed perpendicular to the joists. The bridging should be secured with construction adhesive on three sides as well as long deck screws or common nails through the joists into the ends of the bridging.

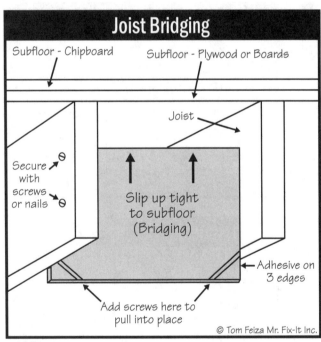

M031

The bridging helps support the subfloor and also stiffens joists as it transfers load and potential movement from joist to adjacent joist. Bridging can be installed in several adjacent areas to stiffen and reinforce a section of the floor.

Special Bracket from Below

Squeak-Relief provides a special aluminum bracket and matching screws and nails specifically designed to secure a subfloor to joists from below. The bracket fits tightly at the joist/subfloor joint, and the screws draw the joint tight without the worry of driving a screw through the finished floor. For a larger area of movement, you will need several brackets. You can find more information about Squeak-Relief through ATCI Consumer Products in the References chapter.

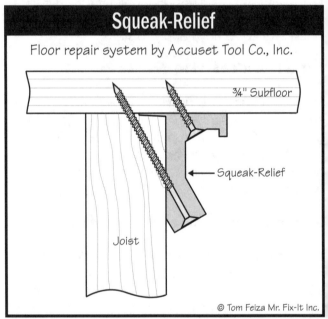

M038

Hardwood Floor Squeaks from Below

If solid hardwood floorboards are moving and squeaking but the subfloor looks secure from below, you can attempt to drive screws up through the subfloor boards into the hardwood. You must measure or carefully estimate the total thickness of the wood floor and subfloor. Try to find an edge or penetration where you can make a measurement. Normally this total thickness is 1-1/2 inches, and a 1-1/4-inch-long screw can be used, but be careful—if the screw is too long, it will penetrate the finished floor.

Select a deck screw, and drill a clearance hole just a bit larger than the diameter of this screw into the subfloor. The clearance hole prevents screw threads from biting too tightly into the subfloor. Drill a small pilot hole into the hardwood floor through the clearance hole. Then, with a heavy weight holding down the wood floor, drive your deck screw (with a washer below the head) up into the pilot hole. It may take several screws in several locations to secure this area. Ultimately, the process should pull the hardwood tightly to the subfloor.

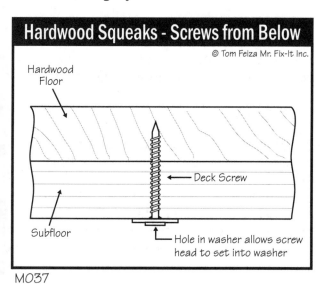

Hardwood Squeaks - Screws from Below

© Tom Feiza Mr. Fix-It Inc.

Hardwood Floor

Deck Screw

Subfloor

Hole in washer allows screw head to set into washer

M037

Hardwood Floor Squeaks from Above

You can also work from above to fix loose hardwood floorboards. Drive finishing nails at an angle through the hardwood floor into the subfloor and joists. Often, to keep the wood from splitting or the nail from bending, you must first create a pilot hole before driving a nail through the hardwood. When you are finished, the small nail hole can be patched with colored wood putty.

You can also drive deck screws or trim screws through the hardwood and into the subfloor or the subfloor and joists.

Trim or finishing screws look like drywall screws with very small heads. You must first drill a clearance hole bigger than the diameter of the screw through the hardwood, and you should drill a countersink hole the size of the screw head. The hole from a deck screw can be filled with a wood plug or colored wood putty. A finishing screw has such a small head that it creates a very small hole which is easily filled with wood putty.

With either method of working from above, you must drive several screws or nails over the areas of movement.

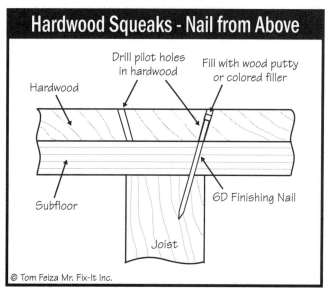

Hardwood Squeaks - Nail from Above

Drill pilot holes in hardwood

Fill with wood putty or colored filler

Hardwood

Subfloor

6D Finishing Nail

Joist

© Tom Feiza Mr. Fix-It Inc.

M035

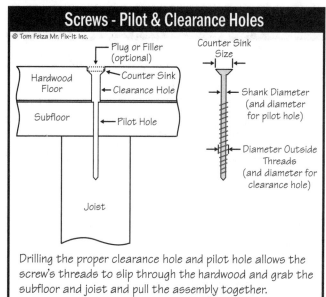

Screws - Pilot & Clearance Holes

© Tom Feiza Mr. Fix-It Inc.

Plug or Filler (optional)

Counter Sink Size

Counter Sink

Hardwood Floor

Clearance Hole

Shank Diameter (and diameter for pilot hole)

Subfloor

Pilot Hole

Diameter Outside Threads (and diameter for clearance hole)

Joist

Drilling the proper clearance hole and pilot hole allows the screw's threads to slip through the hardwood and grab the subfloor and joist and pull the assembly together.

M032

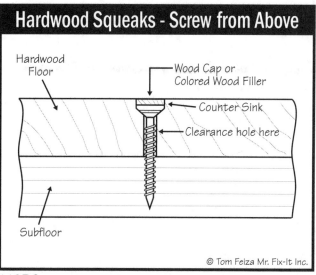

Hardwood Squeaks - Screw from Above

Hardwood Floor

Wood Cap or Colored Wood Filler

Counter Sink

Clearance hole here

Subfloor

© Tom Feiza Mr. Fix-It Inc.

M036

Hardwood Floor—
Special Screws from Above

You can also secure hardwood floorboards from above with a special screw and bracket called Counter Snap from ATCI Consumer Products, in the References chapter.

With Counter Snap, you first drill a pilot hole, then drive a screw through a small bracket that holds the screw head away from the floor. The screw secures the hardwood to the subfloor. This special screw has a notch in its shank, and after you have driven in the screw as far as necessary, you break off the screw at this score line, just below the surface of the hardwood. The remaining hole in the floor is almost invisible.

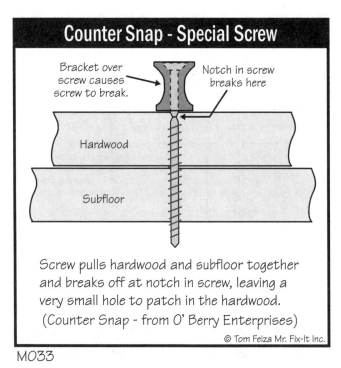

Counter Snap - Special Screw

Bracket over screw causes screw to break.

Notch in screw breaks here

Hardwood

Subfloor

Screw pulls hardwood and subfloor together and breaks off at notch in screw, leaving a very small hole to patch in the hardwood. (Counter Snap - from O' Berry Enterprises)

© Tom Feiza Mr. Fix-It Inc.

M033

No Access from Above or Below with Carpeting

At times there is just no access to the offending floor squeaks. In many cases, you must simply wait until you replace the carpeting or vinyl and then screw the subfloor to the joists. Once the floor covering is removed, use many, many long deck screws to pull the subfloor to the joist. You could drive a screw every 6 inches along the framing.

You can attempt to work through the carpeting, but there is a slight risk to the carpet fabric, and it is

almost impossible to locate floor joists. This will work if you can locate joists or if there are two layers of subflooring. You can attempt to locate the floor joist by drilling a small hole through the carpet and subfloor and then using a thin wire to search for the edge of the joist.

Another way to locate a floor joist through carpeting would be to use a high-quality deep-scanning stud finder. You would need to support the stud finder on still, flat cardboard as you scan the surface. I have had some luck with this method on thinner carpet.

After you locate the floor joists, you can attempt to secure the subfloor through the carpet. Pull the carpet fibers back and drill a small pilot hole through the subfloor at an angle into the joist. Follow up with a deck screw, pulling the subfloor to the joist and pulling the head of the screw through the carpet and pad. There is some risk to the carpet, so try to keep the fibers away from the screw as it twists into the wood.

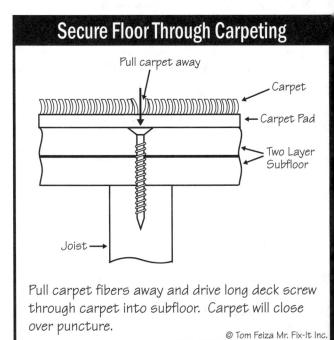

Secure Floor Through Carpeting

Pull carpet away

Carpet

Carpet Pad

Two Layer Subfloor

Joist →

Pull carpet fibers away and drive long deck screw through carpet into subfloor. Carpet will close over puncture.

© Tom Feiza Mr. Fix-It Inc.

M039

Special Screws from Above

A screw and bracket made for securing a floor through carpeting is Squeeeeek No More, available from ATCI Consumer Products.

The screw is driven through a bracket, directly through the carpeting, and set partially into the floorboards. The screw is then broken off at a score line, just below the top of the subfloor.

They'll Be Back

Once you understand the mechanism for squeaks and the basics of framing and construction, you can approach almost any squeak. Special screws and brackets can simplify the repair. Remember that since wood is a natural product, it might continue to move and squeak despite your best efforts. In that case, you may have to resign yourself to the thought that a squeak helps you keep track of the teenagers late at night.

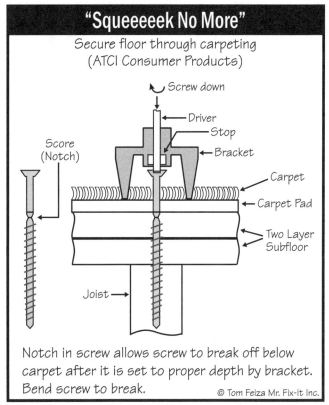

"Squeeeeek No More"

Secure floor through carpeting
(ATCI Consumer Products)

Screw down
Driver
Stop
Bracket
Score (Notch)
Carpet
Carpet Pad
Two Layer Subfloor
Joist

Notch in screw allows screw to break off below carpet after it is set to proper depth by bracket. Bend screw to break.

© Tom Feiza Mr. Fix-It Inc.

M034

Chapter 30 – Ice Dams

Remember those snowy winters? Beautiful snow and ice made for great winter beauty and fun. But then, as the weather warmed a little, that beauty became an ugly, damaging, watery mess inside some homes. In many cases, ice dams were the culprit. Let's talk about winter ice damming and how to prevent problems.

What Is an Ice Dam?

An ice dam is a ridge of ice that builds up along the edge of a roof. The ice creates a dam that backs water up and under the roof shingles. Once the water is deep enough, it penetrates the roofing system and creates water damage inside the home.

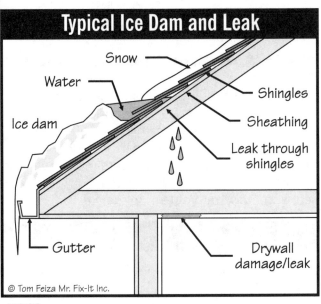

Typical Ice Dam and Leak

Snow

Water

Ice dam

Shingles

Sheathing

Leak through shingles

Gutter

Drywall damage/leak

© Tom Feiza Mr. Fix-It Inc.

R002

To recognize an ice dam, look for a bulge of ice attached to the eaves or overhang of a roof. There may be icicles ("Aren't they pretty!") hanging from the edge, and you may see stains on the siding. The rain gutters may be overflowing with ice.

Often, the bulge of ice is covered with several inches of snow, so you may not see it. Under the buildup of frozen snow is the melting snow and ice—water that is entering your home. If interior damage has already occurred, you will see a wet ceiling and wall or water flowing into windows.

Related Damage

Beneath the ice dam, undetectable damage is occurring in the attic and wall cavities. The wood framing is wet and may be rotting. Insulation is soaked, which makes it inefficient. Mildew and mold can grow in hidden spots, causing odors and other problems inside your home.

Soaked framing and insulation will take a long time to dry out and will continue to contribute to wall damage and interior moisture problems. Uncorrected, the water can cause serious structural damage.

Under Cover: A Close Look at the Cause

Ice dam problems are most common in snowbelt regions. They begin when snow accumulates on a roof. Generally, deeper snow and colder temperatures increase the formation of ice dams. North or northwest winds usually accompany snowfalls, so more snow is deposited on north and west roof planes. Complex roof structures that trap snow compound its depth and the problems it creates.

Once the snow has built up on the roof, it acts as an effective insulator. (Light snow has a insulation value of about R-1 per inch.) Heat from the attic warms the underside of the roof and melts the bottom snow into a slush/ice/water mixture. This mixture slides under the snow cover and runs down the roof till it meets a cold surface like the overhang. The slush then re-freezes. As more slush accumulates, the layer becomes thicker and thicker, creating an ice dam. All of this action occurs hidden from view under the snow cover.

Once the ice dam is high enough to overcome the pitch of the roof, water seeps under asphalt shingles. Standard roof shingle construction is not designed to resist the attack of water pooling on its surface. The alternate freezing and thawing that occurs under these conditions can increase the magnitude of roof leaks. Once the water has penetrated the shingles, it flows under the siding and eaves and leaks through the framing into your home.

"It Never Happened in the Good Old Days"

What seasoned homeowners say is true: ice dams were not a problem before the '30s or '40s. Back then, builders used a totally different type of construction. Homes had steeply pitched roofs. Wooden shingles were installed over spaced boards for sheathing so the shingles could breathe and dry. Spaces between the shingles and deck ventilated the attic and cooled the roof deck. Many families did not fully heat the home's second story, or they heated it just enough to keep water from freezing in a drinking glass. (I grew up in one of those homes.)

In newer homes with good heating systems, the attic was often excessively warm because energy was cheap and so homes were not well insulated. This excessive heat rapidly melted the snow on the roof. Usually a small line of ice existed only at the gutter or eaves, and even that cleared on warmer days. Water penetration did not linger, and ice dams as we know them today did not exist.

Then, in the 1930s and '40s, we began to tighten up our homes and use new materials. Roofers began applying asphalt shingles, and building paper, plywood, insulation, and vapor barriers came into use. Central heating was made very effective, and all the living spaces were heated. These changes triggered new problems with moisture and ice dams. Attic ventilation slowly became the standard.

Good Advice on Preventing Ice

To prevent ice dams, your first step should be to eliminate heat buildup in the attic space below the roof deck. You can do this by (1) improving insulation, (2) stopping air "bypass," and (3) increasing ventilation. The temperature in the attic space below the roofing should be nearly the same as the outside temperature. This "cold roof" concept has proven effective in modern construction.

Phase One: The Insulation Situation

Add insulation to improve the thermal envelope and slow heat transfer to the attic. Surfaces between the attic and the heated living spaces beneath it should be insulated to approximately R-38 or more. R-38 is equivalent to approximately 12 inches of quality Fiberglas bat insulation. Eliminate any gaps or openings in the insulation, and insulate all access doors to the attic, too.

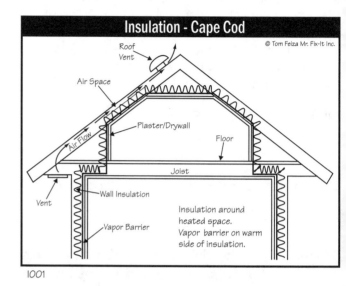

Insulation - Cape Cod

© Tom Feiza Mr. Fix-It Inc.

Roof Vent

Air Space

Plaster/Drywall

Floor

Air Flow

Joist

Vent

Wall Insulation

Vapor Barrier

Insulation around heated space. Vapor barrier on warm side of insulation.

I001

Phase Two: Stop Hot Air "Bypass"

You must also seal any opening that allows heated air to "bypass" the insulation and rise into the attic. The warm air in your home will always try to rise and will push through any small opening. Not only can this warm air movement create major heat losses from the living space, it's also a major source of heat and moisture problems in the attic.

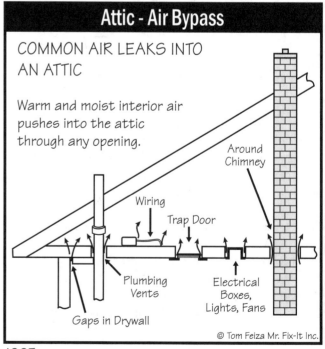

Attic - Air Bypass

COMMON AIR LEAKS INTO AN ATTIC

Warm and moist interior air pushes into the attic through any opening.

Around Chimney

Wiring

Trap Door

Plumbing Vents

Electrical Boxes, Lights, Fans

Gaps in Drywall

© Tom Feiza Mr. Fix-It Inc.

I005

The attic door should be weather-stripped even better than an exterior door. All penetrations of wiring, piping, and wood framing into the attic should be sealed with caulk, sheet metal, or expandable foam insulation. The spaces around most chimneys should be sealed with non-flammable material.

Exhaust fans should not empty into the attic, and the area between the frame of the fan and the ceiling should be tightly sealed. If there are heating ducts in the attic, seal and insulate all duct surfaces exposed to attic air. Look for kitchen or bath soffit spaces that may have gaps and openings in their plaster or drywall.

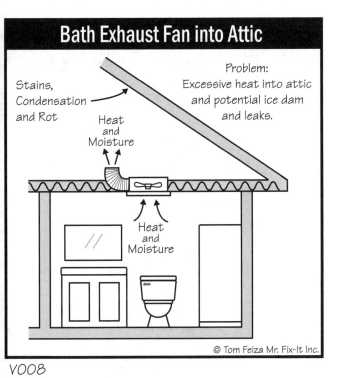

Bath Exhaust Fan into Attic

Stains, Condensation and Rot

Problem: Excessive heat into attic and potential ice dam and leaks.

Heat and Moisture

Heat and Moisture

© Tom Feiza Mr. Fix-It Inc.

V008

Phase Three: Improve Ventilation

Good ventilation is the second half of your ice dam prevention strategy. As you inspect and fix the attic insulation, avoid blocking any vents with insulation.

Increasing the attic's ventilation will cool the space and remove unwanted moisture. The best ventilation system is balanced between low-intake ventilation from the overhangs (soffit) and high-exhaust vents on the attic roof. Most experts agree that the best system is a continuous soffit and ridge vent, although this is not always possible or necessary.

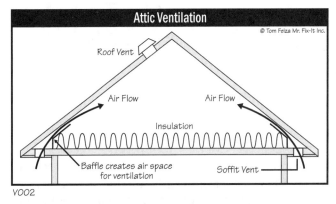

Attic Ventilation

© Tom Feiza Mr. Fix-It Inc.

Roof Vent

Air Flow   Air Flow

Insulation

Baffle creates air space for ventilation   Soffit Vent

V002

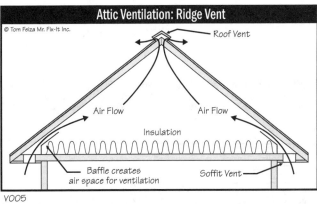

Attic Ventilation: Ridge Vent

© Tom Feiza Mr. Fix-It Inc.

Roof Vent

Air Flow   Air Flow

Insulation

Baffle creates air space for ventilation   Soffit Vent

V005

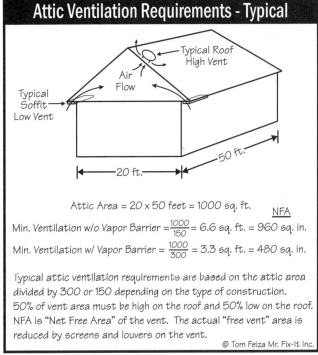

Attic Ventilation Requirements - Typical

Typical Roof High Vent

Air Flow

Typical Soffit Low Vent

20 ft.

50 ft.

Attic Area = 20 x 50 feet = 1000 sq. ft.

NFA

Min. Ventilation w/o Vapor Barrier = $\frac{1000}{150}$ = 6.6 sq. ft. = 960 sq. in.

Min. Ventilation w/ Vapor Barrier = $\frac{1000}{300}$ = 3.3 sq. ft. = 480 sq. in.

Typical attic ventilation requirements are based on the attic area divided by 300 or 150 depending on the type of construction. 50% of vent area must be high on the roof and 50% low on the roof. NFA is "Net Free Area" of the vent. The actual "free vent" area is reduced by screens and louvers on the vent.

© Tom Feiza Mr. Fix-It Inc.

V042

The *minimum* ventilation ratio of 1 square foot of ventilation for 300 square feet of attic space (1/300) is a guideline for newer homes with effective vapor barriers. Older homes need a *minimum* ventilation ratio of 1/150. Half of the ventilation should be in the ridge and 25 percent in each soffit. This is the ideal situation that can rarely be accomplished. When in doubt, add more ventilation. In general, a continuous ridge and soffit vent provides three times the 1/300 ventilation ratio and performs very well. Extra ventilation can't hurt unless you have excessive air bypass that allows excessive warm air to be drawn into the attic.

Remember, a 1 foot by 1 foot grill does not provide a full square foot of ventilation. The grill and screen covering detracts from the "free vent" area by as much as 50 percent. Sometimes the free vent area rating appears on the grill. When in doubt, assume that 50 percent or less of the vent is available as a free vent area.

Attic Ventilation Grills - Typical NFA

Typical Undereave Vent

8"

Louvers/ Screen

Area: 16 x 8 = 128 sq. inches
NFA: 56 sq. inches

16"

Typical Metal Roof Vent (Round)

Screen

NFA: 50 sq. inches

14"

The actual "Net Free Area" (NFA) is reduced significantly by grills and screens. Most vents will have the NFA indicated on the vent. It is often less than 50% of the opening in the sheathing.

© Tom Feiza Mr. Fix-It Inc.

V027

When Do Ice Dams Occur?

If ice dams have already developed on your house, you may be able to wait out the problem and work on insulation and ventilation in the spring—if the water damage is not excessive. You may reach the damaged area through the attic and try to catch some of the water. You may also wish to punch small or even large holes in the drywall or plaster to drain the water, thus limiting damage.

In severe water damage cases, it is possible to chip away the offending ice down to the roof deck to allow the ice/water to drain. Use caution, howev-

er, because removing snow and ice from a pitched roof is a dangerous operation at best. Walking on a frozen roof and chipping away the ice will surely cause some roof damage, but this may seem a reasonable alternative to further interior damage when you see water ruining your fine windows and woodwork.

Melting the ice with snow melting chemicals (not rock salt) is an option in a emergency situation. You can also fill old nylon stocking legs with the snow melt chemical and lay it across the ice dam to cut a groove through the ice. The melting "sock" will continue to keep the groove open as the chemical is activated by moisture.

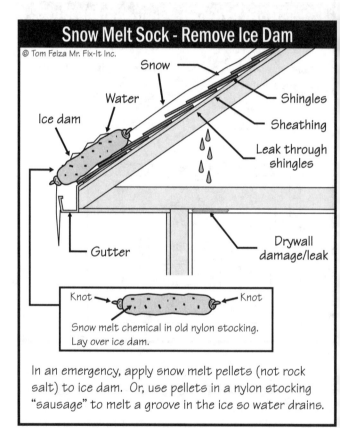

Snow Melt Sock - Remove Ice Dam

© Tom Feiza Mr. Fix-It Inc.

Snow

Water

Ice dam

Shingles

Sheathing

Leak through shingles

Gutter

Drywall damage/leak

Knot — Snow melt chemical in old nylon stocking. Lay over ice dam. — Knot

In an emergency, apply snow melt pellets (not rock salt) to ice dam. Or, use pellets in a nylon stocking "sausage" to melt a groove in the ice so water drains.

M024

Preventive Measures

You may be tempted to use electrical snow- and ice-melt cables, but often these just move the ice dam further up the roof. The cables are hard to maintain, and often they're unsightly. They must be fastened by putting new holes in your roof—not a good idea.

It's possible to remove snow from the problem areas before an ice dam develops if you can reach the area from the ground or the roof edge. You can buy a long-handled snow rake and carefully remove the snow. Remember, though, that you could easily damage the frozen roof, and it's a cold and dangerous job besides.

Snow / Roof Rake

© Tom Feiza Mr. Fix-It Inc.

Snow Cover

Snow / Roof Rake

Working from the ground, use snow / roof rake to remove snow from roof to help prevent ice dams.

M023

Water Shield Provides Help

During major roof repair or replacement, you can add a water shield under the shingles in problem areas like overhangs. The water shield or membrane is a rubberlike adhesive sheet applied to the roof deck under the shingles. The membrane, about as thick as a shingle, is applied as a continuous roll about 36 inches wide. Soft and sticky, it covers nail penetrations and seals the roof deck. If water is forced up under the shingles by an ice dam, the membrane prevents water penetration below the roof deck. The membrane should extend at least two feet into the living space.

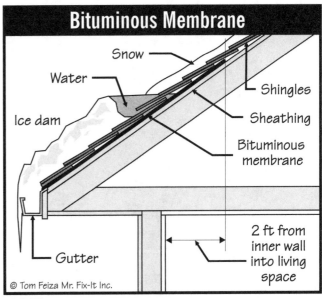

Bituminous Membrane

Snow

Water

Ice dam

Shingles

Sheathing

Bituminous membrane

Gutter

2 ft from inner wall into living space

© Tom Feiza Mr. Fix-It Inc.

R007

Proceed With Caution

If you have any questions or concerns, consult a professional. Improper insulation or sealing around light fixtures, metal flue pipes, and chimneys can create a fire hazard. Also, ventilation can be tricky to achieve. In general, attics are not friendly places—one misstep and you can fall through the ceiling.

Confused? Where to Get Help

All manufacturers of insulation, ventilation, and roofing materials offer technical material. Your local utility or university extension may have free or low-cost information. Or rely on professional contractors for product information and technical literature from manufacturers.

As with any home-related problem, don't panic. If you had minor ice dams once in ten years, I would carefully monitor the problem area and try insulation and ventilation. If you are considering a roof replacement, the continuous membrane under the edge of the roof is good insurance against problems.

Index

Index

Notes

Notes

_____   _____

_____   _____

_____   _____

_____   _____

_____   _____

_____   _____

_____   _____

_____   _____

_____   _____

_____   _____

_____   _____

_____   _____

_____   _____

_____   _____

Notes

Notes

Notes

Notes

_____   _____

_____   _____

_____   _____

_____   _____

_____   _____

_____   _____

_____   _____

_____   _____

_____   _____

_____   _____

_____   _____

_____   _____

_____   _____

Notes

Notes

_____   _____

_____   _____

_____   _____

_____   _____

_____   _____

_____   _____

_____   _____

_____   _____

_____   _____

_____   _____

_____   _____

_____   _____

_____   _____

Notes

Notes

_____   _____

_____   _____

_____   _____

_____   _____

_____   _____

_____   _____

_____   _____

_____   _____

_____   _____

_____   _____

_____   _____

_____   _____

_____   _____

Notes

Notes

_____   _____

_____   _____

_____   _____

_____   _____

_____   _____

_____   _____

_____   _____

_____   _____

_____   _____

_____   _____

_____   _____

_____   _____

_____   _____

_____   _____

Ordering Information

Books by Tom Feiza

Mr. Fix-It's books are available through book retailers, from Internet bookstores, and from Mr. Fix-It, Inc.

How To Operate Your Home – Second Edition (ISBN 0-9674759-3-7) $24.95

The ultimate guide for operating your home—just like an owner's manual for your car. Answers all those questions about how a home works and how you should be operating your home. Provides operation and maintenance schedules to keep your home in top shape and prevent disasters. Full-color cover, 352 pages, over 400 illustrations, service checklists for contractors, equipment tags, and much more.

Home Systems Guide (ISBN 09674759-4-5) $12.95

A shortened, 128 page "systems only" version of How To Operate Your Home with a full color cover and over 250 illustrations. Includes the first seven chapters of How To Operate Your Home. The ultimate guide for operating your home—just like an owner's manual for your car. Answers all those questions about how a home works and how you should be operating your home. Provides basic information you need and more.

Home Journal – How To Operate Your Home (ISBN 0-9674759-2-9) $19.95

Understand and keep track of the important aspects of your home. This book explains all basic home systems and their operation. Includes maintenance schedules and requirements, as well as space to record information on your home's maintenance and improvements. Provides tags for all your equipment and information for responding to home-repair emergencies. Full-color cover, paperback, over 200 illustrations, 138 pages.

Just Fix-It (ISBN 0-9674759-0-2) $14.95

The absolute best home repair tips—hundreds of tips that Tom has gathered in over 15 years of providing radio and print "how-to" advice. How do you remove that rust stain on the driveway? How should you paint dark paneling? How can you make your old countertop look like new?...and much more.

Ordering Books From Mr. Fix-It?

To order books from Mr. Fix-It, send the cover price plus $3.00 shipping and handling for the first book and $1.00 shipping and handling for each additional book. Wisconsin residents must add 5% for sales tax. For an order form and more information, please see www.misterfix-it.com or www.htoyh.com (also: www.HowToOperateYourHome.com). The order form is on the reverse page.

Send your order and payment (cash, check or money order) with complete return address to:

Tom Feiza, Mr. Fix-It Inc.   Or fax order form to Tom at 262-786-7877
P.O. Box 510724   Office phone: 262-786-7878
New Berlin WI 53151

You can also contact Tom and find great home repair information at his websites:
www.misterfix-it.com and www.htoyh.com

Order Form – Tom Feiza – Mr. Fix-It, Inc.

1. Send check or money order payable to:
   Tom Feiza "Mr. Fix-It" Inc.
   4620 S. Raven Lane
   New Berlin, WI 53151

2. Credit Card Orders:
   Fax Form to: (262)786-7877
   Phone Order: (262)786-7878
   Toll-Free: (800)201-3829

Please send copies of the following books:

_____ How To Operate Your Home (Second Edition) @ 24.95 each = $ _____

_____ Home Systems Guide @ 12.95 each = $ _____

_____ Home Journal – How To Operate Your Home @ 19.95 each = $ _____

_____ Just Fix-It @ 14.95 each = $ _____

Wisconsin residents please add 5.1% sales tax $ _____

Subtotal $ _____

Shipping: $3.00 for first book, plus $1.00 for each additional book Shipping $ _____

Total $ _____

Ship To:

_____
Name:

_____
Address:

_____

_____
Phone:

Payment Method: Cash or Money Order $_____   Check # _____   Charge_____

Credit Card Payment: VISA ____   MasterCard ____

Card #_____ Expiration Date_____

_____
Name on Card:

_____
Signature:

Thank You For Your Order!

Information is also available at www.htoyh.com or www.HowToOperateYourHome.com.